11 · 19 · 03

Laurie :

Knowledge supports
the project practetioner.
Good luck .

Joan

SUCCEEDING IN PROJECT-DRIVEN ORGANIZATIONS

SUCCEEDING IN PROJECT-DRIVEN ORGANIZATIONS

PEOPLE, PROCESSES, AND POLITICS

JOAN KNUTSON

PMSI • PROJECT MENTORS
PART OF THE PROVANT SOLUTION

JOHN WILEY & SONS, INC.

New York • Chichester • Weinheim • Brisbane • Singapore • Toronto

PMSI • PROJECT MENTORS
PART OF THE PROVANT SOLUTION

Published by John Wiley & Sons, Inc.
Published simultaneously in Canada.

No part of this publication may be reproduced, stored in a retrieval system or transmitted in any form or by any means, electronic, mechanical, photocopying, recording, scanning or otherwise, except as permitted under Section 107 or 108 of the 1976 United States Copyright Act, without either the prior written permission of the Publisher, or authorization through payment of the appropriate per-copy fee to the Copyright Clearance Center, 222 Rosewood Drive, Danvers, MA 01923, (978) 750-8400, fax (978) 750-4744. Requests to the Publisher for permission should be addressed to the Permissions Department, John Wiley & Sons, Inc., 605 Third Avenue, New York, NY 10158-0012, (212) 850-6011, fax (212) 850-6008, E-Mail: PERMREQ@WILEY.COM.

The author gratefully acknowledges the generosity of the Project Management Institute in granting permission to reprint excerpts from publications. Various terms are adapted from the *Project Management Body of Knowledge (PMBOK).* Many of the chapters of this book are loosely adapted from Joan Knutson's "Executive's Notebook" column in the Project Management Institute's magazine, *PM Network,* 1994–2001.

This material is reprinted with permission of the Project Management Institute Headquarters, Four Campus Boulevard, Newtown Square, PA 19073-2399; phone: (610) 356-4600; fax: (610) 356-4647, Project Management Institute (PMI) is the world's leading project management association with over 70,000 members worldwide. For further information, contact PMI Headquarters at (610) 356-4600 or visit the PMI Web site at www.pmi.org.

"PMI" and the PMI logo are service and trademarks registered in the United States and other nations; "PMP" and the PMP logo are certification marks registered in the United States and other nations; "PMBOK," "PM Network," and "PMI Today" are trademarks registered in the United States and other nations; and "Project Management Journal" and "Building professionalism in project management" are trademarks of the Project Management Institute, Inc.

Chapter 6 is adapted from, and the Chapter 6 Performance Support Tools are reprinted from, Chapter 5 of "Developing Winning Proposals," by Joan Knutson, in *Project Management Handbook,* edited by Jeffrey K. Pinto (San Francisco: Jossey-Bass Inc., Publishers, 1998).

This publication is designed to provide accurate and authoritative information in regard to the subject matter covered. It is sold with the understanding that the publisher is not engaged in rendering professional services. If professional advice or other expert assistance is required, the services of a competent professional person should be sought.

ISBN 0-471-38034-2

Printed in the United States of America.

10 9 8 7 6 5 4 3 2 1

In 1976, I founded a company called Project Mentors. That company was named for my first three bosses and the best mentors any new project manager could have asked for:

Bob Shinberg, who to this day says that he "invented" me,

Bob Bozeman, who allowed me to run like a thoroughbred, and

John Chay, who taught me "How" to be a professional project manager.

It is no surprise that a book titled *Succeeding in Project-Driven Organizations* should be dedicated to the three most professional mentors that have helped me be successful in project-driven organizations.

ABOUT THE AUTHOR

Joan Knutson is a prominent project management consultant, executive coach, and trainer for Fortune 500 corporations ranging from finance and banking to pharmaceuticals, telecommunications, and high-tech industries. She has developed project management courseware and computer-based training materials for managers at all levels and is the author of several books on project management, as well as the "Executive's Notebook" column of *PM Network,* published by the Project Management Institute (PMI).

Ms. Knutson founded Project Mentors in 1976 and grew her project management training and consulting business into a multimillion-dollar firm, which was acquired in 1999. She is currently president of PMSI-Project Mentors, a part of the Provant solution. She also writes a column titled "PM Guru" for PMI's Information Systems Special Interest Group. Applying the knowledge that she has acquired over 35 years in business to her work with distinguished clients and publications, Ms. Knutson is widely recognized as a leader in the discipline of project management.

Ms. Knutson is a contributing editor of *Project Management for Business Professionals: A Comprehensive Guide* (John Wiley & Sons, 2001).

CONTENTS

Part III   Processes

Part IV   Politics

Part V   Conclusion

PREFACE

This book draws on a long career in project management coaching and training to make available in one volume the most comprehensive, state-of-the-art, and readily useful guidance on all aspects of managing projects. Distilling the lessons learned and wisdom gained in executive consultations with scores of Fortune 500 companies and presenting the best of the seminars and trainings that have been given across the country, this practical book offers readers at all levels in all fields a complete orientation to the essentials of successful project management.

This book is designed for all managers of projects—those who wear the official title and bear the explicit job description and those who assume by default the ad hoc challenge of managing a wide array of team efforts. This book gives readers the knowledge, tools, and insights to successfully meet the challenge of project management, whether for the launch of a new product, introduction of a new system, or any other discrete effort that requires the sensible, intelligent practice of team management. It begins with a firm belief that, as a serious discipline that is becoming the new paradigm, *project management* requires a more rigorous approach. This is explored in depth here. It is my hope that as corporations continually reinvent themselves, individuals with project management responsibilities will not only possess the skills to carry on effectively but will be recognized for their talent in governing these processes.

The writings and courseware, from which this text evolved, have been applied widely in finance, banking, pharmaceuticals, telecommunications, and high-tech industries; and the tools contained in this volume are applicable to any industry or environment in which project management is or will be a cornerstone. Today, those environments run the gamut, from the traditional world of construction, architecture, engineering, and capital improvement to the world of Internet startups and specialized consultancy, in industries ranging from travel to managed care. Today, in virtually every field, managers of projects need to see themselves as consultants who are experts in project management, bringing their wealth of problem-solving and analytical skills to their business environments. This book gives those managers the benefit of a lifetime in the front lines of project management to empower them to refine those skills into a well-developed discipline. Its melding of no-nonsense tools with sophisticated yet simply presented theory makes this book as vital to the business classroom as to the hands-on practitioner of project work.

Beginning with an historic overview of the fascinating evolution of organizations from traditional to project-driven, the book is organized around the four arenas that must be fully managed to succeed in project management: the project people, the project processes, the project politics, and the measurements of project success.

Part I defines the contemporary corporate paradigm—the project-driven organization. It presents the concepts of the discipline of project management; how it evolved; the forms that it takes; and the processes, procedures, tools, and terms that it employs.

Part II acquaints the reader with the human behavioral aspects of project management, exploring the many, sometimes surprising roles of participating project players and managers, as well as the keys to successfully managing performance and building teamwork, even in long-distance teams and with less-than-committed clients and customers.

Part III delves into the highly developed processes that support the discipline. They include proposal and portfolio management, planning, execution, and control with special emphasis on the imperatives of good communications, the management of risk, and the rigorous analysis of project closeout.

Part IV charts a sane course through the politics, or organizational platforms, that arise in conducting project management, from gauging the current climate of a corporate culture to nurturing the management effort through the three stages of the evolving entity called the *project office*.

Part V saves for last the most critical issue of project management. As the discipline of project management becomes more visible, top management and clients alike will demand that it not only succeed but that it add significant value to the organization. The final part of this book presents four prospective yardsticks for the measurement of project management success and a set of essential measurement procedures. This complex system is as rigorous in its approach as it is essential to the discipline. By the time readers have arrived here, they will be well prepared and eager to prove not only their own mettle but the profound value of the innovations of the project management discipline.

While newcomers to project management will want to read this book from start to finish, more seasoned managers may find particular chapters of special value—certainly those that tackle subjects not often covered in other references and professional guides. The discipline of project management encompasses a progressively broader share of the work of organizations.

Greater emphasis has been placed on project management concerns such as communications and portfolio management, as well as the development of the project office. This volume focuses on the state of the art of project management and in so doing offers fresh perspectives on a variety of subjects that are covered only sparingly if at all in the major texts on the subject.

As part of the effort to speak in plain English, with as little jargon as possible, frequently used project management terms are defined when first used and gathered in the Glossary at the back of the book. Introduced with brief anecdotes drawn from decades in the field, each chapter ends with one or more Performance Support Tools—a total of 32—all designed to allow managers of projects to apply the information given in the chapter to their unique workplace or project. These tools include benefit statements to present to top management, project client's and other problems/solutions checklists, outlines of essential procedures, worksheets, templates, and report forms. Designed to give the reader a head start in practicing the techniques in this book, whether it is a process for project selection, creating a successful proposal, evaluating a vendor, scheduling a project team, reporting a risk, or writing one's own job descriptions, these time-tested performance supports have won countless satisfied clients over many years. These tools can be accessed electronically at the PMSI-Project Mentors' Web site: http://www.pmsi-pm.com. The author and publisher authorize the reproduction of these tools for organizational use.

Differing significantly in style and approach from the current standard references on project management, *Succeeding in Project-Driven Organizations* is directed not just to the project manager, project client, or project team member curious about the changing landscape of the discipline but to all business professionals who want to enhance their knowledge and improve their techniques in up-to-the-minute project management.

JOAN KNUTSON
President, PMSI-Project Mentors
Part of the Provant solution

San Francisco 2001

ACKNOWLEDGMENTS

Thank you to PMSI-Project Mentors and to our parent company, Provant, for allowing me the time to write this book.

Thank you to the Project Management Institute for giving me permission to use articles that I have written for their *PM Network* magazine as the basis for much of the content.

Thank you to Ilene Shapera-Fenton for taking my homey verbiage and turning it into real English and for being one of the best project managers that I know.

And thank you for colleagues such as Jerry Brown, Betsy Guthrie, Alan Gump, Jane DeYoung, and Karen Borst-Rothe for advice and counsel on specific areas within the book.

J.K.

PART I

INTRODUCTION

CHAPTER 1

The Project-Driven Organization

Project management is a discipline that requires discipline.

The first use of the word *discipline* in the preceding sentence refers to the structured business system that is known as project management. This business system consists of people, processes, and politics. Some of these elements are documented; others, handed down from one generation to another, are informal.

The second use of *discipline* in the sentence suggests that there must be rigorous support of management. A buy-in of all the project players is needed to make project management successful within any organization. Only with this level of discipline can the processes be followed, the people be managed, and the politics, in the form of organizational structures, be positioned correctly.

This book looks at both the discipline of project management and the discipline needed to make project management a viable and applicable business system.

CHAPTER AND BOOK OVERVIEW

This chapter introduces the concepts, benefits, expectations, processes, procedures, practices, tools, and terms that constitute the discipline of successful project management. All of the terms and processes introduced here are fully explored throughout this comprehensive book.

A substantial amount of scope and detail is condensed in these opening pages; they present an overall blueprint for success in project-driven organizations. First, we consider the evolution of traditional organizations into project-driven units. We compare types of organizational structures, including the multiproject environment. Then we examine the rationale and critical success factors of project-driven organizations. Product and project development processes or life cycles are then introduced and outlined in some detail. Other approaches to project management, and coverage of the evolving role of managers of projects complete the topics in Part I.

Part II explores the sociological or people-oriented aspects of succeeding in project-driven organizations: the roles, interactions, performance standards, and team dynamics of the project players. From the top down, those players include management and project clients; managers of projects; resource managers; project team members; and third-party vendors. In Part III, we study the processes of successful project management, from managing proposals, portfolios, planning, execution, and communications, to managing risks and then carefully bringing closure to the project effort. Part IV considers the political ramifications of project management and how to successfully fit the discipline into the corporate culture and create a sensible project management structure that matches the needs of an organization.

The book concludes with discussions of the measurements by which the success of project management can be evaluated. Practicing what is preached, each chapter is accompanied by practical performance support and assessment tools that readers can apply to their own unique environment. All of the Performance Support and Assessment Tools referenced in this book are available for download at www.pmsi-pm.com.

We begin by tracing the path to where we are.

EVOLUTION FROM A TRANSACTION-DRIVEN ORGANIZATION TO A PROJECT-DRIVEN ORGANIZATION

Many businesses have always been project-driven. Organizations dedicated to construction, high technology, and consumer products do projects exclusively. Construction companies build a single building or a complex of buildings. They create roads, lay pipelines, and dig tunnels. They plan, organize, and manage their work. High-technology companies are creating new hardware or software products. They too must plan, organize, and control their work. Similarly, consumer product companies are generating new products that range from cereal to bug spray or gloves. Each of these new products equates to a new project that must be planned, organized, and managed.

Service organizations and information companies have always been transaction-driven. For example, banks process checks, insurance companies process claims, hotels and airlines process reservations, and the stock exchanges process buys and sells . These transaction-driven organizations have just recently recognized that in today's business world they are project-driven.

Processing transactions is a necessity that keeps these companies alive. They have been doing this basic processing for so long that it is no longer a challenge. But every time a new process is implemented, or a new system is installed, or a new product or service is introduced to the marketplace, a project is initiated. New projects keep these organizations growing and competitive in the marketplace.

As you can see in Figure 1.1, traditional organizational structures arrange a business into areas of similar expertise, such as finance, manufacturing, and marketing. The principal function of each area is to support a specific activity within the business. Finance supports the planning and management of funds; manufacturing assembles the product; marketing sells the product; and so on. However, the projects that help these organizations to grow require input, support, and buy-in from many functional departments simultaneously. The traditional organizational structure does *not* support projects that cross many functional lines and require contributions from various functional groups. The traditional structure fosters silos or "stovepipes" that are empires in and of themselves. Think of them as serfdoms that have surrounded their town with a moat. People are allowed in only if someone lets

Figure 1.1   Traditional Organizational Chart

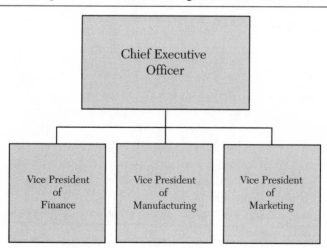

down the drawbridge and invites them in. The rulers are generally so concerned about maintaining their own serfdoms that they have no time to consider other serfdoms' concerns, interests, and projects.

The chain-of-command rule is a classic management philosophy. For many years, it was suggested that each employee should have one boss, and only one boss, as the responsibility is delegated down the chain of command. With the advent of project-driven organizations and project organizational structures, this chain-of-command rule was negated. Project organizations imply that the project team members, and even the manager of the project, have multiple bosses.

Let's consider an example. The branch personnel officer who is helping to install a new product line for the customer may have two bosses: (1) the manager at the branch where he or she works, and (2) the manager of the project at corporate headquarters—the person who is coordinating the rollout of the new service.

Project management has the advantage of open communication links and better utilization of human resources. However, working within a project confers the inherent frustration of having to contend with two bosses, not to mention the questionable level of authority that is sometimes vested in the manager of the project.

Most projects cannot be performed within the confines of the functional department. They require a project-driven organization—one that can support the interdepartmental involvement of team members from widely varied disciplines.

WHAT IS A PROJECT?

A project is the organized development of an end-product. If the focus is on the end-product, that discipline is product management. If the focus is on being organized, that discipline is project management.

A project is also a discernible effort that has a discrete beginning, a discrete end, and a discrete deliverable. It is not a routine, repetitive transaction-driven effort, such as producing cars off an assembly line or processing invoices through an Accounts Payable department. However, retooling the line that manufactures those cars, or automating the Accounts Payable system, would be considered a project.

To be more specific, the basic criteria for work that lend themselves to project management are:

- A *well-defined deliverable* that is neither vague nor ambiguous documented in a scope definition or statement of work.
- A *collection of activities* that will culminate in the end-product. These activities will be documented in a to-do list called a work breakdown structure (WBS). This list of work activities also designates who will be responsible for producing the deliverables from each activity.
- *Activities with start and finish points.* The finish points represent specific deliverables that have a measurable standard of performance criteria. Time and cost estimates are made for each of these activities. "I don't know how long it will take" or "I don't know how many iterations are required" are unacceptable. A best guess is required.
- *Activities that can be ordered.* Certain activities must be conducted serially, or in sequence. Others can go on in parallel, or simultaneously. The sequence is documented in a network and/or a schedule chart.

Projects may originate from the top of an organization, as a result of the strategic planning process. They may also come from the bottom; an individual or a group may initiate a project because of a belief that it will add organizational value in some way. Some projects are initiated externally by a customer or a client. Let's look at how each type is related to project management.

- *Strategic projects.* Top-down projects are business initiatives that have already been assigned high priority, having been identified through a high-level management process that support the long-range strategic plan.
- *Bottom-up projects.* Many good ideas are generated from the people who work in the trenches. If the folks doing the day-to-day operational work do not have a forum *and* a process for putting forward their suggestions, either they will not be motivated to make things better within the organization, or they might proceed informally with no approval.
- *External projects.* A third possible category of projects are derived from external sources; for example, a Request for Proposal (RFP) may be received from a potential customer or client.

Whether organizations have been project-oriented for their entire history or are transaction-oriented and are simply converting to a project-driven style, organizations have one thing in common: They must deal with multiple projects simultaneously. Let's consider the issues surrounding working in a multiproject environment.

A Multiproject Environment

The words "managing projects in an organization" can bring fear into some souls. It means juggling more than one ball at a time, and that feat is even more difficult in an organizational environment where the manager of the project typically does not have official authority. No matter how good the juggler, he or she occasionally will drop a ball. The job requires not dropping too many too often. When one is dropped, it must be picked up quickly, so that as few people as possible will notice.

The existence of multiple projects in an organization forms a system, much like a galaxy of stars, moons, and planets. These celestial objects are related to one another because they occupy the same universe at the same time. If one of them goes off course or if it collides with another orbiting object, the impact will reorder the scheme of things—even if no serious damage is done. In a similar way, multiple projects exist precariously within a business environment. Each project rotates in its own orbit and is fine as long as there are no collisions with any other projects. Thus, this galaxy of projects does or does not work together because there is order within the larger scheme. In a multiproject environment, the job of a project-driven organization is to keep order within the scheme of things. How can this be done?

Multiple projects come in a variety of shapes and forms. The simplest variation is a large program composed of several smaller projects. The program has a single business objective, and all the individual projects contribute to that end-goal. This type of multiproject management situation has a known focal point, and there are reasonably obvious interfaces. However, when the manager of the project is asked to manage multiple *unrelated* projects, the effort becomes much more difficult. Often, the resources required by these multiple unrelated projects are located in different geographic areas and different time zones, and are conducted within different cultures. The effort to manage and coordinate these projects rises almost beyond the capability of any one human being.

Various factors make managing multiple projects different from managing a single project. Handling only one project allows a singleness of purpose; a sole objective is to be reached. A defined resource pool and a select reporting mechanism focus on one to-do list, the work breakdown structure (WBS). In a multiproject environment, the changes are significant. Each project has its own purpose, its own objective. Resources are drawn from a myriad of functional areas; some originate from the same departments and some do not. Each project requires planning, monitoring, and tracking, which, in turn, necessitates an individual report reflecting the status of a unique series of activities.

Strategies for Managing Multiple Projects

Does the manager of the project approach multiple projects differently? Yes, very differently. The following list illustrates the differences in the project environment and in how the manager of the project must act when dealing with multiple projects.

Focusing on Efficiency

In a single-project world, efficiency is important. In a multiproject environment, there simply is no room for wasted time or misplaced energy.

Focusing on Long-Term and Short-Term Goals

A manager of a single project might be able to survive by managing predictable events that will occur one or two weeks in the future. A manager of multiple projects, however, must be able to anticipate events occurring over a longer term, and to gauge the achievement of the long- as well as the short-term goals.

Responding Proactively rather than Reactively

The focus of a single-project environment allows some reactive responses. But managing many projects, especially if long-term management is required, necessitates proactive project management skills, such as providing long lead time to request and acquire resources.

Considering Broader Organizational Issues

Inevitably, multiple projects extend their tentacles into more areas and encounter more political potholes. The manager of the project must be sensitive to the potential problems in these extended team relationships.

Introducing Greater Consistency and Communication of Decisions

A multiproject environment deals with changing priorities, unexpected contingencies, and greater political implications which cause project team members to describe the manager of the project as being inconsistent, erratic, and even irrational. The manager of the project must work at being as consistent as possible. This requires communicating decisions quickly, clearly, and with explanations.

Balancing Flexibility and Stability

A multiproject environment requires a balance between flexibility—successfully meeting the inevitable changes in the projects themselves—and stability—connoting control to the project client, the functional manager, and the project team members.

Practicing Greater Delegation

In a single-project environment, the manager of the project often can do much of the work. In a multiproject world, the manager of the project is forced to fulfill that title in the truest sense and cannot afford to get too embroiled in actually doing the tasks.

Competing, Sometimes against Oneself

Each project requires resources: people, and, possibly, equipment and materials. The resource pools are limited. The manager of the project often competes for the same constrained resource pool (labor, equipment, and materials) that supplies all the other projects within the organization. A manager of multiple projects may require support for each project from the same resource pool, which means competing with himself or herself for the same resources.

To work in this project-driven environment, managers must understand the rationale for its existence and be able to "sell" it to those around them.

RATIONALE FOR A PROJECT-DRIVEN ORGANIZATION

Managers who are attempting to sell the concept of a more structured project management approach to their corporate management and/or their customers should read this section very carefully.

Management, in the literal sense, includes those who manage resources to accomplish a specific purpose. Individuals in management roles often have dual motivations: (1) to do business in the most efficient, effective, and productive manner possible; and (2) to get a quality job done as quickly as possible and for the least amount of money. If the environmental culture in which management works gives the second motivation a higher priority than the first, then, even with the best of intentions, it will be difficult for management to buy into a process such as project management. When the focus is exclusively or primarily on maximum speed and economy, project management can appear to add tremendous overhead in time and resources, without an obvious immediate return on investment (ROI).

A *customer* is someone who buys something from someone else. In the project management world, the customer is referred to as the *project client*. An internal or external project client may buy the deliverable(s) produced from a project process. Whether a project client is internal or external, he or she has one motivation: To get the highest-quality deliverable, as quickly as possible, for the least amount of money. This is often where management gets a second push back. Because of the time, expense, and quality motivation, project clients cannot easily buy into a process that appears to add overhead and therefore might slow down their job.

Project practitioners are often asked: "Can you give me some arguments that will convince my management/customer that project management is the way to go?" Or: "I've been assigned to implement project management in my firm and have been asked to prepare an executive briefing. Do you have any *sell* terms that will get management to buy in?"

The answer is *Yes*. This section presents a cogent series of defensible arguments that help sell project management, and interjects some expected rebuttals from the ever-present resident cynic. To sell, one must understand what the customer is buying. Revlon representatives are noted for stating, for instance, that they are not selling cosmetics; they are selling hope. What are project practitioners selling?

Because bosses/customers do not like surprises, perhaps the most appropriate term to describe the advantages of project management would be *reassurance;* business reassurance. Planning and controlling are integral parts of project management, and, by definition, they reduce the risk factors of dealing in a rapidly changing environment.

Today's changing environment is asking each manager of projects to plan, monitor, track, and manage schedules, resources, costs, and quality. The project management process provides the tools and orchestrates the environment in which those variables can be managed in the most professional manner possible. Let's see how this is accomplished.

A typical project discipline ensures that the following benefits exist. A concise yet definitive project scope statement is generated, and it details the specific project deliverables and outcomes expected from the project, as voiced by the project client. A work breakdown structure (WBS) is also prepared, enumerating a thorough to-do list of the activities to be performed. These two efforts reduce the risk of misunderstandings or omissions. Of necessity, the project client participates in the process via a project team organization. This ensures the beginning of a partnering relationship through good communication.

The schedules, project budget, and quality/defect reports inherently position checkpoints for reevaluation. These status-reporting tools also offer communication and keep all interested parties informed of progress. Quality and control, plus the involvement and commitment of all project players, are built in through this monitoring, tracking, and reporting process.

Because the tracking process reveals deviations from the plan in the early stages, management is provided with sufficient lead time to weigh the ingredients of quality, cost, and time, and to make decisions that will ensure reaching the original goal—or, if necessary, a satisfactory alternative. As a substitute for panic (the *What-do-I-do-now?* syndrome), this early-warning system or proactive management mitigates the more drastic actions that might be required later, if the project were to get into management by crisis.

A by-product of the efforts described above is the creation of a history or metrics base of future planning. The WBS template, network model, and estimating base all create a springboard from which to generate a faster and more accurate plan for the next project. These normalized history bases go beyond scar tissue and provide a prototype plan for future similar projects.

As a corollary benefit to this process, if the manager of the project or any team member leaves the team, documentation is in place to continue business as usual for the project. Documentation and team organization offer the best failsafe or contingency plan for these inevitable changes.

Among the intangible benefits of project management are the experience and professional development that the project team achieves by working in a cross-functional team environment. Growth and development are gained from exposure to the various disciplines represented by subject-matter experts from different parts of the organization. Networking is established, synergy is heightened, and *esprit de corps* is encouraged. Because primary and secondary responsibilities are assigned for the completion of each task, roles are clear, accountability is understood, and staff members are groomed to grow within the organization.

Our resident cynic stated: "But what about all the additional paperwork, time, and structure imposed by project management?" None of these negative conditions needs to occur in a well-implemented project environment. With (1) the implementation of a project management process that presents a consistent way of doing project management, and (2) a project management organizational approach that supports doing project management business efficiently in each group's culture, the environment is positioned to accept and support the project management discipline.

The principal disadvantages of project management may be listed under the heading of approach: unclear, inconsistent, and disorganized. Serious thought, effort, and orientation preceding the implementation of the project management process can negate any of a cynic's negative observations.

This is the goal that motivates both our management and our project clients: to get a quality job done as quickly as possible for the least amount of money. The project management process helps that motivation; it does not hinder it. The time and effort invested in planning and organizing the project before it begins will offset the time it would take to rework, replan, and renegotiate once the project is under way. During the project, early warning signals allow us to reevaluate and respond in a sensible and professional manner. When the project is over, we have in place the mechanisms needed to become a true learning organization—we can learn from our successes and failures and archive these lessons so that others can take advantage of our experiences. Furthermore, cross-functional teams can be formed and reformed to take the best advantage of the resource pool at our disposal. In a cross-functional team environment, the project succeeds and so do the people who participate in it. They learn, grow, and become more productive for themselves and for the organization as a whole.

The key "sell" factors of project management are:

- Communication
- Quality and Control
- Risk Reduction
- Proactive Management
- Involvement, Commitment, Buy-In
- History Bases for Future Projects
- Failsafe Contingency Planning
- Staff Development
- Accountability
- Assurance

At the end of this chapter is Performance Support Tool 1.1, "Selling Project Management to Management/Customer." Review this list and check off those benefits that you think will help you "sell" project management in your project community.

CRITICAL SUCCESS FACTORS

An effective project management discipline is reliant on these five components:

1. Awareness
2. Organization

3. Processes
4. Tools
5. Education

Let's look at each one separately. We will first describe the component more clearly and then define the steps necessary to implement that component within a project environment.

Awareness

The discipline of project management succeeds if there is an awareness of: the rudiments of the discipline, the benefits that the discipline brings to the organization, and management's expectations of project management as they relate to other disciplines at work in the organization.

To ensure awareness, the following steps need to be taken.

Synthesize Management's Vision

Management must articulate a vision for project management within the organization. Is project management merely a data-gathering function that is necessary to disseminate the status of stand-alone work efforts that are under way? Or is project management the mandated mode by which all non-operational work is going to be conducted? There is quite a difference.

Disseminate Management's Vision

After management has solidified the role that project management will play in the organization, this vision must be documented and disseminated to everyone who has a need to know. This can be done at a massive meeting; or by functional managers of operational departments, during weekly staff meetings; or via an executive memo, an internal newsletter, and/or a videotape playing in the cafeteria or auditorium.

Inspect the Discipline

A requirement of proof that the discipline is being used is the only way to ensure that project management is being applied consistently and correctly throughout the organization. Reports, scheduled status meetings, and surprise briefings are ways to keep people mindful of doing business using project management.

Maintain the Focus

With many initiatives, all goes well in the first few weeks or months after implementation, but the energy and focus dissipate after some period of time.

The last job in building awareness of project management is to keep the focus and energy alive. Refresher memos, awards, and recognition can reward good project work, and brown-bag lunches can be scheduled as a forum for continual growth and learning. This is a time to be creative, to keep awareness of project management from dying through neglect.

Organization

The organizational structures that support projects differ from the structures that support recurring day-to-day operational, transaction-driven efforts. Teams drive project management. Teams require a clear definition of the organizational structure in which they are expected to work. To define the company's unique organizational entity, take the following steps.

Reevaluate and Solidify the Correct Structure

Evaluate the current structure under which projects are performed, analyze its effectiveness, and reengineer (as necessary) the clustering of skill mixes, the reporting relationships, and the differentiation of operational responsibilities versus project responsibilities.

Clarify Accountability and Authority

This step is crucial. Mistakes are made not because people are unwilling to buy into the project management discipline but because they are unsure of precisely what they will be held accountable for and, specifically, what authority they have to meet their accountabilities.

Develop Job Descriptions

That which is not written down is not real; therefore, the project management roles, responsibilities, accountabilities, and authorities of each and every project player must be documented for all to see and follow.

Set Up Reward Systems

Reward systems should correlate to job descriptions and be both tangible and intangible. Tangible rewards take the form of salary increases and bonuses. Intangible rewards take the form of recognition and additional challenge.

Position a Performance Management System

Each person deserves a tentative roadmap that shows where current performance is going, what goals are supposed to be reached, and what management is going to do to support the roadmap. Performance management consists of job expectations, tangible metrics that indicate success, and specific advancement potentials if these metrics are attained.

Processes

Project management is directed and facilitated by processes that codify how the project work is to be performed. Two major processes support project management: (1) the *product development process or life cycle* (how to create the deliverable from the project), and (2) the *project management process or life cycle* (how to plan and control the product development process). Let's explore both of these processes.

Establish a Product Development Process

This process delineates project tasks, their associated deliverables, and the responsible parties. A unique detailed task list is produced for the development of each product. The development process for a software product might include: perform feasibility study, generate requirements, program, test, and install. The product development life cycle for an advertising campaign might be: conduct market survey, correlate data, prepare artwork, test market, and roll out. The product development process identifies the actual and unique work efforts that are required to move the project from start to finish.

Establish a Project Management Process

These possible processes provide the standards and procedures that aid in the management of the product development process described above. The project management processes include some or all the following: proposal management, portfolio management, planning, execution, communications, risk management, and closeout. All these processes are integrated within the product life cycle discussed earlier. The chosen project management scheduling and tracking tools are discussed in the next section. Life cycles are further explored later in this chapter.

Part III, "Processes," gives more information on the project management processes.

Tools

When we talk about tools, we are often referring to automated software tools. Typical off-the-shelf scheduling software can be modified to integrate the product development process and the project management processes, including forms, guidelines, and the archiving of historical metrics. The following steps should be taken to enable this component of the project management discipline.

Standardize to a Tool

One tool, one reporting portfolio, one communication vehicle allows all parties to be comparing apples to apples and to be speaking the same language. It is strongly recommended that only one tool be used (or two tools, a micro and a macro, which import and export data between them).

Integrate the Product Development Process in the Tool

Enter the detailed product developmental tasks into the tool, and make this template of the WBS the mandatory starting point for all new projects.

Integrate the Project Management Processes (Including Forms) into the Tool

Customize the tool (to the degree possible) to provide guidance and reminders of the project management processes. Utilize the tool as the repository for all the information concerning each and every project.

Standardize Report Outputs

One size of report does not fit all; however, a standardized series of reports designed for specific audiences will ensure consistent and meaningful communication.

Expand to a Suite of Software

Often, the scheduling tool alone is not adequate for the company's enterprisewide requirements or for its information needs. Therefore, as your last step in building the tool component, consider and implement add-on pieces of software that will create a complete, automated project management system.

Education

Project management requires that the project players possess its unique set of competencies, which are learned in and outside of the classroom. Education offers the correct skill via the correct mode at the correct time. Here are the steps that must be provided.

Set Up Classroom Education

Determine whether classroom education is necessary, and, if so, what types of classes are appropriate. Classes include Project Management Principles of Planning and Control; application of specific processes (e.g., risk management or estimating), the Use of the Automated Tools, as well as Working in Teams.

Acquire Self-Study Education

Self-study computer-based or paper-based education is used as a review and reinforcement of the skills learned in the classroom or as an alternative mode when geography, timing, or budgets cannot justify classroom education.

Enable Performance Support

Be sure that a mechanism is in place to ensure the transfer of skills back to the workplace. Skills transfer can be simple: Provide all the functional managers (or students) of the projects with a guidebook that gives directions for implementation. Skills transfer can also be sophisticated: Provide a software tool that allows students (in an automated environment back on the job) to immediately apply their skills and competencies through charts, graphs, checklists, and worksheets. Education is like a newly planted tree. It takes frequent attention immediately after the planting, and ongoing care throughout its life.

This section has put forth the critical success factors or enablers that need to be in place if project management is to be successful. First, an awareness of the position, benefits, and expectations of project management needs to be cultivated. Second, an appropriate organizational structure, including job descriptions, reward systems, and performance plans, needs to be established. Third, processes of product development *and* project management must be created so that everyone understands what is supposed to be done and how they are supposed to do it. The fourth component, tools, is optional. The correct tools should be given to the people who are accountable for performing the processes. Fifth and last, the players in this environment need to be educated in how project management relates to the organization, the processes, and the tools. Only then can they contribute to the success of each project and, more importantly, to the discipline as a whole.

Review your current project management discipline. Has your organization built each of these components? Has it taken each of the steps to ensure that project management is being built on a strong foundation?

LIFE CYCLES

The preceding section mentioned that the key features of the project management discipline are the two life cycles that provide the framework on which the people, processes, and politics can be built. The first life cycle, the *product development process* or life cycle, describes how to create the deliverable from the project. This cycle delineates the tasks, their associated deliverables, and the responsible parties. It includes the actual and unique work efforts that are required to move the project from start to finish.

The second life cycle, the *project management process* or life cycle, maps out how to plan and control the product development process. The project management processes provide the standards and procedures that aid in managing the product development process.

Let's look more closely at both life cycles.

The Product Development Life Cycle

The product development life cycle focuses on the product or the deliverable that is to be produced by the project. This life cycle also includes tasks such as defining the specifications of the product, designing the product (a widget, a software system, a marketing campaign), managing the work to develop/produce the product, and at the end of the project evaluating the product and the lessons learned in its development.

There are 11 phases in a generic product's developmental life cycle:

1. Initiation Phase
2. Definition Phase
3. Macro/Conceptual Design Phase
4. Micro/Detailed Design Phase
5. Development Phase
6. Testing Phase
7. Quality Control Phase
8. Implementation Phase
9. Post-Project Review Phase (Closeout)
10. Production/Distribution Phase
11. End of Life

These phases are presented in sequential order, but a previous phase need not be completed before the next phase can begin. In reality, these phases overlap each other and should be envisioned that way. Several of the phases may be condensed into a single phase. For example, the testing and quality control phases could be consolidated. On the other hand, one phase could be broken into several other phases. For example, the macro/conceptual design phase could be divided into a phase that concentrates on the concept design and another that addresses the general or macro design.

Phase 1: Initiation

The initiation phase creates a problem/opportunity statement that addresses the viability and feasibility of the product or service being considered. The objective of this phase is to investigate, analyze, and recommend whether a specific problem or opportunity is worthy of the required investment of time, resources, and dollars.

Phase 2: Definition

In this phase, the problem/opportunity statement is defined in greater detail. The requirements are translated into evaluation criteria that detail what is and is not wanted from the chosen solution. Alternative solutions are matched against the criteria, and a recommendation is determined. If there is a viable recommendation, the project is formally approved and prioritized. If a viable alternative is not found, the project is canceled.

Phase 3: Macro/Conceptual Design

This phase addresses the major conceptual design issues. It is important that all parties who will be required to develop the product/service or will be using the product are involved in this phase. The output describes the functionality and design criteria on which this deliverable will be built, from both a technical and a business perspective.

Phase 4: Micro/Detailed Design

This phase documents in detail the specifications required to develop the end-product. The specifications produced from this phase will be used to manufacture the product, to code the program, or to produce the marketing campaign in the ensuing development phase. At this point, the specifications are frozen. If there are to be any changes in the specifications, those changes will be processed through a change control system.

Phase 5: Development

The development phase details the steps to be taken by the project players (the director of manufacturing, the software programmer, and/or the product manager) who will be involved in the actual production of the product. The detailed specifications are translated into the deliverable/actual product.

Phase 6: Testing

In the testing phase, the product is tested to ensure that it meets the specifications developed in the previous phases.

Phase 7: Quality Control

The quality control phase is the final testing effort before the product or service is implemented/shipped. The activity in this phase extends beyond testing the technical functionality of the product. This phase also tests the documentation, functionality, and maintainability in a production/customer environment. The product is tested to ensure that it meets both the test criteria and its projected business/marketing requirements. This phase confirms whether the product will be reproducible and maintainable when the project is completed.

Phase 8: Implementation

In this phase, the transition from the project environment to the operational environment is completed. The product or service is now turned over to production.

Phase 9: Post-Project Review (Closeout)

The post-project review evaluates the immediate success of the project and the processes used to create the product. The product is evaluated to confirm that it has been implemented properly and is meeting functional requirements. The achievement of the process goals by the participants is reviewed and discussed with the purpose of rewarding success and discussing any reasons for failure. This is officially the end of the project but not of the product life cycle.

Phase 10: Production/Distribution

This phase might not be applicable to each type of product. This ongoing operational effort ensures that the product/service continues to be marketed, produced, maintained, and/or shipped.

Phase 11: End of Life

In this phase, the product/service is found to no longer be financially or competitively viable and is discontinued.

Now that we have looked at the product development life cycle, let's review how the project management life cycle plans, organizes, and controls the product life cycle.

The Project Management Life Cycle

A Project Management (PM) life cycle emphasizes the process used to manage a project rather than focusing on the creation or generation of the product. This life cycle is a generic process that is applicable in any industry and in any project-driven organization. The generic PM life cycle has four major phases: (1) the initiation and definition phase, which sets the objectives and scope of the project; (2) the planning phase, which establishes the baselines; (3) the execution (and controlling) phase, during which the plan is monitored, tracked, and revised, as necessary; and (4) the closeout phase. Let's look at each phase more closely.

The Initiation and Definition Phase

The life cycle begins when top management or the customer (i.e., project client) articulates a need. In conjunction with the manager of the project, the project client sets quantifiable project objectives. The following questions are answered: What is being requested? What is the scope of the effort? Why now? Why ever? In addition, time, resources, and costs may be estimated at a rough order of magnitude. If a thorough analysis is performed here, the project life cycle as well as the product life cycle is off to a good start.

The Planning Phase

Next, an integrated or more detailed project plan is developed. The quality of the product and the work effort to achieve it will be closely scrutinized. The specific tools needed to produce this plan are described next.

Because the project will be reduced to the lowest common denominator, the work breakdown structure (WBS) provides the most logical and manageable task structure. Network and Gantt (schedule) Charts are used to plan and control the work effort. Their format allows alternatives to be explored if the work effort must be compressed to meet tight deadlines. The Human Resource Matrix and Resource Loading Chart provide the media from which personnel assignments are developed, as well as a macro approach to overall corporate staffing strengths and weaknesses. These tools help determine, from a strategic and tactical viewpoint, whether the project is siphoning off too many skills that are required for day-to-day corporate operations, thereby diluting the staff necessary to meet daily needs. The project objectives are now detailed, to permit tracking the cost of the project/product against the perceived opportunities in the marketplace, or the value to the user of a product that will be utilized in-house.

Upon completion of the integrated project plan, a management review is conducted to evaluate the initial scope, costs, schedules, and resource allocation. This review provides the data needed to renegotiate the plan (if necessary) and to obtain final approval to proceed. This step in the life cycle sets the baselines. From the conclusions and resulting reports developed through these efforts, final management approval of the detailed Project Plan may be secured, and work begins. (These planning tools are discussed in more detail in Chapter 8, "Project Planning.")

The Execution/Controlling Phase

Essential to the overall success of the generic approach is the implementation of a formal plan to monitor, track, and control work in progress. Through close monitoring of the progress of the project schedule, budget, and resource allocation requirements, future problems can be anticipated, analyzed, and resolved. When future developments are anticipated, roadblocks can be removed, and the information necessary to negotiate conflict resolution can be made available.

As work continues, periodic reports of progress must be generated to evaluate human resources, anticipate any need for schedule changes, foresee cost variances, and ensure conformance with quality standards. Each factor must be examined in depth and reviewed in context. Enlightened trade-offs may be created after necessary approvals are obtained. This information is recycled when the changes are substantial. Through the project management process, a modification of the integrated plan may be recommended. Typical recommendations to modify the plan are: reallocate resources, extend the time estimate, increase the funds allocated, modify the concept of the end-product, or phase in the segments of the end-product.

The Project Closeout Phase

When the end-product is completed, it is appropriate to perform a post-project review or an audit. This process evaluates actual time, total cost, and quality of the product. A significant benefit of the post-project audit is that management receives a precise comparison of the assets actually expended on the project and the amount that was estimated. Management should be informed of (1) the actual and the expected future impact of the project on annual recurring operating expenses and/or income, and (2) whether the paybacks or savings that were contemplated will be realized. This critique also addresses the quality of the product to ascertain whether additional work effort is required and/or justified.

The post-project review provides an opportunity to refine the project management process. A comparison of the plan to the actual facts gives the manager of the project documentation and information for assessing and perhaps improving his or her planning skills. The closeout phase provides critiques that offer managers of projects a substantive learning experience.

Deconstructing the project into the four-phase life cycle described above makes it easier to contemplate the tasks of project management. Each phase has a purpose. Each phase employs the knowledge and lessons learned in the previous phase. Each phase needs to be understood by the manager of the project, the team, and the project client. Only then can support of the project management effort be complete.

In summary, the life cycles both product development and project development are vital to the success of a project. The two are interdependent. Each begins with initiation and definition and ends with closeout.

The Rolling Wave or Phased Approach to Project Management

How often, when you have been asked for estimates of the duration and cost of a project, have you given answers before you fully understood the scope of the effort? How often have you been correct? Although you were assured that your estimates need only be ballpark figures, how often were they set in concrete, never to change?

This section discusses how such a scenario develops, why this approach seldom works, and what can be done to structure a more realistic alternative. To address this issue, imagine that you are an expert mountain climber. You are standing at the bottom of an imposing mountain that you have never seen before. It is your job to climb to the peak of this mountain and to descend to the other side of its base. During the Initiation and Definition Phase of the Product/Project Life Cycles, the person who is funding your expedition asks you, "How long will it take you to get to the other side of the mountain, and how much money do you need?"

You ask yourself, "How do I know how long it is going to take to get to the other side or how much money it will cost? I have never seen this mountain before."

Would answering "I don't know" satisfy your sponsor? Probably not. You were hired because of your expertise in mountain climbing, and you are therefore expected to be able to give some answers. On the other hand, if you shoot from the hip, the accuracy of your best guess will be weak, and sooner or later you will have to confront your error. You seem to be caught in a lose–lose situation. Is there an alternative?

Consider the Rolling Wave, or phased, approach—a method that will both satisfy your sponsor and add a sense of integrity and credibility to your commitments. The Rolling Wave approach to project management suggests that the project planning effort rolls out detailed plans for the *foreseeable* future and, as the project evolves, periodically reevaluates the completion dates and the total dollars needed.

Let's reexamine your mountain climber role. You are standing at the bottom of the mountain. You have minimal knowledge of what is confronting you. But with your mountain climbing background and experience, and given the data you have gathered from other people who have tried to climb this mountain, you *approximate* the time and resources required.

NOTE The operative word is "approximate," not "estimate." Your approximation should be presented so as to provide you with all the flexibility possible. For example: "It will take six to nine weeks to get over the mountain, will require 10 to 12 people, and will cost $50,000, plus or minus 10 percent."

Simultaneously, you provide the sponsor with a detailed plan and a list of everything required to prepare the party to start moving up the mountain. Your plan shows that you have determined the necessary equipment, pinpointed the right people, acquired and studied all available information about this particular mountain, and plotted a route of travel. This is called *scheduling through the first planning horizon.* A planning horizon is described as planning as far ahead as you can see. This target may be stated as the next phase of the Product Development Life Cycle.

Thus far, you have provided your sponsor with (1) an approximation of the time and resources needed to finish the total effort, and (2) a detailed schedule for the first planning horizon or Product Life Cycle Phase.

Now the benefits of Rolling Wave come into effect. You track to the detailed plan that was established for the first planning horizon. At the end of each product phase, many unknowns have been resolved, and many decisions have been made. In our mountain climbing analogy, once the equipment and people required to make the climb are selected and the route is mapped, the planning for the next phase begins. This step, which is to acquire the resources and prepare for the start of the climb, becomes relatively easy. Furthermore, at this stage, the approximation of the total time and resources can be refined with a higher level of accuracy and with greater confidence. At each subsequent reevaluation, the projection of the final deadline and the total dollars becomes more realistic. There will come a point in time when you have enough information available to render further reevaluations unnecessary.

This approach may be logical to other managers of projects, but how can we sell it to our management and project clients? First, let's consider the premise that the old way has not worked. It has not been realistic to formulate a series of time, staffing, and budget commitments and, on Day 1, set them in concrete. Even when estimates have been requested or mandated, or baselines have been announced, the Rolling Wave approach provides a practical methodology for evaluating and reevaluating the validity of commitments, and a means to support refinement of those commitments, if and when appropriate.

THE MANAGERS OF PROJECTS

You may have noticed that we have not once used, nor do we use in this book, the term "project manager." Many people are managers of efforts that have a discrete beginning and a discrete end, and produce a discrete deliverable, but these people do not have the title of "project manager." Their organizations may not have authenticated the job of managing projects, or the job may be too small to be on the radar screen as a bona fide position but may still require the discipline associated with project management.

Therefore, we have chosen to change the title of the individual in question and to include everyone in the organization who plans, organizes, and manages projectlike work. The title "manager of the project" accomplishes that objective. What is the role of the manager of the project?

A Role as an "Intrapreneur"

Think of a project as though it were a microcosm of the organization. It absorbs the organization's resources and, as payback, it creates a deliverable that will provide the organization with a return on that investment: a salable or cost-saving product or service. If this is true, then the manager of the project and his or her project team are running an enterprise; a small microcosim of the business. And as a manager of the project of an enterprise, this person is an "intrapreneur."

What is an intrapreneur? It is a person whose tasks are like those of an entrepreneur but who works within an organization. An intrapreneur should have the same mindset as an entrepreneur: a desire to run the enterprise cost effectively and productively, to gain the most return. Thus, if the manager of the project is willing to be accountable for managing the enterprise, he or she should be given the autonomy and authority to do the job to the best of his or her ability.

The Role of Managers of Projects

A manager of a project must plan, organize, and control the schedules and budgets of that project and must manage an entity called a cross-functional team. In *Productive Workplaces,* Marvin Weisbord suggests that, in this instance, the following conditions must exist simultaneously:

- *Interdependence.* The team is working on important problems in which each person has a stake.
- *Leadership.* The leader wants so strongly to improve the team's performance that he or she is willing to take risks.
- *Joint decisions.* All team members agree to participate.
- *Equal influence.* Each person has a chance to influence the team's agenda.[1]

Today, a project environment that will support a high-performing, cross-functional team is marked by more freedom, less micromanaging, challenging goals, freedom to take risks, patience with ambiguity, and minimal information.

To allow this supportive environment and the above team conditions to exist, the attitude of top management must undergo a shift. Management must:

- Trust
- Encourage trial and error
- Position cross-learning and transfer of learning
- Support assembling the right mix of people, not just a mix of skills
- Encourage getting out of the office to clear the cobwebs and to dream
- Establish reward systems based on individual and team performance

CONCLUSION

Project management is a discipline that requires discipline. As a discipline, PM has become more prominent in the business community. Transaction-oriented organizations are moving toward a project-driven orientation. This is occurring because transaction processing allows the company to survive, but the project discipline lets the company grow and compete.

What is a project? A project is an endeavor that has a discrete beginning, a discrete end, and a discrete deliverable. There are three types of projects:

1. Strategic projects come down from the top. Top-level management conjures them up during a strategic or long-range planning effort.
2. Bottom-up projects are dreamed up by the people in the trenches.
3. External projects, found at some companies, are initiated by an outside customer.

This generally means that multiple projects are in progress within any organization at any time. It is not easy to work in a multiproject environment.

Focus and patience are required. It is also helpful if all the project players have bought into the process of project management. Project players buy in because this way of doing business is a logical utilization of resources to reach common goals with meaningful end-products. Project management facilitates communication, quality, control, risk reduction, and, most importantly, assurance to all the players that project business is being conducted in the most professional way possible.

In positioning this project management discipline, there are five critical success factors:

1. Awareness of the discipline
2. An organization that supports the discipline
3. Processes that prescribe how the discipline is to be conducted
4. Automated tools that support the processes
5. Education in how to use the tools and processes as well as how to work within a project-driven organization

The project-driven organization is built around two different life cycles: a product life cycle and a project life cycle. The product life cycle describes how to create the deliverable produced from the project. This life cycle consists of the actual and unique work efforts that are required to move the project from the beginning to the end.

The project life cycle lays out how to plan and control the product development life cycle. But how do you plan an entire product life cycle at Day 1 of the project?

You don't. You use the Rolling Wave or phased approach to planning, organizing, and controlling a project. You plot the first planning horizon in detail and map out the rest of the project at a high level. At the end of the first planning horizon, you revisit and modify the project parameters of time, staffing, and cost (if necessary), and you detail the plan for the next planning horizon. The project management discipline is an iterative approach.

And who runs this entity called a project? The manager of the project. Although many organizations call this person a "project manager," we have chosen to refer to him or her as a manager of the project. This recognizes that personnel who are not officially given the title of "project manager" are often held accountable for running project work. It also broadens the spectrum of people to whom this book applies and who should be reading this book.

With this information in hand, we offer you Performance Support Tool 1.2, "Gap Analysis," which allows you to determine the current state and imagine the future state of project management in your organization, and to work toward closing whatever gap exists between them. The goal is to identify the barriers and the solutions needed to overcome them so that your organization can reach the future state.

NOTE
---

1. Marvin R. Weisbord. 1987. *Productive Workplaces: Organizing and Managing for Dignity, Meaning, and Community.* (San Francisco, CA: Jossey-Bass).

Selling Project Management to Management/Customer

Project management is a discipline that promotes an environment of performance, profitability, effectiveness, and efficiency.

Below are a series of cogent arguments, which will help you convince your management and/or your customer that project management is a discipline worth investing time and money in.

Here is how to use this performance support tool. First: In Section 1, describe the person/group to whom you are trying to sell project management, then read each of the alternative benefits in Sections 2A, 2B, and 2C checking off those arguments that will help substantiate your case. Finally, in Section 3, summarize a Benefits Statement which can be presented in a proposal to your management or to your customer.

SECTION 1: TO WHOM ARE YOU SELLING?

1. Name of person (title) or department
2. Current use of project management, if any
3. Possible reluctance to accept project management
4. Indications of acceptance of project management

SECTION 2: ALTERNATIVE BENEFITS   CHECK HERE
2A. BENEFITS RELATIVE TO MANAGEMENT   IF APPLICABLE

2A.1   Project management requires a concise project definition and specific deliverable(s). Management must thoroughly evaluate the rationale for any project that is submitted for approval and must justify producing the deliverable(s). This analysis allows management to develop a perspective on how this project relates to the intermediate and long-term goals and strategies of the organization. Management can then appropriately prioritize the project and the effort that it takes to produce the deliverable(s).   _____

2A.2   Quality and control are built in through scheduled management reviews and go or no-go decisions. Management becomes involved at appropriate junctures to review the quality of the deliverable and reevaluate the current status of the justification. If the project no longer will produce the expected benefits, then management has an obligation to terminate the effort.   _____

2A.3   The scheduled interactions with management ensure a continued involvement, particularly for the project client. Project clients should not envision projects as arm's-length endeavors for which they place an order and come back later to pick it up. Projects are not like ordering a pizza. You may request particular toppings, but if the deliverable is less than perfect or indicates substitutions, you'll eat it anyway. Projects are more like ordering a tailored suit. You try it on again and again to make sure it will fit and to have adjustments made as needed. The discipline of project management encourages the project client, the end user, the manager, and the bill payer to remain involved throughout the entire process.

2A.4   Project management provides a historic bank of data and project models for future planning. The future planning can be in the realm of strategic planning regardless of whether the organization has wisely or unwisely expended its money in the past. The project management historical database will provide insight and guidance as to where management should be expending funds in the future.

2A.5   From another and more immediate perspective, a formalized project history base stores data from which more accurate estimates can be made for future projects. New project teams, if provided with models and templates of work breakdown structures (WBSs), sequences, and time estimates, are more likely to prepare realistic plans in which project parameters of time, resources, and scope can legitimately be met.

CHECK HERE
IF APPLICABLE

2B BENEFITS TO THE PROJECT

2B.1   Project management is a discipline that requires discipline. The latter discipline refers to building a foundation to visualize the project through time and to determine the tasks to be performed, the people who need to be involved, and the time frames that must be met. This disciplined approach to planning helps to avoid costly and time-consuming mistakes.

2B.2   A well-conceived plan facilitates timely identification of potential problems in order to take corrective action. Project management can turn a reactive style of management into a proactive one. The warning signals are manifest to all. Decisions relative to alternative actions can be based on reliable data rather than on subjective emotions.

2B.3   Up-front analysis of tasks and time schedules encourages the project team to thoroughly investigate the product requested and the project plan for producing the product, thereby reducing the potential for disasters. Time may be scheduled for documenting status, holding review meetings, and conducting quality control procedures throughout the process. Conservatism may be built into the project plan through scheduling of reviews, reevaluation, rescheduling, and revision of tasks.

2B.4   If subcontractors, vendors, or consultants are involved in the projects, special care must be taken in scheduling their interfaces with the project schedule. Project management compels the subcontractors and the client to think through their relationships, to understand the work effort each must perform, and to agree on acceptable time frames for delivery.

2B.5   If and when the plan goes awry, the manager of the project, the project client, and the team can quantify the impact of the variance on the plan. They can then consider the appropriate trade-offs of time, resources, and/or technical objectives. For example, if the project is slipping behind schedule, the manager of the project may want to order up a cast of thousands to attack the problem. As Frederick Brooks observes in *The Mythical Man Month*, a woman can have a baby in nine months, but two women cannot do it in four and a half months. In a project scenario, it takes time for the new recruits to come up to speed, and they burden the senior people on the team during that process. The sooner the trade-offs of time, resources, and/or technical objectives are initiated, the more effective and less costly they will be.

_____

CHECK HERE
IF APPLICABLE

2C. BENEFITS TO PEOPLE

2C.1   Have you ever picked up a project from a manager who had no documented plans, no written project goals, no technical objectives? How many weeks did it take you just to figure out where the project was, much less where you were going? For the benefit of new managers who may have to take over projects in progress, the organization should require each manager of projects to maintain up-to-date records.

_____

2C.2   A manager of projects wants to be mobile and promotable. An organization can not afford to promote someone who carries entire projects in his or her head. Do that and you may have painted yourself into a career corner with no way out.

_____

2C.3   When you are in trouble and need management support, can you reasonably expect to be allocated additional dollars and/or resources when you have no defensible proof that you are truly in trouble? Approaching management with statements that begin with "I feel . . ." or "I think . . ." is not convincing. Take along appropriate project management data and you can approach management with a confident assertion: "I have the facts for you and the alternatives that I can recommend. I know what I need, when I need it, and for how long I need it." This approach engenders confidence and support.

_____

SECTION 3: BENEFITS STATEMENT

Taking into consideration all the Alternative Benefits which you checked off in Section 2, develop a Benefits Statement which will convince your management or your customer of the justification of the implementation of the project management discipline.

PERFORMANCE SUPPORT TOOL 1.2
Gap Analysis

The Gap Analysis is a series of interviews or focus-group sessions intended to meet the following objectives:

- To determine the current state of project management
- To determine the future state of project management
- To determine the gap between the current and the future state of project management
- To identify the present barriers and the solutions needed to close the gap and reach the future state

A. What is the current state of project management?

To determine the answer to this question, answer the following:

1. What type of projects account for most of the project-related effort in this department?

   _____

2. How are projects presently managed (i.e., formally vs. informally)?

   _____

3. Is there a project management methodology in place?

   _____ Yes   _____ No

   If yes, how is it used?

   _____

4. What constitutes project success in your organization?

   _____

5. What are the rewards of a project's success?

   _____

6. What are the consequences of a project's failure?

   _____

7. How are projects prioritized?

   _____

8. Is top management supporting the project management initiative?

   _____ Yes   _____ No

   If yes, how? If no, why not?

   _____

9. What is the driving/gating project parameter: time, resources, budget, or quality? In other words, if the project team focused its energy on meeting one of these parameters, which one would it be?

   _____

10. In your opinion, what is the team's perception of the driving/gating parameter? Is it time, resources, budget, or quality?

_____

B. What is the envisioned future state of project management?

To determine the answer to this question, answer the following:

1. In your opinion, who/what will be your organization's future customers/markets?

_____

2. How can your organization's use of project management serve these future customers/markets?

_____

3. How will project management fit into the strategic plan of your organization?

_____

4. How will project management fit into the tactical plans of the functional departments?

_____

5. What other vision might project management support?

_____

6. What has prompted your company's interest in project management (e.g., project failure, a top-management directive, or competition)?

_____

C. How wide is the gap between the current and the future state of project management?

1. What is your perception of the current state and your vision of the future state of project management?

_____

2. In your opinion, what is causing the gap between the two?

_____

D. What are the barriers to reaching the future state?

To determine the answer to this question, answer the following:

1. Who are the key players in the implementation of project management?

_____

2. How do you envision their role in the implementation process?

_____

3. What resistance, if any, do you anticipate in this project management initiative? On what history do you base your concern?

_____

4. What are your expectations of a successful project management implementation?

_____

5. How do you expect top management to support the project management initiative?

_____

6. What barriers/obstacles might interfere with the implementation of project management in your organization?

_____

7. What needs to be done to remove those barriers and obstacles?

_____

E. Again, what is the gap between the current and the future state?

1. Based on your perception of the current state and the future envisioned state of project management in your organization, describe the gap between the two.

_____

PART II
PEOPLE

CHAPTER 2

The Project Players

In times past, project teams performed as if they were in a relay race. A runner took the baton, ran his or her stretch of the race, and then passed the baton to the next runner. The problem was that any one player could lose the race by running too slowly or by unsuccessfully handing over the baton. Patterning a project as if it were a relay race was highly risky. Performing the work in sequential order just took too long.

Projects today are conducted more as if they are rugby games. Each player has a specific skill. All players are involved in the game and truly committed to winning. They get to know each other's strengths, weaknesses, roles, and responsibilities so well that, as a team, they can instinctively move the ball down the field and score a point. The success of the team then depends on each player's maximizing performance in his or her respective position and understanding and relying on the expertise and skill of the other players on the team.

CHAPTER OVERVIEW

The roles of the players on a rugby team correspond to the roles of the major players in the project environment:

- The project client is the "owner" of the team, the person for whom the team is playing. He or she gives them direction and judges whether they have been successful.
- The manager of the project is the coach of the team, the coordinater of the plays on and off the field.

- The resource manager is the players' agent, the person who determines on which team(s) his or her staff will play.
- The project team members, the "athletes" who play the game, contribute their specific skills or experience. The composite of the players' different skills makes them a team, and they work together to get the job done. Each individual is crucial to the project's success and has a distinct role within the project.

Within the project environment, here are the key players:

- The *project client* is the person in the organization who wants the project accomplished and can influence the organizational units that are affected.
- The *manager of the project* is responsible for the coordination of the project team and, ultimately, for managing the project plan to enable the successful completion of the project on time, within budget, and at the expected level of quality.
- The *resource manager* is responsible for having available a department of subject-matter experts: engineers, software programmers, lawyers, or other professionals and service providers. They form the resource pools from which the manager of the project staffs his or her project.
- The *project team member* is a representative of a functional department and a contributor to the project team. He or she reports directly to the resource manager yet works to support the effort of the manager of the project.

This chapter focuses on the roles, responsibilities, and interplay of the project players in today's project management game. We will first examine the roles of the four critical project players and the additional management and support groups that contribute to the project's conclusion. Two key project players—the resource manager and the project client—often get less attention because of the traditional focus on the manager of the project and the team.

The most frequently forgotten project player is the resource or functional manager. He or she is a member of the management staff of the organization and is the immediate supervisor of the project team members. Even though the resource manager is not officially on the team, he or she maintains control of the resources needed by the manager of the project to staff the team and get the job done.

The next key player we will examine in depth is the owner or customer of the project—the project client, for whom the manager of the project and the project team are performing the job and by whom the completed project will be evaluated. Identifying the appropriate individual as the project client, and engendering his or her sponsorship, is a crucial element of the job of the manager of the project.

The Performance Support Tools included in this chapter are "Project Client's Checklist," which can help the manager of the project to strengthen project sponsorship, and "Project Role Problems/Solutions Checklist," which can help the manager of the project to overcome hurdles caused by unclear roles and responsibilities of the players on the project team. These Performance Support Tools are available for download at www.pmsi-pm.com.

THE ROLES OF KEY PROJECT PLAYERS

Each of the four key project roles has responsibilities that contribute to the project community. The summaries below describe each job in the project environment. While not all-inclusive, these summaries of responsibilities suggest areas of potential overlap and conflict, particularly in assigning resources, estimating time duration and budgets, and tracking progress.

Project Client

The project client is the individual from the client organization who champions the project, and who should be thought of as the customer.

The role of the *project client* is to:

- Communicate the project's purpose and value to the business management.
- Ensure that the project team has the time and resources needed to achieve success.

- Commit specific resources from a relevant area of the business community, and influence others to do likewise.
- Pave the way for cultural change, caused by the project, in the affected organizational units.
- Finalize and approve any changes to the project's objectives, scope, and success criteria.
- Participate in major project reviews, and approve key deliverables.
- Make key project decisions.
- Ensure timely resolution of issues affecting project success.

Manager of the Project

The manager of the project assumes the primary leadership role in planning and implementing the project, including pulling together and coordinating the project team, and is responsible for project success.

The role of the *manager of the project* is to:

- Identify the skills needed on the team, and negotiate with the resource managers for assignment of appropriate people.
- Coordinate tasks on the work breakdown structure (WBS).
- Negotiate the time frames in which tasks are to be performed.
- Develop and consolidate project plans.
- Track milestones, deadlines, schedules, resource utilization, budgets, risks, changes of scope, quality of deliverables, and other project elements.
- Act as a liaison with top management and the project client.
- Issue status reports and conduct status review meetings.
- Coordinate with outside subcontractors, consultants, and vendors.
- Recommend changes to schedule, resource requirements, and budgets, when required.
- Establish and maintain *esprit de corps* within the team.

Resource Manager

Resource managers "own" the resources that will be assigned to projects. Their job is to assign appropriate skilled people to do projects, to ensure these people contribute to the projects as promised, and to monitor the quality of the deliverables produced from their function.

The role of the *resource manager* is to:

- Hire, fire, train, discipline, and motivate the functional department's employees.
- Generate performance reviews for these employees.
- Develop and manage within departmental budgets.
- Plan the allocation of resources.
- Interpret upper-management's direction, and implement its policy.
- Solve problems as they arise.
- Assign people to the project team.
- Develop and provide a challenge to employees.
- Set and maintain productivity standards.
- Accept accountability for a quality product that is to be delivered on schedule.
- Be proactive when possible and reactive when necessary.
- Validate time estimates for tasks.
- Monitor project work.
- Represent the functional group to the rest of the organization.

Project Member

The project team members contribute their time and effort to the project either on a part- or full-time basis working on assigned tasks producing quality deliverables as scheduled.

The role of a *project team member* is to:

- Act as a liaison between the resource manager and the project team.
- Report back from the project team to the resource manager.
- Provide input regarding project objectives and scope.
- Define/design/perform assigned tasks, or assign people to do so.
- Determine time estimates for tasks that are to be performed.
- Identify potential functional problem areas, and find solutions.
- Interact with other functional areas and other team members.

The seeming similarities among these roles can be dramatic. The role of each player implies that each is responsible for assigning work, estimating how long tasks will take, and monitoring schedules. The assignment of roles can cause dissent if the manager of the project does not distinguish at what level of detail tasks are to be handled by which players. To be sure that conflicts over roles and responsibilities do not arise within the project community, the manager of the project can hold a meeting with all constituencies and ask them to discuss and refine how they view their respective roles and duties within the project environment.

Beyond these key players, the manager of the project relies on *top management, internal support,* and *third-party support* to complete the project. Top management, which includes the chairman or president and the operating committee, has line responsibility for all projects within the organization and for directing the strategies and growth of the enterprise. Internal support is provided by groups within the organization, such as computer operations, drafting, advertising, and other related functions. Third-party support—from independent vendors, suppliers, contractors, and consultants—is often needed to produce the final product. Obstacles to defining the responsibilities of each of these additional players may emerge in the project environment.

The actions that the manager of the project can take to overcome these obstacles are listed in Performance Support Tool 2.2, "Project Role Problems/Solutions Checklist," at the end of this chapter.

Now that we've broadly defined the key players in the project environment, let's explore in more depth the resource managers' critical position.

THE RESOURCE MANAGER—THE "FORGOTTEN" PLAYER

Although allocating competent resources to projects is among the most crucial issues that confront projects today, this is not the job of the manager of the project. It is the job of the resource manager to whom project team members report. The resource manager's most important function is to devise an effective resource management process and ensure that people who have the right talents are assigned and available to the right projects at the right time.

The resource manager is a critical person in the world of the manager of the project. Yet managers of projects seldom make a special effort to have one-on-one meetings with their resource managers, or to bring together all resource managers for project briefings especially designed for them, or to invite resource managers to the training classes that are being held for the project team. The resource manager is often a forgotten cog in the project management mechanism; yet, if the resource manager is not doing his or her job well, the manager of the project—and the project itself—will suffer.

The resource manager's overall job is to see that the employees in his or her department or division are successful and that the department meets its objectives. In support of relevant projects, the resource manager is responsible for ensuring that:

- Employees follow the approved product development processes and produce a quality product.
- Employees are properly trained and prepared to contribute to their assignments.
- The functional area has the necessary staff to perform its own operational work as well as the work of the projects.

In meeting these responsibilities, the first challenge is whether providing qualified resources to projects in a timely manner is perceived as a functional departmental objective. If the organization does not see this as one of the resource manager's major objectives, it will be more difficult to elicit the resource manager's attention to the needs of projects. For the sake of this discussion, we assume that top management recognizes the need to run a project-driven organization and that the resource manager has been invested with accountability to help meet project objectives.

Key Concerns

Resource managers' three key concerns in supporting the project management discipline are: (1) scheduling, (2) development, and (3) working in a matrixed context. Resource managers must schedule their staff to accommodate the needs of their own department as well as the anticipated projects. They must also hire, fire, and develop their staff to meet their own functional growth plans even as they support future projects. And they must amiably support projects and other functional managers in a matrixed or cross-functional project environment. Top management and managers of projects can take specific steps to assist resource managers in meeting their project-specific responsibilities in all three areas.

Scheduling

Resource managers perform three resource allocation roles. At the *most strategic level,* they staff their department to accommodate project work in addition to the functional area's operational work. It is their job to determine the departmental head count for the period of time addressed in the budgetary process. During the functional budgeting process, they must predict the staff size and skill mix needed to accomplish the operational work of the department as well as to accommodate the needs of current and upcoming projects.

At a *more tactical level,* resource managers assign the right individuals—those with the right skill mix—to the appropriate projects. In conjunction with the managers of the projects, the resource managers determine who is to be assigned to what projects. This decision requires a comprehensive knowledge of the skills and personalities of staff members and a sound understanding of the various projects' needs. Resource managers must also clearly understand that staffing projects is as important as performing their department's operational functions.

At the *day-to-day working level,* resource managers prepare and track schedules that respond to changes in the staffing plan and move the pertinent team members accordingly. Along with their staff, resource managers develop a weekly schedule. As projects slip beyond their schedules, or people become unavailable, or priorities change, tactical staffing plans may become invalid. Resource managers must be fluid enough to respond to these changes intelligently and sanely, and to reschedule tasks and people accordingly.

What Can Top Management Do to Help?   Management can share with resource managers the strategic business plans, opportunities that are being evaluated, constraints and assumptions relative to each operating department, and the projected start dates of the various projects that are in the queue. This is a top-down information flow. Management can inform resource managers of the priority of each of the projects, try to avoid changing project priorities too frequently, and, when priorities do change, communicate those changes as quickly as possible to the resource managers and the managers of projects.

What Can Managers of Projects Do to Help?   From the bottom up, managers of projects can keep management and resource managers informed of their resource needs: the number of full-time equivalents, the skill mix, and the time frame during which they will require certain skills.

Hire, Fire, and Develop

In conjunction with developing the staff schedule, resource managers identify the skills, knowledge, and competencies required to deliver the next project work in the queue. They match available skill sets and perform a gap analysis. They then take action to close the gaps by doing whatever is required to get the best bodies on board. This may mean hiring, negotiating transfers from other internal parts of the organization, identifying subcontracting resources, and/or training current staff.

As the business changes, the needed skill mix may change. Certain resources may no longer be competent to accomplish the anticipated workload. In a best-case scenario, these resources/staff will have been groomed to possess needed *new* skills. If not, the resource managers have the unpleasant job of phasing them out of the organization.

After the anticipated work has been broken down into major assignments, resource managers are responsible for grooming, training, and challenging their staff. This career development effort needs forethought and preparation to ensure that the staff members have time allocated in their schedules to participate in their own professional development and are motivated to remain with the organization.

What Can Top Management Do to Help?   To assist in resource planning, top management can inform resource managers, well in advance, of the introduction of any new technologies or new clients that would require added staff or training of current staff in new skills. Management needs to understand that it takes time and money to bring new people on board and/or to provide training that will satisfy future skill requirements.

What Can Managers of Projects Do to Help?   To assist in resource development, managers of projects can offer to perform mentoring in project management. They can be specific as to when new technical skills will be needed on what project(s), and how many full-time equivalents who possess those skills will be required.

Working in a Matrixed Environment

Resource managers tend to stay very focused on their own empires because they are typically appraised and evaluated within that context. However, to support the project management discipline, resource managers need to be willing to function in a *matrixed organizational structure,* which requires lending their people to projects run by various managers of projects, who often report outside the resource managers' sphere of influence. Therefore, their staff are reporting to them and performing work for their functional area while also working for another manager, the manager of the project.

Resource managers must be flexible in supporting other areas, knowing when to place project goals ahead of departmental goals, and discarding any "them-versus-us" attitude in favor of a resource manager–manager of project relationship that is nurtured as a partnership.

What Can Top Management Do to Help?   To help harmonize resource and project management, top management can orchestrate the matrixed environment so that it is understood by all. Cross-functional communication is not suggested—it is required. Management can think through and present clearly the roles, responsibilities, accountabilities, and authorities held by both the manager of the project and the resource manager.

What Can Managers of Projects Do to Help?   To work most effectively with a resource manager in a matrixed environment, the manager of the project should be very sensitive to the conflicting pressures on the resource manager and work with him or her to alleviate those pressures when possible.

In summary, the area of resource management is viewed as the common ground of the resource manager and the manager of the project. The goals of both are: to manage resources properly, to be able to forecast resource needs, to aid in the hiring process, and to contribute to the performance appraisal process as well as the growth and development of the staff.

Bringing the Resource Manager into the Project-Driven Organization

If an organization is convinced that the resource manager is crucial to the success of the manager of the project and that a project-related resource management process needs to be put in place, two initiatives need to be taken: provide the resource manager with (1) appropriate training and (2) the necessary support tools.

The Training Initiative

To initiate the resource management process, the first step is to provide, for resource managers, a seminar that explains the resource management process and resource managers' role in the project management discipline. The course should be positioned not only as a skills course to support the project effort but also as a partnership course for the manager of the project and the resource manager. The focus should be on roles and relationships, not methodology.

Training might cover topics such as: tools to support planning; reports to achieve better communication; understanding roles, responsibilities, and the link between strategic planning and tactical work; knowing how to be flexible yet maintain control; just-in-time recruitment; and maintaining and growing resources. A training program designed uniquely for resource managers will position them to be active rather than passive players in the project arena.

Providing Support Tools

A class, by itself, is not adequate. Some topics discussed in the class will require support tools that can turn concepts into realities. For example, to perform intelligent staffing, one must understand the concept of *resource loading* and *leveling*. As described in detail in Chapter 7 ("Portfolio Management"), resource loading is the mathematical calculation of the effort each individual is exerting on various tasks within a single time frame. When all the resources/staff have been loaded onto a schedule chart, some individuals may be found to be overcommitted. The staffing plan must then be leveled; in other words, one or more of the team members' schedules must be changed to ensure the availability of the right resources at the right times.

Imagine, when the training class is over, that the participating resource managers understand the mathematical premises of resource loading and leveling. They go back to their jobs with the desire and the knowledge needed to manage staff schedules more intelligently, but they lack the software to support them. They may try, and fail, to perform these tasks manually or with inadequate software; or they may not even make the attempt and simply grow more frustrated, knowing how to fix the problem but being unable to approach it without the right tools. The organization needs to provide its resource managers with the appropriate tools to perform their job. In this case, an appropriate tool is an automated system that can perform enterprise-wide resource allocation.

Managers of projects often say that they have no control over resource managers because they usually report to different bosses. This may be true, but it does not lessen the dependence of managers of projects on resource managers. Nor does it absolve managers of projects from doing everything in their power to influence resource managers and support them in performing their jobs to the best of their abilities.

Keep in mind that resource managers control the most important part of the manager of the project's world. They allocate and manage the people who will do the work needed to complete the project. A manager of a project owes resource managers serious attention.

THE PROJECT CLIENT—THE "OWNER"

Another key player who is critical to the project is the project client—the person who champions the project effort and works directly with the manager of the project to acquire the needed resources and adherence to the project management process. The project client in a project community is the person who is accountable for sponsoring a project. He or she represents the entire business, not any one constituency. Although many constituencies may be involved in a project, one person is chosen to be the focal point for arbitration, mediation, and decision making.

This primary project client is consistently referred to in singular, not plural, descriptions. Cosponsorship is not recommended; conflicting interests between two clients may put the project in a stalemate or otherwise jeopardize its success. The project client is chosen because he or she (1) has the greatest vested interest in having the project succeed, (2) has the best skill mix to oversee the project, and/or (3) has the needed political clout to obtain the support needed.

The term *client* is often used incorrectly to refer to the original proponent (or requester). The logical primary project client is the person in the organization who both wants the project accomplished and can influence the organizational units that are affected. In short, the project client is the person who can make it happen.

Key to the success of the project is the ability of the project client to ensure that the project participants are focused on and committed to a common purpose and vision of success. The manager of the project can achieve this within the project team, but the primary client must expand that commitment to include the larger business community and support functions.

Usually, the primary client (an executive or member of management) champions the project, finds funding for it, and makes sure the cultural changes are assimilated into the affected business units. Therefore, this person needs to possess an organizational authority that spans the sphere of influence of the project.

Should there be serious doubt about the value of the project to the company or about its chances of success, the project client must bring this to the attention of the authorizing management body and make a recommendation.

This is not an enviable position, nor is it the time for the project client to fade into the woodwork.

The Manager of the Project/Project Client Partnership

The manager of the project must *know what effective sponsorship looks like.* Many primary project clients have little understanding of this role, and it may fall to the manager of the project to educate them on their responsibilities and on the time commitment associated with sponsorship. First-time clients typically underestimate the amount of time involved. Seasoned managers of projects will be prepared with estimates and experiences from other project clients.

One approach is to work with the project client and develop an agreement that clarifies the client's role and specific responsibilities. This is particularly important when day-to-day sponsorship has been delegated to a secondary client while other responsibilities remain with the logical (original) project client.

Next, the manager of the project should take steps to *develop an effective working relationship* with the project client. This should include talking with the project client about his or her working style. Some clients will have a hands-on approach; others will be more removed. The manager of the project might pose to the project client the following questions for discussion:

- What kinds of issues/problems do you want to be involved in?
- How should progress be communicated to you and to business management? What is the best means of communication? The best time?
- Which deliverables do you want to approve?
- How do you want to be involved in requested changes to the project?

The manager of the project can take specific steps to *keep the project client involved* throughout the life of the project. Again, knowing what the client should be doing, clearly stating those expectations, and following through on them is an important corollary. The manager of the project can help maintain project client involvement in the following ways:

- As the project moves from one phase to another, discuss with the project client what to expect and what questions he or she should consider. (Refer to Performance Support Tool 2.1 at the end of this chapter.)
- When deliverables are submitted for review, indicate the kind of feedback that is needed.
- Involve the project client in preparations for major project reviews, and emphasize the decisions to be made.

- Inform the project client promptly of issues needing sponsorship resolution. Provide some background, pros, cons, and recommendations.

Potential Sponsorship Problems

The most serious sponsorship problem is *not having a project client*. Project sponsorship is a matter of organizational policy. If an organization has not reached the point where every project is required to have a client, managers of projects can only articulate the benefits of having one and the risks of not having one. If, on the other hand, project sponsorship has been adopted as a policy but, for various reasons, a project client has not been named, the managers of projects should keep the issue alive and press for resolution. They might even recommend that the project be canceled or postponed until a primary client is named.

The next most serious sponsorship problem is *having the wrong person as the client*. Usually, this means that the person chosen does not have organizational authority commensurate with the scope of the project—that is, he or she is not high enough in the management hierarchy. *Authority* and *hierarchy* are not popular words in these days of flattened organizations and empowered teams, but it is still a fact of life that people resist change. Occasionally, after all other persuasive means have been used unsuccessfully, it may be necessary to say, "This is the project initiative we are going to take. If you cannot support it, you need to go elsewhere." That statement requires organizational authority.

The opposite problem can sometimes occur: The client is too high in the organization. He or she may be an appropriate client who has *insufficient time*. Delegation to an acting client may then be the answer. Or the project client may be too far removed from the scope and objectives of the project to give effective direction. The suggestion in this case is to review the sponsorship responsibilities with the person and decide on an alternative—a more suitable client, and a means of keeping the original person involved (if desired) at a more appropriate level.

At this point, the manager of the project needs to decide carefully how to proceed. The three potential problems described above are among the most delicate problems that the manager of the project is called on to handle. He or she may be tempted to avoid dealing with them, but the price for not acknowledging them may be high. A clear statement of the problem, the risks involved, and some possible alternative actions will help considerably.

Finally, the manager of the project needs to know how to respond if a change in project client occurs during the project. This is another high-risk situation. At the very least, the new client may have no personal commitment to the success of the project; in fact, he or she may think it is a waste of company resources and call for it to be canceled. Such clear opposition, however, is far preferable to the worst-case scenario, in which the new project client has expectations that differ from those of the original client but fails to articulate them clearly.

When there is a change in project client, the most urgent responsibility of the manager of the project is to *review and discuss in depth,* with the new client, the project's background, objectives, scope, anticipated benefits, and specific success criteria. It may be necessary to rewrite the project definition completely to express the new client's desires, but this outcome is better than proceeding with unclear expectations.

An effective project client can make the job of the manager of the project immeasurably easier. Clear objectives, the commitment of the business community to the project's success, adequate funding and resources, quick resolution of issues, and cooperative project clients are critical to successful project management. A smart manager of projects cultivates sponsorship—the client's firm commitment to the project—to achieve these ends and to ensure the ultimate success of the project.

Will the Real Project Client Please Stand Up?

Several years ago, the author had the opportunity to hear a dynamic manager of projects speak about her experiences. She described her confusion and her ultimate enlightenment when she discovered that one particular project client was in fact not the only person she had to satisfy. She had taken over the job of Facilities and Construction Manager for a large health care institution in the San Francisco Bay Area. She was not in the construction trade, but she had worked with this health care institution for many years. She knew the players and had experience working within this political network.

In her new role, one of her first large projects was the renovation of a nearby residence into a specialized doctors' clinic. Her approach was to go to the doctors who were to occupy the building and ask them how they wanted the building refurbished. Decisions had to be made concerning the decoration of the interior, the sign that would be posted outside, and the landscaping. She listened carefully to the doctors and worked with her internal facilities people to generate a design, which the doctors approved.

Her internal staff and several contractors completed the work, but, before long, two serious complaints were voiced. The employees who worked in the clinic lodged the first complaint. They claimed that the room layout and the placement of equipment did not facilitate efficient processing of patients or paperwork. To be seen and treated, patients were moved upstairs, downstairs, and all around the building. It was tiring for patients and staff.

The second complaint was more compelling. The manager of the project was called into the next board of directors' meeting and criticized, on two counts, for the renovation of the clinic. First, the interior was done in a southwestern motif, with turquoise and pink tones. The board said that the motif and colors were not appropriate for a health care institution and did not conform to the atmosphere of similar buildings on the existent campus. Second, the landscaping and signage gave the clinic the appearance of a commercial place of business—an absolute violation of the wishes of the neighbors. Years before, the community had obtained an agreement from the nearby hospital that if private residences were to be used for hospital business, the neighborhood would remain residential in appearance, and the hospital property would blend with the surrounding homes.

In due course, the building was completely redone. The layout was made more efficient, the new interior was consistent with other facilities within the hospital complex, and the exterior was in keeping with the rest of the neighborhood.

What had the manager of the project done wrong? She had gone to the primary users of the project. She and her staff interviewed them thoroughly and had them sign off on specifications. She produced what the doctors had requested, and she obtained written approval from them. However, in this scenario, there were multiple project clients whom she had not considered, one of whom was the *operational project client.* The employees who had to function within the building should have been consulted from an operational point of view so that the facility afforded them a layout in which they could work productively. Even more important was the *strategic project client,* who controlled the purse strings. In this case, the strategic project client was the board of directors, which had ultimate responsibility for adhering to the strategic goals and policies of the organization. (A turquoise-and-pink interior color scheme and neon signs were prohibited.)

The lesson here is: Make sure you ferret out all three project clients—the primary client, the operational client, and the strategic client—before thinking that you have successfully completed the project scope definition, and before work begins on the project.

The "owner" project client is being increasingly viewed as a major key to the success of project management. Jane DeYoung, Senior Consultant with

The Project Clients

PMSI-Project Mentors, a part of the Provant solution, noted in the Project Management Institute's periodical, *PM Network:*

> More and more project managers are becoming aware of the importance of having a committed and "savvy" project client. Those who have led projects both *with* such a client and *without* almost always cite effective sponsorship as a critical success factor. But many project managers, especially those less experienced, are woefully unaware of the difference sponsorship makes.[1]

A lack of committed sponsorship is sometimes mistaken, vaguely, for insufficient management support (too little focus on the vital role of the project client). A manager of projects who knows what sponsorship should be is more likely to gain the full benefit of it and to recognize its absence. This person will know how to work effectively with a client and how to handle sponsorship problems.

CONCLUSION

For a project team to succeed, each of the project players must understand and play his or her role to the best of his or her ability and in concert with all of the other team players. To build effective teamwork, the manager of the project works with the players—refining the responsibilities appropriate to each, and providing the tools and techniques that enable the players to fulfill their roles. The project client, who has requested the project and can be seen essentially as the project customer, must be carefully identified and actively engaged in sponsoring the project. This occurs through the development of an effective partnership with the manager of the project, who works with the project client to establish performance criteria and keeps the client involved throughout the life of the project. Similarly, the manager of the project, as well as top management, can work proactively with the resource managers. Finding a staff with the expertise needed to get the project done, making sure that they have all the information they need, and scheduling and developing the staff to meet project deadlines are the key responsibilities.

Managing the project team requires a commitment to resource managers in the form of training and support tools. And the entire project team process requires that the manager of the project overcome barriers to the fulfillment of all project roles by communicating effectively with every member of the team.

The Performance Tools that follow provide aid in that communication. The Project Client's Checklist gives the manager of projects a comprehensive set of questions that can engage the project client in understanding his or her role, as well as the project parameters from project initiation through planning, execution, and review. The Project Role Problems/Solutions Checklist helps the manager of projects overcome barriers to defining responsibilities among all the players by identifying potential pitfalls and critical issues that require discussion.

NOTE

1. Jane DeYoung, PMSI-Project Mentors, a part of the Provant solution. March, 1995, Vol. 8, No. 9. In "The Importance of Project Sponsorship." *PM Network* (Upper Darby, PA: The Project Management Institute).

PERFORMANCE SUPPORT TOOL 2.1

Project Client's Checklist, Beginning to End

PROJECT DEFINITION AND PLANNING

Your most important job during project initiation is to ensure that the project objectives are clear and that the cost-benefit analysis makes it a good investment of the company's resources. You will normally work through the portfolio management process, together with the management body that approves projects, to clarify the potential benefits, and with the assigned manager of the project, to understand what is required and determine the estimated costs. As the project client, you will want to answer the following questions:

- Why is this project needed? What's the problem being solved or the opportunity to be seized? How does it support our corporate goals?
- What are the objectives? What will the end result look like?
- What are the benefits? How will life be better when the project is over?
- How will we measure success? What is our baseline? What is our target?
- What areas of the organization will be affected? In what ways will they be affected?
- Who needs to be involved? And how?
- What are the boundaries or what is the scope of the project?
- What are the constraints in time, money, and quality?
- What can be achieved realistically within those constraints?
- Roughly, how much will it cost and how long will it take?
- What are the risks? Can they be managed?
- Should we proceed?

PROJECT EXECUTION AND CONTROL

During the life of the project, you will want to stay involved, not in the day-to-day details, but in weekly or biweekly updates with the manager of the project and possibly the core project team. You will want to see progress tracked against the approved work plan and schedule, and see key deliverables at defined milestone review points. You can also expect to make decisions regarding suggested changes in the project scope and/or deliverables. These are some pertinent questions to pose:

- Are we accomplishing what we planned to accomplish? Within the planned time frame? With the planned resources? Within budget?
- Is there anything I can do to facilitate your work?
- Are you getting the cooperation you need from the resource managers?

At the same time, you will be the project spokesperson to the rest of your organization. You may need to do some marketing, persuading, and negotiating, especially if there is resistance to the changes the project is bringing. If there are any signs that the project is in trouble, you will be fact finding, problem solving, and maybe sticking your neck out. Consider these three important questions when facing a problem:

- Can we still achieve the objectives? Are they still of value to the organization?
- What are our alternatives? What are the pros and cons?
- Should the project be stopped?

PROJECT CLOSE-OUT

As the project nears completion, you will focus primarily on transition management. The project team should have a documented implementation plan. You may need to commit extra resources in the affected functional areas, and set their expectations for some degree of disruption. Plan to be available to troubleshoot and resolve issues. As the project client, you will have valuable contributions to make to the post-project review, and you can pose these important questions:

- Did we accomplish what we planned to accomplish? Within the planned time frame? With the planned resources? Within budget?
- How did we perform based on our success criteria?
- Are plans in place to measure the predicted benefits?
- What lessons did we learn?
- What remains to be done?

Source: Jane DeYoung, PMSI-Project Mentors, a part of the Provant solution. Reprinted with permission.

PERFORMANCE SUPPORT TOOL 2.2
Project Role Problems/Solutions Checklist

BARRIERS TO DEFINING CLEAR PROJECT ROLES AND RESPONSIBILITIES

Project management is more than tools and techniques. It is based on the appropriate people being capable and motivated to use these tools and techniques. Project players must be given clear roles and responsibilities, as well as organizational and management support, to be capable and motivated. Listed below are checklists of the problems various members of the project team might present to the manager of the project, followed by summaries of potential solutions.

Top Management

Top management consists of the individual(s) who have line responsibility for all the projects within the enterprise. This group includes the president and the operating committee, which is the body of individuals that heads each functional unit of the corporate or government structure. Top management directs the strategy and the growth of the enterprise.

Problems

Certain traits that often characterize top management can blur its roles and responsibilities. Check those that apply to your top management:

☐ Unavailability for meetings
☐ Making unrealistic demands
☐ Wanting to become too involved in project details
☐ Failing to understand enough of what is expected
☐ Giving the project team an unclear picture of what is expected

Solutions

To avoid these pitfalls, the manager of the project can take the following course of action to define and reinforce top management's roles and responsibilities throughout the life of the project:

• Develop detailed project plans and thorough project objectives that must be approved by top management during the early phases of the project
• Develop a status-reporting methodology so that management is periodically informed of the progress on the project
• Include the dollars involved in every negotiated trade-off alternative
• Start by asking and then insist on getting top management's attention
• Communicate

Project Client

The project client is the management individual from the client organization who champions the project. The project client should be thought of as the customer of the manager of the project. If the manager of the project provides expertise and a service, the manager of the project is truly working for the project client.

Problems

The project client may pose barriers to a successful project in the following ways. Check those traits that apply to your project client:

☐ Resisting change by insisting, "We've always done it this way before."
☐ Failing to understand project management's special jargon and buzzwords
☐ Having no real knowledge of or respect for project management
☐ Asking the project team to drop everything to service them first
☐ Questioning the credibility of the manager of the project because he or she may not be a technical subject matter expert
☐ Failing to know what he or she wants from the project
☐ Failing to provide realistic time and dollar constraints
☐ Having limited or no time to talk
☐ Being reluctant to sign off on project milestones
☐ Being uncooperative
☐ Continually introducing scope changes
☐ Assuming the role of expert and micromanaging the effort rather than allowing the manager of the project to do his or her job
☐ Lacking a concrete understanding of project success criteria, by which to determine whether the final product is acceptable and meets necessary performance/quality levels

Solutions

To mitigate these and other project client-imposed obstacles, the manager of the project can do the following:

• Get to know the project client's business as well as possible
• Make sure the project client becomes the accountable manager in the project
• Do his or her homework as manager of the project before talking to the project client
• Involve the project client as much as possible
• Define the project's success criteria in quantifiable terms
• Communicate

Project Team Members

Project team members contribute their time and effort to the project either on a full-time or part-time basis and are actively involved in working on the project. They may be at the same managerial level or higher in the organization than the manager of the project. These individuals have a vested interest in the final product; however, unlike the manager of the project, they do not assume leadership of the project team, nor do they have the responsibility for the ultimate success of the project. These folks are often referred to as individual contributors or core team members.

Problems

The success of the manager of the project in orchestrating the work of the team can be weakened by the following impediments to the role of the manager of the project. Check those challenges that apply to you:

☐ No direct control over team members
☐ Difficulty measuring the team members' productivity
☐ Political brushfires involving team members, such as team members having other priorities that prevent them from contributing to the project
☐ Leadership differences: The manager of the project may have one set of performance criteria by which he or she is measured while another guides the project team members

Solutions

To remove these barriers to effective project team leadership, the manager of the project can do the following:

- Establish direct leadership and gain and exhibit respect for all team members prior to starting the project
- Take a professional approach to his or her relationship with these team members
- Involve team members from the initiation of the project and at every phase of the project to its completion
- Create an effective reporting mechanism to get information to and from all team members
- Become the team members' decision-authority focal point for the project
- Establish frequent review dates
- Provide frequent feedback to all team members
- Give team members goals and standards of performance for accomplishment
- Demonstrate a positive attitude
- Communicate

Support Groups

Internal support is provided by groups within the organization that are part of the project team and contribute to the success of the project but have no vested interest in the final product. Examples of support groups are computer operations, drafting, advertising, and other related functions. Managers of projects need these internal support groups to contribute in order to create the project's end deliverable. However, because the support group team members need neither the manager of the project nor the final product(s) that the team is creating, the manager of the project may have no real leverage.

Problems

The following obstacles may impede the contributions of internal support. Check those that apply to your internal support groups.

☐ Inadequate understanding of the various priorities of the organizational units that need their support

☐ Conflict of interest in how their time should be used
☐ Lack of interest in the final product
☐ Questionable performance quality
☐ Failure to identify requirements that they can accommodate
☐ Being caught in the middle, between what their resource manager needs and what the manager of the project needs
☐ Being told by the manager of the project and core project team that what they are producing was "needed yesterday" (that is, having unrealistic timetables imposed on them)
☐ Involvement in the effort too late to make an optimal contribution
☐ Receiving no recognition for above-standard performance

Solutions

To remove these obstacles and optimize the contributions of internal support groups, the manager of the project can do the following:

• Require early planning and involvement of the support groups
• Generate more personal interaction with the support groups
• Give the support team member reason(s) to participate, such as intellectual challenge
• Communicate

Third-Party Support

External groups are often needed to help develop and produce a final product. These third parties include vendors, suppliers, independent contractors, and consultants who are on the payroll of neither the project client nor the manager of the project.

Problems

The manager of the project will need to consider these critical factors in enlisting third-party support. Check the issues that apply to you:

☐ Determining whether the project has a real need for a third party
☐ Assessing the impact on the rest of the team of bringing an outsider into the project
☐ Ensuring that the most suitable third-party supplier is chosen during the selection process
☐ Pulling the third parties into the communication network
☐ Educating the third-party group about the scope and requirements of the project
☐ Continuously evaluating the third party's performance

Solutions

The manager of the project can do the following to optimize the contributions of third parties to the project:

• Clearly identify the third parties' tasks
• Put them through a thorough bidding process in which they contractually commit to a final time and dollar amount
• Educate them about the project and its final product

- Conduct periodic performance reviews
- Communicate

Primary Objectives of Communication

In the manager of the project's relationships with top management, project client, project team, and internal and external support, communication is the common thread. Managers of projects must, first, develop a communication system that they will not allow to disintegrate, no matter how burdened they become with day-to-day work. Second, managers of projects must communicate the following to each group and individual at the beginning of the project:

- Their roles and responsibilities
- Their tasks
- How their tasks relate to the tasks of others within the project team
- The scheduling and timing of the individual project player's contribution to the whole project and the budget within which they are to work
- The quality of performance they must achieve for the final product to meet or exceed the required standard

Keys to Establishing Good Communication

If good communication is established from the beginning of the project and managed professionally throughout the project, the project management community will benefit from improved teamwork and cooperation, and they will ultimately produce better project results. The six keys to establishing the needed communication between the manager of the project and all the project players are:

1. Build relationships first.
2. Communicate project goals and requirements clearly.
3. Know the needs and expectations—yours and others'.
4. Plan with others early.
5. Establish formal communication plans.
6. Continually work toward common understanding and agreement.

Read Chapter 10, "Communications Management," for more information on how to create a project communications infrastructure.

CHAPTER 3

The Manager of Projects

"This is Jane speaking. I just found out that our company is having a singing contest at the Project Management conference this fall. I think it would be a great idea if we, as a group, competed. We here in San Francisco think it is a great plan. Beauregard in Atlanta and Pierre in Paris, I hope you think it is a great idea, too.

"I can't quite hear you, Pierre. It must be the static over this teleconference phone. Well, anyway, since the conference is in Long Beach, I thought that one of the Beach Boys' hit songs would be just right. I'll take over as manager of the project and send out a project plan and a rehearsal schedule by the end of next week. We're hanging up here in San Francisco. Talk to you all soon."

How do you suppose Jane's team fared in the singing contest? Teams aren't cohesive just because someone says they are. All team members have to work at it.

—————————— CHAPTER OVERVIEW ——————————

As traditionally organized businesses evolve into project-driven organizations, management is seeing the role of managers of projects in a new and different light. Management wants tangible results from projects—results derived from the development of quality deliverables that translate into a favorable time-to-money ratio and more competitiveness in the marketplace. Management is also looking for help in managing growth, change, and performance. Instead of traditional project planners and status-report producers, management needs proactive people with today's professional skills for executing project management in all projects and simultaneously helping to integrate the project management discipline into day-to-day operations.

The role of managers of projects needs to change. Managers of projects need to see themselves as consultants who are experts in managing projects and who bring problem-solving and analytical skills to their business environments. Managers of projects must offer comprehensive project-specific solutions, which may be product-, process-, or people-oriented. They must also take primary responsibility for gradually inculcating the values of project management throughout the enterprise.

Managers of projects can accomplish all of these changes by expanding their roles to include both consulting and mentoring. A manager of a project might begin by mentoring, coaching, and consulting a cross-functional team of people on a single project. To maintain mentoring and consulting roles, managers of projects must involve themselves in facilitating strategic planning, process and procedure development, intervention, and audits wherever those skills are needed within the enterprise. By focusing not only on the processes but also on the cultural interventions that support project management, managers of projects will meet management's expectations.

Because project management is a discipline that requires discipline, additional efforts are needed to ensure that processes and project-specific endeavors are performed effectively and efficiently, using project management tools and techniques. A manager of projects must play a consulting role and interact with the project players within their unique business environments. The manager of projects must also fulfill the role of a mentor who, in concert with all project stakeholders, brings management processes and expertise to the project. The vision of the project management discipline must be expanded beyond the context of simply the next project and become *a way of doing business.* In consulting and mentoring roles, managers of projects take applicable approaches from the project management discipline and the organizational sciences and apply them to their environment to improve project and team behaviors, processes, and methodologies.

The manager of projects coordinates the effort of producing a deliverable that has been requested by a project client and carried out by a project team. At the start of each job, the manager of the project is asked to listen to the project client's needs and wants, and to translate them into results, just as a consultant would. The role of a manager of projects mirrors that of an internal or external consultant working for a client or customer.

A manager of projects may be an internal consultant representing a function within the organization or may be contracted out by an independent firm to assist an external client organization. In either situation, the manager of projects is performing a consultative role as a facilitator and mentor, not a doer and manager. Within the evolved discipline of project management, the role of the manager of projects is transformed from sage-on-the-stage to guide-on-the-side.

This chapter explores the new consultative and mentoring roles of managers of projects. The accompanying Performance Support Tool 3.1, "Mentoring Session—Special Topics List," suggests special mentoring-meeting topics to strengthen team relationships. All Performance Support and Assessment Tools referenced in this book are available for download at www.pmsi-pm.com.

THE BENEFITS OF A NEW PERSPECTIVE

The project client for whom the manager of the project works has certain implicit expectations to which the manager of the project must respond. One benefit of this new consulting/mentoring approach is that the client and the project community as a whole are provided with a comprehensive means of negotiating and fulfilling expectations.

Providing Real Solutions to Real Needs and Wants

The manager of the project should not presume that making a high-tech presentation or delivering a 50-pound report to the project client is good enough. The manager of the project's role is to provide, in answer to the client's problems and needs, solutions that will create meaningful and measurable change. Furthermore, the implementation of the change must meet the real needs and wants articulated by the project client. The manager of the project may have to subtly prod and probe to ensure that what the clients say they want is what they truly want, and more importantly, that it is truly good for the organization as a whole.

Minimizing the Analysis

How many times have the people in your organization been interviewed, invited to be part of a focus group, or given survey questionnaires, and then discovered that the questions being asked were identical to those asked during previous data-gathering sessions? Is it any wonder that the people involved in defining project requirements grow weary of the process? To streamline the organizational effort, instead of starting all over again, a smart manager of projects asks to see the results of previous similar interviewing efforts. Then, after doing some homework, the manager of projects asks only those questions that have not already been answered, and words them precisely, to yield the most useful information. The manager of projects can make the preliminary data-gathering effort short and sweet. The people being interviewed will appreciate the brevity and, in turn, will cooperate more readily during the project.

Making the Project Client a Partner

In a consulting/mentoring role, the manager of the project changes from being merely another pair of hands brought into the project to do the grunt work to becoming a partner with the project client. If the perception of the manager of the project is that of a "go-fer" (someone who goes for this and goes for that), that is exactly how the project client will use the manager of the project. This type of relationship hazards the risk that the project client will ultimately discard the manager of the project because he or she is not meeting the project client's expectations. Managers of projects need to be cleansed of the magical thinking that impels them to believe that they have the power to make everything all right without the full cooperation of the project client and all involved stakeholders. The manager of the project's relationship with the project client should be collaborative, not prescriptive.

Customizing the Project

In creating deliverables, it is OK to start from a model or a template that has worked in the past. However, it is *not* acceptable to use a one-size-fits-all prescriptive approach. The project client wants to feel special because he or she and the problem to be solved are special. The manager of the project, in a consultative role, needs to customize the steps, processes, and techniques used for each project client.

If a project deliverable is labeled "DRAFT" in big and bold letters on the cover, it should only mean that the content is not finalized. It does not excuse any product that has been thrown together unprofessionally. Impressions count. When readers are distracted by obvious mistakes, they discount the validity of the content. The manager of the project must proofread, check, verify, and validate *any* document before it is given to the project client or anyone in the project community.

Going the Distance

The manager of a project often starts a job with great energy. Then, as newer, more pressing, or more lucrative demands arise, the manager of the project may let up and start concentrating elsewhere. A manager of a project in a consultative role treats each project client as if he or she were the most important customer. That project client is the only focal point while the manager of the project is with him or her. The energy level remains high, and the attention given is seemingly single-minded.

THE CONSULTATIVE ROLE

The consulting role of the manager of the project may consist of identifying areas of concern and positioning the project client or the team so that problems are moved toward solution. In other situations, the project client or the team may have already identified the issues and defined specific interventions for which they need facilitation and/or project management expertise. These assignments may be long term—for example, the development of a business process—or short term, such as conducting one or more project-specific planning sessions. In such instances, the manager of the project must provide the skills, talent, and experience to collaborate with the project players. His or her job is not to recommend solutions but to aid in implementing those solutions, and to recommend courses of action or create structural remedies that the key players can implement. The manager of the project is the person who takes strategies through to action and results.

If, in response to a specific request, managers of projects keep the entire business enterprise in mind, they can, with the extensive involvement of the project players, ensure the greatest opportunity for success. This comprehensive—or holistic—approach engenders success not only for the project as a whole but for the process and the management of people. By maintaining a broad perspective, the root causes of problems—not just the symptoms—can be tackled, and substantial improvement can be institutionalized.

By maintaining the perspective of a consultant, the manager of the project can ensure management that the people involved will gain the practical ability to better manage projects themselves. In a meeting, for example, the manager of the project's position as a consultant/facilitator frees the team members and project client to focus discussion on the assignment rather than the mechanics of the meeting. Those involved can also observe the techniques that the manager of the project employs and use them in future meetings. The manager of the project is not just doing the work to get the job done. His or her objective is to transfer skills and implement practical solutions and processes for future projects and future teams. In a consulting role, the mission of the manager of the project is to deliver timely, responsive services to all the project constituencies and to improve the project management environment throughout the enterprise.

Figure 3.1 portrays the efforts undertaken within the manager of the project's consulting model. The upper portion of the circle refers to project-specific efforts; the lower portion refers to efforts affecting the entire enterprise. The enterprise-wide efforts have been broken down into process-related and culture-related interventions. Let's take a closer look at both the project-specific and the enterprise-wide efforts.

Project-Specific Consultative Efforts

The tasks performed in a project-specific consultant's role are very similar to those the manager of the project is currently performing, but they have a different perspective. The tasks might consist of:

- Participating in monthly status meetings
- Facilitating specific planning efforts
- Coaching and mentoring members of the project team

Figure 3.1   Consultative Efforts of the Manager of Projects

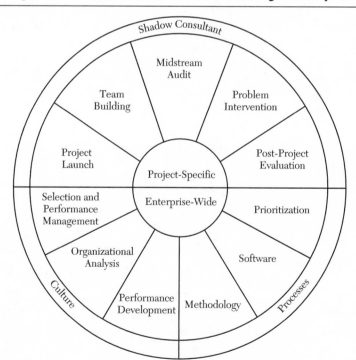

In a consulting role, the manager of the project reviews project plans, status reports, and other project-related documents in order to provide expertise, guidance, and direction. The manager of the project works closely with the project team members and offers individualized reinforcement of sound project management principles. He or she can also advise the project team members on alternatives that were considered successful in previous similar situations.

When the manager of the project adopts this consulting role, the organization is provided with an objective review that helps the team members step back from the political and procedural minutiae and concentrate on completing their tasks as planned. This benefits the team members, most of whom may also have technical roles. The manager of the project, in this consultative role, teaches the team members how to focus strictly on critical project issues and gain time to maintain their core technical roles. Some of the project-specific consultative tasks that the manager of the project might perform are shown in Figure 3.2 and are detailed in the following sections.

Project Launch

This effort involves creating the basic project team structure and project plan components of a new project. The manager of the project guides the intact team through the project planning process and produces a project mission statement, a map representing project relationships, a team communication strategy, a work breakdown structure (WBS), a task responsibility matrix, a project network, a schedule, and risk management plans—to name a few of the possible deliverables. At the end of a series of work sessions, the manager of

Figure 3.2   Project-Specific Efforts of the Manager of Projects

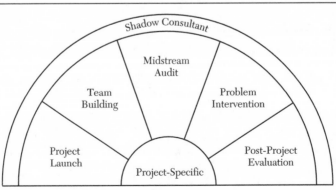

the project has aided the team in outlining a game plan to address the monitoring, tracking, and controlling of the project once it gets under way.

Team Building

This effort entails building team effectiveness. In a consultative role, the manager of the project works with the project client and project team members to build a strong foundation for effective personal interactions. This highly customized effort is essential to the cohesion of the team. Team-building sessions should be designed to include a variety of instruments, exercises, and techniques to deal with specific cultural issues and meet predefined interpersonal objectives. The manager of the project will need to do some homework before moving into this consultative endeavor. Consult someone trained in human resource development, or any of the excellent books that contain exercises on team building. Team vision, strategies for interacting during a project, tactics for being accessible and available, team-generated agreements for expected behaviors, a map of interdependencies, and role/responsibility/authority issues should all be discussed and a consensus reached. By increasing team effectiveness and cohesion, tangible project goals can be met with a minimum of conflict or organizational disruption. In the consulting role, the manager of the project can facilitate the behavioral and communications dynamics essential to the team's coalescence.

Project Midstream Audit

This effort involves evaluating existing project plans and progress reports, identifying problem areas, and determining appropriate strategies for refocusing plans and revitalizing the project team. Several months into a major project, the project client and the team members may begin to lose interest or focus. This can have a devastating impact on project results. Key problems, issues, and roadblocks must be identified and analyzed to determine their causes and impacts. The entire team (or individual subteams) needs to be coached by the manager of the project, acting in his or her consulting role. Together, they can create action plans, revise the project plan, and/or review the risk management plans that allow for making changes, solving problems, and removing barriers to progress. Those participating in the Project Midstream Audit should leave the session(s) with a clear sense of direction and renewed readiness to face the project with vigor and energy.

Specific Problem Intervention

This effort entails analyzing a current problem situation to determine its cause and related impact, and devising appropriate corrective actions. The assumption is that the project is in trouble. The project players must determine what is causing the problem and suggest an appropriate action. Taking on the mind-set of a consultant, the manager of the project can assist the relevant players in analyzing the problem from several perspectives in order to understand the potential solutions and their impacts. After the problem is thoroughly understood, the project group, with the manager of the project acting as a facilitator, can develop alternatives and choose a recommended solution. The goals are: gain a perspective on the problem, and devise appropriate corrective strategies.

Post-Project Evaluation

This final effort involves reviewing and evaluating a recently completed project so that lessons learned can be identified as growth experiences for the project team and documented for use by future teams. Everyone working on a project learns and somehow benefits from the experience. But does the organization benefit from what is learned by individual project participants? Often, it does not. This evaluation process ensures that team members assimilate project lessons learned and that the information benefits others as well. For more information on this subject, see Chapter 12, "Closeout Management."

The above efforts focused on project-specific consultative endeavors, which address one specific project and one unique project team. There are, however, other concerns that affect the entire organization. They require what we call *enterprise-wide consulting.*

Enterprise-Wide Consultative Efforts

As presented in Figure 3.3, another set of concerns must be addressed by the manager of the project in this new consulting role. These are enterprise-wide efforts that will support the project management initiative throughout the organization. As you can see from the model, these consultative endeavors can be divided into those that address the culture and those that relate to project management processes and procedures.

Cultural Endeavors

Three types of consultative project management activities relate to the overall, ongoing culture, or people-focused emphasis, of the organization. These are: selection and performance management, performance development, and organizational analysis. Support of these activities appropriately enables the manager of projects to build into the organizational culture a culture of project management.

Figure 3.3   Cultural Efforts of the Manager of Projects

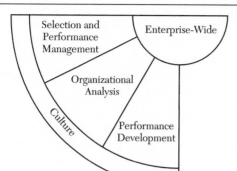

Selection and Performance Management.   This effort involves finding and preparing the right people for the right jobs. In his or her consulting role, the manager of the project can manage these critical human resources needs by selection, assessment, and performance management. Project team members may be selected from various cross-functional departments within the organization, or qualified subject matter experts may be hired or subcontracted from outside the company. The manager of the project can contribute to the interviewing and selection process. He or she can also work to create an internal skills inventory database of potential project team members within the organization. On a broader scale, the manager of the project can work with the human resources department to prepare job descriptions, assessment tools, and interviewing selection criteria to be used when hiring new managers of projects and project team members into the company. The manager of the project can also help to design performance appraisal review forms used exclusively for project players.

Organizational Analysis.   This effort involves assessing project management organizational structures and barriers that impede the implementation of project management. An effective project management strategy requires an appropriate organizational structure to support it, and an environment conducive to the discipline of project management. The manager of the project may need to analyze and recommend organizational structures that best support a project environment relevant to a specific project or even a specific phase within a unique project. He or she may need to offer suggestions to remove barriers that are negatively impacting project management within the enterprise. Additional changes within the organization, and/or in how the role of the discipline of project management is communicated throughout the organization, may be required.

Performance Development.   This effort involves devising a means to orchestrate a personalized learning environment for the project team members, and to transfer the learning once people are back on the job. All project players need to keep developing and growing, learning more about both their technical and their interpersonal roles in project management. This can be done through classroom training, self-study, or on-the-job coaching. In their consultative role, managers of projects should consider it their job to make recommendations and to institute, within their level of authority, mechanisms for personal development for all their project team members. But what ensures that the skills learned will be brought back to the job, cultivated, and encouraged until they become reality and habit? The manager of the project must provide a performance development skills transfer program to ensure that these new skills will be applied back on the job.

Process-Related Endeavors

In his or her consultative role, the manager of projects must undertake three areas of activity to support enterprise-wide, process-related efforts. As Figure 3.4 shows, these concern methodology, software, and the prioritization process.

Methodology.   This effort consists of creating a project management methodology or a series of guidelines that apply uniquely to project management in the project client's organization. These guidelines permit the manager of the project to reengineer the work processes and the way in which all project

Figure 3.4   Process-Related Efforts of the Manager of Projects

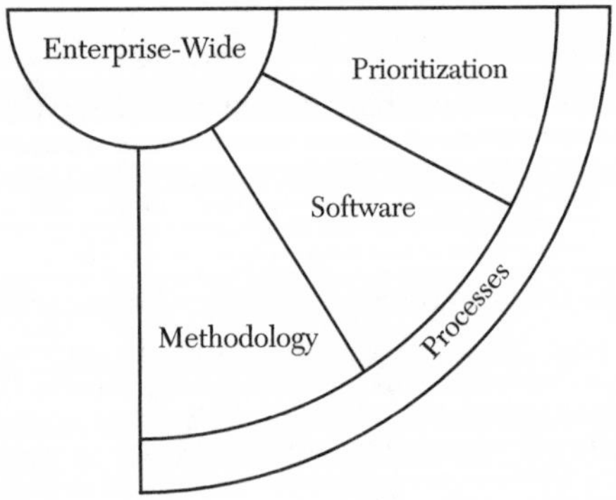

players approach their jobs. Few companies have escaped the need to rethink their project management strategies and to see that these processes and procedures are correctly documented and disseminated to all the people who engage in project work. Managers of a project can work with existing off-the-shelf methodologies or may choose to build their own. The purpose of these methodologies is to clarify the processes, procedures, and methods by which project management work will be done.

Software.   This effort focuses on integrating the scheduling tool of choice into the business processes that are already in place. This integration will maximize the company's investment in project management software and in the efficiencies that the software can generate for the enterprise as a whole. Today's project management software, used as a tool in exercising the project management discipline, has the inherent power to transform data into information and, ultimately, convert information into action. The manager of the project's ability to take on the role of consultant in the choice and implementation of this software provides the bridge that links project management methodologies, the learning process, and the integration of project management tools into the day-to-day work environment. Strategically, the manager of the project can help evaluate, choose, and implement not only the scheduling tool but also companion products to enhance the functionality of the chosen scheduling tool. Tactically, the manager of the project can aid in the customization of this suite of project management tools creating templates, charts, and reports specific to the needs of project players while also working within the standards established for the entire organization.

Prioritization.   This effort entails assisting the organization in developing and implementing a project solicitation, selection, and prioritization process. Using an off-the-shelf project prioritization template, or creating one from scratch, the manager of the project, along with a top-level management team, can solidify a model to assess the viability of a project. If viability is established, the project can be assigned a priority in relation to other projects in progress. Project requesters are educated about the method for presenting a new project so that their project proposal will receive the most favorable consideration.

Summary

In their roles as consultants, managers of projects need to work with their designated contacts—the team leaders, the team members, the project client, and top management—to define boundaries and establish goals prior to any work being performed. To pull these constituencies into collaboration, the manager of the project might use questionnaires, focus groups, individual interviews, or a combination of these methods. Throughout the process, the manager of the project should model the behavior he or she needs to enable members of the organization to apply the principles of project management to future assignments. The manager of the project should also maintain the broad view of a consultant to oversee the management of both project-specific and enterprise-wide tasks. In a consultative role, the manager of the project pursues project-specific tasks, such as facilitating the creation of project plans; enterprise-wide initiatives, such as developing project-related job descriptions and reward systems; and process-related initiatives, such as developing the rollout of a project management methodology and its attendant tasks, deliverables, roles, and responsibilities, throughout the project's life cycle.

In the assignment itself, the manager of the project must involve all the appropriate players in creating, interpreting, and validating the deliverables. The project outputs are often accompanied by the manager of the project's reports, but the organization owns the tangible products of each endeavor of the project. The manager of the project acts as a facilitator to see that the effort is accomplished with credibility and integrity.

Managers of the projects face unique challenges. They must acquire the consultative skills that are necessary to perform this new role. They must also broaden their perspective. Formerly tactical problem solvers, they must become designers and implementers of meaningful changes in the enterprise's approach to doing business. Only then can they best serve the organization, the project, and their careers.

THE MENTORING ROLE

This section explores the mentoring role of the manager of the project. *Mentoring* is establishing and maintaining a personal relationship with the team leaders and/or the core team members, who, in turn, use the same mentoring techniques to establish and maintain a relationship with their team members. We will first look at the concept, purpose, and objective of mentoring, and will then explore a process for creating the mentoring relationship.

Purpose and Objectives

In the most simplistic terms, a mentoring role requires setting up a process for ongoing communication in which the manager of the project can give guidance and advice to the project team members. Consider mentoring as part of the manager of the project's coaching job. Coaching is not just cheering players on, nor can direction and guidance be provided in a vacuum. The manager of the project can't just sit down one day with a team member and say, "Okay, I'm here. What would you like to be coached on today?" Building a relationship in which coaching efforts are accepted and assimilated into each team member's style takes work. Communication must be regular and structured. Ideally, the manager of the project should meet with each core team member once a week—or semimonthly, at the least. The best form of meeting is face-to-face, one-on-one. If a face-to-face session is occasionally not possible, a phone conversation can be substituted. Ideally, the manager of the project should spend thirty to sixty minutes each week, one-on-one, with each member of his or her team.

Mentoring sessions should be structured so that topics discussed at previous meetings are reviewed each week, and one unique "topic-of-the-week" is then initiated by the manager of the project. Each of these elements has a purpose. The review of earlier topics allows the team members to be thinking ahead and preparing their responses. The comfortable and safe exchange of familiar information helps them to become partners in a trusting personal relationship. It also alerts the manager of the project to trends in the issues, problems, and successes, which will be revealed in the responses and in the level of the team's energy and enthusiasm. In addition, keeping to the topics allows all the project team members, as they compare notes, to see that this mentoring effort has a consistent approach. The unique topic then adds spontaneity to every meeting.

Again, the purpose of the meetings is not to perform a status review of the tasks for which each team member is accountable. The goal for the discussions is an exchange, between the team member and the manager of the project, of good news and bad news, frustrations, dreams, goals, and expectations.

Mentoring Sessions

Now that we've established the purpose of the mentoring sessions, let's consider a model agenda that the manager of the project can follow to facilitate building a mentoring relationship with the project team members.

The agenda is divided into five topics:

1. Organizational Issues
2. Relationship Building and Personnel Development
3. Open Dialogue

4. Vision/Dream
5. Action Items

Each topic is explored next.

Organizational Issues

This topic involves posing and answering variations of the following questions:

How is the job going?

What accomplishments have been made?

How is the special project-of-the-month progressing?

Is there any need for clarification of roles and/or procedures? This segment of the discourse is repetitive and is addressed during each meeting. It is broken into three subsets: (1) the job, (2) the special project of the month, and (3) roles/procedures.

The Job.   Open the dialogue with the topic that is nearest and dearest to both of you: the job that the team member is doing. The first question is: "What accomplishments did you achieve last week and what insights, if any, did you gain from achieving them?" Accomplishments can relate to completion of the project, a better working relationship with project stakeholders, or a more efficient use of a process.

Next, ask about any stumbling blocks that the team member encountered during the previous week. This gives you, as the manager of the project, an opportunity to resolve those problems or to add to the list of action items any efforts needed to resolve the problems. Then address lessons learned and/or support needed. The support might be in the form of a tangible tool, political lobbying, or information or knowledge presently unavailable to the team member. Notice that the above topics unearth possible problems while they are still small and manageable. Documentation of these issues, problems, and successes becomes the base for a continuous improvement report, which you will need to present during close-out at the end of the project. This report presents a blow-by-blow record of what went right and what did not go right. The lessons learned will be helpful for any similar or future project that you or an associate may have as an assignment.

Special Project of the Month.   This special team-related project is not a task within the project's work breakdown structure (WBS). It is an effort that can help the total project. Every team member is asked to take on one unique contribution to the team itself—for example, researching the technology being used and making a presentation to the entire team, or refining the status reports to make them more meaningful to all the constituents on the distribution list. This personal project should be something that can be accomplished in 30 days or less. Its purpose is threefold:

1. Focusing players on certain short-term but meaningful activities that will help the project and the project team as a whole.
2. Teaching players how to initiate and execute projects within limited time constraints, thus practicing good project management skills and practices.
3. Having players contribute their efforts on behalf of the better operation of the team.

Each team related project should begin with a project request that is reviewed and approved by the manager of the project. It need not be formal, but it should follow the project management process. This may be a learning experience for project team members who have never had an opportunity to create a project request. Once the projects are under way, the manager of the project checks their status and ensures that each special project will result in a quality product within a designated time frame. When a team related project is about to be completed—the manager of the project and team members begin setting up the next team-related project.

Roles/Procedures.   The last part of the organizational issues segment of the weekly mentoring meeting is to ask the team member if he or she needs any clarification relative to his or her role or anyone else's role within the project. This is also the time to find out whether the team member is confused about the process or the specific procedures that the team is being asked to follow.

Although role clarification and procedural definition are dealt with during the launch of the project, changes do occur, and what may have been clear at the beginning of the project may become muddy as the project evolves. Confusion and misunderstandings could undermine the assignment; this meeting affords a time to bring to light any issues needing resolution. After the manager of the project and the project team member have thoroughly reviewed the job, the team-related project-of-the-month, and any possible misunderstandings in roles and procedures, it is time to move on to a behavioral subject.

Relationship Building and Personnel Development

This agenda item concerns posing and answering variations of the following questions: "How do you feel about . . . ? What are your views on . . . ? Can you think of ways to improve . . . ?" A new and different topic should be introduced each week. The focus here is on the people-management part of the manager of the project's job. The goal is to help team members build their knowledge of the organization as a whole and of their own project, and solidify their relationship with you, their manager of the project. This enlivens meetings and builds the bond that creates the synergy necessary to make the sum greater than the total of the parts.

The following eleven topics for this agenda item are discussed in detail in Performance Support Tool 3.1, "Mentoring Session—Special Topics List," at the end of this chapter:

1. What the project team looks like to you
2. Your role within the project
3. The five major tasks that you perform
4. A communication plan
5. A stakeholder's analysis
6. Responsibility, accountability, and authority
7. Operating agreement
8. Values
9. Paradigm shift
10. What do you want to be remembered for
11. Walk a mile in the other person's moccasins

Choose topics with which you are comfortable and which, you truly believe, will add value to your relationship with your team members. As you add to the agenda, be consistent with each of the team members with whom you meet. After you and the team member have discussed organizational and personnel issues, allow time for some unstructured dialogue.

Open Dialogue

This agenda item poses and answers an open-ended question: What, if anything, do we want to talk about? Open dialogue is a dealer's choice. You and your team member direct this part of the conversation as you see fit. Bring up any "By the way, . . ." or "I've been wanting to talk to you about . . ." subjects that seem to never find the right time or place to be aired.

Vision/Dream

This agenda item concerns the following scenarios: "If I could . . . , I would . . ."; "If we as a team could . . . , we would . . ." In an attempt to end every meeting on a positive note and to encourage your team to be creative, encourage each team member to think about what utopia would be within your project. You may get answers like "If I could learn more about XYZ project scheduling product, I could use the reports better," or "If we could have some time as a group, offsite, we might get rid of this them-versus-us feeling." This topic should be a consistent feature of each meeting. You may be surprised at how spontaneous and genuine people are with their responses. It is like asking people what they see in an inkblot; they often share some astounding insights.

Action Items

This final agenda item concerns the question: As a result of this meeting, what has either the manager of the project or the team member promised to do? Action items need to be tracked, to ensure their closure. It becomes very important that you keep track of these action items and see that they are completed. If you have made a promise, keep it. If the team member has signed up for an action item, be sure that it really happens.

In summary, project mentoring involves building a relationship with the key players—the people the manager of the project relies on to get the project done. This relationship is not built on platitudes but on serious, hard work. The manager of the project takes the time and effort to establish a solid communication link with the team members. The mentoring role initially solidifies the relationship, and then reenergizes the connection between the manager of the project and the team members.

CONCLUSION

Dr. Owen C. Gadeken, of Defense Systems Management College, presented an excellent paper, "In Search of Excellence: Leadership Lessons from DoD's Best PMs," at PMI's 1997 conference. He observed that the best managers of projects possess the following qualities:

- Strong commitment to their mission
- Long-term and big-picture perspective
- Systematic and innovative thinking
- Ability to find and empower the best people for their project team
- Selectivity in their involvement in project issues
- Consideration of external stakeholders
- Focus on relationships and influence
- Proactive information gathering and insistence on results[1]

These are traits that any top management would want a consultant to bring to a project. It is equally important that managers of projects establish and fulfill the expectation that they will service projects with a professional consulting and mentoring approach that embraces all the project players in their sphere of influence—from project planning and launch to team building, midstream audit, performance development, organizational analysis, human resources planning, corrective intervention, and post-project audit.

NOTE

1. Owen C. Gadeken. 1997. "In Search of Excellence: Leadership Lessons from DoD's Best PMs." *Proceedings of the Project Management Institute,* presented at PMI's 1997 conference.

PERFORMANCE SUPPORT TOOL 3.1
Mentoring Session—Special Topics List

This Performance Support Tool provides an 11-week special topics list that is to be used in mentoring meetings to build relationships and develop team spirit. The objective of these discussions is to allow an exchange of good news, bad news, frustrations, successes, dreams, goals, and expectations between the team member and the manager of the project.

The suggested topics, which can be organized in any order, provide a forum in which the manager of the project can start to build rapport. By providing the manager of the project with an opportunity to learn more about project team members, this forum helps to determine actions that may motivate each contributor and make the team a more powerful entity.

WHAT THE PROJECT TEAM LOOKS LIKE TO YOU

To establish a context for the discussion, ask each team member to draw a picture of how he or she fits into the project team. Encourage them not to use a traditional, hierarchical organization chart. Tell them that they can and should make the picture as creative as possible. (One player, for instance, drew an old frigate. All the project players had some role in sailing that ship.) Ask each team member to include anyone and everyone who is seen as having a part in the project, not just the team members and the project client.

To facilitate the discussion, pursue where the team member feels he or she fits into the rest of the team organization. Try to discern whether the project team member is expressing a positive or negative feeling relative to the team as a whole or to how he or she relates to the other team members. All stakeholders should be acknowledged. Are there people whom the team member has not considered as active contributors to the project when in fact they should be included? You need not get into too much depth here. (More specific issues relating to roles and responsibilities are discussed in the subsequent topics.)

YOUR ROLE WITHIN THE PROJECT

Ask the team member this hypothetical question: "If you were at a party and a stranger asked you what you do for a living, what would you answer, in twenty-five words or less?" After the team member has responded, suggest that the response might have been: "I am a team member working on XYZ project." Then ask: "If the person at the party then asked you to define the term *team member,* how would you respond and how would you describe the kind of project you are working on?"

To facilitate the discussion, encourage the team member to avoid generalizations, dig deep, and try to explain his or her participation in the project and precisely what the project is meant to accomplish. Consider playing the role of the stranger at the party; ask probing questions. Pay attention to misconceptions, but do not attempt to refute the statements. Clarify your questions by restating them in a positive way.

THE FIVE MAJOR TASKS THAT YOU PERFORM

Ask the team member to share with you the five most important tasks that he or she performs within the project team. Suggest inclusion of tangible tasks, such as contributing subject matter expertise to the work, and consideration of the more intangible nontechnical jobs that he or she performs, such as attempting to be peacemaker when needed. Enumeration of the tasks on the work breakdown structure is not an appropriate response.

There are ways to facilitate this discussion. First, don't let the team member get away with reciting the first five things that come to mind. Ask him or her to spend some quiet time writing down on paper every task that he or she performs, and then to pick the most important five and share them with you. The team member might also write on a blackboard all the things that he or she contributes to this project and then identify and explain the top five contributions. Encourage all of the team members to be specific and honest with you and with themselves.

A COMMUNICATION PLAN

Communication is the crux of any positive relationship. Most problems between two people occur because there was no communication, or communication was faulty or misleading. By preparing a plan, the manager of the project and the team members can establish a channel of communication and maintain it at a high level. The product of this channel is a dialogue between the manager of the project and the team member—a change in the *modus operandi*. Until now, the project team member has been doing all the talking and the manager of the project has merely probed and searched for more information. This time, the topic brings about an exchange. The communication plan is an agreement on the answers to these four questions:

1. What do we need to communicate about, to keep the relationship healthy?
2. How frequently do we need to communicate?
3. What medium should we use: e-mail, voice mail, one-on-one meetings, reports?
4. What feedback will ensure that the communication has been received and understood?

Keep in mind that less interpersonal forms of communication, such as memos and e-mail, can be used routinely if they are sent more frequently. On the other hand, important issues, such as reporting problems that have occurred, should be communicated through a more personal medium, such as a phone conversation or a face-to-face meeting. (This type of communication is needed less frequently.)

A STAKEHOLDER'S ANALYSIS

Look at the various stakeholders, including the project team members, project client, resource managers, and strategic clients. What are their relationships to one another? At the start of this session, identify all the stakeholders in the project. Revisit some of the previous meeting notes, or the picture of the project team. The first objective is to reach consensus on your relationships with one another. Refer back to the communication plan. Decide what you, as the manager of the project, need to give to each team member if the relationship is to stay healthy. In return, what will you need to get from each team member? For example, a team member may ask the manager of the project to keep him or her informed as soon as the project client asks for a change in the scope of the end-product. Or, the manager of the project may ask a team member to let him or her know if any other priorities are interfering with putting the promised effort into the project work. When these needs and wants have been articulated, the manager of the project and the team member should resolve to keep each other informed in a timely manner.

After the need for communication has been clarified, the manager of the project should encourage the team member to consider every stakeholder with whom he or she interacts, and to define specifically what the team member needs to give that stakeholder and what the stakeholder should give in return. After the team member has completed this analysis, he or she should arrange a meeting with each of the stakeholders, share the information, and reach a final agreement on a personal communication plan. This spreads the relationship building beyond the manager of the project and the team member.

RESPONSIBILITY, ACCOUNTABILITY, AND AUTHORITY

Responsibility is an ethical commitment to accomplish work on time, within budget, and of the quality promised. *Accountability* may bring a consequence or, if the responsibility for meeting the commitment is attained, a reward. We are often confused as to what other people see as our responsibilities and what they are holding us accountable for. Responsibility has a moral and ethical basis; accountability has more of an ownership, succeed-or-fail tone.

Discuss the team member's opinion regarding the difference between being responsible and being accountable. For many people, the distinction is not clear. When you have reached consensus on what each of these words mean, ask the team member to consider what he or she is responsible for within the project and what he or she will be held accountable for during and after the project. If time allows and the topic is applicable, the discussion might cover what *authority* (formal or informal) the team member has, to ensure that he or she meets the prescribed responsibilities and accountabilities. To bring others into this consensus-building, suggest to a team member that he or she should share this input with his or her resource manager.

OPERATING AGREEMENT

In this session, you and the team member are going to develop an *operating agreement* to which both of you will adhere throughout the rest of the project. Each of us has issues that bother us in a personal/business relationship, and other conditions and circumstances that we appreciate (and sometimes require) in a personal relationship. For example, a manager of a project might react negatively if someone presents a project request that has no cost justification or offers no benefits to the organization. On the other hand, that same manager of the project may like people who are creative, take initiative, and think ahead.

Spend a few quiet minutes in which each of you writes down the things that you like and dislike about working with other people—for example, you can't stand it when a meeting starts late because someone hasn't been considerate enough to show up on time. After you have both completed your lists, share them with one another—one item at a time, in a round-robin fashion, and write them on a blackboard. Discuss them, clarify any confusing items, and push back at each other when necessary, but work hard at understanding each other's point of view. At the end of the discussion, pick five items that are most important to each of you, and reach a consensus that these will be the rules by which the two of you will attempt to work during the rest of the project.

If you have access to personality profiles such as the Myers Briggs or Performax DISC profile, and if you believe that these instruments have credence, use them as tools to stimulate discussion of team members' personal styles and how they complement or conflict with other team members' styles. Research some of the excellent 360° evaluation systems for managers of projects and project teams. Consider investing in one of these systems if you feel it can provide some structured feedback to your project team members.

VALUES

Our personal values set the tone for how we, as individuals, act and react. Let's say that my key set of values is based on achieving success, power, and wealth. However, because the person with whom I am working has values such as peace of mind, family, and personal time, we might have a difficult time understanding one another and working well together. Is either of us wrong? No. However, everyone is different. This session is designed to help the team member and the manager of the project understand and respect these differences.

This is a rough session for you, as manager of the project, especially if you believe that everyone on your team should have (or even *must* have) the same values that you do. Sorry; reality differs. It may be difficult for you *not* to belittle a team member's set of values or to try talking the person out of his or her values and into yours. The only way to be successful during the discussion is to be prepared to accept the other person's values. The purpose of this session is to talk about ways in which your expectations, based on your values as the manager of the project, can be satisfied without asking the other person to change his or her values.

PARADIGM SHIFT

Every project goes through changes. Changes can be triggered internally, as the project moves through the various phases of the product/systems development life cycle. The goals, objectives, and tone may change. The atmosphere during the design phase is much different than it is during the testing phase. Changes can also be caused by external factors; for example, the project client could resign, leaving the project with no replacement for three months. This session offers an opportunity to talk about what the team member perceives as either internal or external changes that he or she believes are impacting the project or the project team either positively or negatively. To facilitate the discussion, ask the team member the following six questions:

1. What do you see as the major shifts or changes that are affecting the project?
2. How do you feel about the changes? Do you like or dislike them?
3. Do the changes affect you personally? If so, in what way(s)?
4. How do you believe the changes will impact the project and/or the project team?
5. What do you believe needs to be done to mitigate and/or enhance the impact of the change?
6. What other changes do you expect in the future?

It is your job as manager of the project to listen not only to what the team member is saying but also to "listen between the lines" to determine what is not being said but is implied. You must also consider that some issues might be too politically sensitive to be expressed in a forthright manner. Use all of your active listening and probing/questioning skills to get to the real issues. Then provide solutions, information, and consolation with honesty and integrity. This discussion may generate action items to be undertaken by you or by the project team member. This is also an appropriate forum for sharing, one-on-one, any paradigm shifts that you can foresee occurring in the future. Do not share conjecture; communicate only facts as you know them.

WHAT DO YOU WANT TO BE REMEMBERED FOR

Ask the team member, "What do you want to be remembered for? If you were able to attend your own wake, and the only attendees were the people with whom you worked (not your personal friends and family), what would you want them to say about you? More specifically, what would you want your project clients to relate to the rest of the audience? How about your resource manager? And lastly, what would you like the people who worked with you on various projects to say about you?"

Suggest, as the team member envisions this scenario, that if the mourners are not saying the things that he or she would like them to be saying, then maybe the team member needs to reevaluate his or her motivations and change them to create a more memorable image. You might also share with the team member how you would like to be remembered. You might want to avoid asking whether the team member would see you as you would like to be seen, but by offering your vision of your legacy, the team member will become more aware of who you are and more empathetic to your inner self. Beware: Don't construct a string of platitudes. Be honest or don't share at all. If your desires are seen as a sham, you may never recover the team member's respect.

WALK A MILE IN THE OTHER PERSON'S MOCCASINS

We all become so engrossed in who we are, what we do, and the problems we face that we often forget to be sensitive to the situations of other persons. Most of the previous sessions have been geared toward explaining oneself to another person. This session is strictly about putting oneself in the other person's place for a few minutes.

Each person is asked to complete this sentence: "If I had the job of (the **role** of the other person, not his or her name), I would like (what) the most and I would like (what) the least." For example, "If I had the job of a project team member, I would like being treated with respect and consideration the most, and I would like being ignored the least." Do not direct your comments to another person specifically; direct them to the job the person holds. When each of you hears how another person views your job, do not try to explain or defend it or to make excuses. Remember that another person's perception is his or her reality. The purpose of this exercise is to exchange perceptions. At the end of the session, each person needs to consider what the other person has said, internalize its meaning, and adjust his or her perceptions accordingly.

ASSESSMENT TOOL

Manager of the Project Assessment

Project Leaders	Response Answer each question in the space provided. Where 1 to 10 are used, 1 = Lowest score and 10 = Highest score.
1. How are project leaders chosen?	_____
2. What criteria are used for choosing project leaders?	_____ _____
3. How is the position of the project leader viewed?	_____ _____
4. How is it rewarded?	_____
5. To what degree is there positive visibility for being a project leader?	High _____ Medium _____ Low _____
6. How much authority do you have over resources (as a project manager)?	1 2 3 4 5 6 7 8 9 10
7. To what degree can you negotiate due dates?	High _____ Medium _____ Low _____
8. How much authority do you have over technical decision making?	1 2 3 4 5 6 7 8 9 10
9. How much authority do you have over the project as a whole: for driving the project, changing its direction, and so on?	1 2 3 4 5 6 7 8 9 10

CHAPTER 4

Performance Management

During the Civil War, President Abraham Lincoln was considering making Ulysses S. Grant commander-in-chief of the Union forces. The members of the cabinet did not support this choice at all. They were attempting to persuade President Lincoln to change his mind. At one point, the President lost his temper, looked at a dissenting cabinet member, and said, "I'll buy that man a keg of bourbon a day, if he can win this *!*! war."

Everyone has strengths and weaknesses. Our job as managers of projects is to bring out and put to good use the strengths of our project team members. It is also our job to recognize their weaknesses and to attempt to redirect these weaknesses so that they do not harm the project. Sometimes, like Abraham Lincoln, we need to abide team members' weaknesses because of the offsetting positive strengths that these members bring to the team.

Another story from history comes to mind. One night, Henry Ford was entertaining, as dinner guests, three candidates for a high-level management position within his corporation. As the entrée was served, Henry picked up the salt shaker and liberally salted his food. He then passed the shaker on to the young man seated at his left, who accepted it and, following the example of Mr. Ford, also liberally salted his food. The man then passed the shaker on to the candidate seated at his left, who mimicked what Mr. Ford and the other candidate had done. He energetically salted his food. The salt shaker was passed to the left again, into the hands of the last candidate. This man put the salt shaker down, tasted his food, and continued to eat without adding any salt to the meal. Can you guess which of the three candidates got the job? Yes; the third candidate. But why? When Mr. Ford asked the last candidate why he did not salt his food as everyone else had, the young man replied, "I had not tasted the food yet, and I didn't know whether it needed salt. When I tasted it, I decided that I didn't want to add salt." Henry Ford claimed that he had set up this test for all three of the candidates. He was looking for someone who could think for himself and would not just follow suit.

In our project teams, some individuals may not be performing their technical tasks or fulfilling their project responsibilities exactly as we would do them, but this variance should not suggest that these folks are wrong or incompetent. We need to let them do their jobs. We should question them or provide criticism only if what they are doing is wrong or will hurt the project. Beyond that, everyone has a right to perform necessary functions as he or she sees fit.

CHAPTER OVERVIEW

"The rung of a ladder was never meant to rest upon, but only to hold a man's foot long enough to enable him to put the other somewhere higher."
—Thomas Henry Huxley, nineteenth-century biologist

Project team members (see A–H on Figure 4.1) occupy a unique place in the traditional organizational structure. Like most employees, they report to a resource or functional manager who is responsible for the allocation of their time and the quality of the technical product/deliverable that they produce, as well as for such personnel-related functions as the annual performance appraisal. At the same time, project team members often perform much of their work for a second manager, the manager of their project, the person who is chartered to interact with project team members in a specific, approved, and funded project effort.

Figure 4.1 portrays a typical project organization structure. The structure is traditional in that functional departments managed by resource managers report to the head of the organization, in this case, the CEO. However, this structure is nontraditional because projects cut horizontally across the functions pulling project team members to contribute to various projects. For example, person A works within a specific function and reports directly to a resource manager. In addition, person A along with persons D and F, from two other functional areas, have been designated to work on project 101 and report to the manager of project 101.

The dichotomy between the reporting and performing relationships can create barriers to optimum performance. Lack of input into the Performance Management System by the manager of the project can result in an incomplete

Figure 4.1   Dual Reporting

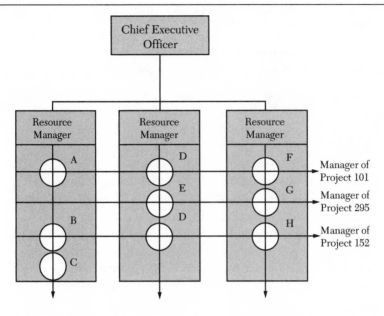

or inaccurate picture of performance, which, in turn, may (1) prevent project team members from creating effective self-development plans or (2) inhibit them from advancing appropriately within the organization.

The question then becomes: Which manager is responsible for improvement of performance and development of skills and competencies? Is that same manager responsible for the annual performance appraisal? If only the resource manager is designated, valuable feedback, coaching, and direction can be lost, and determination of compensation may unfairly exclude input from the persons with whom the project team member has the most day-to-day contact. A lack of reinforcement and reward for good project management practices can then lead to the loss of individuals who could have contributed substantially to the company.

This chapter presents a *performance management system* that formally brings together input from resource managers and from managers of projects; requires input from the project client; and gives project team members opportunities to set realistic performance expectations and personal developmental goals by which their achievement can be more objectively measured. This system will repay a company's investment many times over because it identifies good project team members and gives them the means to grow and develop effectively within the organization.

The performance management system described in this chapter encompasses much more than an annual performance appraisal. Two components of the system are covered in detail:

1. The performance improvement process
2. The performance appraisal review process

As part of the performance improvement process, a Performance Expectations Agreement and a Personal Development Plan are established at the beginning of the review year. The expectations and the goals of the plan are revisited as part of a formal system of interim dialogues between the project team member and the two managers (the manager of the project and the resource manager). The interim dialogues, which are scheduled at predefined checkpoints, gauge attainment of the established expectations and goals.

The performance appraisal review process, which is performed within the company's scheduled time frames, measures and rewards the attainment of these goals.

This chapter describes a Performance Management System (Figure 4.2) designed specifically for project team members. It consists of the following sections:

- The Performance Improvement Process
- The Performance Expectations Agreement
- The Personal Development Plan

Figure 4.2   Performance Management System

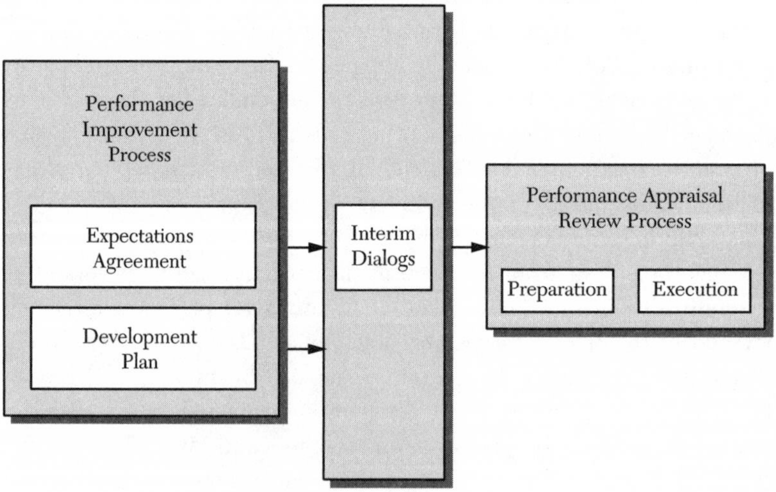

- Interim Dialogues
- The Performance Appraisal Review Process
- Preparation
- Execution
- Conclusion

In addition, at the end of the chapter Performance Support Tool 4.1 ("Performance Management System for Project Team Members") offers a worksheet to aid in the completion of all the deliverables discussed in the chapter. All Performance Support and Assessment Tools referenced in this book are available for download at www.pmsi-pm.com.

A sound performance management system develops and rewards good project management within an organization by fulfilling the following goals:

- Define clearly the performance responsibilities and expectations of the project team member, and associate these expectations with quantifiable metrics in the form of a Performance Expectations Agreement.
- Encourage every project team member to develop his or her capabilities and to acquire new knowledge and skills according to his or her Performance Development Plan.
- Include the appropriate people—in this case, the manager of the team member's project and their functional (i.e., their resource) manager—in the dialogue and feedback process.
- Ensure that every project team member receives accurate, timely, and beneficial feedback about his or her performance, and that all managers of projects in the organization follow the same equitable process.
- Recognize individual contributions and efforts that further the goals and commitments of the project(s) being implemented.
- Promote the success and well-being of project management within the organization.

Overall, the performance management system gives an organization the means to train and retain good managers of projects and committed project team members by providing them with a fair and motivating work environment.

THE PERFORMANCE IMPROVEMENT PROCESS

The first part of the performance management system is the performance improvement process. During the performance improvement process, the project team member develops two tools with which to gauge his or her progress:

(1) the Performance Expectations Agreement and (2) the Personal Development Plan. The Performance Expectations Agreement consists of a series of measurable performance and productivity criteria. The project team member will work toward meeting those performance standards during the year. Consequently, he or she will be reviewed at the end of the predetermined review period (usually 12 months).

The second document that results from the performance improvement process, the Personal Development Plan, is established for each team member. It defines skill and/or behavioral goals and suggests the types of education, study, and mentoring efforts that will be undertaken. Each plan is implemented unilaterally, with the support of the company, so that the project team member is able to meet the performance criteria established in the performance improvement process.

To ensure that this process is successful, the project team member must:

- Buy into the Performance Expectations Agreement and the Personal Development Plan.
- Agree to the metrics used for evaluation and be willing to be accountable for meeting the stated goals.
- Be willing to assume ownership for each of his or her plans. It is not the organization's responsibility to see that the goals are met. It is the responsibility of the project team member, with the assistance of the organization.
- Foresee the payoff of knowing in advance how he or she will be evaluated.
- Be able, to some degree, to control his or her own fate.
- Be assured that resources will be available, from the organization, to attain the results agreed to in the plans.

Now let's take a look at the two deliverables from the performance improvement process.

The Performance Expectations Agreement

The Performance Expectations Agreement consists of a series of quantifiable criteria toward which the project team member will work and upon which he or she will be evaluated at the end of the review period. The Performance Expectations Agreement is negotiated among the project team member, the manager of his or her project, and his or her resource manager.

The development of a Performance Expectations Agreement is based on three premises:

1. The organization has made a commitment to its goals and strategic plans, and from those strategic plans evolve the business objectives of all divisions that ultimately create projects. The organization has recognized that it is a project-driven organization.
2. The organization, management, and team member all recognize that a valid performance review is based on measurable behavior rather than personality.
3. A project team member's performance will be evaluated in terms of results measured against established, unique goals developed by the manager of the project, the resource manager, and the individual project team member—not simply against the common goals of all project teams.

If these premises are not accepted by all parties involved, the performance review process loses value because it *does not* measure progress toward attainment of business-relevant goals, include measurable and attainable objectives, and assess relevant achievements.

Steps and Guidelines

Let's first review the steps needed to produce a Performance Expectations Agreement and discuss in more detail the guidelines necessary to generate meaningful goals with strong success metrics.

The steps to generate a Performance Expectations Agreement are shown in Table 4.1. (These steps are also given in a template that can be used on the job; see Performance Support Tool 4.1 at the end of this chapter.)

The most important part of this process is the creation of the key results and their associated quantifiable measurements. When generating a Performance Expectations Agreement, follow these guidelines:

- Start the key result with an active verb such as "*Conduct* effective cross-functional meetings."
- Identify a key result for every job responsibility within the project team member's job description, focusing on project-related responsibilities.
- Convert each key result into a goal that is attainable yet stretches the project team member. In other words, create goals that provide the project team member with a challenge, such as: within a six month period "Run four monthly meetings involving the representatives of the five user groups from around the country, to ensure their continued agreement with the system results and their requirements." Running one meeting within the six months would not be much of a challenge.

Table 4.1   Steps to Generate a Project Management Performance Expectations Agreement

Step	Parties Involved	Action
1	Resource Manager Manager of Project	Solidify the project team member's job description with the project team member.
2	Project Team Member	Identify and document five to ten key results that would demonstrate success.
3	Resource Manager Manager of Project	Review key results and comment on areas that need further discussion, adding, deleting, and/or modifying.
4	Resource Manager Manager of Project Project Team Member	Reach consensus on three to five key results that will become the project team member's goals. Set dates for the accomplishment of each goal as well as the dollars needed to support the goal.
5	Resource Manager Manager of Project Project Team Member	Agree upon the success metric or measurable criteria upon which each of the goals or performance expectations will be monitored and evaluated throughout the year. Further, determine how these will be maintained once the goal is reached.
6	Resource Manager Manager of Project	Document the Performance Expectation Agreement along with a periodic interim dialogue plan.
7	Resource Manager Manager of Project Project Team Member	Sign the document indicating agreement on the goals and their associated metrics at this moment in time. (After signing the document, these goals and metrics may still be renegotiated during the review period.)

- Set a day, month, and year when the goal is to be accomplished. The target date does not always have to be at the end of the review period. Stagger the completion dates throughout the review time frame so that there are successes throughout the entire period.
- Identify the costs (in dollars, time, materials, and/or equipment) needed to meet the goal, and commit those funds for the project team member to use at his or her discretion. For example, "Transportation for 10 people to these meetings, and access to meeting facilities and necessary computer support to demonstrate the system."

- State verifiable criteria that signal when the goal has been reached, such as: "A sign-off on the system prototype to date by all five user representatives, or a sign-off on the necessary Change Control documents by all user representatives if the prototype is still in development due to requirement changes."
- Agree on the quantitative standards that are expected to be maintained after the goal has been reached, such as "Continued agreement on the system requirements and performance by all five user representatives, obtained on a monthly basis."
- Be sure that the goal is controllable by the project team member. For example, it should be assumed that the user group representatives do not change their requirements without going through a formal change control process. It should also be assumed that the system's engineers and developers maintain complete and open communication with the project team member.
- Do not establish more than 10 goals; having only three to five would be preferable.

Common Pitfalls

The five common pitfalls of setting performance expectations are as follows:

1. *The project team member to be assessed does not have clear knowledge of his or her areas of accountability and expected deliverables.* Experience shows this is more often the case than not. A project team member will benefit if the manager of the project and the resource manager agree on areas of accountability and expected deliverables toward each goal, and set specific interim milestones.
2. *Specific goals and success metrics, as well as target dates, are not agreed on by all parties.* This is often caused by conflicting priorities among projects but also may occur when functional responsibilities conflict with project responsibilities. In the latter case, the manager of the project and the resource manager must agree on the relative priority among the areas of accountability assigned to the project team member. The more difficult this agreement is to achieve, the more the organization needs an overall prioritization process for projects and a clear division of responsibility among managers of projects, resource managers, and the project team member. Conflicts in priorities, not project management incompetence, most often cause project failures in organizations.
3. *Goals and success metrics are incorrectly expressed in terms of activities rather than in terms of concrete results.* There is a well-known

truth among project practitioners: "Don't confuse activity with progress." Results lead to the achievement of organizational objectives; activities do not.

4. *Goals are developed without the input of the project team member.* A
   project team member who is not allowed an opportunity to express his
   or her thoughts about the goals, key results, and success metrics that
   will be used to measure his or her performance will never be fully motivated to achieve them. Remember that the achievement of goals is up
   to the project team member, and strong inner drive and commitment
   are therefore essential motivators.

5. *The goals do not encompass all areas of the project team member's
   work, such as personal development, methods and procedures, personal relationships, and production.* Many studies suggest that the
   characteristics of a successful and effective project team member include not only the ability to manage their task assignments but also
   considerable interpersonal skills. Among those are the ability to communicate, establish, and maintain trust; to take risks; and to inspire
   other team members. They also include ongoing self-development.
   These characteristics can all be measured. By recognizing and rewarding them, the organization will encourage them among all employees.

Reaching Consensus

After the goals and success metrics are determined, the project team member, the manager of the project, and the resource manager need to reach consensus. Answers to the following questions will determine whether the goal
and its associated success metrics are achievable and are accurate measures
of a project team member's skill and effectiveness:

- Does the project team member have the authority and resources to
  achieve the goal? If not, what recourse does the project team member
  have? The Performance Expectations Agreement should include a set
  of explicitly stated assumptions that protect the project team member
  from being held accountable for goals that cannot be achieved due to
  circumstances beyond his or her control.
- Do the goal and the success metrics measure a major segment of the
  project team member's responsibility and accountability? If not, can
  the project team member reach the goal easily or will he or she have
  to stretch beyond previous performance to do so? The goal must not
  be set so high that it is unattainable nor so low that it is too easy.

- Does the goal conform to the business objectives of the project team member's project manager and resource manager, and to those of the department? Does the goal also conform to the business objectives of the project and of the project management discipline?
- Is there a way of providing the project team member with feedback relative to how he or she is progressing toward the goal? If not, can the goal be clearly measured at the end of the review period?

Agreement on these questions will establish a firm foundation for the rest of the performance management process. The goal of the Performance Expectations Agreement is ultimately to develop criteria that are relevant, achievable, challenging, measurable, and mutually agreed on.

Sample Criteria

Table 4.2 gives a sample list of criteria that might be used to set performance goals and ensure that all the relevant activity areas are included.

After performance expectations have been established and agreed on, the next step in the process is the writing of the team member's Personal Development Plan. This plan details the types of education, study, and mentoring efforts to be undertaken by the project team member to improve his or her skills and help toward attainment of the goals set in the Performance Expectations Agreement.

The Personal Development Plan

The Personal Development Plan, an offshoot of the Performance Expectations Agreement, defines the types of development efforts the project team member must make, either independently or with the support of the company, to attain his or her goals. With a full understanding of the job description and the Performance Expectations Agreement, the project team member and his or her manager can design a Personal Development Plan that will help the project team member to grow during the next 12 months, to attain the metrics in the Performance Expectations Agreement, and to prepare for taking on more project management responsibility in coming years.

SWOT Analysis

One way to approach the creation of a Personal Development Plan is to ask the project team member to enumerate his or her **S**trengths, **W**eaknesses, **O**pportunities for improvement, and **T**hreats perceived as barriers to

Table 4.2   Sample Criteria for Setting Expectations Goals

Category	Characteristics	Sample Criteria
Performance	Displays observable behavior that leads directly to positive project results.	• Employs the project management tools appropriately. • Works independently. • Solves problems. • Takes initiative. • Is innovative and creative.
Communication	Is able to send and receive information using appropriate media and level of detail, including observable efforts to ensure that messages are understood correctly by the sender and the receiver.	• Communicates clearly and in a timely manner. • Understands the project management process. • Uses the appropriate tools to communicate.
Interpersonal Skills	Is able to work effectively through others and to inspire motivation in others.	• Works well with other project team members and project stakeholders. • Has a professional relationship with project client(s).
Attendance and Work Habits	Models professional behavior on the job that indicates respect for others' schedules and work needs and for the organization as a whole.	• Is punctual and has minimal absenteeism. • Is on time for meetings and participates/facilitates them professionally. • Meets requirements as defined in the job description of a project team member. • Applies project management knowledge/skills to the projects. • Shares knowledge/skills with other members of the project team. • Aggressively seeks out knowledge and new/enhanced skills.

improvement. This assessment, commonly called a SWOT analysis, provides a starting point based on the project team member's own assessment of his or her self-development needs in the context of the project work environment. It is important to encourage project team members to include all facets of their work in their SWOT analysis: personal development, methods and procedures, and interpersonal relationships, to name just a few. One of the major pitfalls in composing Personal Development Plans and Performance Expectations Agreements is failure to encompass all these areas. A focus that includes only the technical and easily measurable areas of project management ignores the wisdom of many studies. Successful project team members need (1) characteristics that transcend the use of technical tools and techniques, and (2) the ability to examine their own strengths and weaknesses in the areas of leadership and self-development.

Table 4.3, a sample of a SWOT analysis, lists a fictional project team member's strengths, weaknesses, opportunities, and threats in terms of his or her project management (technical) skills, team leadership, and self-development.

A SWOT analysis can be lengthy and should be revised as often as necessary, depending on the volatility of the project team member's environment. Changes in opportunities and threats need particular attention. For example, if the portfolio of projects in which the project team member is involved changes every quarter, then the opportunities for self-development will change just as often. On the other hand, if the project team member is handling projects lasting longer than a year, the opportunities will tend to remain more stable. The "planning horizon" of the SWOT analysis should be negotiated among the project team member, the manager of the project, and the resource manager. It is important to address opportunities and threats/barriers to keep the project team member motivated and to maintain a meaningful performance management system. Interim dialogues between the project team member and the manager of the project will provide a chance for these discussions.

After the SWOT analysis is complete, a Personal Development Plan can be created based on the feasibility of the opportunities and threats identified by the project team member. Such a plan provides a road map for plotting personal learning and professional growth. It helps the project team member to develop and stretch, intellectually and interpersonally, and thus prepare for more responsibility. Using the Personal Development Plan, the project team member, the manager of the project, and the resource manager can create a strategy that may include off-site training, on-site self-study, time with a mentor, and personal self-development.

Table 4.3   A Sample SWOT Analysis

SWOT Factors	PM Skills	Team Leadership	Self-Development
Strengths	Understands and attempts to use project management tools and techniques, including project schedules.	Received training in assessment of personality styles and in conflict management.	Attends local chapter meetings of the Project Management Institute (PMI). Reads one project management book every quarter.
Weaknesses	Can't do all the scheduling manually, and doesn't know how to use project management software.	Does not lead meetings effectively.	Would like to get Project Management Professional (PMP) certification.
Opportunities	Class in the company's scheduling package offered next quarter, new project beginning next quarter would allow application of skills.	Another employee has offered to mentor me in leading meetings.	PMP review class offered by PMI next quarter.
Threats/Barriers	Software not installed on computer.	Need opportunity to lead meetings.	Does not have money to take PMP exam review class.

REMEMBER   It is not exclusively the company's job to provide a project team member with training. The project team member has a responsibility to invest some of his or her time in personal growth and development for the future.

The Progressive Levels of Personal Development

"Personal development" is a broad term that can be seen as a progression through four levels:

1. Knowledge
2. Skill
3. Competency
4. Mastery

Generically, in the education profession, the established model for personnel development is called the professional growth model. First, the learner must attain knowledge about a technical or interpersonal concept. This knowledge base is transformed into a skill, which then becomes a competency. Over time, a competency evolves into a mastery of that competency. The growth is progressive, as shown in Figure 4.3. A person's development begins at the bottom of the triangle and moves toward the top.

Let's relate this framework to project management. Knowledge, such as that in the *Project Management Body of Knowledge (PMBOK)*, is learned first by reading and understanding concepts, and memorizing definitions and facts. As this project management knowledge is practiced, in a classroom or on a job, it becomes a skill. As the skill becomes a habit and is incorporated into daily life; it then becomes a competency. Finally, individual style is added to the competency and, with repeated experiences, it evolves into mastery.

Development and Assessment of the Levels of Personal Development

For a project team member to progress through the professional growth model, behaviors critical to his or her success must be identified. *Each individual*

Figure 4.3   Progressive Developmental Model

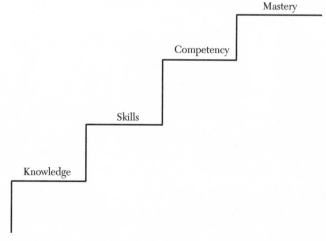

project team member has unique job strengths and weaknesses relative to the project management discipline. Each person will need to exhibit a unique combination of traits to perform in a particular project environment and become successful. Some behaviors relate to technical actions such as producing and reading Gantt charts; other behaviors focus on the human dimensions of the equation, such as negotiating or leading.

After the behaviors are isolated, an assessment can determine the project team member's level in the progression from knowledge to mastery. When an initial assessment is completed, a Personal Development Plan is prepared and that person moves from a current level of performance into the next one. Each level of the professional growth model includes a final assessment to ensure that the project team member is ready to advance. The performance progression is a spiral process of developing a behavior and then assessing whether it has been attained, before moving up to the next level.

Let's trace the professional growth model from knowledge to mastery.

Knowledge: Development.   *Acquiring knowledge* is learning in the truest sense of the term. It involves gaining understanding of a behavior, and its associated activities, by cognitive processes. Knowledge is gained by reading and understanding concepts and by memorizing definitions and facts. It is acquired by reading and/or listening to information and absorbing that information into one's retentive memory. Knowledge can be accomplished by attending a class, working through a computer-based training product, watching/listening to a videotape or audiotape, reading a book, or observing a demonstration.

> **Example**   A project team member wants to develop his or her skill in managing meetings, particularly status review meetings. This can be done by reading a book on meetings management and observing a well-run status meeting.

Knowledge: Assessment.   Attending a class or reading a book does not necessarily ensure learning a new behavior that can be applied on one's job. The traditional assessment relative to ascertaining a level of knowledge is typically a test. This test might be a traditional examination with answers in the form of true–false or multiple-choice questions; an essay; or a more sophisticated assessment in which one responds to various scenarios imbedded in a case study or performs a series of behaviors in a computerized simulation.

> **Example**   A mentor who is assigned to the project team member questions the project team member concerning the essential skills of

"meetings management" as they have been learned from a book and observed in at least one status meeting.

After the team member has proven cognitive understanding of a behavior, he or she moves up to the level of "skills" development. Let's look at the development of a skill and at how to assess whether it has been adequately developed.

Knowledge

Develop by:

1. Awareness
2. Cognitive understanding through reading/listening
3. Retaining information

Assess by:

- Taking a test
- Case study
- Perform via a simulation

Skill: Development.   A *skill* is developed by repeated practice. The beginning of this effort is practicing the knowledge that one has acquired. It can occur in the classroom environment; however, a classroom does not offer enough time to review and fully reinforce a behavior so that it becomes a refined skill. To progress, the project team member needs to create a personal schedule in which opportunities to practice this skill are coordinated with the manager of the project and the resource manager. The schedule provides explicit assurance, from the manager of the project and the resource manager, of a commitment of time for the project team member's performance growth. It also ensures that the project team member can expect greater visibility and recognition as the skill develops.

Skills can be developed in the following ways:

- Working with a mentor or coach
- Working through additional practice tools, such as computer-based training
- Integrating a skill consciously into one's everyday work effort, with the help and support of a manager of projects and a resource manager

Example   The project team member has learned the steps required to facilitate a meeting and understands the tips and traps. Now the project team member needs to apply that knowledge so that it is transformed into a skill. This can be done by immediately applying what has been learned. For example, the manager of the project may assign the project team member to lead specific small meetings. If these formal opportunities are not present, the project team member may need to orchestrate a scenario in which he or she can facilitate an event—for example, call and conduct a meeting. Informal group meetings attended by the project team or by peers, and directed toward a specific objective, such as monthly luncheons for sharing best practices, would suffice.

Skill: Assessment.   For a skill to be assessed, it must be observed, evaluated, and critiqued by a highly capable person. The student's manager of projects (or an objective subject matter expert) might watch the project team member perform the behavior or review the deliverable produced and provide feedback and constructive criticism. This sequence of feedback and constructive criticism should be repeated until the mechanics of the skill have been learned and can be applied correctly. In another approach, the project team member submits to a peer review. The peer group evaluates an output or a behavior and provides advice and counsel in an egoless, nonthreatening environment.

Skill

Develop by:

- Repeated practice
  - —Starting in classroom
  - —Continuing on the job
  - —A mentor or a coach
  - —Practice tools (i.e., CBT)
  - —Assignments from manager

Assess by:

- Observation
- Evaluation
- Critique
  - —Provide feedback and constructive criticism until performed correctly

Competency: Development.   *Competency* is achieved by incorporating a skill into one's everyday life. This means not only applying the skill in a variety of different ways but consciously modifying one's behavior until the skill becomes comfortable and second nature to perform.

Example   A project team member has been given opportunities to facilitate many meetings, practice meeting management skills, and become more confident with each experience. The project team member's manager of projects, resource manager, and others, have seen his or her performance and have provided advice when appropriate. Now, the manager of the project is giving the project team member more opportunities to facilitate larger meetings, and the project team member is simultaneously orchestrating opportunities to manage other meetings.

NOTE Knowledge becomes a skill by being practiced. For a skill to become a competency, the behavior must be performed frequently enough to become inculcated into the core of one's life.

Competency: Assessment.   The best way to assess one's competency is to perform a 360° assessment, which involves asking various people who have observed the competency—project clients, team members, vendors, and customers—to fill out an assessment or to be interviewed. The report generated from this assessment is then provided to the student with helpful comments for further development. This is the last formal review and assessment of a behavior in the professional growth model.

Example Team members and project clients are asked to judge how well a project team member handles meetings related to one or two current projects. They reply via an interview form that probes effectiveness in meeting preparation, control, and follow-up. The results are shared with the project team member, who then consolidates the suggestions for improvement and develops strategies to implement those improvements.

The base of knowledge has been transformed into a skill by structured practice experiences. The skill has been applied repeatedly, has improved with adequate feedback, and has become a competency. Now, as time passes, that competency evolves into mastery.

Competency

Develop by:

- Translating a skill from what is consciously performed into an unconscious habit
- Performing the skill frequently enough to be incorporated into the core of one's life

Assess by:

- 360° assessment
- Functional manager or mentor feedback

Mastery: Development.   To *master* a behavior, one has to make it one's own. A team member must not think that just because he or she has become competent in a behavior, full development has been achieved. There is always more to learn and there are always more approaches for refining and upgrading every behavior. To gain mastery, one must continue to do the following:

- Read about and observe others performing a similar behavior (gaining more knowledge).
- Practice new variations of the behavior (improving one's skill).
- Incorporate these modifications into one's style of performing the behavior (becoming more competent).

Mastery involves mentoring others and helping them through their performance progression in this specific behavior. In this way, the behavior is further mastered each time it is performed.

Example   A project team member now has become known for his or her ability to facilitate a group of people and is asked, upon occasion, to manage either large or politically difficult interactions. However, the project team member has not stopped watching other successful facilitators and incorporating their nuances into his or her style of meeting management.

Mastery: Assessment.   Mastery is more appropriately assessed by the individual rather than by others. However, one can tell whether an individual has gained mastery of a behavior when the following conditions prevail:

- He or she is comfortable and confident when performing the behavior.
- Others compliment the individual on the behavior.
- Others request performance of the behavior.
- He or she is asked to teach others how to perform the behavior.

Mastery is the self-actualization of a new behavior. It is evidenced by successful performance and creation of the desired result for oneself and for others.

Mastery

Develop by:

- Making it one's own
- Continuous attention
- Mentoring others via performance progression:

  —Reading

  —Observation

  —Trying new variations

Assess by:

- Personal evaluation

  —Comfortable performance

  —Receive compliments

  —Requested to perform

  —Asked to teach others

Moving Through the Levels of Personal Development

When project team members begin this progressive growth spiral, they cannot estimate their level of personal incompetence. Leading a meeting looks easy. Why do some people have such a hard time? As participants, they were in a blissful state of *unconscious incompetence.*

The experience of trying to run a meeting proved that it was not easy. With this first disastrous attempt, a level of *conscious incompetence* was reached. In other words, they knew what they didn't know. They took a class (or read a book or looked at a videotape). And with the knowledge that they acquired, they cognitively understood the guidelines, hints, and traps of managing a meeting. They understood the meeting management process and "learned" the textbook solutions. In other words, they had become *consciously competent.*

They then were given the opportunity to use this knowledge to facilitate a variety of different types of meetings, such as status review meetings and project kick-off meetings. With that practice and the feedback that they were given, their knowledge was transformed into a skill. After more practice in preparing for and conducting meetings, what had been a frightening and uncertain experience became an easy, ingrained competency.

In the skill and competency levels of the performance progression, they reached a stage of *unconscious competence.* They didn't have to think consciously about the steps or the traps. They performed the job of meeting management without thinking about the specifics that they had learned. As time went by and more and more opportunities to run meetings occurred, they started to create their own personal facilitation techniques. They became so proficient at managing meetings that other people were asking them to run their meetings or to coach their people in how to manage meetings. They had truly reached a level of unconscious competence. They did well without thinking about it. They attained the mastery of this behavior, and they will never stop refining the skill. To improve their style, they will continue to observe others who facilitate groups and serve as role models for developing new and better techniques. They will continue to read and to examine their progress, always attempting to get better at this behavior.

And, just as Sisyphus, who struggled so hard to push a boulder up a mountain and, when he finally reaching the top, took a deep breath and raced back down to select another boulder, so too our project team member will find another behavior, another technical or interpersonal incompetence that he will want to improve, and he will start the professional growth model all over again.

In summary, managers of projects and resource managers have the job of orchestrating the development of project team members' technical and human skills. It is the responsibility of the manager of the project and the resource manager to work with project team members to accomplish the following goals:

- Help with the progression from the acquisition of a knowledge base, and assist in finding opportunities that allow practice in transforming that knowledge into a skill.
- Encourage the repetitious performance of the behavior and provide feedback so that the skill becomes a competency.
- Recognize a person's success in performing a skill so that he or she is encouraged to gain a greater mastery of the behavior.

We have now completed the exploration of the performance improvement process. We have created a Performance Expectations Agreement and a Personal Development Plan for the project team member. This is not a one-time effort. The Performance Expectations Agreement and the Personal Development Plan must be reviewed, revisited, and refined before the performance appraisal review process begins. Let's look at how these interim dialogues are to be conducted.

INTERIM DIALOGUES

The key to the success of both the Performance Expectations Agreement and the Personal Development Plan is constant dialogue between the project team member and his or her manager of the project. The following guidelines can assist a manager of projects who is responsible for orchestrating these personal development dialogues:

- Invest time in producing a proactive meeting schedule, and review the plan with your project team member. Do not cancel or reschedule these meetings. If you do, the project team member may infer that he or she is unimportant in your eyes.
- Create a file for the project team member. Document the Performance Expectations Agreement and the Personal Development Plan, along with notes of conversations and issues that occur in the interim.
- Schedule regular meetings with the project team member. Ask these questions:
  —What is moving the project team member toward the metrics as defined?
  —What hurdles is the project team member encountering?
  —What can be done to remove those hurdles, or does the metric need to be changed?

—Is the developmental plan being followed?

—Is the project team member being given the time to learn and grow, and is he or she being given an opportunity to use the new skills and knowledge?

• Refer periodically to this file, to keep yourself and the project team member on target.

The scheduling of these interim dialogues will depend on the timing of the goals established in the Performance Expectations Agreement. To check on progress and resolve any outstanding issues, at least one meeting should be scheduled prior to the dates set for achievement of each goal. Some project team members may need interim dialogue meetings every few weeks; others may need them every few months. As a general rule, to keep motivation high and to catch problems before they make achievement of the goals difficult or impossible, no more than two months should elapse between meetings. In general, it is better to make small changes to keep the Performance Expectations Agreement and the Personal Development Plan current; you should not have to rewrite them.

The culmination of the performance management system is the performance appraisal review process. This process is tailored to each individual project team member and requires serious preparation to ensure its effectiveness.

THE PERFORMANCE APPRAISAL REVIEW PROCESS

At the end of a 12-month period, it is time to create and conduct the Performance Appraisal Review. This is a review of the success and failure of the project team member for the purpose of providing constructive feedback, communicating financial rewards, and setting the baseline for next year's performance management system.

Conducting a Performance Appraisal Review for a project team goes beyond filling out the same generic appraisal review documents that are used for all other employees in the organization. Since it is based on a Performance Expectations Agreement and a Personal Development Plan, the Performance Appraisal Review is uniquely designed for the specific role that the project team member plays.

The Performance Appraisal Review dictates the financial remuneration of each project team member. The connection between outcomes of the performance improvement process and discussion of the project team member's financial remuneration within the performance appraisal review process is subject to discussion, as is the relative timing of these events. Some schools of thought maintain that (1) the Performance Expectations Agreement and the Personal Development Plan are the bases on which bonuses and merit increases are determined and therefore should be tied together, and (2) the discussion of dollars and performance should be conducted at the same time. Others believe that if these two discussions are conducted at the same time, the persons being reviewed will pay too little attention to feedback and expectations regarding their performance. Primarily, they will be waiting to hear only how much money they are going to receive. If they do not receive the increase they expect, some important information that would help their professional growth can be negated.

The performance improvement process within the performance management system has been positioned as an ongoing, scheduled dialogue of growth in and attainment of predetermined performance metrics. Because discussion of salary increases and bonuses culminates all previous discussions and translates them into financial remuneration, the salary discussion should be presented to the project team member during a separate meeting.

As discussed above, the performance improvement process employs quantifiable performance expectations and definable developmental metrics. Success or failure in meeting these expectations and metrics is the basis for financial reward—either a salary increase or a bonus. It is strongly recommended that the project team member's manager of projects be a partner in the performance improvement process so that his or her input will contribute to the determination of financial remuneration. In addition to attainment of the success criteria defined in the performance improvement process, the employee's length of time in the position and adherence to industry standards—and the company's performance—are considered when making these financial decisions.

Input into the appraisal process can be expanded by communicating with people with whom the project team member has been working—the manager of projects, the resource managers, peers on the project team, project clients, and representatives of vendors and suppliers. This type of 360° assessment employs documents and prescribed delivery and feedback processes that can either be purchased off-the-shelf from independent companies or developed internally.

Preparation

The performance appraisal review is an interactive communication process. Prior to completing a written review, it is critical to obtain the project team member's input concerning his or her performance. The following steps are often needed:

1. One month before the review is due, the appraising manager sends the project team member a Self-Appraisal Form and requests its return within one week. Attached to the form is an announcement of the date, time, and location of the appraisal meeting. The goals established in the Performance Expectations Agreement are the basis for the appraisal.
2. The appraising manager discusses the self-appraisal with the project team member, introduces his or her own observations, shares information gathered from project clients and other relevant sources, and completes the appraisal at least one week before the date of the appraisal meeting.
3. The appraising manager develops the preliminary appraisal and reviews it with the manager of the project before meeting with the project team member.
4. The appraising manager and project team member meet in person (or, if necessary, over the telephone) to discuss the appraisal. During this meeting, the project team member's strengths and weaknesses are discussed candidly. He or she has the right to question the appraising manager's feedback and to ask for postponement of the review or for escalation of the review to another level of management.
5. The appraising manager writes the final appraisal, based on the previous steps, and forwards it to the manager of the project for signature.
6. The final document is sent to the project team member, who then has five days to respond to the appraisal and to return it to the appraising manager. The project team member must sign the final document as an indication that he or she received the appraisal and accepts the information that it contains. Written addenda may be attached by the project team member.
7. A copy of the final, signed appraisal is sent to the project team member, and the original is placed in his or her personnel file.

The Self-Appraisal Form

The best way to solicit employee feedback is through a Self-Appraisal Form and discussion. Typically, the Self-Appraisal Form contains the following sections, to which the project team member is expected to respond:

- A summary of my project performance responsibilities includes the following:
  —Three to five primary performance expectations and goals that were projected I would accomplish

—One to three strengths in the form of goals met, achievements, and contributions made

—One to three improvement/developmental opportunities met

- Other considerations may include the following:

  —What could [my company/department] do to better utilize my skills and strengths?

  —What specific barriers could be removed to aid me in reaching my goals?

  —Comments/suggestions that would help either the manager of my project and/or my resource manager evaluate my performance or my team's performance next year.

  —Suggestions to support my professional development or the building of my team during the coming year.

Input from the Manager of the Project

The manager of the project should be answering the following questions concerning the working relationship with the project team member:

- Describe your official working relationship with [the project team member]. What work packages has [the project team member] run for you, or to which projects has [the project team member] contributed? Describe those efforts briefly.

- What is your experience of [the project team member's] performance? For example, describe his or her professional and project management capability (such as quality of work, quantity of work, ability to follow project management procedures, suggestions for creative solutions, and accountability). Give specific examples wherever possible. Comment on areas of strength and areas that need improvement.

- What is your experience with [project team member's] interpersonal skills? What is he or she like to work with? Consider communication skills, sense of humor, professional attitude, collaboration, and teamwork. Give specific examples, and comment on strengths and on areas that need improvement.

Execution

The actual performance appraisal session need not be tense or stressful for either the project team member or the appraising manager. The appraising manager should create and maintain a nonconfrontational atmosphere. Information should be exchanged in a way that avoids defensiveness and emphasizes the need for the project team member to grow and develop as a result of

Table 4.4   Guidelines for Receiving Performance Review Feedback

Performance Reviews: How to Receive Feedback

When it comes to performance appraisals, most of the attention is focused on how bosses give feedback. Many believe, however, that how employees receive feedback is equally important. These guidelines can steer those being appraised toward a constructive response:

- *Feedback is a gift.* Consider others' reactions to be a gift, requiring commitment and effort from the giver.
- *Giving feedback is a risk.* Thank and reassure the giver.
- *Perception is reality.* Accept the impact of your behavior as the other's reality. You do not have to agree with it.
- *Distinguish impact and intent.* Focus on being curious about your impact, not defensive about the presumed intent.
- *Look for the "germ of truth."* Adopt a "What can I learn from this?" posture.
- *Check your understanding.* Paraphrase back to the appraising manager to verify what you hear, and clarify anything about which you are unsure.
- *Put the message in perspective.* The feedback relates to just one aspect of your behavior, not your worth as a person.
- *Assume good intent.* Assume that the giver values and wants to improve your performance, even if the feedback expresses temporary dissatisfaction.
- *Separate consideration from action.* Take time to think about what's been said before reacting.
- *Be responsible for yourself.* You decide how much you can take, at what rate, and what you will do with the information.
- *First impressions are valid.* Do not dismiss first impressions from new people because "They don't really know you yet." First impressions are important and provide some useful data or insights you wouldn't otherwise have.

Source: Darrel Ray and Howard Bronstein. 1995. *Teaming Up: Making the Transition to a Self-Directed, Team-Based Organization.* (New York: McGraw-Hill.) Reprinted with permission.

this feedback. In essence, the final appraisal session should contain no major surprises for either participant. Table 4.4 lists the guidelines that can be distributed to project team members before their appraisal sessions, to provide a constructive context for the experience of being critiqued.

CONCLUSION

At the company picnic, one of the many competitions was a tug of war. In the middle of a long sturdy rope was tied a large knot. The knot was placed on a marker on the ground, and one group of us was told to line up and grab one end of the rope while another team lined up and grabbed the other end. The objective was for each team to pull as hard as they could so that they pulled the knot over the marker toward them. The first team to pull the knot over the marker won. As I was pulling as hard as I could, I couldn't take my eyes off the knot. Suddenly, I had a terrible vision: I became the knot in the middle, being tugged in opposite directions by forces that I couldn't control. This image made me think of my job back home.

I work in a project-driven organization, and I am in the unenviable position of having two bosses. One is my functional manager or, as we call them in my organization, my resource manager. Her name is Jeanne. She is a good boss. She requires that we perform our jobs at a high level of performance and produce quality deliverables that meet out department's standards. She is fair, gives good direction, provides room to grow, and keeps me highly motivated. In addition to performing my operational duties for my department, I spend about 50 percent of my time as a team member on Jeff's project. This project is highly visible. I work with team members from other functional areas, such as manufacturing and research and development. It's fun and I really feel that I am contributing to this effort.

There is, however, one major problem. Jeff's project schedule requires that I get a key deliverable done in the next two weeks, but Jeanne wants me to be working on the department's annual budgets for the next two weeks. We have a project status review meeting scheduled for Wednesday afternoon, but an all-staff meeting is scheduled for the same time.

Jeanne says my departmental responsibilities are the most important, while Jeff is adamant that my effort is needed on his high-priority project. What do I do now? Who do I satisfy? My survival instincts tell me that I should satisfy Jeanne because she writes my performance appraisal review. I feel as though I'm caught in the middle of a tug of war. Will my resource manager and my project manager ever work out a staffing plan that has no conflicts? How then do the project manager, Jeff, and the resource manager, Jeanne, deal with this scenario?

Whether the project team member is a full-time or part-time contributor to the project, project management work requires specific efforts, skills, competencies, and political acumen that are not needed in his or her everyday operational work. Project management must be addressed, evaluated, and rewarded according to the needs of each project. A performance management system that utilizes both a performance improvement process and a performance appraisal review process focusing on the project management part of their job accomplishes this objective in a collaborative and supportive environment.

Use of this system strengthens the project team members and the project management culture throughout the organization. The time and effort spent in developing a formal performance improvement process, interim dialogues, and a performance appraisal process will let ambitious project team members see that project management is rewarded and recognized. The time and effort spent on the system will not be lost on resource managers, who are required to make conscientious efforts to track and report on project team members' accomplishments and contributions to their individual projects.

PERFORMANCE SUPPORT TOOL 4.1

Performance Management System for Project Team Members

Name: _____

Period Beginning: _____ Ending: _____

Resource Manager: _____

The Manager of the Project: _____

_____

_____

_____

Created On: _____

Reviewed On: _____

_____

_____

_____

**Performance Management
System Process**

1 Performance Expectations

2 Developmental Plans

3 Interim Dialogues

4 Performance Appraisal Review

Performance Improvement Process

1. ☐ **Check box when job description is complete**

2. **Performance Expectation Agreement**

	Key Result (Project Team Member)	Comments (Resource Manager)	Goal (Consensus)	Success Metric
1.	_____	_____	_____	_____
2.	_____	_____	_____	_____
3.	_____	_____	_____	_____
4.	_____	_____	_____	_____
5.	_____	_____	_____	_____
6.	_____	_____	_____	_____

3. **Interim Dialogue**

Goal	Interim Metric	Checkpoint (Date)	Revision
1.	_____	_____	_____
2.	_____	_____	_____
3.	_____	_____	_____
4.	_____	_____	_____
5.	_____	_____	_____
6.	_____	_____	_____

Development Plan

1.	SWOT Analysis

Strengths

Weaknesses

Opportunities to Improve

Threats or Barriers to Improvement

2.	Developmental Goals

Goal:

Means of Improvement
Interim Dialogue(s)

Goal:

Means of Improvement
Interim Dialogue(s)

Goal:

Means of Improvement
Interim Dialogue(s)

Goal:

Means of Improvement
Interim Dialogue(s)

Performance Appraisal

1.	Self Appraisal		

Achievements and Contributions

Performance Expectations	Actual Attainment	Comments

Development Goals	Actual Attainment	Comments

CHAPTER 5

Team Dynamics

The Wave is the epitome of a motivated body of people exerting effort to reach a common goal. For readers who are unfamiliar with it, the Wave is a phenomenon seen at a sporting event—a baseball, football, or hockey game. With spontaneity, thousands of spectators, in one section and then in the next adjacent section, stand up and wave their arms over their heads. The action is repeated as the Wave ripples around the stadium or arena. What triggers it? What motivates people to stand up, catch, and then pass along the Wave? What inspires them to exert this extra energy over and above simply watching the game? Whatever its origin, leaders in a project environment need this same magic to generate positive energy within cross-functional project teams.

By definition, a team is a group of people who possess diverse expertise and experiences and are collectively, collaboratively, and congenially focused on completing a single common goal. The Wave fits that definition but it is a momentary phenomenon of spontaneous energy that soon dissipates. This chapter examines how all the project players assume responsibility for the energy and focus of the team from the day the project starts until the day it ends.

CHAPTER OVERVIEW

Team dynamics is an ever changing kaleidoscope. Each combination of human beings has its own chemistry, its own personality and character. Today, it might feel synergistic, cohesive, and bonded. With a shift in the wind, the team atmosphere can change from positive to negative. A change, from either within or without, can modify the chemistry and thus the personality of a group of people.

The manager of projects needs to be aware of these changes in tone and attitude. However, the care of the team is not only this manager's job. It is the job of every project player who contributes to the team or who comes in contact with its members. When the team is energized—doing its own version of the Wave—productivity occurs. When the team is apathetic or demotivated, focus and creativity are diverted away from the delivery, on time and within budget, of a quality product or service.

This chapter explores several facets of the dynamic project team with the objective of giving all the project players techniques to direct the energy of the group toward productive rather than destructive efforts. First, we look at who is being managed. You may be surprised at the priorities managers of projects should set in managing their time. Next, we consider how they are being managed—what techniques motivate and energize people on the project team. In the section titled "Cohesive, Productive Distance Teams," we delve into the peculiarities of motivating a remote or virtual team that crosses geographic and sometimes cultural borders. The chapter concludes with discussions of "What Can Impact the Dynamics of a Team?" and "Ways to Create a Strong Project Team."

Performance Support Tool 5.1, at the end of this chapter, describes a five-session process for creating a team charter. Team charters set the guidelines for how project teams will work together for the duration of the project. All Performance Support and Assessment Tools referenced in this book are available for download at www.pmsi-pm.com.

Before you read further, complete the Project Team Assessment tool at the end of this chapter so that you can make a personal determination as to the current status of your organization.

WHO ARE YOU MANAGING?

The people being managed can be seen from two points of view: (1) the manager of projects might consider the various stakeholders in the project environment and set an order of priority beginning with who is the most important, the second most important, and so on; or (2) the primary focus could be on one of those stakeholders, an actual project team member. Let's take a careful look at the parties in whom the manager of projects should be investing time and energy.

Among Stakeholders

Imagine that you are an executive who manages a staff of managers of projects. You have called a coaching meeting—one of many that you hold—with the specific agenda of talking about the people whom managers of projects are managing. Next week, you plan to call a second meeting and discuss techniques for managing and motivating those people. You are now in the small conference room with your cadre of managers of projects. Instead of starting with a long preamble, you start by asking a question: "Whom do you think you are managing?"

Everyone in the room looks around at everyone else. This does not sound like a trick question, but everyone is reluctant to answer it. Shortly, someone takes the plunge and says, "We manage project team members."

You smile and answer, "You're right, but they're not the most important people that you manage. *The most important person that you manage is yourself.*" You only have so many hours in the day and so much energy to expend in those limited hours. The most important thing is the work that you do, when you do it, how much time you take to do it, and how efficient you are when you do it.

It is critical that you set priorities. Time management philosophy prompts us to do the "A" list first, the "B" list second, and then somehow make the "C" list go away. The "A" items are those that have the greatest impact on the success of the project. They are usually the most difficult and often the most unpleasant, but if you do not do them, the project could falter, technologically or politically. If you have time after you have finished your "A" list, you move on to your "B" chores, which are the semicritical efforts that add efficiency and productivity to your project. The "C" tasks are usually easy and give immediate personal gratification but contribute little to the real success of the project. They include copying, collating, and distributing the monthly status report, or spending inordinate time on the phone. Do not do these tasks. Get someone else to do them. Maintain your self-control. Keep focused. Manage yourself first.

Now that you have made your first point, you pose the question again, "If the first person you manage is yourself, who else do you manage?" Now you are in for real trouble. You have tricked your managers of projects once; they won't want to be hoodwinked again. Nonetheless, eventually, someone will probably say, "Next, we manage project team members."

You respond, "You are right, but not quite yet. *The next person that you manage is your management.*" Your management can be impatient, unbelieving, and either overinvolved or underinvolved. This is the time to explain that you are talking not only about yourself but also about the project client, the customer, and the steering committee—the people directly involved in the project and above you in the pecking order.

All of these important folks need to be managed—but not necessarily in the traditional sense of the word. Lessen their frustration by delivering timely information and notifying them of problems in time to react in an intelligent manner. The information must be not only timely and honest but in a format that allows management to understand the situation without digging through masses of data. With today's scheduling software and associated companion products, managers of projects have no excuse other than laziness for not designing meaningful and accessible information. And what do you do about the executive who is either overinvolved or underinvolved? Talk to him or her about it. Do not avoid the issue. Do not hide behind the "but-they're-more-important-than-I-am" excuse. Management consists of real people who have probably walked in your shoes at some time in their lives. Be tactful and diplomatic, but frank. Most of them will work with you. Manage your management as you would like to be managed if you were in their shoes.

Twice now, you have asked your managers of projects to identify the people they are managing, and you have told them that (1) they are managing themselves, and (2) they are managing their management. Do you have enough nerve to ask again? Sure you do. You say, one more time, "Managers of projects, who are you managing?" Cynicism and snickers will abound. They will know you are toying with them, but one person will inevitably be sure that the time is right to answer, "We manage project team members." Be gentle. "You are right, but not quite yet. *The third group that you must manage are your peers.*" These are the folks who share the same level with you. You have no direct authority over them, and they have no authority over you. They could be other managers of projects, or functional managers who dedicate the resources that you need on your project, or third-party suppliers.

Why is this group so important? For the reason given above: You need them or something that they have, yet you cannot force them to work with you. This is where your strong influencing skills come into play. Bargain or collaborate with them, convince them, but never ignore your peers.

This is a good time to get some suggestions from the group as to the best way to manage peers. Examples might be: treat them with respect; anticipate a favor and offer it before being asked; listen to their side of an issue; and give them due credit when they have been supportive toward a project. You may need a peer's cooperation and possible favors in the future. Manage your peers with gentle, loving care.

Unless you are a reincarnated kamikaze pilot, do not ask your question again. It is time to agree with everyone's initial instincts and to address the common answer to the question: "Managers of projects, who are you managing?" The group that came to mind first is really the fourth group (after self, managers, and peers). *The manager of projects manages the project team members.*

This ends the first meeting. As the attendees leave, remind them that next week's meeting will consider *how* to manage project team members. So, during this executive coaching session, the mangers of projects and their boss have explored the question: Whom do managers of projects manage? The answer: themselves, their managers, their peers, and, last but not least, their project team members.

Before the next meeting on the topic of how to manage project teams, we may want to consider if we have the time to concentrate on motivating the entire project team. If not, then which constituencies will offer the greatest return?

Among Team Members

Managers of projects should address their attention to all members of the project team but, given limited time, some distinctions must be made in the amount of effort one exerts in managing different levels of commitment within the team. A typical project team is composed of three segments of people:

1. *Committed team members.* Those who are totally committed to project management and to this particular project
2. *Antiteam members.* Those who are cynical about project management and/or are averse to this specific project
3. *Neutral team members.* Those who have no strong opinion. They are neither adamantly for nor against the project and/or the discipline of project management.

On which group would you expect the manager of projects to be focusing his or her attention? Instinctively, you may reply, "The antiteam members," but consider the argument below before making your choice.

As you can see in Figure 5.1, these three types of project team members can be portrayed in a normal bell curve distribution. The committed team members and the antiteam members are at opposite ends of the bell curve. The majority of team members are neutral. They fill the large area in the middle.

How can you gain the greatest return on investment? *Invest your time and energy in the largest group. The neutral team members will make the most difference.* The committed team members are already with you. They should not be ignored, but they do not require the same care and feeding as the other two groups. The antiteam members are going to be tougher and will require a more compelling argument, which may or may not be successful. The

Figure 5.1   Where to Invest Your Time

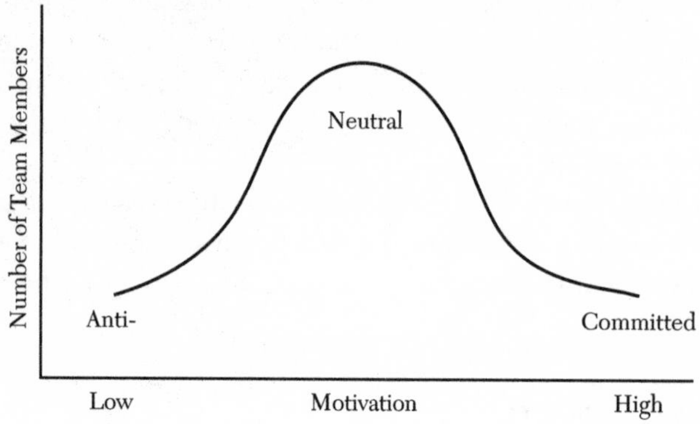

neutral team members, the largest group of people, are at least receptive to project management and/or to the project at hand. Go after the neutral team members, with gusto.

Now that we have considered the segments of people and the time and effort the manager of projects should invest in each group, let's consider how these folks are motivated or energized.

HOW ARE YOU MANAGING?

A week later, you and your managers of projects are having another coaching session. Remember, as a kid, how you played softball with the gang? Everyone showed up on the field. Sometimes you got to be captain; sometimes somebody else got the nod. Captains took turns picking players for their teams, starting with the person who was "the best." The player picked last was begrudgingly accepted onto the team. Remember how badly you wanted to be picked early and how demoralizing it was if you were picked last?

Building a project team is quite different. Businesspeople are not anxious to be picked. Managers of projects must cajole and induce people to be on their teams and, once chosen, to play hard to win. Our business culture does not encourage people to become productive team members. This section of the chapter provides suggestions or techniques for developing a strong and coordinated project team.

A computer hardware manufacturer in the Rocky Mountains has created the ultimate teamwork environment. Project players are encouraged to ferret out their next assignment. They interview managers of projects. They attend project team meetings to get a sense of the chemistry of the group. And once they decide on which team they want to play, they apply for the position and often actively vie for the opportunity. Can you imagine the difference in atmosphere when a team member really wants to be picked for a team rather than being forced into service?

How can you motivate a cross-functional project team to be as high-performing as possible? Let's first look at what does *not* motivate a team and then consider some potential motivators.

Demotivators

The following conditions or events do not motivate team players:

- Extensive and unexplained overtime
- Turnover among the managers of projects and/or project clients
- Too many players on the team, which negates interaction
- Incompetent project players
- Constant change of players
- Continual change in the project's scope
- Unclear goals relative to the project's deliverables and the expectations of the team

Motivators

At the most basic and important level, project team members need to be able to answer the question, "What's in it for me?" (This is known as WIIFM, pronounced "Wiff-um.") In a recent survey, team members reported that the following positive factors are important to them:

- Secure work environment
- Bonuses or other tangible rewards
- Sincere recognition (the operative word is "sincere")
- Satisfaction of meeting goals
- Promotions when warranted
- Respect for their need for outside areas of interest and time with family
- Managers' leadership by example

A variety of factors will motivate a project team member. The following list is composed of the factors that most individuals regard as important for their personal job satisfaction. Each factor translates into a positive motivator for working well on a project team. Because each team member is different and is motivated by different things, consider each person individually as you read the list. What will or will not energize him or her? Assuming that salary/income as a motivator is realized at an acceptable level, these factors are the critical motivators for project team members and all the project players:

1. A *respected reputation* within the discipline and/or the industry
2. *Status and recognition* within the organization
3. *Genuine appreciation* from the project client and from the team member's own management. This appreciation must be earned, not just "given."
4. The *appropriate authority* to make decisions and run one's own show (to a reasonable limit)
5. *Pride in the quality* of what one produces, whether it is a report, a widget, or a software product; in other words, the knowledge that what has been created is the best that he or she is capable of producing
6. *Working in a synergistic and professional relationship* with other members of the project community
7. A *"stretch" assignment* that challenges one's knowledge, skills, and experience
8. A *competitive environment* in which one can raise the bar, competing with one's associate(s) in a friendly and professional way
9. Feeling treated as a *unique* individual by one's management

So far, in this chapter, we have explored what team members see as their reward ("What's in it for me?") for being a collaborative, congenial, cooperative team member, and what motivates them to work synergistically. In the following section, we explore ways of meeting the challenge of motivating team members who must collaborate over a geographic distance.

COHESIVE, PRODUCTIVE DISTANCE TEAMS

The term "cohesive project teams" almost sounds like an oxymoron when you add the word "distance." Managers of projects may be so preoccupied with the schedule and the production of a quality deliverable that they forget the nuances of managing a remote team. This section of the chapter addresses (1) the difficulties of managing a remote team and (2) eight rules that will enhance the cohesiveness and productivity of distance teams.

Difficulties When Managing a Remote Team

Distance teams are legitimately named when there is significant geographic distance between where at least one team member works and where other folks on the team work. We most often think of this geographic space as separating one country from another. However, a distance team can be located within one country or on different campuses within the same town.

The distance between the project players begets the problem. "Distance" can mean the time spent shuttling back and forth to different buildings, or it can extend across time zones where face-to-face meetings are not an easy option. With differences in time zones come difficulties not only in scheduling conversations during everyone's normal workday but also in dealing with the different cultures that are familiar to the various project players.

The specific problems that arise in distance teams include:

- Difficulty communicating
- Different or conflicting ways in which people are accustomed to doing business
- Lack of patience to engage in the processes needed to make distance teams productive
- Travel that results in lost work time
- Different languages, expressions, and slang
- Erroneous assumptions and unfounded fears
- Not-invented-here (NIH) resistance
- Overreaction to the perceived "distance team problem," which suggests a bureaucracy that constrains innovation

As you can see from this list, two basic factors affect distance teams: (1) the logistical complications caused by the geographic distance that separates the members of the teams, and (2) the varied organizational and/or national cultures at each location. The eight rules presented in the next section can mitigate these difficulties.

Rules for Managing Distance Teams

Rule 1. Be Sensitive to Culture

Culture dictates the acceptable protocol for how one behaves and communicates. Protocols differ, depending on where and how one was raised or on the unique culture that has evolved within an organization and is being perpetuated by its leaders. There are no correct or incorrect protocols. What one person may perceive as incorrect may be absolutely the most appropriate behavior for someone else.

When we speak of culture, we often assume that we mean different cultures based on borders separating countries. That is a valid assumption. But there are other cultural differences besides nationality—differences of style, of industry, of region, of class, of gender, of ethnicity to name a few.

To address this issue, being sensitive is most important. This means thinking before we speak; asking whether what we have said or done is acceptable; building a trust level at which persons from each culture can be open and honest when confronted by situations that are confusing or annoying.

If the cultural difference is national, it is worth researching the likes, dislikes, conventions, and protocols of the pertinent countries. At the same time, don't forget to send the team members in those countries some good books about your culture. Consider seminars in which folks from the different locations convene not only to learn but to get to know one another. The seminar might be focused on cross-cultural education, but it does not necessarily need to be. Whatever the topic, the team members' participation in the same experience will facilitate cross-cultural learning and better personal relationships. You can take this option one step further by considering colocating team members. It might be wise to send some of your people on expatriate assignments for three months or more, to immerse them in the culture of the other organization and its distant locale.

Rule 2. Coordinate Face-to-Face Meetings

No amount of expense is too much for this important tactic. Having the entire team meet at least once, face-to-face, is critical. Knowing what team members look like and their mannerisms when they talk; observing what makes them laugh; seeing pictures of their kids, pets, and homes—these contacts bring people closer together.

When speaking over the phone, a person who is brusque in his or her responses could be considered officious. Over the phone, you cannot see facial expressions, or the environment in which the person is speaking. In person, however, you may get a far different and more accurate impression. The person may be shy, not gregarious, and the pressure under which he or she works may not allow for long conversations.

A face-to-face meeting, scheduled periodically, establishes relationships that can withstand the test of distance for long periods of time. If face-to-face interaction is thoroughly impractical, coordinate remote group meetings via videoconferencing.

Rule 3. Provide Consistency

When members of a project team work down the hall from one another and one of them gets tied up and asks for a 15-minute postponement of a meeting, no one gets too upset. But when one or more of the team members are several time zones away and have planned their day (if not also their night) to be available for a conference call, 15 minutes can become a major annoyance.

What a distance team needs most is stability. Meetings set for the same time on a prescheduled day create some stability. Agendas remain generally the same, with only minor changes. Status reports maintain the format established at the beginning of the project.

When this level of consistency can be attained by the team as a whole, it creates, at the very beginning of the project, a communication protocol that should be honored to the letter unless the team as a whole agrees to change it. (See Chapter 10, "Communications Management," for further information.)

Rule 4. Establish Roles and Responsibilities

Who are you? Who am I? What do I do? What do you do? Where does my metaphorical project territory begin and end, and where does yours begin and end?

Understanding and respecting the roles and responsibilities of each team member is a crucial rule for the success of all teams; but it is even more important when teams are at remote locations. When we are all in one place and someone steps on my toes, I can go into that person's office, or we can go out to lunch, and talk it over. I cannot do that when a ragged relationship develops with someone who is miles away.

Setting up (1) clear roles within the context of the team and (2) specific responsibilities relative to each of the tasks within the work breakdown structure can prevent many misunderstandings that would otherwise fester into rifts between team members and, ultimately, between different geographic locations.

Rule 5. Identify a Single Point of Contact for Each Location

This is a delicate issue. Should everyone at every location be encouraged to talk to everyone at every other location? Imagine the number of interruptions (e.g., phone calls and e-mails). Did you know that, according to time management theory, every time you are interrupted, you lose approximately 10 minutes of productive time just getting refocused on what you were doing before the interruption?

Would it not be more productive to have a single person serve as the point of contact at each location? His or her job would be to filter questions and issues that he or she could handle, and then funnel the remainder, in a batch mode, to the appropriate people for response.

Do not take this rule too literally. If there is an immediate need for communication, then, of course, there are exceptions.

Rule 6. Initiate Inclusive Celebrations

One of the most tangible events that make a team cohesive is a planned celebration. Yet we often forget to include the team members at the remote locations. What is worse, on the next conference call, those of us who attended the
celebration tend to make all kinds of reference to the fun that was had, and to
hint at inside stories about what went on. This can be cringingly thoughtless.

There are ways to include the folks at various locations. At a preset time,
everyone can hook up through a teleconference or videoconference so that
everyone cuts the cake at the same time or drinks a champagne toast together. The rest of the celebration can go on where it is, but those few minutes of connection will make a difference.

Also remember that the trinkets that often become part of a project's mi-
lieu should be sent to everyone. These trinkets can range from an embroi-
dered shirt to an engraved paperweight. *Everybody* gets one. Another idea is
to have pictures taken of all the subteams at different locations and find a
central bulletin board in each location on which to hang them.

Be creative. Lots of different ways can be found to capture a positive
team feeling. But remember that doing it once is not enough. Team spirit
needs to be reenergized frequently—without doing the same thing over and
over. Try all kinds of approaches.

Rule 7. Provide Training in Teleconferencing, Videoconferencing, and E-Mail Skills

Because the modes by which the groups at various locations can communicate are limited, it is important for management to provide remote teams
with the best technology available, and for the people using the technology
to be well informed on how to make each type of communication most productive. Information and training on the use of teleconferencing, e-mail,
and, if appropriate, videoconferencing should be made available to all project team members. And why not set up a Web-based chat room on specific
topics or an electronic bulletin board?

Rule 8. Add Time and Budget to the Plan, to Cover Distance Teams' Issues

As you can tell from Rules 1 though 7, managing a cohesive and productive
distance team takes additional time, effort, and money. The manager of
projects must set up the necessary protocols to bind and hold the team together, and team members must invest in this relationship. The budget

must allow for the trips, technology, and creative perks that help build the desired synergy.

In summary, the manager of projects must work at creating and maintaining the entity that we call a team. Each organization is different, and each configuration of a team presents different issues and problems. Do not expect these problems to go away without external intervention, and do not imagine that the challenge of working with a distance team is not important enough to address. An out-of-control, dysfunctional team can bring down the entire project enterprise, no matter how brilliant the concept of the deliverable or how perfect the project plan. The variable of a cohesive and productive project team is crucial. Take it seriously.

We have looked at what motivates and energizes project players individually and as members of a team. Even among the most thoughtfully managed teams, some external influences over which we have no control can impact team dynamics. In the next section, we'll look at four of them.

What Can Impact the Dynamics of a Team?

Several external influences can impact productivity within a project team. Among these are: (1) poor performers, (2) turnover, (3) overstaffing, and (4) the effect of overtime. Their ramifications are explored next.

Poor Performers

Not all projects are blessed with superstars. Many projects are not even blessed with average performers, and some projects are destined to have more than their share of poor performers. In *Controlling the Software Project,* Tom DeMarco suggests that 3 of every 10 team members could be poor performers. DeMarco calls this "spoilage" and suggests that "taking a poor performer off your team can often be more productive than adding a good one."[1] On almost every project, there are people who introduce more spoilage than the value of their production.

This follows the bad-apple-in-the-barrel philosophy. As one bad apple decays and disintegrates, it blemishes all the other apples with which it comes into contact. So it is with spoilage. Not only are poor performers not productive, but they distract and drag down the good performers around them.

This philosophical concept is readily accepted by most of us. The question is: What can be done about it? How does a manager of projects get rid of a poor performer? There are several responses to that question. The first response is to determine whether that person is performing poorly because he or she is incompetent. This may not be the case. The person may simply be the wrong person for that job. If the person were assigned to another task, he or she might perform more effectively. Or maybe that person does not have the skill-set needed for the task, but some form of training might turn this poor performer into an adequate performer. Is that person unaware that he or she is perceived as a poor performer? If this is the case, counseling may result in improved performance.

If none of these three options is appropriate, it is the responsibility of the manager of projects to remove the poor performer from the project by returning them to their resource manager. If it is not politically feasible to remove the poor performer from the project, the best alternative is to isolate the poor performer so that he or she causes minimal degradation of the team.

Turnover

If there is turnover during the project, there will be a negative impact. If the project loses a team member and introduces a replacement, additional time and effort must be expended to orient that new team member and bring him or her up to speed. The amount of lessened team productivity depends on two factors: (1) the point at which the turnover occurs, and (2) the role of the person who has left the team.

If the turnover occurs in the early stages of a project or the early stages of a ramp-up of a phase of the product life cycle, the impact on productivity is minimal. However, if the turnover occurs in the latter part of the phase or of the project, the impact is greater because other team members may be so engrossed that they do not have time to orient the new team member. In addition, by this time, the new team member must absorb more information if he or she is to be productive.

Another question has significant bearing on the impact of turnover: Who has left the team? Some studies indicate that the loss of the manager of the project, or of the project client, has the greatest effect on the ability of the project team to bring the project in on time and on budget. The loss of a team member, a project administrator, or a resource manager will have a less substantial impact. According to some studies worthy of note, the loss of the project secretary has the third greatest impact (after the loss of the manager of the project and/or the project client).

Turnover may occur when a project team member leaves the company for another job. Other than keeping this person engaged and motivated in the first place, very little can be done about this situation. However, transferring a team member out of one project team and into another, even though still in the company, causes a negative impact that can be addressed. Many approaches are available for dealing with or avoiding the transfer of project team members. In the process of developing the project plan, the manager of projects exerts a considerable effort to involve the members of the project team in the process, to build commitment to the plan, to motivate the team members to achieve the plan targets, and to inspire the team members to develop a sense of ownership of the plan. The dividends from this effort are felt throughout the execution of the project. The effort generally results in a better plan and the retention of team members.

It is impractical, however, for the manager of projects to seek a guarantee that the same personnel will be available throughout the entire project. No resource manager or supervisor can offer such a guarantee and have any expectation of being able to honor it. Priorities change, emergencies arise, personnel are offered promotions or new opportunities, and transfers of project team members are required. The procedure for transfer of a member of the project team needs to give the manager of projects an opportunity to take exception to a proposed transfer or to have adequate time to facilitate a transition.

Four lessons must be learned by anyone managing team turnover:

1. If you can control turnover, accomplish it early in the project.
2. If turnover is in the position of the manager of the project, project client, or project secretary, expect a significant impact.
3. When turnover is official, prepare and exercise a well-orchestrated transition plan.
4. When turnover occurs, immediately reevaluate and renegotiate the time and budget required to complete the project.

Overstaffing

Bringing additional resources onto the project team will have an impact on the productivity of the resource model. There is a law of diminishing returns when adding personnel to the project team. Adding one more person may reduce the time needed to complete the project. Adding another person may further reduce the time. However, somewhere in the progression of acquiring additional resources, the time needed will increase.

In *The Mythical Man-Month*, Frederick P. Brooks, Jr., suggests that this phenomenon occurs because the addition of new personnel requires that additional communication channels be established and maintained.[2] Brooks presents this formula:

$$I = \frac{E(E-1)}{2}$$

where I equals the number of interfaces or communication channels that must be established, and E is the number of elements or people on the project team. For example, using the formula, if there are 10 elements (E) or people on the project team, 45 communication channels (I) must be established and maintained. (10 times 9 divided by 2 equals 45.) If you add one more person, so that the team now has 11 people, 55 communication channels will be required ($11 \times 10 \div 2 = 55$). You may be more convinced when you calculate the actual number of people on your team.

There is a point beyond which the introduction of additional resources to the project is nonproductive. Frederick P. Brooks, Jr., cited earlier in this chapter, coined the adage, "A woman can have a baby in nine months, but two women are not going to have a baby in four and a half months." Or, to use another adage, throwing the Mongolian hordes at a project does not work.

Effect of Overtime

There are several philosophies concerning overtime. One of them holds that no amount of overtime is good. Another point of view is that overtime is effective, if it is required only for short intervals. Project team members are willing to rise to the occasion and accept overtime under two conditions: (1) if they see the end of the overtime, and (2) if they understand why the overtime is necessary. When overtime becomes a way of life, it is no longer productive.

In *Advanced Project Management*, F.L. Harrison suggests that if one were to work six days at 12 hours per day, one would be approximately 88 percent productive.[3] In effect, that person would give the project $72 \times 88 = 63.4$ effective hours. However, if the same person were asked to work 7 days at 12 hours per day, or 84 hours, he or she would be only 77 percent productive. In other words, the person working 84 hours would provide the project with only $84 \times 77 = 64.7$ effective hours. By having one team member work an extra 12-hour day, the project would gain only 1.3 hours of effective effort. Whether you agree with Harrison's percentages or not, it goes nearly without saying that the productivity of people who work too much consecutive overtime is reduced.

If you are certain that you will ultimately be requiring overtime for completion of the project, it may be wiser to schedule it at the beginning of the project, if possible, rather than at the end. This may sound like blasphemy, but think about it. During the latter stages of a project, people are becoming tired. They may have been worn down by problems and slippages and are now looking forward to their next assigned project. How productive can they be? On the other hand, at the beginning of the project, a person is energetic, fresh, and enthusiastic. Imagine how much more productive his or her additional time might be.

In summary, management of project team resources is not purely a mathematical exercise, nor is it merely a matter of determining whether the resource histogram (as discussed in Chapter 8, "Project Planning") is showing an over- or underutilization of the staffing plan. Many managerial issues—poor performers, turnover, overstaffing, and the effect of overtime—affect resource models. As project players, we cannot always avoid these factors. However, we can be sensitive to its effect on the project team and take positive action in anticipating and managing that impact.

WAYS TO CREATE A STRONG PROJECT TEAM

Whether working with a distance team or motivating team members in the same location, several techniques can be used by managers of projects, and their project team leaders, to create and maintain strong project teamwork.

Build a Broad-Based Team

Choose the best people available to be part of your team. The "best people" are team players who are known to get the job done and who bring a diverse set of skills, experience, and personality to your project. If you are not given a choice but are told who will be assigned to your project, familiarize yourself with each individual. Observe and listen. Evaluate outside input, but make your own judgment.

Ascertain the Strengths and Weaknesses of Each Individual on the Team

Because there is no perfect team player (including you), becoming familiar with and accepting each person's weaknesses and strengths will make it easier for you to work with your team. However, if some persons on your team cannot hold their own, have them reassigned, for both your benefit and theirs. In some cases, this may be easier said than done. Attempt to reassign them to their functional/resource manager in exchange for qualified players and/or future draft choices. If this is not feasible, move them to another assignment where they can be more productive.

Establish a Formal Leader

Note the article "a" and the adjective "formal." The "a," of course, denotes singular. Project team members cannot divide their loyalty among different captains. One, and only one, person must run the project. "Formal" means that this leader has been officially delegated the leadership responsibility and authority. If you are the manager of the project, make sure that everyone on the team understands your role, who assigned you this role, why it is necessary to have a single point of control, and how you plan to exercise your authority as the manager.

Prepare a Project Plan

As discussed in Chapter 8, "Project Planning," the project plan lists all the tasks that need to be performed, the role each player will take in each task, when it will begin and end, what deliverable will be produced, and how much money or effort has been estimated for the tasks. Project management tasks must be included as well. Although the project plan is a technical project management tool, it also facilitates communicating to each team player the role and responsibility he or she is to assume. In a baseball manner of speaking, it indicates the correct batting order and what area each outfielder has to defend.

Involve Team Members in Decisions

This technique is closely related to the previous one. During the creation and management of the project plan, the team members should be consulted. When it is necessary to revise plans, inform the team members of the scope and the potential impact of the problem. They may have thoughts on how to resolve the problem. Their expertise could make the difference.

Keep Team Members Informed

Nothing is more frustrating to team members than having the game plan change without their knowledge. Be sure that each project player is informed.

The manager of the project must have the respect of the team, in case it becomes necessary to change the game plan quickly, without providing immediate, detailed explanations. This sort of change should be undertaken only in situations where the players trust the manager of the project and the manager does not abuse the privilege.

Build and Maintain Team Spirit

If the manager of the project becomes apathetic, the team will become apathetic. Each negative development does not have to be shared with the team. If it does not impact the team members' ability to perform the job successfully, keep the downside to yourself. If you are not a natural cheerleader, do not pretend. You can still impart a sense of professionalism and positive energy. However, you might want to find someone on the team who can be a cheerleader. That's the person who sets up the Milestone Party or the Friday beer bust. A well-timed and deserved thank you can go a long, long way.

In summary, a strong team is the nucleus of a project and can ensure its success. The season is a long one. The team members are asked to play in close quarters, sometimes under great stress. Give them your technical guidance, your project management expertise, and a significant intangible: your enthusiasm and support of them as team members.

CONCLUSION

Even though most managers of projects may instinctively say that they manage only project team members, this is rarely entirely true. Managers of projects manage three groups of people other than their project team members:

1. Themselves, by determining what they do, when they do it, how much time it takes them to do it, and how efficient they (and others) are when they do it.
2. Their management—people who are above them in the political hierarchy: their immediate supervisor, the project client, the customer, the steering committee, and anyone who is directly involved in the project and is higher in the pecking order. These people are managed by being provided with appropriate information and knowledge about problems in time to react in an intelligent manner.
3. Their peers—the folks who are at the same level as the manager of projects or at a level that has no direct authority over the project.

To successfully manage one's peers, one needs to treat them with respect, anticipate a favor and offer it before being asked, listen to their side of an issue, and give them due credit when they have been supportive to the project.

Managers of projects also, of course, manage their project team members. They do this by offering appropriate recognition, true respect, interesting challenges, and career and intellectual development. They must work hard, and employ specific strategies, to keep project team members motivated and working together dynamically as a team. The strategies include building a broad base of team members, establishing a formal leader, preparing a plan, involving team members in decision making, keeping team members informed, and building team spirit.

Managers of projects must also pay special attention to the needs of distance teams. This requires being sensitive to diverse cultures, providing consistency, clearly defining roles and responsibilities, identifying a single point of contact at each location, being inclusive in celebrations and other events, training team members in many forms of long-distance communication, and budgeting time and money to cover the exigencies of long-distance teamwork.

Finally, managers of projects must be prepared to address the many influences that can negatively affect the team, including dealing with poor team performers, avoiding or minimizing the negative effect of turnover, and exercising caution in the addition of resources and in the scheduling of overtime.

NOTES

1. Tom DeMarco. September 1982. *Controlling Software Projects: Management, Measurement, and Estimation* (New York: Yourdon Press).
2. Frederick P. Brooks, Jr. July 1995. *The Mythical Man-Month: Essays on Software Engineering* (New York: Addison-Wesley).
3. F.L. Harrison. 1981. *Advanced Project Management* (3rd ed.) (Hants, England: Gower).

PERFORMANCE SUPPORT TOOL 5.1
Creating a Team Charter

This tool is designed to help managers of projects and project team members create **a team charter**—not a corporate charter or department charter or even project charter—by understanding and applying the charter concept at the team relationship level.

Generically, "charter" is defined as "a document issued by a body outlining the conditions under which a body is organized and defining its rights and privileges" or as "a document defining the formal organization of a body." In its *Guide to the Project Management Body of Knowledge,* the Project Management Institute defines a project charter as "a document issued by senior management which provides the manager of projects with the authority to apply organizational resources to project activities." The team charter might therefore be defined as a document issued by managers of projects, in conjunction with project team members, that provides the group with the guidelines by which they will interact and will keep the entity energized and focused throughout the evolution of the project.

It is customary to prepare a project charter document that defines the mission and the deliverables of the project. It is equally important, however, to recognize that the team as an entity also needs a charter representing its *raison d'être,* its goals or mission as a group, the roles individuals must fill within the team, and the operating agreement under which the entire team will work.

Following the directions in this Performance Support Tool, you will create a team charter that will include:

- A team model statement
- A team values statement
- A team mission statement
- A team goals statement
- A team operating agreement

Let's work through the process that leads to a team charter.

THE FIRST SESSION: POSITIONING

The team begins by cultivating an atmosphere and attitudes that facilitate deeper discussions in the future. A meeting should be called to discuss two issues: (1) how to address the project, that is, the results-oriented job the team is taking on, and (2) how to start getting to know one another as future team members. This meeting will set the stage for the future development of the team charter.

The first step, during this kickoff session, is to state or restate the project's charter or mission statement. It is crucial that all members of the team understand, accept, and are committed to the stated background, goals, and deliverables of the project.

When an acceptable level of comfort concerning the overt, tangible focus of the job has been reached, the team can begin to establish the more intangible team relationships and dynamics. Here are some ways to set the tone for this process:

1. Have the team members describe the best and the worst team that they have ever been on; for example, the best team always treated each other with respect, or the worst team always felt tense and unfamiliar.
2. Draw a picture of what a team might look like—perhaps a ship with a captain, a navigator, and a crew—or any appropriate model of teamwork.
3. Provide a metaphor for a successful team and the elements that make it successful—possibly related to sports or family or music. For example, a project team is often described as a symphony orchestra with a conductor (the manager of projects), first chairs (the team leaders), and musicians (the subject-matter experts on the team).
4. Ask the team members to share some personal activity or trait, e.g., "I'm a skydiver," or "I'm addicted—to M&Ms." These small tidbits are the beginning of recurring and friendly themes.

The real purpose of the first session is to have the team members look at what makes effective or ineffective teams and at how this team's interactions will differ from their day-to-day operational environment. Take the information that the team has shared, and create a description of "an effective team," such as: "An effective team is one that works toward a common goal in a professional manner, with mutual respect and consideration for all involved." By the end of this first session, you will have created a statement or model of what your team members believe is an effective team.

Toward the end of this kickoff meeting, discuss the steps needed to generate a team charter—a statement of expectations. You might discuss:

- *Why the team needs a charter:* Share with the team the appropriate rationales, and add any others that you consider pertinent.
- *What areas will be covered:* The team will develop (1) a values statement, (2) a mission statement, (3) a goals statement, and (4) an operating agreement.
- *How the charter will be used:* The charter will be made into posters and will hang on the wall during team meetings. If the stated values, mission, goals, or operating agreement are violated, the team will either change the charter or correct the team's actions to comply with it.

THE SECOND SESSION: VALUES STATEMENT

It is difficult to ask someone, out of the blue, "What are your values?" Often, people respond with personal goals, such as "To be successful," or with results, such as "To create the best end product." These are laudable, but they are not values. This session is designed to determine what values are basic and meaningful to the people on this team and then to transform those overall generic values to a set of values that will be appropriate to all the team members.

To help team members focus on values, direct them to finish several of the following sentences:

- The three people whom I most admire are _____ , _____ , _____ .
- The characteristics that I most admire in each of these three people are _____ , _____ , _____ .

- The traits in other people that irritate me most are _____ , _____ , _____ .
- The values of the company in which I want to work are _____ , _____ , _____ .
- The qualities that I most appreciate in people with whom I work are _____ , _____ , _____ .
- I am most proud of myself when I _____ .
- I am trying to improve the following personality traits in myself: _____ , _____ , _____ .

This self-analysis should reveal, to each of the team members, a recurring theme. In effect, they have identified the characteristics and values that are important to them—for example, respect, professionalism, common courtesy. By now, the team members should feel comfortable about sharing these personal values with the group.

Stating these values allows deeper insight into each team member's likes and dislikes. Consolidating these values creates a blueprint for a "team value statement." Such a statement might include some of the following elements:

- We will follow the golden rule: Do unto others as you would have them do unto you.
- We will attempt to leave our silos and work for the good of the team.
- We will support other people, even if there is no direct credit to come our way.

THE THIRD SESSION: MISSION STATEMENT

The team mission statement describes what the team is trying to accomplish—not relative to the project's deliverables but as a vision of the unique chemistry that they as a group can create. The types of questions that the team needs to answer about the mission are:

- What are we doing as a team, beyond the obvious creation of a thing or a service or a system?
- Why have we been chosen as a team to do this particular project?
- What can we uniquely do to affect the success of this project?
- What can we uniquely do to affect the success of the project management discipline within the organization?

This might be a perfect time to have the team members go away and consider how they would write the team's mission statement and return with a draft from which to work. Here is a template to provide some direction: "This team is to (do what) in order to accomplish (what purpose) so that (result)."

When the team members come into this meeting, provide them with large stick-back note pads. Ask them to create, on separate notes, fill-ins for "do what," "what purpose," and "result." Then ask everyone to come up to the wall and put their three notes under the corresponding heading: "Do What," "What Purpose," and "Result." Review these three parts of the mission statement, consolidate similar concepts, and discard irrelevant suggestions. The team then refines the surviving candidates until a final team mission statement is completed. Here are two surviving statements, to serve as examples:

- We will establish a communication plan that will set a company precedent *in order to* ensure the dissemination of the most timely and accurate information concerning the project *so that* our project client is totally satisfied with our performance.
- We will create an environment in which lessons learned are shared and captured *in order to* establish an archive of project information *so that* this information can be used by future projects within the firm.

THE FOURTH SESSION: GOALS STATEMENT

After the team has envisioned the mission of its contribution to the organization as a whole, the next step is to create goals for the team members themselves. These goals focus on the short term (within the duration of the project) and the long term (after the team is disbanded). Examples of each follow.

Short-Term Goals

- We will enjoy each other and work hard when it's time to work and play when it's time to play.
- We will support other people's learning relative to each other's discipline or to each other's organizational unit within the business.

Long-Term Goals

- We will want to work with each other again after this assignment ends.
- We will show the rest of the organization that project management tools and techniques are helpful when running a project.

THE FIFTH SESSION: OPERATING AGREEMENT

At the final session, the team decides how they are going to work together. What are the rules of the road? Certain things may grate on people's nerves, but either they never pinpoint them or they never have a forum to articulate them, even if the irritation has been going on for some time. The beginning of the project is the best time to get those potential irritations out on the table.

The issues that the team members ought to be thinking about as they develop the team operating agreement include:

- What do we need to give to/get from each other in order to be able to do our own individual jobs within the project?
- What are the rules around meetings?
- What are the ways in which we will or will not treat each other?

Listed below are some "rules" that might be included in a team operating agreement:

Meetings

- Meetings will start on time and end on time.
- Food and drink are/are not allowed.
- Agenda will/will not be passed out ahead of time.

- Interruption will/will not be permitted.
- People must/need not stay until the meeting is concluded.

Communication

- Identify and communicate possible conflicts clearly and immediately.
- Notify the team about any schedules or budgets that may not be met by a 10 percent variance.
- Don't assume—ask questions.
- Be responsive to communications—that is, respond within 24 hours.
- Be ready to back up all statements with facts.
- Respect confidentiality.

Personal Courtesies

- Nothing is a fact until proven; avoid premature conclusions.
- Treat each other with respect.
- Corporate rank does not exist within the team, especially in meetings.
- Only constructive criticism, presented tactfully, is allowed.
- Agree to disagree.
- Be flexible and willing to change if properly influenced.

By the end of this process, the team will have created a doctrine, or team charter, by which to work. This team charter includes:

- A team model statement
- A team values statement
- A team mission statement
- A team goals statement
- A team operating agreement

The process of creating the team charter is as important to team building as it is to creating the deliverables. People get to know each other. They become sensitive to each other's likes, dislikes, values, and principles. What better way to rivet a group of people together than to empower them to build their own "civilization"—the norms upon which a body of people organize themselves and the precepts upon which they operate and grow?

Take the time to allow your team to establish its own civilization—its own basic premises of group interaction, which will allow your project team members to thrive and flourish.

Project Teams Assessment

General Questions	Response
	Answer each question in the space provided. Where 1 to 10 are used, 1 = Lowest score and 10 = Highest score.
1. How are project teams formed?	
2. Who chooses members?	
3. What is a typical team size?	_____ Persons
4. How often do you get the right skills and the right people?	Very often ___ Sometimes ____ Seldom ____
5. How are resource conflicts (who should work on which projects now) resolved?	
6. What types of team building approaches do you use?	
7. How often do you call team meetings?	Very often____ Sometimes ____ Seldom ____
8. What are the meetings used for?	
9. How much attention do you pay to the following? • Building and following an agenda • Producing minutes after the meeting	 1 2 3 4 5 6 7 8 9 10 1 2 3 4 5 6 7 8 9 10
10. What is the perceived value or benefit of meetings?	
11. How much time do you spend per week in meetings?	_____ Hours
12. What communication do you conduct with other regional offices?	
13. How well does the communication work?	

PART III

PROCESSES

CHAPTER 6

Proposal Management

Imagine that you are a vendor who is looking to sell a specific product to a prospective client. The client's search has been narrowed down to two potential vendors: you (Vendor A) and your strongest competitor (Vendor B). The client wants the product to possess a required list of features. You have Feature 1; Vendor B has Feature 2. Features 1 and 2 are comparable, and neither will be the tiebreaker for the client. You have assigned your best salesperson to this account. But Vendor B also has a very charismatic sales rep doing the best that he or she can do to get the sale. Vendor B assures the prospective client that his or her firm will support the implementation of the product. The client has asked you about your implementation support, and you have given assurance that your firm is the best in the business.

Let's review the situation. The prospective client easily gives Feature 1 and Feature 2 equal value. Both salespeople are pros, and both promise strong implementation support. However, how does the prospective client differentiate between two unsubstantiated promises of strong implementation support?

What is the differentiating factor from the viewpoint of the client? You can promise competent and professional implementation assistance but to differentiate yourself, your proposal must show how you will keep that promise. You will include in the proposal:

- A template of the tasks that will be performed during the implementation, indicating which tasks will be done by the client and which tasks are your responsibility;
- A communication plan describing the project management reporting that you will be providing on a frequent basis;
- A biography of several qualified managers of projects who would be available to manage the project from your side.

With a project management model describing how the project will be handled, it becomes clear that you, Vendor A, should be the vendor with whom the prospective client will want to work. The services or products that many vendors are selling are often comparable—maybe a little stronger in one facet and a little weaker in another—and each vendor's sales staff may be professional and charismatic. Ultimately, the sale comes down to what the selected vendor will provide over and above the tangible product—the intangible support that will differentiate you from your competition, as demonstrated in Figure 6.1. A promise to provide support has no substance without a documented methodology demonstrating the credibility and integrity of the promise.

The differentiator for which the customer is looking is a tried-and-true process that the vendor will employ to plan, organize, and manage the assignment. This is project management.

CHAPTER OVERVIEW

In a dramatically changing business environment, certain markets disappear for some companies and new business opportunities appear for others. Both

Figure 6.1   Comparative Vendor Analysis

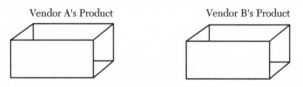

Vendor A's Product   Vendor B's Product

Feature/Service	Vendor A	Vendor B
Feature 1	✓	
Feature 2		✓
Implementation/ Installation Support	✓	✓
Project Management	✓	

situations suggest that prospective clients/customers who issue a Request for Proposal (RFP) or a Request for Information (RFI) can expect highly competitive responses from organizations. Many factors can separate the winner from the loser in this bidding process. They include, but are not limited to, the degree of prescience within the organization concerning changing industry trends; the degree to which the response to the request, stated in the RFP/RFQ, is cogent and targeted; the professional appearance of the proposal document; the responsive attitude of the salesperson; and, last but not least, how project management is positioned within the proposal. It is incumbent upon managers of projects who are involved in the bidding/proposal process to become sharper and more professional in analyzing business opportunities as they relate to the generation and preparation of a proposal.

When competition was not so fierce, responding to a request for a proposal may have meant merely filling out some tedious paperwork to be awarded the job. Today, actively choosing the most appropriate business opportunities and then generating a highly professional proposal may mean life or death for an organization. In addition, the way that project management is positioned within the proposal and how project management is used during the proposal process can be viewed by the prospective client/customer as a positive differentiator from your competition. This chapter offers a blueprint for fulfilling the objectives, and the goal, of successful proposal management.

The chapter is divided into three sections. "Proposal Management—The Process" covers how to analyze potential business opportunities and then how to generate winning proposals. The second section, "Proposal Management and Project Management," covers how project management can help sell your products and services; in other words, how project management is imbedded in the Proposal Management Process. The third section offers a "Vendor Evaluation Matrix" that you can give to your prospective client as an aid in evaluating all vendors equally and fairly.

Although the chapter uses the terminology of a large consulting firm or major defense contractor, the concepts are germane to everyone in project management who must pitch projects to management, to users, or to a boss, with the understanding that business opportunities can be internal as well as external. Typically, we think of the competitive bidding process in terms of consulting firms, government contractors, and architectural/construction firms. But this trio is not the entire picture. An information systems division issues proposals to obtain funding for projects that will support its community of users' requirements; a marketing division is taking the pulse of its customers and presenting to its management proposals for funding new or enhanced products; an engineering division may bid a job so that the functional divisions within its company do not go to the external competition for engineering expertise. It is our job, as good managers of projects, to be looking for business opportunities wherever they occur, and then to be able to write a proposal, cost/benefit analysis, business case, or white paper to justify those projects.

PROPOSAL MANAGEMENT—THE PROCESS

This section provides an overall, generic model to be used by organizations— small and large—when they must decide whether to propose, and, if so, how to present their proposals when prospective clients may range from a multinational enterprise to a steering committee within a small firm. Readers will interpret this model differently, depending on their industry and their competitive position within their marketplace. Regardless of how strong you think your company/division is in the marketplace, misjudging business opportunities or submitting a less-than-quality proposal can lose business that is needed for growth and, in some instances, for survival.

In this generic model, we look first at finding potential business opportunities and deciding whether to compete for the business—that is, whether to prepare a proposal. If the business opportunity is worth pursuing, we explore how to write and critique a proposal.

Analyzing Business Opportunities

These steps should be considered when analyzing potential business opportunities:

- Identify new business
- Evaluate opportunities
- Posture to win new business
- Establish/maintain contacts
- Develop strategy
- Perform business risk assessment
- Obtain Request for Proposal (RFP)
- Make the transition to the proposal writing phase

Each of these steps is divided into specific focus topics. For each step, a list of questions that must be posed and/or additional issues that must be considered are presented for your review.

Step: Identify New Business

Requests for your services do not automatically come to you. You must be positioned to be invited into the bidding process. Here are some resources to consider when you are attempting to entice new business.

Sources of Information.   These can be formal or informal. They can be found in formal publications, such as the Government Clearinghouse (it publishes contracts that are being let, ranging from creating training to building missile silos). Prospective customers who are aware of your existence may send you an RFP or an RFI. A Request for Information (RFI) is a customer's fishing trip. The question is: How much time and energy should be spent responding? Base your decision on the qualifications of the prospective customer, the size of the job, and your perception of the potential return on investment if you were to be considered and eventually got the bid. Informally, look to your network of friends, the local newspapers, and the minutes from your own company's steering committee.

Follow the Competition.   Although the competition may not always be right, you would be wise to keep an eye on your opponents. If they are bidding, then you may want to find a way to bid as well. If you lose a bid to a competitor, don't be too proud to ask the customer, "What did the competitor do to get the job?" or "What can we learn that would make us more competitive next time?"

Who Is Responsible?   Seeking out business opportunities does not just happen. Someone in the organization must take that responsibility. By default, it is often the top executive of the group. This does not necessarily make sense. Other people may have interests and talents that can contribute to marketing the organization's expertise.

Step: Evaluate Opportunities

Every opportunity may not be worth pursuing. Some opportunities are good; some are bad. The following guidelines can help you to decide whether to invest time and effort in chasing a particular opportunity.

To Bid or Not to Bid.   As an opportunity presents itself, evaluate whether you want to "take the wave." In some instances, it may be wiser to pass it by. Some years ago I was acquainted with a firm that was in the data processing consulting and training business. The owners seized an opportunity to start a data entry–keypunching business, which turned out to be a bad decision.

The new business was not consistent with their mission statement, they lacked the necessary expertise, and they diluted their energy and financial resources, which adversely affected their growth. It is as important to determine what *not* to pursue as it is to decide what to pursue.

Assess the Chance of Success Realistically.   Don't be a gambler if you don't have the financial and physical reserves to absorb a loss if you were to win but were unable to make the venture profitable.

How to Evaluate a Business Opportunity?   Take the time to make a sound business decision. Remember that it is not prudent to bid on every job that comes your way. Filter out opportunities that will not be good business decisions by conducting your own B-A-N-C analysis:

- *Budget.* Does the customer have the budget (funding) to pay for the job? If not, when will the funding be available? If the overall position is negative, this still might be a good future business opportunity. Don't lose touch with the prospect, but don't put a lot of time and effort into writing a lengthy proposal.
- *Authority.* Does your contact person have the authority to approve the project? If not, how far up the line of command does your prospect have to go to obtain approval? If your contact is not a decision maker, does not have formal or informal power to fund the project, or has only indirect access to a decision maker who can fund the project, this business opportunity may not be worthy of a lot of effort now. Maybe later, but not now.
- *Need.* Is there an identified need on which everyone is in agreement? If not, can you help define the need? And will you and/or your customer contact be able to sell the need once it is substantiated? Furthermore, can your organization satisfy the need with your current expertise or products? If not, how much risk is involved in acquiring the skill/products to fulfill the contract without exceeding the time and dollar requirements? If the evaluation is negative, indicating an unfavorable risk/reward on this venture, it is preferable to pass up this situation. However, keep tracking the opportunity. When the need is truly defined *and* the risk is acceptable, be there to offer your products/services.
- *Cycle.* When will the client act? Is enough money left in this year's budget to pay for your project? Has money been allocated for your type of project, or will funding not be made available until the next quarter or maybe the next fiscal year? The further away the budget cycle, the

less time you want to spend now; however, when that cycle becomes imminent, be ready to take the wave and ride it.

For detailed guidance, see Performance Support Tool 6.1, B-A-N-C Worksheet, at the end of this chapter. This Support Tool and all others referenced in this book are available for download at www.pmsi-pm.com.

In the proposal management process—which is, in essence, the initiation phase of a project—a tremendous amount of effort and care is required just to obtain authorization to vie for an opportunity. Be sure to invest enough time to work through this part of the process professionally and thoroughly.

Step: Posture to Win New Business

What does it take to be considered for new business opportunities and to win that new business? The following issues must be resolved.

Marketing versus Technological Issues.   Recognize the ongoing struggle between the sales function and the creative function of the business. Don't try to market what you can't make. Conversely, don't make what you can't market.

Customer Contact Plan.   Make a conscious decision to build the infrastructure required to create visibility in your potential marketplace. Build an assertive sales force, become very active in professional organizations, go on speaking tours, attend trade shows, create a Web presence. Best of all, complete successful jobs to earn respect for your firm and visibility in your area of business.

To Team or Not to Team.   If you do not have all the expertise required to respond to an opportunity, do you want to co-venture with another firm? The up side is that the other firm brings essential expertise and may help you get the contract and break into a new area of business. On the down side, co-ventures have many of the characteristics of a marriage. If it doesn't work, breaking up is hard to do.

Step: Establish and Maintain Contacts

Awareness of your existence is paramount. When new business opportunities arise, potential customers must think of you as a viable candidate. This step profiles three types of viable contacts.

Current Customers and Solid Prospects.   Keep in constant contact either through advertising, newsletters, periodic mailings (we call them "wave mailings"), and phone calls, or by stopping in and saying hello. Your current customer base holds the best potential. Your clients know you and, hopefully, respect the work that you do. Penetration selling—selling to your current client base—is proven to be the most productive. Solid prospects are waiting for the right time to bring you into their organization. Keep your name in front of them.

Colleagues in the Industry.   Cultivate a network of people who are willing to recommend you and may use your talents when needed. Be gracious with tangible and intangible recognition of their help.

The Competition.   Make your competitors aware of what you're doing. They may want to team with you at some point. Perhaps they may not be able to handle a particular project and, as a show of good faith to their client, they may recommend you. Contrary to popular belief, Macy's did send people to Gimbel's.

Step: Develop Strategy

If a business opportunity is worth winning, make a conscious decision as to how you are going to acquire the contract. Consider both of the following important strategies.

Identify Capture Plans.   Consider optional capture plans such as pricing lower than other competitors, providing better quality. Selling is often based on the *relationship* between the vendor and the prospect. Develop strong personal relationships.

Gauge the Customer's Position in the Procurement Cycle.   Ascertain where the customer is in the procurement cycle; for example, is the company conducting a needs analysis, defining requirements, or searching for bidders? Has the funding been allocated, and is the client ready to sign a contract? The closer the customer is to the end of the procurement cycle, the more you want to offer.

Step: Perform Business Risk Assessment

If the business opportunity still seems enticing after you evaluate your strategy, stop and take a realistic look at the potential risk involved. Following are the areas of risk to evaluate.

Risk of Losing the Bid.   How much do we risk by making a significant investment in developing the proposal and then not being awarded the contract? Don't kid yourself. Producing a winning proposal takes time and energy. It is not worth undertaking unless you are convinced that you have a good chance and you want to get involved in that type of business opportunity.

Risk of Winning and Not Being Able to Deliver.   If we are awarded the contract, what is the risk of not being able to produce the end product? Your desire to win the contract can cloud your good sense. Don't pursue a business opportunity to which you may not be able to respond. Not only is it embarrassing to the client, but your lack of follow-through can get around in the industry.

Risk of Winning but Not Making Money.   If we are able to produce the end product, what is the risk of not making a profit? If an adequate level of profit is not guaranteed, pass up this business opportunity. Many companies undertake jobs in which there is a possibility of a loss. Instead of saying "No" and extracting themselves, they lose their objectivity, perhaps because of ego or political reasons, and they end up paying the piper. Know how to, and when to, resist a potentially unprofitable venture. There is, however, one exception to this rule: If you want to move into a new marketplace or a new line of business, a conscious decision to take a loss on the first few projects may be acceptable.

Step: Obtain Request for Proposal (RFP)

If you have cultivated your prospects correctly, you will receive plenty of requests for your products/services.

Step: Make the Transition to the Proposal Writing Phase

By considering the evaluation criteria established in your portfolio management process (see Chapter 7), you will choose only those opportunities that are worthy of your bid. Your next move is into the proposal writing effort.

We have explored the first phase of the proposal management process: analyzing business opportunities. Let us now suppose, hypothetically, that we have received a viable invitation from a prospective customer/client to bid on an opportunity to sell our product or our service. We must produce a compelling proposal that will entice the prospective client to choose us over our competition.

Generating Winning Proposals

When writing a successful proposal, the following discrete steps should be taken:

- Organize for a successful proposal effort
- Understand the customer
- Establish protocols

- Identify evaluation criteria
- Prepare proposal
- Critique (verify/certify) proposal
- Submit proposal
- Be awarded the contract!

As in the previous section, each step in this model is accompanied by sets of specific questions to ask, related steps to take, and documents to produce, so that the client/customer can make informed decisions about which projects to approve, which assignments get priority, and, in some cases, which bidder is awarded the job. These steps pertain to all managers of projects, whether they are consultants, defense contractors, or project management experts.

Step: Organize for a Successful Proposal Effort

Taking the time to plan the work that needs to be done during the proposal writing phase will allow the effort to go forward more efficiently and effectively. Listed here are the tasks that need to be done first.

Determine the Levels of Authority.   Who has the authority to write the proposal? Who has the authority to sign the proposal as a representative of the company? Most important, who has the authority to approve the dollars and conditions established in the proposal, which can be construed as an official offer of services and/or product? If your offer is not well conceived because the wrong people prepared it, or wrong assumptions were made, or unreal commitments are established, these mistakes can have a broad range of embarrassing consequences and legal implications.

Staff the Proposal Team.   Pick the right people for the proposal team. Choose them for any or all of the following reasons: they have submitted successful proposals in the past, they are intimately familiar with that part of the business, they know (or have worked for) the customer in the past, and/or they are skilled estimators. Create a balance of business professionals and technicians on the proposal team.

Ensure the Proposal Team's Compatibility.   The members of the proposal team need to be acceptable to the proposal team leader, to management, and to each other. If the people on this team cannot quickly reach a synergistic working relationship, the proposal either will not get out on time or will not be a winning proposal.

Assemble External Advisory Teams.   Everyone whom you may want to become involved in the proposal team may not be available full time; therefore, establish advisory teams that will help prepare and/or critique the proposal as their skills are required.

Set Milestone Targets for Preparing the Proposal. A high-level schedule of major due dates will keep everyone focused on getting the tasks performed so that the proposal will be delivered on time and with minimal stress.

Step: Understand the Customer

Selling requires building a relationship. To build a successful relationship, you need to learn everything you can about the other person. To sell a proposal, learn as much as you can about your prospective customer. As you research the customer's background, focus on the following activities.

Compile History. Pull together every piece of documented history about the project and the client/customer that you can find. Carefully review the RFP and critique any similar proposal that has been submitted in the past. You can learn from proposals that failed as well as from those that were successful. The history of previous similar projects can provide background for schedules and/or costs. Also gather any documentation about the customer: what you (or other firms) have done for it in the past, its style of management, and what the trade journals or periodicals say about it. Get a copy of its annual stockholders report to determine where it is strong and where it needs help. This research may seem laborious, but it can make the rest of the process of generating a winning proposal much easier.

Learn from Past Experiences. Past experiences with the client and with producing proposals can give good direction. Does sending people off site work well within your organization, or is it preferable for each group to produce its part of the proposal independently and then submit it to the proposal team leader for consolidation? Does producing a quick draft of a proposal, and then having a "red team" tear it apart and build it back together, work better than attempting to prepare each section meticulously the first time?

Assess New Players, Policies, Predicaments, and Predilections. Time may have elapsed since the evaluation of this opportunity was conducted or since a decision was made to bid on the job. Stop and take a look at what may have changed. If there are new players in the client organization, there may be a new ball game. Get their input immediately. New policies, organizational changes, or changes in the business environment—yours or the prospective customer's—should be taken into account.

Differentiate Incompetence (in Customers) from Personal Arrogance. Never deceive yourself that you are smarter than your customers. A customer will make a decision based on having a vendor with whom the firm wants to work. The customer has a vision of its needs. Its perception is its reality.

Either bid the job for which it is asking or bid the job that you think it really needs. If you choose the latter, be prepared to lose. If you know you will lose and therefore cannot ethically bid the job for which the customer is asking, don't bid at all.

Step: Establish Protocols

Protocols are the disciplines that must be followed during the proposal process. These disciplines allow each of the players to do its part of the work and to be assured that all the pieces will fall into place when the proposal is completed. These protocols—the rules that will be followed—often fall into the following categories.

Dos and Don'ts.   The dos and don'ts are the rules that will be followed. They might include: no dollars will be discussed with anyone outside the team; every person (or only one person) will review the drafts of the proposal; meetings will be conducted Tuesdays and Thursdays from 1:00 P.M. to 4:00 P.M., and all members are required to be present.

Administrative Disciplines.   This is the time to establish the systems that everyone will use while putting the proposal together. For example, all materials will be submitted in a preestablished format produced on a specific model computer using a specific word processing software; or all dollars will be figured on a 10-year payback period.

Leaders.   Writing a winning proposal is a project. Put together a project plan that assigns specific efforts, and choose leaders who represent different parts of the organization, including marketing, manufacturing, and finance. Another approach is to assign leaders who control different parts of the proposal, such as "Reasons why our firm is the one to choose," the financial bid, and the Statement of Work.

Step: Identify Evaluation Criteria

The prospective customer has determined a series of criteria on which it will evaluate the bidders. The proposal team's job is to ferret out those criteria and respond correctly, appropriately, and thoroughly. Evaluation criteria determine how the customer will make its decision.

Locate Grading Criteria.   Evaluation criteria are part of the Request for Proposal. If the first phase of this proposal process—analyzing the opportunity—was done well, those criteria were extracted and thoroughly understood. If there was no Request for Proposal, then there should have been—and there needs to continue to be—long, probing conversations with the prospective customer to be sure that the criteria on which the bid is to be evaluated are completely understood by the proposal team.

Understand the Grading Criteria.   Grading criteria become the tiebreaker if there is a tie. Find out which criteria will be given heavier weighting. Sometimes pricing overcomes adherence to requirements; sometimes, a slick presentation of the document triumphs over content. Although obtaining the grading criteria may be difficult, attempt to persuade the client to share them with you.

Step: Prepare Proposal

When preparing the proposal, the format and the content must be chosen carefully to make the most positive impact possible on the prospective client. Refer to Performance Support Tool 6.2, at the end of this chapter, for a template of a professionally designed proposal. The following sequence of activities can generate a world-class proposal.

Address Three Sections: Management, Technical, and Financial.   The emphasis and the sequencing of these three sections is dependent on the weighting of the evaluation criteria set forth by the client or by the format specified in the RFP. The management section describes the history of the company: What is unique about this company that should justify its winning the contract and the credentials of the team and the manager of the project who will be assigned? The technical section answers the prospective client's question, "How well does the vendor understand my business situation and has it recommended a viable solution?" This section also includes a high-level project plan with clear roles and responsibilities delineated between the vendor and the customer. The financial section expresses the one-time developmental costs and the associated payment conditions and recurring or ongoing costs, if any. It may be presented as a fixed price bid, time and materials, or cost plus.

Price the Bid to Win/Lose.   Position the proposal to be realistic but persuasive. It might include a risk/reward analysis, a cost/benefit evaluation, or a cost comparison of different approaches. *Be realistic.* That advice cannot be emphasized enough. No bid is worth winning if you ultimately lose money or do not professionally meet your commitments to your customer. Although this may sound blasphemous, there may be situations in which you price the bid to lose. One reason might be that you feel that your company/division should bid on the job, but the job is truly out of your area of expertise. Bid high enough that if you get the job, there will be sufficient funds to buy the expertise, technology, and time to do the job right.

Pick a Proposal Theme.   Pick a theme for the proposal: "We are the best in the business and will supply you with the strongest talent available on this job," or "We have a better financial bid," or "Look at how strong we are technologically and at the variety of options we are presenting," or "Isn't our proposal the most professional document you have ever seen?" Keep coming back to the theme throughout all the sections of the proposal. If you try to juggle multiple themes at one time, you will probably only confuse the customer. Pick the theme that you think will sell.

Emphasize Past Performance.   Emphasize your past performance—with this client or with similar clients—in performing similar types of projects. Give as references those who are going to say only wonderful things about you. All prospective clients are expecting you to give them nothing but good references. Surprise them by listing a client whose contract you lost but who will tell a positive story about how your firm conducted itself when it lost. Remember to have the courtesy to tell your references that they will be receiving a phone call from your prospective client. Include any samples or examples of similar work you have done. The customer is trying to find some *tangible* reason why you should be chosen above all others.

Work with Subcontractors.   If you don't have the talent needed to cover all facets of the assignment, don't try to fake it. Find within your network other people or firms who can team with you or to whom you would be willing to subcontract. Keep in mind, however, that when you subcontract, you are not totally in control. Be careful whom you pick to subcontract. Because the subcontractor needs to have a say in the proposal, be sure to leave enough preparation time for your subcontractor to be involved.

Process through the Approval Levels.   Various stages of proposal preparation require various levels of approval. In the initial stages, be sure the areas of the company that are going to contribute to the job have given you accurate prices. When the proposal is near completion, the finance department should review the financial data; the legal department should review the legal issues, and so on. Lastly, have the highest level of management review the proposal from an all-business perspective to determine whether the organization is willing to commit to the stated promises, and whether your firm has used every technique it can to win the contract.

Choose the Type of Bid.   This is a complex subject in and of itself. Fixed-price bids are the most binding but they make the customer most comfortable. Cost-plus bids are best when there are many unknowns but, for the customer's sake, establish some not-to-exceed limits. Incentives/penalties (for positive and negative performance) are worth considering. These incentives can be based on schedule, cost, and/or quality. Take some time to consider the correct type of bid/contract for this assignment and this particular customer.

Employ Parametric Pricing.   Take advantage of all the history that is available relative to pricing the job. Use past job logs, personnel/payroll reports, change control logs, and so on.

Conduct a Risk Assessment.   Risk assessment can be mathematical as well as subjective. Anticipate any contingencies that can be expected. Think of all the factors that caused extra expenditures of dollars or hours in past similar projects, and take those into account when estimating the job. Look at areas of unknowns where innovation, technology, or just good luck is involved, and be sure you have factored those into the time and cost equations.

Step: Critique (Verify/Certify) Proposal

Almost as much time needs to be spent on reviewing the proposal as on preparing it. Check once for typos and for mathematical errors. Check a second time for logic and consistency errors. And check a third time to be sure that what you are bidding is what the prospective client is requesting. Be sure that your review includes the following tasks.

Verify That the Statement of Work Is Totally Responsive to the RFP.   For the hundredth time, go back to the RFP and be sure the proposal addresses the requests and requirements. For example, is there a need for proof of insurance or for minority status? Read each sentence. An important issue that the customer wants addressed may have been buried somewhere in the text.

Focus on the Right Criteria.   Did the customer mention, verbally or in the RFP, a specific criterion on which the proposal will be evaluated? If the criterion is financial, then don't include 20 pages describing the fantastic qualifications of every consultant/technician on your staff.

Recheck for Accuracy.   Nothing so destroys all the work that you have done than to have the customer find a mathematical error. Have several people check the data for the slightest error. Review the proposal for statements that are illogical or unsubstantiated, or do not jibe with other statements. Find someone with good analytical skills to perform this check.

Use a Compliance Matrix.   Prepare a compliance matrix that graphically shows what the customer will be responsible for and what your organization will be responsible for. Also indicate what test or products will ensure compliance, how they will be measured, who will do the measuring, and who will sign off that compliance has been attained.

Red Team the Proposal.   Now that you, the proposal team, and your advisory group have reviewed the document until you are sick of it, go off site and review it again. Bring some other people who have not been involved before now. The rule of thumb is: Have several people review the proposal—someone old, someone new, someone borrowed, and someone blue—in other words, someone who has worked on the team, someone who knows nothing about the proposal, someone borrowed from finance or the estimating group, and your resident cynic, that nitpicker who will find the slightest error. Consider inviting some high-level management. Leave your ego at home. The document will probably be substantially changed by the time the "red team" is done with it, but it will be a better proposal.

Step: Submit Proposal

Getting to the church on time is crucial. Most bids have absolute due dates. If your proposal is late or you are not available for the presentation, you will be out of the running. The following media are used for submitting the proposal.

Written Proposals.   Print it, bind it, be sure the pages are in the right order and not upside down; give whatever ritualistic blessing you use, and send it off. Call in a few days to be sure that it has been received. The phone call serves two purposes: (1) the proposal might get lost, and you want to be sure it gets into the customer's hands prior to the deadline, and (2) it shows your interest in getting the job.

Oral Proposals.   Show up on time, be prepared, and do not just talk from the proposal document. Have a stand-alone presentation prepared—the proposal is then a leave-with document. Finally, listen. Don't do all the talking.

Bidders' Conference.   This is the most difficult hurdle of them all. Anyone who watched the presidential debates has seen the lose–lose situation in which candidates can find themselves when they are pitted against a competitor. Being too aggressive, or badmouthing your competitor, leads to failure. Being too soft and nonassertive also is unsuccessful. Keep reminding yourself, "Be professional, be professional." That demeanor will contribute to winning the contract.

Step: Be Awarded the Contract!

Bravo! All that hard work paid off. You and your organization have been awarded the contract. Your job has just begun. Here are the first two steps.

Conduct a Post-Mortem Debriefing.   Answer these questions: What did we do wrong? What did we do right? What will we do better the next time? Give yourself time to work through this process. It will be invaluable in how you relate to your now-current client and in developing the next proposal for future clients.

Even if you lose the bid, go through this process to learn what you did wrong so that you will never do the same thing again.

Make the Transition to Project Management.   One does not automatically walk from the award of the job into the doing of the job without some rest, followed by serious project planning for the project launch and a higher level plan for the entire project. The time to rest will give you the wherewithal to move into the actual project, and the time taken to prepare a plan will give you the tools to monitor and manage the project.

The objective of your proposal is to differentiate yourself from the competition. Make sure your proposal stands out and is memorable in a positive way. Think about using graphics, pie charts, project plans, and models. You may find proposal preparation software that can help you with the organization and visual presentation, and with price estimating and reporting. If you are generating proposals for large projects or making proposals to government agencies, consider investing in software that systematizes price estimating and cost report generation.

Do not confine yourself to an exclusively paper-based product. Depending on your type of work or the type of client, you may want to include a video or CD presentation that visually displays what your firm can do. For a prospective client who is on the road a lot, you may even consider creating a cassette with an audio proposal. However, don't let creativity compromise the clarity or the professional appearance of your proposal.

This chapter has so far presented the basics of attracting business and getting your firm in the running for new business; evaluating whether to pursue specific new business opportunities; and generating a winning proposal. A major contention of this book is that using project management in the sales process can help an organization "sell" its products and services. The next section explains how.

PROPOSAL MANAGEMENT AND PROJECT MANAGEMENT

In a conversation almost two decades ago, one of IBM's regional directors was lamenting the fact that IBM no longer could just sell computer equipment—it had become important, almost necessary, to sell installation support as well. Today, companies that sell products and/or services are expected not only to provide installation or implementation assistance but to provide this assistance using the project management discipline. The customer expects to have the product or service, of the quality promised, delivered on time and within budget. The only way to meet these expectations is to plan, organize, and track the delivery in the most professional way possible. That means using the discipline of project management.

William Doey, Jr., the president of IKON Design, a document-imaging company located in the San Francisco Bay Area, observes in his customer newsletter: "Recently, we began reviewing the 'value' we bring to our clients, which is something I believe we offer that is in addition to our core products. . . . [W]e deliver conversion plans that go beyond project-to-project thinking. . . . We call this value *Performance Beyond Expectations*. . . . We do this by investing in engineering and project management skills." Doey and his entire organization are committed to working every job as though it were a project and to employing project management in every client engagement, so that the customer is assured that the job is being planned, monitored, tracked, and managed to the best of IKON's ability.

This section of the chapter (1) discusses how project management can be a differentiator which can aid a company in selling its product/service, and (2) offers an external plan to position project management as a differentiating sales factor, and (3) offers an internal plan to employ project management to meet the commitments as sold.

How Project Management Is a Differentiator

Potential customers will see the use of project management by a vendor/supplier as a differentiating factor in terms of time, money, quality, and ease of delivery and implementation. Why?

The Time Difference

The customer wants the job done on time. He or she has advertised internally, and sometimes externally, that this product or service will be available, or will have accomplished its objectives, by a certain date. Advertising the due date makes the project and the customer very visible. A late delivery date becomes an embarrassment to all those who were responsible for the choice of and the interaction with the vendor.

The Money Difference

The customer has requested, from its management, funding of a specific amount or at least a range of potential expenditures that will not exceed a certain amount. Therefore, the customer is relying on the vendor to perform the work within the preestablished budget. Having to return to management to ask for more money is embarrassing. The assumption on management's part is that either the wrong vendor was chosen or the vendor relationship was not well managed. Either way, the onus falls on the folks who chose the vendor and/or those who are managing the assignment.

The Quality Difference

The customer has announced that the product or service is to perform in a certain way. There is a preconceived expectation of quality on the part of those who will use the product or those who will be exposed to the service. If this expectation is not met, the failure is visible not only to management but to everyone who comes into contact with the end deliverable. Again, who looks bad? The person(s) who chose the vendor and/or the person(s) who managed the engagement.

The Difference in Ease of Change

The customer implicitly expects that the assignment will be carried out with as little upheaval to the organization as possible. This benchmark is not as quantifiable as matters of keeping to schedule, budget, and quality; however, it can be more important than all three. Implementing a new product or purchasing a service heralds a change in the environment. Not only will a cadre of employees be involved in the implementation/installation, but an even larger group of people in the organization will be using the new product, or the concepts introduced through the service, once the vendor has left the scene. Therefore, the bumpier and less controlled and managed the effort, the more dissonance it causes within the organization. Again, those who chose the vendor and who worked to manage the vendor are seen as the responsible parties.

In all of these instances, the persons who make the final decision on a vendor and the persons who manage the relationship with the vendor are putting their reputations on the line. If the vendor is unsuccessful, the blame falls not only on the vendor's shoulders but also on the shoulders of those who chose and/or managed the vendor. The vendor leaves the stage, but the person who chose him or managed the engagement stays and endures the consequences. Using the project management discipline can help satisfy the customer's expectations of getting the product/service on time, within budget, of the desired quality, and with minimal upheaval—thus setting up as superstars the people involved in the vendor's selection and management. (See Figure 6.2.)

Figure 6.2   Customer Expectations

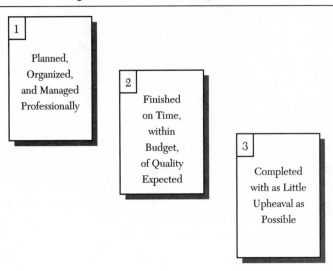

Customers need more than just a promise that project management will help vendors meet their expectations. As summarized in Figure 6.3, they need to see that vendors are walking their talk—that they are employing the project management discipline during the sales process, the launch, and throughout the endeavor. In other words, they are taking the following steps.

Figure 6.3   Project Management as a Differentiator

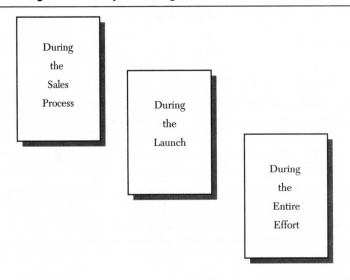

During the Sales Process

The proposal must clearly describe the project management tools and techniques that will be employed. Conducting the proposal effort as a project is particularly persuasive. It shows the prospective client how the discipline can really add value to the future engagement. Together, planning the preparation of the proposal, letting the client know the steps in this process, and keeping to the delivery dates increase credibility and reliability. Good project management makes the entire interaction between client and vendor more professional and more mutually beneficial.

During the Launch

After being awarded the contract, the vendor's first few interactions set the tone and establish its reputation as "easy to work with" or "troublesome." The first interaction is a well-organized project kickoff meeting during which members of the customer's organization and the vendor's organization accomplish several tasks. They develop a project plan. They also agree on roles and responsibilities, and they establish a mutually agreeable communication plan consisting of reports and appropriate meetings. First impressions count. The impression created during the launch sets the stage for a successful ongoing relationship and for managers of projects to drive the ongoing work effort.

During the Entire Effort

It does little good to show that project management won the job and launched the job and then excused itself from the discipline once the engagement got under way. During the project, vendor and client truly see the return on investment of applying the project management discipline. Customers need to see that their vendor of choice has inculcated project management within its own organization and has trained its staff to use the tools of the project management discipline throughout the process, as described in the following external and internal plans.

An External Plan to Position Project Management as a Differentiating Factor

The outputs of the external plan that positions project management as a differentiating, competitive factor are the deliverables that are seen by the world. They are tangible items that position project management as a way to do business. Some are imbedded in the sales and marketing collateral; others are identified uniquely as project-management-related differentiators. Your company needs to parlay the use of the project management discipline in its marketing collateral, its bid proposals, and during the engagement.

In the Marketing Collateral

Create collateral that sells not only the product/service and implementation/installation support, but project management as well, as shown in Figure 6.4. This sales collateral should include a customer-oriented Project Management Benefits Statement, plus convincing biographies of your cadre of managers of projects, highlighting their technical and project management experiences. Project management is a consultative job, and consultative jobs are typically dependent on the personal relationship between the manager of the project and the customer. Therefore, seeing an impressive presentation of the qualifications of the person with whom the customer will be dealing may lead the customer to make a choice based on the person and therefore the company that should be entrusted with the job.

In the Bid Proposal

As shown in Figure 6.5, a compliance matrix includes a description of the roles and responsibilities of all the players from both the vendor's and the customer's organizations. The roles and responsibilities listing serves two objectives: (1) it informs the customer that the manager of projects is not just a "pair-of-hands" acting as liaison between customer and vendor but a professional who possesses the skills and the authority to actively manage the

Figure 6.4   Project Management Promoted in Collateral

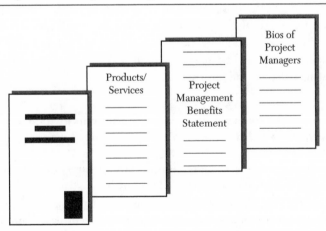

Figure 6.5   Project Management Compliance Matrix Included in the Bid Proposal

Compliance Matrix Roles and Responsibilities		
Task	Customer	Vendor
Job Related:		
_____	X	
_____		X
_____	X	
_____	X	X
Project Management:		
_____		X
_____		
_____		X
_____		X

project; and (2) it differentiates, in the mind of the customer, the various roles and gives a clear understanding of what the vendor will be doing and what the customer must do to get the job done.

As shown in Figure 6.6, it is advisable to generate in the proposal a communication plan that identifies the type of information that the person in each role described above needs to give and to get; the mode in which this communication will be delivered; and how frequently these communications will occur. Key features of this plan are: it makes the manager of projects the focal point of communication with the customer, and it establishes procedures for when and how this communication will occur.

In the Kickoff Meeting

As shown in Figure 6.7, as part of the kickoff meeting with the customer, include a session on the importance of project management in fulfilling the customer's requirements and an overview of how project management will be employed throughout the engagement. This presentation reinforces the differentiating factor that helped sell the job, gives the customer reassurance that the job will be handled professionally, and sets expectations for the working relationship between the vendor and the customer.

Figure 6.6   Project Management Positioned in Proposal Communication Plan

Communication Plan				
	Customer Liaison	Vendor Project Manager	Mode of Communication	Frequency
RE: Product/Service				
1._____	P			
2._____	S	P		
3._____		P		
4._____	P			
RE: Implementation				
1._____	P			
2._____		S		
3._____	P	S		
4._____				
RE: Project Management				
1._____	P			
2._____		S		
3._____	S	P		
4._____				

P= Prime Responsibility
S= Support Responsibility

Figure 6.7   Project Management Positioned in the Kick-Off Meeting

I. _____

• _____

• _____

II. _____

• _____

• _____

III. Project Management

• Importance

• How It Will Be
Employed

Rationale:

• Reinforces
Differentiating Factor
That Helped Sell the Job

• Reassures a Professional Job

• Sets Expectations for the
Working Relationship

In the Customer Survey

An important project management procedure that can be employed throughout the engagement is conducting customer surveys—questioning the customer on the timeliness and quality of interim deliverables as well as the supportiveness of the project team. (See Figure 6.8.) This brings to the customer's attention not only your desire to provide excellent service but the ways in which the discipline of project management is affecting the success of the assignment and the relationship with the customer.

In Customer/Vendor Meetings

Finally, throughout the engagement, conduct face-to-face meetings with the customer whenever possible. In these meetings, review schedules, budgets, and the quality of deliverables being produced, from both the vendor's and the customer's perspective. Project management meetings unearth problems before they can negatively affect the job.

The efforts listed above offer a variety of ways to display the discipline of project management explicitly to the customer. Charge the customer for this project management effort. Something given for free is often perceived as having no value. Managing the effort using the project management discipline has immense value and should be recognized and compensated accordingly.

Figure 6.8   Customer Survey to Determine Satisfaction with Project Management

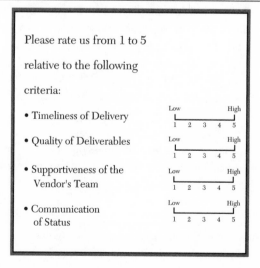

Now let's look at subtler but equally meaningful efforts to ensure that the promised results that won you the job are actually being delivered.

An Internal Plan to Facilitate Project Management as a Differentiating Factor

To ensure that promises about the benefits of project management that were made during the sales process are met during project execution, a variety of processes and organizational commitments are required, as follows.

Product or System Development Life Cycle Template

Create a template that defines the steps needed to implement or install your product or service. Share this template of tasks with your customer as the model work-breakdown structure—the framework for the project plan. Modify it with the customer so that both of you feel comfortable that all work efforts that need to be done are scheduled to be performed. Be sure to include all the project management efforts, such as project planning, project kickoff, project status meetings, and project closeout.

As part of the communication plan presented in the proposal, include a component that clarifies that *all stakeholders are required to inform all other stakeholders of any changes* in the scope of deliverables or in priorities. Include consequences for failure to do this, and rewards for maintaining good communication.

Continuous Improvement Process

Establish a continuous improvement process to pass on lessons learned to new project teams. This can be done by building a project history base, using the actual data from past project schedules, budgets, change control logs, and staffing plans. This historical data can then be used to increase accuracy in bid proposals and confidence in projected plans for future projects.

Project Management Lexicon

Produce a project management lexicon of terms. This will allow employees from various divisions, and customer representatives, to learn and speak the same project management language.

Rolling Wave Approach

Consider a rolling wave approach to project management: Perform a formal project management review at predetermined checkpoints. In this way, the customer is officially informed of any problems and lessons learned while appropriate actions can still be taken.

Updating Project Plans

Maintain the rigor of creating and updating project plans. This requires discipline on the part of all stakeholders, both within the vendor's organization and at the customer's site.

Quality Plan

Establish a proactive quality plan by instituting many interim quality assurance checkpoints during the project plan. This ensures a timely and quality deliverable.

Performance Management System

Institute a performance improvement, appraisal, and development process for managers of projects, based on following the project management discipline, managing the financial budget commitments, optimizing customer satisfaction, and other criteria.

Summary

If project management is to be seen as a differentiating, value-added service to your customer, it is essential that (1) project management be prominently positioned within the sales process and utilized during the launch of the engagement, and (2) the vendor organization adheres to the rigor of project management throughout the job. Project management can make the installation or implementation of a company's products or services more efficient, more effective, and more successful. Put the limelight on the project management process and use it to sell your wares. More importantly, build on the success of previous jobs and view project management as a way to sell the next job.

VENDOR EVALUATION MATRIX

Many prospective clients are not prepared to deal with the selection process. A stack of proposals may accumulate on their desks, but they often aren't quite sure how to differentiate one vendor from another, except maybe on the vendor's recommendations of solutions to problems, price, and, hopefully, a good project management plan. There are other considerations in selecting vendors. Performance Support Tool 6.3 at the end of this chapter provides a generic vendor evaluation matrix that you can offer your prospective clients. It is a list of criteria on which multiple vendors can and should be evaluated.

The vendor evaluation matrix is designed to focus on the following perspectives:

- Evaluation of the vendor company in terms of its stability and reputation
- Evaluation of financial issues, including the pricing of the product/service and of other auxiliary materials or support for the future
- Verification of a product/service as set forth in the proposal
- Evaluation of how responsible the vendor has been during the proposal management effort and how responsive it promises to be once the project gets under way
- Evaluation of the vendor's sales approach—whether it has been professional and collaborative

The matrix is designed so that prospective clients can weight each of the selection criteria relative to their view of its importance. The matrix also contains columns in which prospective clients can check off which vendors met which criteria. A sample matrix is displayed in Figure 6.9.

It is amazing how many prospective clients do not have this type of evaluation form and how grateful they are to be given a template from which they can tailor their own. Offering your clients this tool for no fee can earn some intangible points.

Figure 6.9   Sample of Vendor Evaluation Matrix

Key:
Vendor 1: Your Company Name
Vendor 2: _____
Vendor 3: _____

Selection Criteria	Response	Weighted Evaluation Criteria	Vendor 1	Vendor 2	Vendor 3
COMPANY EVALUATION					
Is the vendor stable? How many years have they been in business?					
Do they concentrate strictly on this product/service? Or do they offer a full range of products/services?					
How long has the vendor been providing this product/service?					

--- **CONCLUSION** ---

During the "Analyzing the Business Opportunity" phase of the proposal management process, the proposal team extracted the evaluation criteria presented in the RFP, asked clarifying questions, and thoroughly understood the client's decision criteria. If there wasn't a RFP, there was a series of long, probing conversations with the client, to be sure the business need and criteria on which the bid was to be evaluated were completely understood.

Once the evaluation criteria were identified, the team sought out the criteria that would be given heaviest weighting. Although obtaining the weighting of criteria can be difficult, the client shared this information because the weighting of criteria might become a tie breaker. The team then balanced the proposal to the weighted criteria. When you wrote the proposal, you restated the customer's requirements as extracted from the RFP and presented three sections: technical, management, and financial.

In the technical requirements section, your technical expertise and response to the client's requirements of the product or service were clearly laid out. The technical response was also detailed in an appendix that responded point-by-point to the requirements in the RFP. Included was a project plan answering these questions: What are the tasks? Who is responsible? What is the amount of effort required? What is the timeline?

You picked a proposal theme and kept coming back to it throughout all the sections of the proposal. The team was tempted but didn't present a series of options. Instead, it took a calculated risk and chose a theme and a recommendation that were tied to the evaluation criteria and would sell.

In the management section, you described what is unique about your company and its products/services. You justified awarding the contract to your team. Company history focused on past performance with this client and similar clients. You also described who would manage the project and provided information on the experience of the project team. To cover some facets of the assignment for which your firm lacks expertise, you carefully selected another firm that could team with you, and you made sure to leave time to allow that firm to contribute to the proposal. You included a compliance matrix that graphically showed efforts for which the customer would be responsible and efforts for which your organization would be responsible. You gave references of clients and people who would offer positive remarks about your organization and alerted them in advance to expect a phone call. You also provided samples of similar work, always guided by the need to help the customer find some tangible reason why he or she should pick your firm.

In the financial section, you took advantage of all of the history that was available relative to pricing the job, using past job logs, personnel/payroll reports, and change control logs, to name a few sources of data. You conducted a risk assessment, defined contingencies, and looked at unknowns where innovation, technology, or good luck are involved. The financial section of the proposal was realistic yet persuasive. It included a risk/reward analysis, a cost/benefit evaluation, a cost comparison of different approaches, and a choice of contract arrangements from fixed-price to cost-plus.

After writing the proposal, you confirmed that it was as tight, accurate, responsive, and appealing as it could be. You double-checked all calculations. You verified that your Statement of Work was totally responsive to the RFP. You went back to the RFP one more time and made sure that your proposal addressed all requests and requirements. Then you formed a "red team," who checked it one more time.

The proposal was printed and assembled in proper order, bound, and delivered on time. You called the client a few days after submitting the proposal, to be sure it had arrived and to show your interest in getting the job. You were able to convince the client to give you time to make a verbal presentation, at which you were prepared with a professional stand-alone presentation and a handout. You were smart enough not to do all the talking but instead asked open-ended questions and listened.

After what seemed an interminable time, you received word that your firm had been awarded the contract. All that hard work paid off. You took some time to celebrate, and then debriefed the proposal process and created an archive of parts of the proposal that could be excerpted for future opportunities. You generated a project plan to launch the project and moved on to conduct the job that you had worked so hard to win.

That is the history of how you analyzed a good business opportunity and generated a winning proposal.

B-A-N-C Worksheet

BUDGET

Does the customer have the budget (funding) to pay for the job?
_____ Yes _____ No

If no, when will the funding be available?
Date: _____

Guidelines: If funding is not available, don't lose touch with the prospect, but don't put a lot of time and effort into writing a lengthy proposal.

AUTHORITY

Does your contact person have the authority to approve the project?
_____ Yes _____ No

If not, how far up the line does your prospect have to go to obtain approval?
Answer: _____

Guidelines: If your contact is not a decision maker, or does not have formal or informal power to fund the project, or direct access to a decision maker who can fund the project, then this business opportunity may not be worth a lot of effort now. Maybe later, but not now.

NEED

Is there an identified need on which everyone is in agreement?
_____ Yes _____ No

If not, can you help define the need?
_____ Yes _____ No

Will you and/or your customer contact be able to sell the need once it is substantiated?
_____ Yes _____ No

Can your organization satisfy the need with your current expertise or products?
_____ Yes _____ No

If not, how much risk is involved in acquiring the skill/products to fulfill the contract without exceeding the time and dollar requirement?
Answer: _____

Guidelines: If the evaluation is negative, indicating an unfavorable risk/reward, it is preferable to pass up this venture. However, keep tracking the opportunity. Once the need is truly defined and the risk is acceptable, you want to be there to offer your product/services.

CYCLE

When will a decision be made?
Answer: _____

Is there money left in the budget for your project?
_____ Yes _____ No

Is the money currently allocated for your next type of project, or will monies not be made available until next quarter or maybe next year?
Answer: _____

Guidelines: The further away the budget cycle, the less time you want to spend now; however, when that cycle becomes imminent, be ready to mount the wave and ride it.

PERFORMANCE SUPPORT TOOL 6.2

Proposal Template

Client: Client contact:
Source: Client decision maker:
Proposal leader:
Phone: Fax: E-mail:

Briefly describe the client's business needs and wants:

Client's Evaluation Criteria (by weight):

1.

2.

3.

TECHNICAL SECTION

Statement of Work:

Deliverables (quantify, if possible):

Exclusions (if any):

Special requests and requirements:

Tasks   Timeline (schedule)

MANAGEMENT SECTION

Briefly describe your company and why it is uniquely qualified:

List the qualifications of the individuals to be assigned to this project (include credentials where possible):

References:
Name   Phone Number   Project Referenced

FINANCIAL SECTION

Task Description	Consultant Name Est. Days $/Day	Support Staff Est. Days $/Day	Other Costs (billable nonlabor costs) Unit $

Contingencies

Progress Payments		
Milestone Date	Deliverable	Invoice Amount

Special Arrangements

Any agreed-on discounts or special arrangements:

PERFORMANCE SUPPORT TOOL 6.3
Vendor Evaluation Matrix

Vendor 1:   [Your Company Name]
Vendor 2:   _____
Vendor 3:   _____

Selection Criteria	Response	Weighted Evaluation Criteria	Vendor 1	Vendor 2	Vendor 3
Company Evaluation					
Is the vendor stable?					
Number of years in business					
Does the vendor concentrate strictly on this product/service, or offer a full range of products/services?					
How long has the vendor been providing this product/service?					
Is the vendor geographically available? Does it have representation beyond this area? Nationwide? International?					
Is there breadth and depth in its client list? Has it had long-term relationships with past/current clients?					
Does the vendor understand our business and the competitive challenges we face?					
Does the vendor have other clients in an industry similar to ours?					
Do you have a good feeling about the vendor's management?					
How long have the principals been with the firm?					
References from past/current clients: Did the job meet requirements? Was it within budget? Was it on schedule? Was the vendor professional in the relationship?					
Has the vendor dedicated the appropriate amount of time, staff, and talent to the job?					

Selection Criteria	Response	Weighted Evaluation Criteria	Vendor 1	Vendor 2	Vendor 3
Are representatives willing to invest time to detail the scope of the engagement?					
Did the vendor provide a project plan for the job?					
Is the vendor's philosophy or concept consistent with, or is it able to be tailored to be consistent with, corporate policies and procedures?					
Financial					
How are products priced?					
Are pricing options available?					
Is pricing available by product?					
Is the vendor willing to negotiate? Are quantity discounts available?					
Are upgrades extra, and if so, how much?					
Does the vendor provide ancillary materials? Do they cost extra, and if so, how much?					
Are any value-added tools or services included with the product purchase?					
Product/Service					
Does the product effectively deliver what it claims?					
Does the design of the product make sense?					
Is the product professional?					
What quality control measures, if any, are taken to ensure the product operates as specified?					
Is the product guaranteed? What guarantees or warranties are offered, if any?					

Selection Criteria	Response	Weighted Evaluation Criteria	Vendor 1	Vendor 2	Vendor 3
Responsiveness					
Is the vendor willing to conduct interviews, to become familiar with our needs/culture?					
Does the vendor have one focal point of contact for the job? At the appropriate level?					
Is our contact "listening" to us?					
Does the vendor show concern for our needs and success? Is it quickly grasping our important concepts and requirements?					
Is the vendor willing to tailor the product to meet our needs? Or, does the vendor create the product such that it can be tailored by our company?					
Is the vendor open to our company's involvement in tailoring the product?					
Is the vendor going to be able to meet our deadlines?					
Is the vendor willing to travel, if necessary?		'			
Has our contact at the vendor returned our calls in a timely manner?					
Does our contact appear to be truly concerned about our needs and not just about making the sale?					
Have the vendor's promises been kept?					
Has the vendor's support staff been professional when we called or visited?					
Sales Approach					
Do the salespeople believe in their product and talk about it intelligently?					
Are the salespeople responsive to phone calls and requests?					
Did they prepare a professional proposal?					

Selection Criteria	Response	Weighted Evaluation Criteria	Vendor 1	Vendor 2	Vendor 3
Have they delivered what they promised, in a timely manner?					
Have they prepared thoughtfully before meetings?					
Have they taken initiative in the process?					
Are they patient and willing to follow our lead (i.e., not a hard sell)?					
Are we comfortable presenting this vendor to management?					

CHAPTER 7

Portfolio Management

A senior executive of a well-known petroleum company was conducting an on-site visit of the company's Louisiana facility. As a development experience, one of the up-and-coming senior engineers was given the privilege of walking the executive through the facility. To be sure that the young engineer was not caught off guard with a question that he could not answer, his boss, a higher-level and longer-term employee, tagged along on the walk-through.

The tour was going quite well. The young engineer had been doing an excellent job of responding to all of the executive's comments and questions. As the three of them were walking from one building to the next, the senior executive noticed several mango trees on the grounds and remarked offhandedly, "I wonder what the correlation is between the presence of mango trees in this part of the country and the production of oil." The young engineer had no immediate response, nor did his manager. They moved on to the next building and to different topics of interest to the senior executive.

The tour ended, and the executive flew back to Chicago. The young engineer and his manager met the next day to debrief. They were very proud of themselves. They had been able to respond to all of the senior executive's queries except "the mango tree question." The engineer and his manager decided that they really needed to address this question. So the senior engineer was given a three-week project: Research the correlation of the existence of mango trees with the production of oil.

When the three weeks ended, the engineer had produced a 50-page report which, in essence, said that there was no correlation between the presence of mango trees and the presence of oil. The two engineers had a big decision to make: Should they send the report directly to the senior executive in Chicago, or should they send it up the chain of command, asking each intermediate manager to review and sign off on the document? Being conservative, they decided to move the document up the chain of command.

For the next four weeks, "The Mango Tree Report" went from one manager to the next higher-level manager, and so on, up the chain of command. Ultimately, it landed on the desk of the senior executive who had asked the question seven weeks earlier in Louisiana.

The senior executive blew his stack. First, he had not been serious about his question. He had just been passing the time of day as they wandered from building to building and was simply musing on a subject that was of no real interest to him or the company as a whole. He had even less interest in the ensuing report. What disconcerted him most? Not only had a senior engineer wasted three weeks conducting the research and writing the report, but five levels of management had taken their time to review the document and sign off on it.

What happened here? There was no process in place to document what was perceived as a project need nor a way to confirm that the mango tree project was approved. In addition, our two engineers had no sense of their other work as compared to this new endeavor. In other words, there was no project portfolio management system in place.

For years, quality management was a key initiative. Quality meant "doing things right." Portfolio management is "doing the right things."

CHAPTER OVERVIEW

When multiple projects are vying for approval and for a limited pool of resources, the discipline of project management can become almost impossible to manage. The portfolio management process restores manageability by providing an organization with a consistent evaluation method that can be applied objectively to each proposed project. Implementing a portfolio management process offers a variety of benefits. Project requesters, otherwise known as proponents of projects, are able to develop better and more appropriate corporate-level project proposals. The Project Review Board, which acts as a selection/prioritization committee, spends significantly less time evaluating unworthy projects. And once the projects are evaluated, the proponents know precisely why their projects were accepted or rejected. Most significantly, the Project Review Board can make careful objective decisions based on the project's merits rather than on the implied urgency of the project, the strength of the proponent's political allies, or the *issue du jour*.

This chapter deals with the five key processes in portfolio management: (1) solicitation, (2) selection, (3) prioritization, (4) registration, and (5) resource allocation. We begin by exploring the up-front phase of how each project starts: An idea is crystallized into a proposal or business case (solicitation). The initiator or proponent then presents the business case to the powers-that-be and receives (or is denied) an approval to proceed (selection). If approved, the project is prioritized relative to other projects (prioritization), and the basic information concerning the approved project is entered into a portfolio database (registration). Lastly, the resource pool available across the entire enterprise is allocated to the projects that are highest on the priority list until no further internal resources are available (resource allocation). If the pool of resources does not accommodate all the projects on the priority list, business decisions are made concerning external resource acquisition or reprioritization of the projects in the queue.

The five-process generic model presented in this chapter can be used by small or large organizations in dealing with internal and/or external project clients. All five processes of portfolio management can be performed formally or informally.

In any exploration of portfolio management, it is important to remember one assumption: Successful enterprise project management is predicated on accurate single-project planning. In other words, if each of the projects within the enterprise is not ultimately planned accurately and managed proactively, the portfolio management process will not create a miracle and make a failing enterprise suddenly successful.

At the end of this chapter, there are two Performance Support Tools. The first, Performance Support Tool 7.1 is a five-page form to follow in order to create the business case produced out of the solicitation process. The second, Performance Support Tool 7.2, is a selection/prioritization criteria list consisting of 33 potential evaluation criteria upon which proposed projects can be selected and ultimately prioritized. These Performance Support Tools are available for download at www.pmsi-pm.com.

Before reading the rest of this chapter, you may want to complete the Assessment Tool at the end of the chapter. This assessment will help you evaluate your organization's strengths and weaknesses in the management of its portfolio of projects.

THE SOLICITATION PROCESS

If a runner doesn't come off the starting line strong, he or she has less chance of coming in a winner. The *Project Management Book of Knowledge (PMBOK)* identifies the starting line of the project life cycle as initiation and defines it as "committing the organization to begin a project phase."[1] In essence, the business case or project proposal for doing the work is created during this initiation phase of the project. As shown in Figure 7.1, this part of the portfolio management process primarily documents ideas so that selection and prioritization decisions can be made in the next two processes.

Solicitation involves documenting the premises on which the expectations of the customer will be based. Examples of these premises include:

1. What are we producing?
2. What justifies the production of this deliverable?
3. For whom are we producing the deliverable?
4. What are the project parameters, particularly in time and cost targets?

More important than the resulting document is the discussion in which the project players reach agreement on the above points. After analysis and logical thinking, the information from this dialogue gets translated into the business case document.

Before beginning the solicitation process, those participating should have a sense of the following:

- Project selection process—Who will review it and how long will it take to get a decision?
- Appeals process—Will there be an appeal process and if so, what is it?
- Consistent format, layout, and content—Which sections will be required to be included in the business case?
- Mode of submittal—Will the business case need to be submitted only in writing or will the proponent be asked to present personally in front of the Project Review Board?

Figure 7.1   Translating Ideas into a Business Case

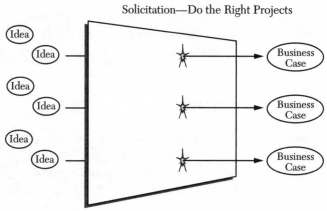

Solicitation—Do the Right Projects

- Specific criteria—What will be the requirements for approving and ultimately prioritizing the project?

After these processes and requirements are known, six steps must be taken to start a project correctly. These steps are the essence of the solicitation process of portfolio management. Management should oversee this process. It must be done thoroughly and completely; if it is not, management must require it to be done again until it is acceptable. The six steps are:

1. Identify and define a high-level statement of work.
2. Define the business justification for the project.
3. Clearly identify all critical stakeholders and their low-level needs and expectations, including the boundaries for the project's budget, duration, and risk.
4. Describe the team infrastructure.
5. Add optional sections and finalize the business case.
6. Map the business case against the evaluation criteria as defined in the selection process in order for the proponent to decide whether to move the project to the selection process.

These steps are presented in Figure 7.2 as a series of six loops in a solicitation spiral: (1) high-level expectations, (2) justification, (3) low-level expectations, (4) infrastructure, (5) optional items, and (6) decision to submit.

The work efforts suggested for each loop in the solicitation spiral are described here in detail. Each organization, however, must tailor the process to its own unique way of doing business.

Loop 1: High-Level Expectations

After noting preliminary discussions with the proponent and any documentation already created or acquired from previous similar projects, *confirm in writing the high-level expectations of the customer,* which should include:

- *Background of this project.* Includes a problem/opportunity statement and strategic alignment with organizational goals and other organizational initiatives. A reason for the initiation of the project at this time—a business need, a customer request, technological advances, or a legal or regulatory requirement—may be included.
- *High-level description of the project's outcome or deliverable.* Describes what the product or service will look like and/or be able to do.
- *Identification of the three project clients.* The primary client provides direction, makes decisions, and serves as the champion of the project.

Figure 7.2   The Solicitation Spiral

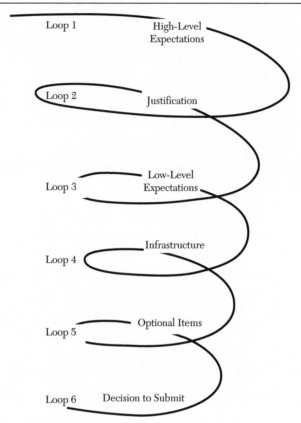

The operational client is the "end-user" of the product or service after is has been created. The strategic client ensures that projects are aligned to long-term organizational goals and that money to fund the project is spent wisely.

- *Strategy for creating the deliverable.* Lists any alternative approaches plus a recommendation (or a process to reach a recommendation).
- *Targeted completion date.* Pinpoints the goal for completing the project and a rationale for that date.
- *Targeted budget dollars.* Presents the budget goal.
- *Areas of unacceptable risk for the proponent.* Defines areas of the business, the product, or the project that could put this endeavor in jeopardy.
- *Suggested priority of this project in relation to all other organizational projects.* Without performing the next stage in this portfolio management

process, suggests that the project should be considered as high, medium, or low priority and why.

- *Delineated constraints.* Defines what has been predetermined versus what the manager of the project can determine alone. For example, one constraint might be that the software must be purchased rather than developed internally.
- *Surface assumptions.* Articulates the presumed givens on which many decisions will be based. An assumption might be that the resources would be made available as need.

To complete this section, refer to Performance Support Tool 7.1, page 1, at the end of this chapter.

Loop 2: Justification

After confirming these high-level expectations, use the following cost/benefit techniques to *justify the project from a business perspective.* Justification of a project may be tangible or intangible.

Tangible

- *Document tangible benefits*—expressed as dollar savings and/or dollar revenue.
- *Estimate developmental costs*—for internal and/or out-of-pocket dollars.
- *Estimate recurring or ongoing costs*—for internal and/or out-of-pocket dollars.
- *Calculate an appropriate breakeven point, ROI (return on investment) and/or IRR (internal rate of return).*

Intangible

- *Document intangible benefits*—those that have no dollar value but are highly desirable; for instance, "better employee morale."
- *Define future opportunities*—those that will be possible when this project is implemented.

To complete this section, refer to Performance Support Tool 7.1, page 2, at the end of this chapter.

Loop 3: Low-Level Expectations

Given the confirmed high-level expectations and the business justification, *identify the detailed or low-level expectations for all the stakeholders in the project.*

This part of the business case is divided into three parts: (1) definition of requirements, (2) more detailed information concerning the triple constraint of schedule, budget, and quality; and (3) identification of specific risks.

Requirements

- *Cursory list of mandatory versus optional requirements*—present a list of requirements; differentiate, in specific, definitive terms, those that are mandatory and optional to the success of the project.
- *Exclusion*—state requirements to be excluded from this project.

Triple Constraint

Quality

- *Success criteria*—specify the technical performance (quality standards) on which the deliverable will be measured.
- *Completion criteria*—pinpoint precisely what needs to be delivered, such as a fully tested system.

Schedule

- *Stakeholder's target completion date*—state a time target for completion that is consistent with the time specified in the statement of work in Loop 1. Express it as a specific date (month/day/year), a range of dates (6 to 9 months), or a specific quarter and year (third quarter, 2002). Include a milestone chart (a schedule for each phase/milestone), as appropriate.

Budget

- *Anticipated budget*—include an acceptable plus-or-minus tolerance; estimated labor and nonlabor costs; plus any contingency funds and/or management reserves, if negotiated.

For each of the triple constraint parameters, also estimate your confidence level for each of your approximations and the consequences, if any, if your approximations prove to be inaccurate.

Identification of Specific Risks

- *Risk identification*—articulate the risks relative to the development of the product or service, and/or the schedule, and/or the assignment of resources.

To complete this section, refer to Performance Support Tool 7.1, page 3, at the end of this chapter.

Loop 4: Infrastructure

Using knowledge of the organization's culture, clarify *the makeup and relationship of the members of the project team:*

Project Manager

- *Role of the manager of the project*—include accountabilities and authority (formal and informal).
- *Percentage of the manager of the project's time*—specify the percentage (or hours) of time that the manager of the project has available for this project.

PM Performance Management System

- *Performance improvement process*—establish the process that will be in place to evaluate the contribution of the manager of the project and the project team, relative to this project.
- *Performance development process*—establish the process for improving the manager of the project's and the project team members' project management competencies while working on this project.

Project Client

- *Role of the project client (sponsor)*—define the role of the "owner of the project" as it relates to the manager and to the leadership of this project, his or her formal and informal authority and time committed to the project.

Team Skills

- *Major skills*—enumerate the expertise required in the project team and whether that skill will be acquired from internal departments or external sources.
- *Skill gaps*—indicate what skills, if any cannot be filled internally or from known external sources.
- *Type of team structure*—suggest an appropriate team structure—for example, a weak part-time matrix, or a stronger full-time project team.

To complete this section, refer to Performance Support Tool 7.1, page 4, at the end of this chapter.

Loop 5: Optional Items

Taking all the information in Loops 1 through 4, finalize the business case document. Add any of the following, if appropriate:

- *Proposed external supplier relationships*—detail who from outside the organization will be involved in the project, such as contractors, vendors, independent consultants, and their relationship, such as strategic alliance or supplier.
- *Proposed internal relationships*—detail interactions with other departments, division, and subsidiaries.
- *Communications plan*—include the purpose, mode, recipients, and frequency of communications.
- *Change control process*—describe how to request a change, how to analyze the impact of the change, and how to obtain approval for the additional funds and/or time needed to implement the change.
- *Issues management*—explain how issues/problems will be isolated, tracked, and resolved.
- *Post-project review plan*—discuss the metrics to be applied, the types of information to be collected, and the methods of assembling and organizing the information so that preparation of the lessons learned is expedited at the end of the project.
- *Methodology*—choose a project management methodology and/or a product development methodology, if appropriate.
- *Risk management plan*—include risk identification, risk abatement planning, and risk monitoring.

To complete this section, refer to Performance Support Tool 7.1, page 5, at the end of this chapter.

Loop 6: Decision to Submit

By the end of the solicitation process, the proponent(s) of the project will have generated the business case as described. In some cases, by performing a mock selection process against the published evaluation criteria, the proponent(s) may realize that their project will never clear the selection hurdle. In other cases, the proponent(s) may realize that even if the project does get through the selection process, it will be so low on the priority list that it will never be allocated the resources to do the job. The proponent(s) may then decide not to present the project for consideration. If this is the situation, the decision not to move forward will save time and effort for those who are selecting and prioritizing projects.

If, however, after going through the mock selection process, the proponent(s) believe that their project is justified, they will move the project into the selection process.

THE SELECTION PROCESS

The Project Review Board becomes the decision-making committee during the selection process. This group of people should represent a cross section of management. Specifically, they should include top managers representing each of the functional areas within the organization. Their job is to select and prioritize each project that goes through the portfolio management system.

An alternative approach to the Project Review Board is to put the proposed project through a tiered progression. With this approach, the proponent's department or division management must approve the project *before* it goes to the top-management selection group. As shown in Figure 7.3, this results in fewer projects from which to select because these projects will have gone through a justification filter. This fuller process of winnowing projects for review saves top management time and effort.

What Happens Overall during the Selection Process?

The Project Review Board performs three jobs. First, it reviews and discusses the proponents' solicitation document (i.e., the business case). In some organizations, the proponent is asked to appear before the Board and present the case on behalf of the proposed project. This process can be iterative; the decision makers may then ask for additional information. Usually, however, clear criteria minimize this type of request.

Second, the Project Review Board evaluates the projects under consideration, using the predefined criteria checklist (see Performance Support Tool 7.2 at the end of this chapter). The checklist is used to consider each project's value relative not only to its financial justification but also to its impact on the staff, other projects, and marketplace image, as well as on the overall synergy with the organization's strategic (i.e., plan). In effect, these evaluation criteria determine how the Board will select the projects for approval. Tangible data, such as financial benefits versus financial costs, resource requirements, or technological constraints, are always considered in the selection process.

Finally, the Project Review Board either approves or does not approve the project. If the project is not approved, the decision-making group must give

Figure 7.3   The Filtering Effect of the Selection Process

Selection—Stop the Wrong Ones

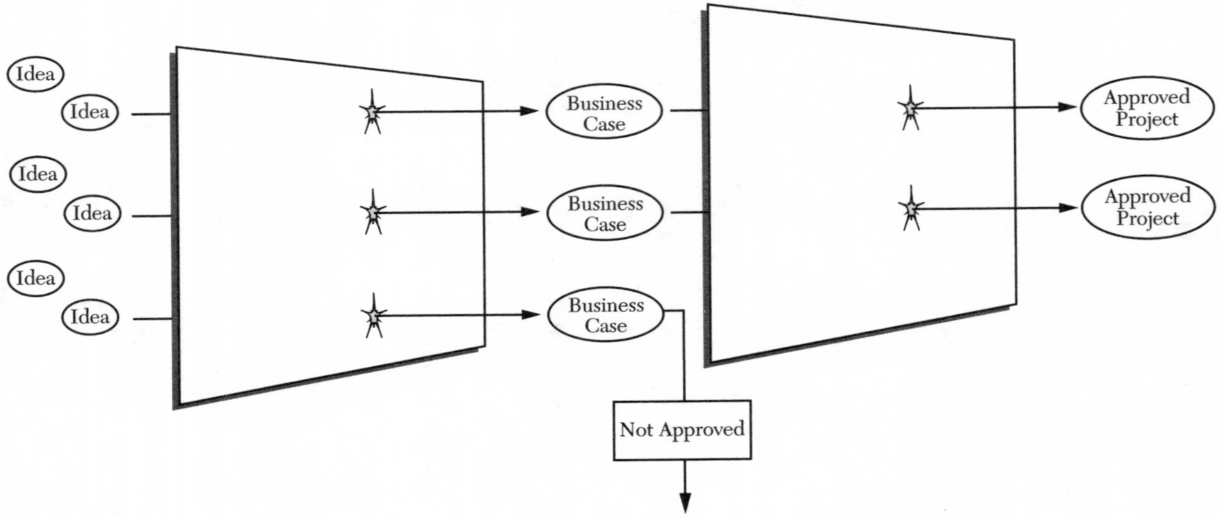

the proponent reasons for the denial. In some organizations, proponents have an appeal process that allows them to escalate their case to another group for a final decision.

Guidelines for the Selection Process

Before the selection process begins, the project management community should be aware of these three guidelines:

1. Protocols must be established and rigorously followed. Making exceptions in favor of or against any particular project is unfair for other projects being reviewed.
2. Proponents who enter the process must understand that their project will be evaluated on its merits, not on the basis of their emotional desire to "win." They need to recognize that their project may not be selected.
3. The Project Review Board must focus on the larger picture of organizational good and must put aside any smaller concerns of their own personal functional area.

Criteria with Scoring Models and Guideline Questions

In Performance Support Tool 7.2 at the end of this chapter, the sample list of 33 criteria is divided into two basic filters:

1. *Watershed* criteria: Three questions that may eliminate projects for consideration.
2. *Ranking criteria:* Nine categories (with 33 subcategories) that prioritize projects according to the scores assigned them.

Filter 1: Watershed Criteria

Watershed criteria constitute a filter that stops totally unacceptable projects from proceeding through the process. For each project, the Project Review Board performs this watershed analysis first. The scoring for watershed criteria is simply pass or fail, but the Board still needs to discuss the details of that decision and reach consensus.

The following three criteria are applied to all projects to eliminate them from further consideration if they fail.

The Watershed Test.   The project is rejected if it:

1. Doesn't fit the corporate mission,
2. Doesn't promote one or more corporate strategies, or
3. Conflicts with the organization's values.

Stated conventionally, the watershed criteria are as follows:

1. Does the project fit the corporate mission? (Yes = Passes; No = Fails)
2. Does the project promote one or more corporate strategies? (Yes = Passes; No = Fails)
3. Does the project conflict with any of the corporate values? (Yes = Fails; No = Passes)

 Criterion 2 above can be waived if the project "promotes" corporate strategies through its relationship with another project.

Filter 2: Ranking Criteria

Ranking criteria are applied to projects that have survived the watershed gauntlet. The criteria are broken into nine categories: (1) organizational factors, (2) cost/benefit, (3) customer satisfaction, (4) relationships with stakeholders, (5) uncertainty of definition, (6) technical uncertainty, (7) risk, (8) cultural change, and (9) impact. Table 7.1 shows the criteria within each of the nine categories used in the evaluation of projects that have passed the watershed test.

Each organization's list of criteria might differ in some respects from the example above. What is important, however, is that the criteria list is developed and serves as the *consistent* basis on which projects are evaluated, selected, and prioritized.

Four General Scoring Models

Four possible scoring models can be used to measure the various criteria shown above: (1) the effect model, (2) the fit model, (3) the impact model, and (4) the financial model.

For each scoring model, we offer a description of the model and an example that includes sample questions that need to be asked when evaluating this criterion.

Model 1: The Effect Model

This one-dimensional model looks at the overall effect a criterion will have. This model ranks criteria on a scale of 1 to 5, with 3 as a neutral point, 5 as a strongly positive score, and 1 as a strongly negative score:

5 Strongly enhances . . .
4 Enhances . . .
3 Has no apparent effect on . . .

Table 7.1   Ranking Criteria for Project Selection/Prioritization

Category	Criteria
1. Organizational factors	A. Strategic importance B. Market demand relative to strategy C. Benefits to the enterprise D. Synergy with other projects E. Organization's capabilities
2. Cost/benefit analysis	A. Internal rate of return (IRR) B. Payback period C. Annual rate of return (ARR) D. Costs: Lost opportunity E. Costs: Compliance penalties F. Costs: Degree of commitments G. Benefits: Supports current line(s) of business H. Benefits: Quality improvement potential I. Benefits: Employee morale
3. Customer satisfaction	A. Incremental impact to customer satisfaction
4. Stakeholder relations	A. Effect on relations with community B. Effect on relations with suppliers C. Effect on relations with board of directors D. Effect on relations with partners/competitors E. Effect on relations with employees
5. Uncertainty of definition	A. Solidity of requirements
6. Technical uncertainty	A. New skills are/are not required B. Specific equipment/hardware are/are not now available C. Software capabilities are/are not now available D. New technology may/may not need to be developed
7. Risk	A. Technical complexity B. Lack of control C. Regulatory environment D. Predictability of market demand
8. Cultural change	A. Change the organization will need to assimilate
9. Impact	A. Magnitude of corporate cultural change B. Impact on existing projects C. Impact on corporate image

2 Has an adverse effect on . . .

1 Has a strong adverse effect on . . .

The following example uses this model to determine the effects on relations with third-party suppliers ("Stakeholder Relations").

Example

Category: Stakeholder Relations

Criterion: Effect on relations with suppliers

Sample Questions: After you determine who the suppliers are, you can use this model to evaluate questions like these: How does the project help the suppliers serve customers? Does it increase supplier loyalty? Does the project create win-win opportunities? Does it promote the quality of partnerships?

5 Strongly enhances relations with suppliers

4 Enhances relations with suppliers

3 Has no apparent effect on relations with suppliers

2 Adversely affects relations with suppliers

1 Results in a strong adverse effect on relations with suppliers

Model 2: The Fit Model

This model looks at how a criterion will fit into a larger picture. It usually relates to issues of strategy. Model 2 is another one-dimensional method of ranking criteria, this time on a shorter scale of 1 to 3 or 4; 3 or 4 is a strongly positive number, and 1 is a neutral score.

4 Strong fit

3 Some fit

2 Minimal fit

1 No fit

The example below uses this model to determine the synergy of the project being evaluated with other projects already approved under the category of "Strategy."

Example

Category: Strategy

Criterion: Synergy with other projects

Sample Questions: How does this project affect other existing or planned projects? Are there economies of scale to be gained by partnering this project with another planned or existing project?

4 Provides significant positive effect on multiple projects
3 Provides significant positive effect on one project
2 Provides some positive effect on one or more projects
1 Provides no synergy with any other project

Model 3: The Impact Model

This model reveals the degree of impact across two dimensions. This model is a two-dimensional matrix. A two-dimensional model is a comparison of two variables, one shown on the x-axis and the other on the y-axis. Each variable is graded from not positive to positive. As the two variables are compared, the weaker combination creates a lower score than a combination of variables that are more positive. Below is a sample of this type of model.

Extent of Impact		Likelihood of Occurrence		
	Medium/Large	3	4	5
	Small/Medium	2	3	4
	None/Small	1	2	3
		None/Slight	Reasonable/Slight	Reasonable/Good

The example that follows attempts to evaluate the predictability of the demand for the product/service within the current marketplace. This criterion falls under the "Risk" category.

Example

Category: Risk

Criterion: Predictability of market demand

Sample Questions: What is the demand for the project's product? What is your evidence for this demand? You should state the demand for the product in quantifiable terms when presenting the evidence.

Extent of Demand for Identified Deliverable		Evidence		
	High Demand	2	4	5
	Medium Demand	1	3	4
	Low Demand	1	1	2
		Anecdotal	Moderate	Conclusive

Model 4: The Financial Model

This model performs financial calculations to arrive at a cost/benefit justification. The example below is used to score the cost of investment and maintenance, the income and profitability—all to determine the Annual Rate of Return (ARR).

The sample project's projected cost is $75,000 with a return of $82,000 in revenue or savings over a three-year period. Thus, the ARR is approximately 3 percent. The project would score a 2 on this criterion.

Example

Category: Cost/Benefit

Criterion: Annual Rate of Return

Sample Questions: What is the total cost? What is the total project revenue or cost saving? What is the profit or net cost savings?
First, let's calculate the Annual Rate of Return for this project.

	Year 1	Year 2	Year 3	Total
Investment	<50,000>	0	0	<50,000>
Maintenance	<5,000>	<5,000>	<15,000>	<25,000>
Income	2,000	50,000	30,000	82,000
Total Costs	<75,000>			
Total Revenue	82,000			
Profit	7,000			

Annual Rate of Return (ARR) = (Profit/Cost) / Years
= (7,000 / 75,000) / 3 = 3%

Now that we have determined that the Annual Rate of Return for this project is 3 percent, let's see whether it scores greater than 3 in this subcategory, which is what is expected by the organization to be viable.

5 ≥ 15% ARR
4 10%–14% ARR
3 6%–9% ARR
2 3%–5% ARR
1 ≤ 3% ARR

As you can see, an Annual Rate of Return of 3 percent scores a 2, which is not great.

REMINDER   A full list of possible criteria and associated scoring models is provided in the Performance Support Tool 7.2 at the end of this chapter. The list illustrates how each criterion is graded or scored. The result is a quantitative, objective selection/priority ranking, rather than a qualitative, subjective opinion.

Measurements achieved through this type of scoring process significantly benefit the organization. They allow managers from various disciplines to work together as a team as they objectively evaluate the worth of the multiple projects that are being proposed.

THE PRIORITIZATION PROCESS

The selection process is only the first hurdle. The next hurdle involves getting the approved projects prioritized at a high enough level so they will get the resources that are needed to complete the project.

Multiple projects must be prioritized relative to the strategic long-range direction of the entire organization. This prioritization is required as soon as the project passes through the selection filter described above. The prioritization process positions the newly approved project relative to other projects. In a multiproject environment, the prioritization process becomes even more critical because each project tends to compete for resources as though it was the single most important project. Furthermore, people often move in and out of projects, and the scope and budget frequently change. Some factors of change are internal and some are external, but the one constant is that priorities do shift. Therefore, a periodic reevaluation process, preferably based on mathematical metrics or standards, is needed.

The prioritization process employs the same criteria that are used in the selection process. The Project Review Board has already evaluated each project relative to a predefined criteria checklist. Each criterion on the list has a quantifiable rating or score attached to it. The Board now needs to review the scoring from the selection effort to ensure that it has remained constant. As shown in Figure 7.4, the scores from each criteria are totaled, and the sum indicates the placement of the new project relative to other projects being considered and current projects that have been prioritized, whether under way or in the queue.

The relative weighting of one criterion to another might also be considered. In Figure 7.5, each of the criteria has been weighted. In this

Figure 7.4 Scoring in the Prioritization Process

Prioritization—In the Right Order

Approved Project	Project Sponsor	Evaluation Criteria				Priority
		Cost/ Benefit	Market Demand	Project Synergy	Supplier Relations	
_____	_____			X		4
_____	_____	X				1
_____	_____		X	X	X	3
_____	_____		X			7
_____	_____	X		X		2
_____	_____		X		X	5
_____	_____	X				6

example, the "synergy with other projects" criterion has been weighted by a factor of 4 thus making it more important than the other two criterion.

After the numbers have been run, the Board looks at the new project priority list and verifies that the new list makes good business sense. All the possible intangible, nonquantifiable variables that need to be taken into consideration are considered. These decision makers have the right to modify the priority list, but they should only do so if they (1) are doing it from a strictly objective business perspective and (2) have every intention of adhering to these modified priorities.

Figure 7.5 Sample of Weighted Project Criteria

Weighting Ranking Criteria

Projects	Relations with Suppliers		Synergy with Other Projects		Predictability with Market Demand		Total
	Score (2)	Weighting	Score (4)	Weighting	Score (3)	Weighting	
Project A	1	2	2	8	1	3	13
Project B	4	8	3	12	4	12	32
Project C	3	6	2	8	1	3	17

THE REGISTRATION PROCESS

After they are merged and prioritized the projects are registered in the enterprise project database (see Figure 7.6). The following information might be input for each project in the project database:

- Assigned project ID number
- Designated project client or champion (who may or may not be the proponent)
- Record of all current project players—their department, telephone and e-mail numbers, and other pertinent details
- The project charter or the statement of work
- Reconfirmation of the project's priority position
- Date approved

This database file then becomes the core record of high-level information concerning the project. Some organizations also include other data fields in this file, including, for example, the criteria in which the projects rated particularly high and low. Some firms then compare the highs and lows for all current projects, sometimes even matching them against the scores of completed projects. Other organizations document who was on the Project Review Board.

The primary multiple-project problem across the enterprise is, most clearly, competition for resources and management attention. Decisions made by the Project Review Board will direct functional managers and managers of projects in their efforts to effectively allocate the organization's limited supply of resources by focusing attention on the most critical needs and priorities. Although this process won't solve all of an organization's challenges, it can avoid political infighting, save time, and minimize uncertainty and frustration for project participants at all levels.

Figure 7.6   The Registration Process

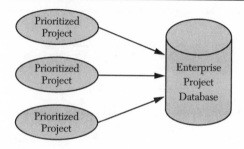

THE RESOURCE ALLOCATION PROCESS

Functional managers "own" the resources. Managers of projects need to "contract" the functional managers' resources in order to get their projects completed. It becomes a push and pull to satisfy both the functional managers' day-to-day operational requirements and those of the managers who are running multiple projects.

Even after a cross-functional matrix organization is implemented and a selection/priority-setting process has been established, multiple projects are not necessarily guaranteed success. If the resources are not available, or the resources that are available have been committed to more work than they can complete, the jobs will not get done no matter what the project database might say. (See Figure 7.7.)

Figure 7.7   Problems if There Is No Resource Planning Process

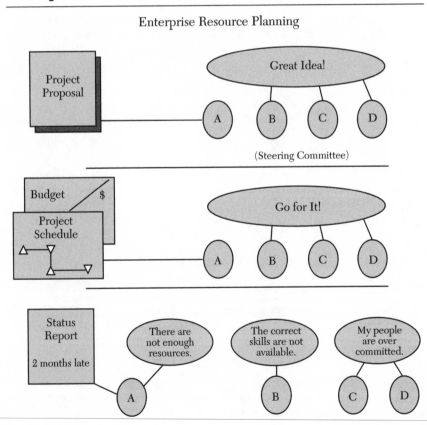

Let's look at a technique to allocate individual resources to multiple tasks possibly across multiple projects during a single time frame and then look at what to do if a resource is over- or undercommitted. When we understand the analytical process, we can consider the best person to analyze resource allocations in a multiple-project environment.

Resource Loading

Resource loading determines the commitment of each resource per task and calculates the total commitment of each resource working on parallel efforts in the same time frame. Given these data, it is relatively easy to determine whether any resource is over- or undercommitted in terms of hours available to work on project-related efforts.

The resource allocation process first calculates the individual effort person by person. This is done by dividing a person's estimate of the effort that will be given to a particular task by the duration of that task. The calculation spreads this individual's effort allocation equally over the duration of the task. The allocation of effort is posted on the corresponding task on the Gantt schedule chart. Then, adding each time window (day, week, or month) determines the total effort committed by each individual. If there is over- or underloading—that is, if the individual's effort allocation is greater or less than the time available—a technique called resource leveling needs to be performed.

Resource Leveling

As summarized in Table 7.2 (and further explored in Chapter 8, "Project Planning"), the following techniques resolve any over- or underloading of resources:

1. Reschedule a noncritical task within its float time, to shift the allocation of effort into a time window that will resolve the problem but not cause an over- or underloading problem with any other resource working on that same task in that same time window.
2. Extend the duration of a noncritical task into its float time, to lower the resource's allocation on a per-unit-of-time basis.
3. Instead of spreading the effort equally across the task, assign the resource unequally over the duration of the task, being sure that the resource has scheduled the total amount of effort required before the task ends.

Table 7.2   Resource-Leveling Options

	Option	Caveat
1	Move task into the float, finding a window resolving the overloading . . .	being sure not to overload any other resource(s)
2	Extend duration of the task (within its available float) to decrease individual commitment . . .	see caveat for Option 1 and never beyond the Late Finish date
3	Allocate effort nonlinearly over the task . . .	keeping minimal commitment if they are to return later in the project
4	Off-load the effort to someone else who has available time . . .	and the right skill mix
5	Break dependencies, either starting sooner or ending later . . .	accepting the business risk
6	Add people, overtime, technology, and so on . . .	accepting the increase to the budget
7	Reduce scope or push out project end date . . .	if the client agrees

Note: The PMBOK refers to the limiting constraints (i.e., caveats) as resource leveling heuristics.

4. Offload the assignment to another team member who has the correct skills and has time available.

These four techniques for resource leveling are just a few of those available. Other techniques might include hiring additional resources, reducing the scope of the project, and/or pushing out the deadline of one or several tasks that may delay the completion of one or several projects.

Now that we have begun to consider methods of allocating resources and resolving overcommitments, we should consider who is the correct person to acquire this information and resolve these problems in a multiproject environment. Should it be a centralized management group, the resource manager, or the team members themselves?

Who Analyzes Resource Allocations in an Enterprise-Wide Project Management Environment?

There are various alternative ways to compile resource allocation data in a multiproject organization. All of the ways described below can be supported by a project management software package with multiproject capabilities. The key question is: Who should assume accountability for performing this analysis? The following three options emerge.

1. Roll-up by Project Office or Project Review Board

The Project Office or the Project Review Board accumulates all the individual project plans that have been resource-loaded and resource-leveled. Then these individual project plans are rolled up into a consolidated resource management plan. The overloading and underloading problems are isolated and solved on a resource-by-resource basis, using the resource leveling techniques described earlier.

2. Roll-up by Functional Area

For each individual resource, the resource manager who owns that resource prepares an integrated multiproject resource plan, determines any problems associated with the people working in his or her area, and negotiates with the respective managers of projects to resolve any over- or underloading.

3. Roll-up by Project Team Member

Each team member analyzes his or her workload and determines whether a personal overload or underload exists. Members who are overcommitted or undercommitted negotiate with either their resource manager or their manager of projects, depending on how the politics of their matrix organization dictate.

In an enterprise-wide project management environment, who should analyze resource allocations? The choice depends on the type of matrix organization that is in place. If a Project Office or a Project Review Board exists, it is appropriate to use option 1.

If the functional areas see themselves as pools of resources that support projects within the organization, the functional manager should assume the responsibility. If neither of these descriptions applies, the project team member, for his or her own survival, needs to figure it out and ask for clarification of priorities if over- or underloading has occurred.

Did you notice that, in the above logic, the manager of the project was not one of the people pinpointed to assume accountability for this effort? Why? Because the manager of the project does not have access to data enumerating what each team member is committed to accomplish for other projects and in his or her day-to-day operational job. The manager of the project must rely on any or all of the above to ensure that resources are available when he or she needs them.

Project management software supports the resource loading and leveling analysis. Products that support multiproject analysis accomplish that end in various ways. Some ask the project planner to set up the multiple projects as though they are subprojects of a mammoth whole. Other products allow the planner to integrate multiple projects, one at a time, juxtaposing each new one with the current project. The software accumulates the aggregate number of resources required by all the projects and indicates overloading situations. With some programs, to resolve the overloading, the planner must put away the current project, call up the other project(s) that require rescheduling, and then change the resource assignment or allocations as necessary. Other products allow multiple projects to reside concurrently in memory and to be modified as required.

Multiple-project control differs from single project management principally in the management of resources. In the planning phase, resources must be loaded into each single project by an individual and then rolled up to ensure that there are enough resources to satisfy every project, with no overloading or underloading of any one resource or resource pool. While the work is in progress, the manager of the project must be sure that the resources are being provided as promised and must track and manipulate the resources to keep the loading level as planned.

So far in this chapter, we have examined the five processes in a portfolio management system: (1) solicitation, (2) selection, (3) prioritization, (4) registration, and (5) resource allocation. Next, we provide an implementation plan to kick off the portfolio management system within your organization.

MAKING IT YOUR OWN—AN IMPLEMENTATION PLAN

Every organization is different. Each has a unique political culture into which this portfolio management process must be assimilated. Therefore, the implementation plan needs to be designed and orchestrated very carefully. The following description of a portfolio management implementation plan can be used as a springboard or a model for any organization, in any industry, to develop its own unique process.

Eight Steps in Establishing a Portfolio Management System

We suggest the following distinct steps to design and implement a process:

1. Establish a top-management Project Review Board.
2. Identify and empower the right working committee to develop the portfolio management process.

3. Brainstorm and categorize the evaluation criteria.
4. Develop scoring models for criteria.
5. Identify a short list of watershed criteria.
6. Develop a weighting scheme for the criteria.
7. Submit two proposals for a trial run through the new procedure.
8. Develop project solicitation/prioritization guidelines for future project requests.

Let's look at each step in detail.

1. Establish a Top-Management Project Review Board

The Project Review Board supports a positive enterprise-wide project environment in a larger sense as Board members agree on overall project selection and prioritization. During the portfolio management process, this Board, using the key priority factors relevant to the unique corporation/agency, evaluates each new project against criteria for assigning values (or scores) for each factor, and then assigns each project priority-values depending on the consensus of the group.

Project selection priorities must be set at a high enough level in the organization to have impact and meaning for affected departments. The Board's goal is to assess projects. Board members need to see whether proposed projects are viable. If they are, they prioritize them relative to other projects competing for the same resource pool.

Members of the Project Review Board must be senior decision makers and must agree to meet on a regular basis—typically, monthly or at least quarterly. It is important that the people chosen to participate on this Board are truly committed to active participation in the committee.

2. Identify and Empower the Right Working Committee to Develop the Portfolio Management System

The Project Review Board decides on the composition of the working committee. This committee should be comprised of representatives from both the community that will be proposing new projects and the group that will ultimately be evaluating projects employing this portfolio management system. Management must give this new working team the authority and responsibility to develop and roll out the process. The operative word in the previous sentence is *authority*. This effort will not be successful if top management refutes and changes the decisions that the working committee makes. The committee needs to feel empowered and supported by the management group and should be assured that what it produces will be used with only minor modifications.

In essence, this working committee is chartered to establish selection/priority standards—criteria, scoring, and priority values—to which all can agree.

3. Brainstorm and Categorize the Evaluation Criteria

The working committee's first job is to establish the categories on which projects will be evaluated. Conducting prescheduled meetings is the best way to ensure that the participants actually participate. And working off-site is the best way to stay focused. Let's put it this way: Run this endeavor as you would any project. Put a plan together and then work toward the plan. In some cases, an outside facilitator can be helpful in keeping side conversations to a minimum and breaking up any bottlenecks that delay making appropriate decisions.

During these sessions, the working team will generate all the relevant categories of criteria that it feels should be included in the evaluation of corporate-level projects. Starting with a boilerplate model, such as the one presented in Performance Support Tool 7.2 at the end of this chapter, can be helpful. Remember that there are nine categories in this model: (1) Organizational Factors, (2) Cost/Benefit Analysis, (3) Customer Satisfaction, (4) Stakeholder Relations, (5) Uncertainty of Definition, (6) Technical Uncertainty, (7) Risk, (8) Cultural Change, and (9) Impact. When the list has been completed, the major subcategories of evaluation need to be reviewed. The working sessions may produce more or fewer of these major categories, and the categories may be differently named as well. However, grouping the criteria into categories helps to clarify their intent, eliminates duplicates, amalgamates some entries, and identifies missing criteria that need to be added to the list.

4. Develop Scoring Models for Criteria

After the categories of evaluation are determined, the working committee needs to establish meaningful, quantitative values or scores for each criterion—all within the larger picture of corporate long-range goals. The committee chooses the scoring models that it considers most appropriate for each of the criteria. (Possible scoring models are described earlier in the Selection Process section. They include the Effect Model, the Fit Model, the Impact Model, and the Financial Model.)

It is appropriate to develop guideline questions to help the project proponent think through the issue and to help the Review Board score the project. These guideline questions are also included in the criteria listed in Performance Support Tool 7.2, at the end of this chapter. Together, all the criteria provide a solid checklist for each proposed project as it goes through the selection/prioritization process. If the process is followed correctly, the whole enterprise scheme of multiple projects is scored, selected, and prioritized in order to choose those projects that will have the most beneficial impact on the organization. Apportioned weights are then assigned to the individual criterion. Lastly, all criteria categories, criterion, and weightings must be examined to ensure that the values correctly reflect the organizational vision and goals.

Of particular importance in establishing project priorities is balancing comparative, quantitative scores with nonquantifiable information. Project scores developed within this process can be used not only for project selection but also for determining the project with the highest priority when several projects occur simultaneously. This balanced process ensures that decisions are not based solely on numeric scores. Part of the prioritizing may be based on gut feelings and past experiences. True consensus also needs to be reached among the members of the Project Review Board. Therefore, the roles and responsibilities of the Board are critical in weighting all these factors.

5. Identify a Short List of Watershed Criteria

This list of watershed criteria should prevent unworthy projects from reaching the more specific evaluations in the rest of the model. If a proposal fails any one of these watershed tests, the proposal is rejected without further evaluation. (Refer to the Selection Process section, and review the recommended watershed criteria.)

6. Develop a Weighting Scheme for the Criteria

The working committee provides a total relative weight to the criteria categories, and then apportions weights to individual criterion within the groups. For example, the team might develop a 1,000-point scale and then use a simple spreadsheet with formulas to convert raw scores to weighted scores and to provide a total evaluation score equaling 1,000. Figure 7.8 provides an example of this process.

7. Submit Two Proposals for a Trial Run Through the New Procedure

To test the validity of the system, the working team picks two proposed projects. These should be similar enough so that there is a horse race to determine which is selected and which might have the higher priority. The Project Review Board will evaluate both projects using the portfolio management process. The purpose is to find the ambiguities, contradictions, and mistakes in the new system, not to necessarily provide a final evaluation or selection

Figure 7.8   Sample Project-Scoring Spreadsheet

Criteria	Points	Max Score	Model
Watershed			
• Fit with corporate mission			Pass-Fail
• Promote one or more corporate strategies			Pass-Fail
• Conflict with corporate values			Pass-Fail
Organizational Factors	210		
• Market demand relative to strategy	70	4	2
• Benefits to the enterprise	70	4	2
• Synergy with other projects	70	4	2
Cost/Benefit	285		
Annual rate of return, $	40	5	4
Costs			
• Lost opportunity; $	35	3	2
• Compliance penalties; $	35	5	2
• Previous commitment; $	35	3	2
Benefits			
• To customers (intangible)	35	5	2
• Quality improvement potential	35	3	2
• Supports current line(s) of business	35	5	1
• Employee morale	35	5	1
Risk	175		
• Uncertainty of the Definition	35	5	3
• Technical complexity	35	5	3
• Lack of control —Make versus buy, strategic alliance, suppliers/subcontractors	35	5	3
• Regulatory environment —Political, legal	35	5	3
• Predictability of market demand	35	5	3
Relationships with Stakeholders	180		
• Effect on relations with community	30	5	1
• Effect on relations with suppliers	30	5	1
• Effect on relations with customer	30	5	3
• Effect on relations with Board	30	5	1
• Effect on relations with partners and competitors	30	5	1
• Effect of relations with employees	30	5	1
Impact	60		
• Magnitude of corporate cultural change required	30	5	3
• Impact on existing projects	30	5	1

or priority decision concerning the two submitted proposals. The trial run may unearth severe logic errors and will provide the team an opportunity to refine the process before implementing it.

8. Develop Project Solicitation Guidelines for Future Project Requests

The final step is to develop a comprehensive set of guidelines for the proponent to follow when he or she is presenting a new project proposal or business case. The guidelines provide the following:

- Standard format for all future project proposals
- Schedule of submission and review dates
- Detailed explanation of the selection and prioritization process
- Map or flowchart of the process
- List of the criteria along with their scoring methods and weights

The goal of the solicitation guideline is to ensure that the proponents know how to write a compelling business case and that they understand how their proposal will be evaluated. It is hoped that knowing the process and the criteria will dissuade project proponents from submitting unacceptable proposals.

NOTE The project solicitation guideline document is created *after* the development of the selection/priority criteria, rather than before, because the solicitation document needs to map to the evaluation criteria.

CONCLUSION

We have discussed three key factors that make multiproject management successful in an enterprise project management organization:

1. The project solicitation process must be understood and adhered to.
2. The project selection/priority process needs to be based on objective, quantifiable criteria.
3. Various techniques for allocating resources over these many projects must be considered.

To successfully manage a business system comprised of multiple projects within a matrix organization structure, three key elements must be in place:

1. An organizational design that assumes accountability for managing multiple projects
2. Organizational processes by which projects are selected and priorities are established and reestablished as necessary

3. Available information, generated manually or via a project management software product, that helps to allocate resources properly over all the projects

If these three critical success factors are in place, the portfolio management process can be managed effectively and efficiently within a matrixed environment.

Although we have not implied that this portfolio management system *should* be automated—it could certainly be a manual pencil-and-paper system—it is easy to see how each of these segments *could* be automated. For example, the project proposal from the solicitation phase could be filled out online using a word-processing package. Use Performance Support Tool 7.1 for this purpose. The criteria based on Performance Support Tool 7.2 used to approve/disapprove and prioritize the project in the selection and prioritization phases could be consolidated and calculated using spreadsheet software. The core organizational information concerning the project within the registration process could be resident in a relational database. And the allocation of resources could be loaded and leveled using a project management scheduling program with a powerful multiproject capability. As long as each of these is linked ultimately to the project identification number, we have begun our project knowledge-based system or our automated project notebook.

To support the portfolio management process, organizations should take the following steps:

1. Ensure buy-in to the new process by involving key departments and individuals in its development.
2. Establish a mechanism for communicating priorities to the parts of the organization that are affected by these decisions.
3. Establish a clear understanding, with functional managers and managers of projects, about how these selection/priority decisions are to be used.
4. Establish a mechanism for revising and updating the project prioritization process itself, including such issues as selecting new Project Review Board members, changing or adding key factors, changing the scoring mechanism, and/or reweighting the scoring system.

Top-level managers are looking for a way to "get a handle" on the portfolio of projects that are being conducted within their enterprise. Establishing a portfolio management system during the initiation phase sets the stage for true enterprise-wide project management. The portfolio management system requires that all new projects across the enterprise be proposed in a consistent fashion (solicitation), chosen under the same criteria (selection), ranked objectively relative to all the other projects in the enterprise (prioritization), and codified in a singular informational database for enterprise access (registration). Finally, before work begins on these projects, portfolio management requires an evaluation to ensure that there are enough bodies (and other resources) available to accomplish the work at hand (allocation of resources).

Stamina, stride, style, and strength at the finish line are all important in winning a race. But if you are the runner and you don't get a good start, it becomes more difficult—and in some cases, almost impossible—to run the race. Thinking through all of the items presented in this chapter will get the project off to the start that it deserves. Such reflection also gives the project every chance of getting across the finish line successfully.

--- **NOTE** ---

1. PMI Standards Committee. 1996. *A Guide to the Project Management Body of Knowledge (PMBOK)*. (Upper Darby, PA: Project Management Institute, 165).

PERFORMANCE SUPPORT TOOL 7.1

Business Cases

(page 1 of 5)

Business Case: High-Level Expectations

Project:

Proponent:

Background:	**Areas of Unacceptable Risk:**
Problem/Opportunity:	
Strategic Alignment:	

Description of Deliverable:	**Suggested Priority:**
	☐ High
	☐ Medium
	☐ Low
	Why?

Clients:	**Constraints:**
Primary:	
Operational:	
Strategic:	

Development Strategy:	**Assumptions:**
Targets:	
Completion Dates:	
Budget:	

Business Case: Justification

Project:

Proponent:

Tangible:	**Intangible:**
Benefits: Revenue: Savings:	**Benefits:**
Developmental Costs: Internal: Out-of-Pocket:	
Recurring Costs: Internal: Out-of-Pocket:	**Future Opportunities:**
Breakeven, ROI, IRR:	

Business Case: Low-Level Expectations

Project:

Proponent:

Requirements: ✓ if Mandatory Optional	**Risk Identification:**
Inclusions:	• Schedule:
	• Budget:
Exclusions:	• Quality:

Triple Constraint—Driving Factor Is:

Schedule	**Budget**	**Quality**
Target Completion Date:	± Tolerance:	Completion Criteria:
Milestone Chart:	Contingency Fund:	
	Category:	
	Labor:	Success Criteria:
	Nonlabor:	
Confidence Level:	Confidence Level:	Confidence Level:
Consequences:	Consequences:	Consequences:

(page 4 of 5)

Business Case: Infrastructure

Project:

Proponent:

Project Manager:

Accountabilities:

Authority:

    Formal:

    Informal:

Time Committed (% or Hours):

Team Skills:	✓ if from	
	Internal Department	External Source

Skill Gaps:

Solution:

Project Client:

Accountabilities:

Authority:

    Formal:

    Informal:

Time Committed (% or Hours):

Team Structure:

☐ Functional

☐ Strong Matrix (Full-Time)

☐ Weak Matrix (Part-Time)

☐ Project Office

PM Performance Management System:

☐ Performance Appraisal

☐ Performance Development

Business Case: Optional Items

Project:

Proponent:

Include any or all of the following:

- Proposed Relationships

  — External Suppliers

  — Internal Departments/Subsidiaries

- Communication Plan

- Change Control

- Issues Management

- Post-Project Review (Project Close-out)

- Risk Management

- Methodology

  — Project Management

  — Product Managment

PERFORMANCE SUPPORT TOOL 7.2
Selection/Prioritization Criteria List

STEP 1: WATERSHED CRITERIA

These criteria constitute a filter that stops totally unacceptable projects from proceeding through the process. For each project, the Project Review Board performs this watershed analysis first. The scoring for watershed criteria is simply pass or fail, but the Board still needs to discuss the details of that decision and reach consensus.

The following three criteria are applied to all projects. If the projects fail, they are eliminated from further consideration.

If the project:

1. Doesn't fit the corporate mission,
2. Doesn't promote one or more corporate strategies, or
   Note: The project needs to promote corporate strategies either in its own right or by supporting other project(s) that promote corporate strategies.
3. Conflicts with the organization's values, the project is rejected.

Stated conventionally, the watershed criteria are as follows:

1. Does the project fit the corporate mission? (Yes = Passes; No = Fails)
2. Does the project promote one or more corporate strategies? (Yes = Passes; No = Fails)
3. Does the project conflict with any of the listed corporate values? (Yes = Fails; No = Passes)

STEP 2: RANKING CRITERIA

These criteria score the project relative to specific differentiating variables: (1) organizational factors, (2) financial measurements, (3) customer satisfaction, (4) employee satisfaction, (5) uncertainty of definition, (6) technical uncertainty, (7) risk, (8) infrastructure risk, and (9) impact. Here are examples of each.

1. Organizational Factors

A. Strategic Importance

Score 3 (high) to 1 (low), as follows:

3   The project directly achieves all or part of a stated corporate strategic objective.
2   The project has no direct relationship to such goals, but is a prerequisite for another project that achieves all or part of a corporate strategic objective.
1   The project has no direct relationship to such objectives but will improve operational efficiencies, which in turn support stated corporate strategic objectives.

B. Market Demand Relative to Strategy

Does the project satisfy the market demand? Score 4 (high) to 1 (low), as follows:

4   Increases market demand with no loss of existing demand; differentiates us from our competitors; responds to major market requests; provides business growth; offensive assertive in nature

3   Meets industry standards; maintains existing market position; responds to some demand; helps us catch up with the market; "defensive" in nature
2   Responds to minimal demand
1   Responds to no demand

C. *Benefits to the Enterprise*

Does the project advance the strategic direction? Score 4 (high) to 1 (low), as follows:

4   Provides significant positive benefit to the entire organization
3   Provides significant positive benefit to one company/division/department
2   Provides some positive benefit to multiple companies/divisions/departments
1   Provides some positive benefit to one company/division/department

D. *Synergy with Other Projects*

How does the project affect other existing or planned projects? Are there economies to be gained by partnering this project with another planned or existing project? Score 4 (high) to 1 (low), as follows:

4   Provides significant positive effect on multiple projects
2   Provides significant positive effect on one project
3   Provides some positive effect on one or more projects
1   Provides no synergy with any other projects

E. *Organizational Capabilities*

The degree to which the organization is capable of carrying out the changes required by the project. Score 6 (high) to 1 (low), as follows:

6   The organization has a well-formulated plan for implementing the proposed outcome of the project; the management structure is in place, as are the required processes and procedures. There is a project client, the product is well-defined, the risks have been considered, and contingency plans exist.
5–2   Values for 5–2 may be adopted for situations that blend elements of preparedness with elements of risk.

	YES	NO	NOT KNOWN
Well-formulated plan			
Management in place			
Contingency plans in place			
Processes and procedures in place			
Training for users planned			
Project client exists			
Product is well defined			
Need for product is clear			

For each No or Not Known, .5 may be subtracted from the score.

1   The organization has no plan; management is uncertain about responsibility; processes and procedures are not in place; no contingency plan is in place; and the product is not well defined.

2. Cost/Benefit Analysis

A. *Internal Rate of Return (IRR)*

IRR is the expected value of a project's net cash flow (expressed as a percentage). IRR measures the percentage rate at which net cash flow is sufficient to repay invested capital and provide a sufficient rate of return on that capital. IRR is evaluated over a five-year period. Score 4 (high) to 1 (low), as follows:

4	200+	=	200% or more IRR over five years
3	100–199.9	=	100% to 199.9% IRR over five years
2	61–99.9	=	61% to 99.9% IRR over five years
1	<60	=	Less than 60% IRR over five years

B. *Payback Period*

Payback period measures the relative riskiness of a project—the quicker the payback, the less the risk. This criterion also measures liquidity, or the amount of time funds will be tied up in the project. The payback period is the expected number of years it will take for the net cash flow from a project to offset the original development expense. Score 5 (high) to 1 (low).

5   Less than 2 years
4   Equal to or greater than 2 years but less than 3 years
3   Equal to or greater than 3 years but less than 4 years
2   Equal to or greater than 4 years but less than 5 years
1   Equal to or greater than 5 years

C. *Annual Rate of Return*

What are the costs to develop and implement the project and to maintain the project for its lifetime? How long will the program last? How much money will the project save or bring in? What is the annual rate of return? Score 5 (high) to 1 (low), as follows:

5   ≥15% ARR
4   10–14% ARR
3   6–9% ARR
2   3–5% ARR
1   <3% ARR

D. *Costs: Lost Opportunity*

A score of 3 on this criterion means that if the project is not undertaken, a significant loss of revenue will result. A score of 2 is given only after all reasonable attempts to attain project revenues have been exhausted, or if the criterion is not applicable. Score 3 (high) to 1 (low), as follows:

3   Significant loss of revenue (>3% of the total revenue generated by the primary business for the same number of years as defined in the ARR criterion)
2   Unknown level of revenue lost or not applicable
1   Insignificant loss of revenue (<3% of the total revenue generated by the primary business for the same number of years as defined in the ARR criterion)

E. Costs: Compliance Penalties

Score 5 (high) to 1 (low), as follows:

5   High $ cost with high negative visibility
4   High $ cost with no negative visibility
3   Unknown cost with unknown visibility, or not applicable
2   Moderate $ cost with no negative visibility
1   No $ cost with no negative visibility

F. Costs: Degree of Commitments

Score 3 (high) to 1 (low), as follows:

3   A signed contract
2   A letter of intent only
1   A verbal commitment only (or less)

G. Benefits: Supports Current Lines of Business

Score 5 (high) to 1 (low), as follows:

5   Strongly enhances current business
4   Enhances current business
3   Has no effect on current business
2   Adversely affects current business
1   Results in strong adverse effect on business

H. Benefits: Quality Improvement Potential

Product-related: Does the project have the ability to address defined opportunities for improving a product portfolio?

Process-related: Does the project have the ability to address defined opportunities for improvement of current processes?
Score 3 (high) to 1 (low), as follows:

3   Provides significant opportunities
2   Provides limited opportunities
1   Provides no opportunities

I. Benefits: Employee Morale

Score 5 (high) to 1 (low), as follows:

5   Strongly enhances employee morale
4   Enhances employee morale

3   Has no effect on employee morale
2   Adversely affects employee morale
1   Results in strong adverse effect on employee morale

3. Customer Satisfaction

Measures the incremental impact to customer satisfaction that a project provides, in terms of the services that are provided. Rate 5 to 1 based on your judgment as guided by the following matrix:

Extent of Impact	None/Slight	Reasonable/Slight	Reasonable/Good
Medium/Large	3	4	5
Small/Medium	2	3	4
None/Small	1	2	3

Likelihood of Occurrence

5   Reasonable-to-good likelihood and medium-to-large impact
4   Reasonable-to-good likelihood and small-to-medium impact OR slight-to-reasonable likelihood and medium-to-large impact
3   Reasonable-to-good likelihood and none-to-small impact OR slight-to-reasonable likelihood and small-to-medium impact OR none-to-slight likelihood and medium-to-large impact
2   Slight-to-reasonable likelihood and none-to-small impact OR none-to-slight likelihood and small-to-medium impact
1   None-to-slight likelihood of increased satisfaction and none-to-small impact if increased satisfaction is achieved

4. Stakeholder Relations

A. Effect on Relations with Community

How does the project meet or fit with the community values? Does it fill a community need without duplication? What is the potential for positive public relations? Does it increase corporate visibility in a positive way? Score 5 (high) to 1 (low), as follows:

5   Strongly enhances relations with community, as either a byproduct or direct result of the project
4   Enhances relations with community
3   Has no effect on relations with community
2   Adversely affects relations with community
1   Results in strong adverse effect on relations with community

B. Effect on Relations with Suppliers

Does the project enhance supplier loyalty? Does it reduce costs? Does it increase the number or promote the quality of partnerships? Score 5 (high) to 1 (low), as follows:

5   Strongly enhances relations with suppliers
4   Enhances relations with suppliers
3   Has no effect on relations with suppliers
2   Adversely affects relations with suppliers
1   Results in strong adverse effect on relations with suppliers

C. *Effect on Relations with Board of Directors*

Does the project help the Board meet its responsibilities? Does it increase the Board's prestige or community standing? Does it help the Board increase its understanding of its role? Does it enhance opportunities to educate the Board? Score 5 (high) to 1 (low), as follows:

5   Strongly enhances relations with Board
4   Enhances relations with Board
3   Has no effect on relations with Board
2   Adversely affects relations with Board
1   Results in strong adverse effect on relations with Board

D. *Effect on Relations with Partners and Competitors*

Does the project further our interests and image within the industry? Does it expand the opportunity for "partnering"? Does it provide an opportunity to convert competitors into partners? Score 5 (high) to 1 (low), as follows:

5   Strongly enhances relations with partners and competitors
4   Enhances relations with partners and competitors
3   Has no effect on relations with partners and competitors
2   Adversely affects relations with partners and competitors
1   Results in strong adverse effect on relations with partners and competitors

E. *Effect on Relations with Employees*

Can the project support team and/or individual contributions? Can the project increase employee understanding of the business? Can it provide an opportunity to grow professionally? Can it increase opportunity, security, and a sense of ownership? Score 5 (high) to 1 (low), as follows:

5   Strongly enhances relations with employees
4   Enhances relations with employees
3   Has no effect on relations with employees
2   Adversely affects relations with employees
1   Results in strong adverse effect on relations with employees

5. Uncertainty of Definition

The degree to which the requirements and/or specifications are known. Also assessed are the complexity of the deliverable(s) from the project and the probability of nonroutine changes. Score 4 (high) to 1 (low), as follows:

4   Requirements are firm and approved. Specifications firm and approved. Deliverable(s) are straightforward. High probability of no changes.

3   Requirements are moderately firm. Specifications moderately firm. Deliverable(s) are straightforward. Probability of nonroutine changes.

2   Requirements not firm. Specifications not firm. Deliverable(s) are quite complex. Changes are almost certain, even during the project's evolution.

1   Requirements unknown. Specifications unknown. Deliverable(s) may be quite complex. Changes may be ongoing, but the key here is unknown requirements.

6. Technical Uncertainty

The readiness to undertake the project. The purpose is to recognize the risk and emphasize the preparedness and preparations needed for project success. Score 4 (high) to 1 (low), as follows:

A. New Skills Are/Are Not Required

4   No new skills required for staff or management. Both have experience
3   Some new skills required for staff, none for management
2   Some new skills required for staff, extensive for management
1   Extensive new skills required for staff and management

B. Specific Equipment/Hardware Are/Are Not Now Available

4   Equipment/hardware is in use in similar applications.
3   Equipment/hardware is in use, but this is a different application.
2   Equipment/hardware exists, but not utilized yet within this organization.
1   Equipment/hardware is still in development; key features are not yet tested or implemented.

C. Software Capabilities Are/Are Not Now Available

4   Standard software is used; straightforward or no programming is required.
3   Standard software is used, but complex programming is required.
2   Some new interfaces between software are required; complex programming may be required.
1   Features are needed that are not supported in current software; therefore, moderate advance in the state of the art will have to be investigated.

D. New Technology May/May Not Need to Be Developed

4   Technology exists with minimal modification required.
3   Technology is available commercially with minimal modifications, or technology is available in-house with moderate modifications, or technology will be developed in-house with minimal complexity.
2   Technology is available commercially, but the complexity is high or the technology will be developed in-house and the difficulty is moderate.
1   To our knowledge, no technology is available in-house or externally. Either an extensive vendor search or a complex design/development is required by internal staff or by a contractor.

7. Risk

A. Technical Complexity

Is this new technology? How stable is the hardware/software? How complex are the internal and external systems required to operate the program? What backup systems are required to provide continuity of service?

Extent of	Medium/Large	3	4	5
Complexity	Small/Medium	2	3	4
	None/Small	1	2	3
		None/Slight	Reasonable/Slight	Reasonable/Good

Likelihood of Technical Problem Occurrence

B. Lack of Control

This criterion includes issues arising from make-vs.-buy decisions, strategic alliances with uncontrollable external entities, and dependence on external suppliers and subcontractors.

Extent of	Low control	3	2	1
Lock of	Medium control	4	3	2
Control	High control	5	4	3
		None/Slight	Moderate	High

Degree of Dependence on Outside Entity

C. Regulatory Environment

This criterion addresses "the influence of legislative factors on the proposed project." What is the timing of the regulations? Are proposed regulations going to interfere? What is the predictability of regulations being enacted?

Extent of	High	3	2	1
Regulatory	Medium	4	3	2
Impact	Low	5	4	3
		None/Token	Moderate	High

Likelihood of Adverse Effects Resulting from Regulatory Change

D. Predictability of Market Demand

The demand for the product should be presented in strong quantifiable terms.

Extent of	High	2	4	5
Identified	Medium	1	3	4
Demand	Low	1	1	2
		Anecdotal	Moderate	Conclusive

Evidence

8. Cultural Change

The degree of nonproject investment necessary to accommodate this project—the degree of change that the organization would need to assimilate in order to make the project successful. Score 4 (high) to 1 (low), as follows:

4   No change in the way that the current organization functions will be required. The deliverable from the project can use existing services and facilities.

3   Small changes in the way the organization functions will be required.

2   Moderate change in the way that the organization functions will be required.

1   Substantial change in the elements of the way the organization currently functions will be required.

Extent of	High	2	3	5
Change	Medium	1	3	4
	Low	1	2	3
		Negative	Neutral	Positive

Benefit to Corporate Culture

9. Impact

A. *Magnitude of Corporate Cultural Change*

Change means change in mission, values, roles, organizational structure, and/or organizational purpose. Evaluate both the extent or magnitude and the benefit of the change that the project will bring to the corporate culture.

B. *Impact on Existing Projects*

How does the project provide an opportunity to combine projects to improve project management efficiency? How does the project affect the ability of other projects to meet objectives (time, budget, quality)? How would this project impede the progress of other projects? Score 5 (high) to 1 (low), as follows:

5   Strongly enhances existing projects

4   Enhances existing projects

3   Has no effect on existing projects

2   Adversely affects existing projects

1   Results in strong adverse effect on existing projects

C. Impact on Corporate Image

Score 5 (high) to 1 (low), as follows:

5   Strongly enhances image of the company with customers and corporate partners
4   Enhances image of the company with customers and corporate partners
3   Reinforces existing image of the company with customers and corporate partners
2   Somewhat negatively affects image of the company with customers and corporate partners
1   Has strong negative effect on image of the company with customers and corporate partners

ASSESSMENT TOOL

Portfolio Management Assessment

General Questions	Response Answer each question in the space provided.
1. Do you develop and use mission statements for each project?	Yes _____ No _____
2. To what degree are project definitions clear?	High _____ Medium _____ Low _____
3. To what degree do you typically understand how the project fits with the company's long-term vision?	High _____ Medium _____ Low _____
4. To what degree is there common understanding of project goals among all participants?	High _____ Medium _____ Low _____
5. To what degree is the end result of each project clear?	High _____ Medium _____ Low _____
6. To what degree are completion criteria (end-point) clear?	High _____ Medium _____ Low _____
7. To what degree are priorities clear relative to the project itself (e.g., time vs. cost vs. scope)?	High _____ Medium _____ Low _____
8. To what degree are product strategy priorities clear? Example: developing a low-cost product by X date versus developing a state-of-the-art solution no matter how long it takes.	High _____ Medium _____ Low _____
9. To what degree are priorities clear, relative to other projects?	High _____ Medium _____ Low _____
10. To what degree are project stakeholders clear?	High _____ Medium _____ Low _____

CHAPTER 8

Project Planning

History shows us many successes and failures related to project planning:

- When the Central Pacific and Union Pacific were linked in the Utah Territory in 1869, there was a serious miscalculation as to where the two railroads would meet. It was discovered that the railroad coming from the east was going to be many miles away from the one coming from the west. Though neither company wanted to take the responsibility for the error, a clearer specification within what appeared to be a nonexistent project plan would have avoided the disaster.
- The Denver airport took many more months and hundreds of thousands over budget to complete.
- The United States sent a crew to the moon and brought them home successfully.
- The pyramids got built but only with the sweat and pain of hundreds of thousands of workers.
- High-technology products that used to take 18 months to get to market are now being designed and produced in six months.
- The "Y2K" conversion and compliance work needed to bring computer systems into the twenty-first century was in the most part accomplished without a major glitch.
- Pharmaceutical products are now moving from ideation through development and clinical trials in the shortest time frame ever.

What is similar among all of these occurrences? They succeeded if there was good planning, and they failed if there was no planning or poor planning.

CHAPTER OVERVIEW

Political campaigns, conferences, weddings, even Thanksgiving dinners are planned. Project managers and their project teams make use of a variety of planning techniques and tools. This chapter presents a toolkit of charts, graphs, worksheets, and mathematical calculations that will help managers of projects to organize their project enterprise and to monitor, track, and control it from the idea stage to its completion.

This chapter also offers a process by which each tool can be created, along with guidelines and an example of the application of each tool. Blank templates of several forms are provided in the Performance Support Tools section at the end of the chapter. The tools contained in this chapter are described as follows:

- The *Work Breakdown Structure* is a decomposition of the project work into various levels of detailed tasks shown on a checklist or in a hierarchical diagram. The breakdown starts with the project's major phases and proceeds to the lowest level of detail. It is the project's "to do" list.
- The *Skills Inventory and Responsibility Matrix* helps to match tasks to appropriate project team members who possess the appropriate skills.
- *Project Task Estimates* consist of both effort and duration estimates. Effort estimates indicate the actual work time required to accomplish each of the tasks. The duration is the elapsed time required between the start of the task and the completion of the task.
- The *Project Network* is created when the interdependencies of tasks are analyzed and portrayed in a diagram that shows which tasks must be done in sequential order and which tasks can be done simultaneously. Seeing task relationships on a Project Network helps project players to envision the roadmap of the work that needs to be performed in the project.
- The *Critical Path* is the longest path within the network diagram. It is created by adding the durations estimates of all tasks on all paths and identifying the longest series of tasks. This analysis determines the duration of the project as a whole.
- The *Project Schedule* (Gantt Chart) is a graph that depicts, on a calendar chart, the relationships of the tasks shown on the Project Network.
- The *Project Staffing Plan* is the analysis that determines whether there are enough people on staff to fulfill all the project tasks in the time frame in which they are currently scheduled. The commitment of each resource is loaded onto the Gantt Chart and summarized on a time-window-by-time-window basis. If any resource is overcommitted,

specific resource leveling techniques are used to resolve those problems and create a realistic Staffing Plan.

- The *Project Budget* is the estimation of the one-time developmental costs that will be incurred by the project. These expenditures are shown on a spreadsheet and possibly a line graph.

Let's now explore each one of these tools and others in more depth.

Before you read further, complete the Project Planning Assessment Tool at the end of this chapter so that you can make a personal determination as to the current status of your organization. All Performance Support and Assessment Tools referenced in this book are available for download at www.pmsi-pm.com.

WORK BREAKDOWN STRUCTURE: THE TASK LIST

A work breakdown structure (WBS) is a hierarchical list or a diagram representing all tasks that must be completed to finish the project. It becomes the foundation on which all baseline plans are built. If the WBS is faulty, all planning from this point forward will also be faulty. According to the

Figure 8.1   Work Breakdown Structure, Tree Chart Model

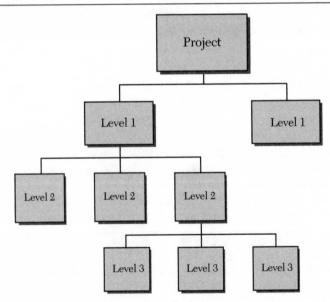

PMBOK, the WBS is a "deliverable-oriented grouping of project elements that organizes and defines the total scope of the project." Figure 8.1 presents a model of a work breakdown structure (tree chart) diagram. Note that each lower level is a decomposition of the level above.

The Process of Creating a Work Breakdown Structure

The process of creating a work breakdown structure benefits from the involvement of project team members and subject matter experts. Gathering input from the project team by using questionnaires, interviews, and/or group session to perform the following five steps:

1. Restate the project objective and confirm that it is correct.
2. Decompose the project into major elements of work (level-1 categories).
3. Decompose each level-1 work element into detailed tasks (levels 2, 3, etc.).
4. Identify a task owner and deliverable for each task at the lowest WBS level.
5. Write a task description for each task.

The major elements of work, also known as level-1 categories, may be organized in a variety of ways. These categories can be chosen to construct level 1 of a work breakdown structure:

- Product life-cycle phases—such as concept design, detail design, test, and ship
- Deliverables—such as a report or a bug-free program code
- Components of the product—such as subassembly A and subassembly B
- Functions—such as compilation or storage
- Organizational units—such as finance or manufacturing
- Geographical areas—such as Singapore, or "the Western region"
- Cost accounts—such as R&D, operations, or personnel
- Time phases—such as "Phase I roll-out in U.S." or "Phase II roll-out in Europe"
- Tasks—such as procure materials, or lay bricks

Figure 8.2 presents a sample work breakdown schedule, which will be used throughout this chapter. The objective of this sample project is to implement a project management scheduling software package within the organization. The name of the project, "Project Management System Implementation," is displayed in the top box of the figure. The next level of boxes displays the level

Figure 8.2   Work Breakdown Structure, Tree Chart

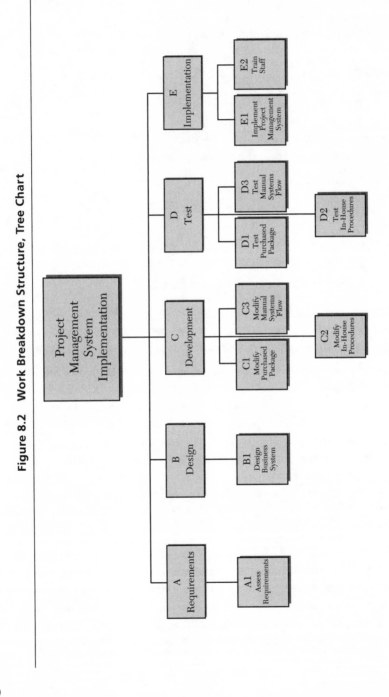

1 or major phases in the product/systems development life cycle that are necessary to install the software. These phases are Requirements, Design, Development, Test, and Implementation. Each of these phases is in turn broken into level 2 activities.

How Detailed to Make the WBS

Not all work elements must be broken down in the same level of detail. Work that has been performed many times before may not require multiple levels of tasks, whereas unfamiliar or especially complex work may require several levels of decomposition.

Generally, you will have sufficiently defined the work to be performed if you can:

- Describe the task using a single action verb.
- Assign single task ownership.
- Describe with a single deliverable.
- Reasonably assign effort estimates.

NOTE *An effort estimate is the actual amount of effort that is needed to accomplish the assignment. The effort estimate is not duration or calendar time.* More detail on task estimating is presented in the "Project Task Estimates" section later in this chapter. Project management standards suggest that you continue to break down the work for the next planning horizon until it will take 40 hours or less to accomplish. This is called the "Forty-Hour Rule." (The Project Management System Implementation sample project is not broken down to the "Forty-Hour" level. It presents only the higher levels of the WBS.)

For people who are not visually oriented or who do not relate to graphic representations of data, the more linear or outline form of the work breakdown structure presented in Figure 8.3, in a list format, may be preferable. When portraying the WBS in a list format, one can add two pieces of information:

1. The list can include the task owner—the person who will be held accountable for coordinating the work in this task.
2. The list can include the deliverable—which is the result that can be expected—from each task, as specified by the task owner. A blank WBS list form is provided as Performance Support Tool 8.1 at the end of this chapter.

Figure 8.3   Work Breakdown Structure, List Format

Project Name: Project Management System Implementation

Project Manager: Joan Ryan

Date Prepared:

TASK ID	Task Name	Task Owner	Deliverable
A A1	Requirements Assess Requirements	Joan R.	Requirements Document
B B1	Design Design Business System	Bob S.	System Design Document
C C1 C2 C3	Development Modify Purchased Package Modify In-House Procedures Modify Manual Systems Flow	Guy R. Marie S. Bob S.	Reprogrammed Package Procedures Manual Flow Charts
D D1 D2 D3	Test Test Purchased Package Test In-House Procedures Test Manual Systems Flow	Guy R. Marie S. Bob S.	Tested Package Tested User Standards/Procedures Tested Operational Procedures
E E1 E2	Implementation Implement Project Management System Train Staff	Joan R. Marie S.	"Live" SystemsLive Systems Trained Staff

It is strongly recommended that a Task Description Worksheet, shown in Figure 8.4, be prepared for each task at the lowest level of detail in the WBS. This worksheet includes a full description of the work to be performed in the task, a clear description of the deliverable produced, and the success criteria—or quantifiable standards of performance on which the deliverable will be measured. The task owner documents, on the worksheet, any assumptions that are made in describing the task. A blank form of this worksheet is provided as Performance Support Tool 8.2 at the end of this chapter.

SKILLS INVENTORY AND RESPONSIBILITY MATRIX

Determining the roles and responsibilities of all project participants is an important step in project planning. It requires careful selection of team members and negotiation of the specific roles each will play as the project progresses. According to the *PMBOK*, organizational planning involves

Figure 8.4   Sample Task Description Worksheet

Project Name: P.M. Systems Implementation

Project Manager: Joan Ryan

Date Prepared:

Task ID: A1

Task Name: Assess Requirements

Task Owner: J. Ryan

Task Description:
  To specify the detailed business requirements by analyzing the current
  system's strengths and weaknesses, by investigating the needs of users, and
  by isolating and prioritizing those needs that are to be implemented.

Deliverable Description:
  The deliverable is a comprehensive requirements document that describes
  the assessment and findings.

Success Criteria (for the deliverable):
  The requirements document should list detailed system requirements
  and priorities for each client group. Current project management practices,
  policies, and procedures should be fully documented including users'
  assessment of what is working well and areas for improvement. Features of
  the new program should clearly correlate to assessment data, and should
  reflect client needs. Each section of the document should contain a
  summary and the supporting detailed information. User groups must sign off
  on the document.

Assumptions:
  Management of each of the user groups will provide knowledgeable
  resources to contribute to the assessment. These resources will be available
  at the outset of the project.

---

identifying, documenting, and assigning project roles and responsibilities,
and reporting relationships.

The Skills Inventory and Responsibility Matrix Process

The skills inventory and responsibility matrix process essentially consists of
the following four steps:

1. List the skills required to complete the project successfully, as determined by task deliverables on the Skills Inventory.
2. Select team members who have the appropriate mix of skills and write their names on a Skills Inventory worksheet.
3. Negotiate roles and responsibilities of team members, relative to each task and gain commitment from the resource managers and individuals involved.
4. Document assignments by task on a Responsibility Matrix.

The Skills Inventory

It is important to assign, to each task, a person who has the correct skill mix. Figure 8.5 presents a sample skills inventory of individuals who are available to work on the Project Management System Implementation project.

The Responsibility Matrix

An understanding of the skills and characteristics of team members assists in the assignment of individuals to the appropriate tasks. Figure 8.6 presents an

Figure 8.5   Sample Skills Inventory

Skill / Name	Programmer 1	Programmer 2	Programmer 3	Analyst 1	Analyst 2	Technical Writer	Trainer	Tester	User	Project Leader
Joan				X		X				X
Seth									X	
Guy		X						X		
Bob	X			X				X		
Jean			X							
Marie						X	X	X		

Figure 8.6   Sample Task List with Responsibility Matrix

Project Name Project Management System Implementation		Prepared by Joan Ryan		Page of 1 1					
Project Manager J. Ryan		Responsibility Matrix				P = Prime S = Support		Effort Estimate	

Task ID	Task Name	Task Owner	Joan R.	Bob S.	Guy R.	Marie S.	Jean M.	Seth K.
A1	Assess Requirements	Joan R.	P	S	S	S	S	S
B1	Design Business System	Bob S.	S	P	S	S		S
C1	Modify Purchased Package	Guy R.			P		S	
C2	Modify In-House Procedures	Marie S.	S	S		P		S
C3	Modify Manual Systems Flow	Bob S.		P		S	S	
D1	Test Purchased Package	Guy R.	S		P		S	S
D2	Test In-House Procedures	Marie S.	S			P		S
D3	Test Manual Systems Flow	Bob S.	S	P				S
E1	Implement Project Management System	Joan R.	P	S	S	S	S	S
E2	Train Staff	Marie S.				P		

example of the WBS task list combined with a responsibility matrix. The *PMBOK* refers to this format as a "Responsibility Assignment Matrix" (RAM).

This form is used to document task assignments and corresponding levels of responsibility. The following guidelines should be followed in documenting commitments to tasks and responsibilities and creating this form.

Guidelines for Creating Responsibility Matrices

From all functional areas and third-party suppliers, a true commitment of personnel should be made at the time the matrix is created. "Promise to accomplish" assignments are always nice to hear, but they are worthless if the staff is unavailable to perform the work. Each commitment should spell out exactly who will perform which tasks. Following are guidelines to follow when creating the Responsibility Matrix.

- In a Responsibility Matrix, tasks should be listed on the vertical axis, and individuals and/or job titles should be listed on the horizontal axis.

- After setting up the matrix, indicate those who will have prime responsibility (the task owner) with a P and those who will have supporting responsibility with an S. Although one person or area of responsibility is primarily accountable for each task, other people or groups often support these tasks. These support people must spell out their commitments as well.
- Consider adding responsibilities beyond prime and support, coded as follows:

  A = Approval required

  R = Reviewer

  N = Notify of significant changes
- Provide a legend so that anyone viewing the chart will know the meaning of codes.
- The lower the level of task detail, the more accurate your resource assignments will be.
- Allocate responsibility in the most logical *and* practical way. The person with the most experience or highest level of skill and/or greatest vested interest should be the person primarily responsible.
- When you know who will actually be involved and the level of each person's skills, your effort estimates will be far more accurate.
- This method of allocating responsibility is not only fair but is also an effective way to introduce less experienced members of the project team to roles and responsibility.
- To make the best use of staff capabilities, enhance staff skills by training, transferring, hiring, or firing; establish performance criteria for each task and each project team member; and manage the project against those criteria.
- As manager of the project, you may assume primary responsibility for some assignments but not for all. If someone else is better qualified or has a vested interest in a certain job, he or she should be responsible for it.

A Responsibility Matrix form is also provided as Performance Support Tool 8.3 at the end of this chapter.

Project Task Estimates

An estimate is a prediction of the time required to complete a task. Two types of estimates are suggested:

1. An *effort estimate* reflects the amount of personal or billable time an individual is planning to devote to a task's completion.
2. A *duration estimate* reflects the expected elapsed time between the start and finish of the task. The *PMBOK* defines duration as the number of work periods likely to be needed to complete each identified activity.

The Effort/Duration Estimating Process

The process of estimating the effort required and the duration needed to complete a task is described in the following steps:

1. Be sure each task has been defined as clearly as possible, including its deliverable and success criteria.
2. Select relevant data to develop baseline effort estimates. Collect effort data from similar previous projects.
3. After considering the level of effort-related variables, which will be described next, develop effort estimates for each task.
4. Determine the nature of each task—either resource-driven or fixed-duration—as follows:
   a. A *resource-driven* task has a variable duration based on the number of resources assigned and how well they work together.
   b. A *fixed-duration* task is not influenced by adding resources but by external factors, such as waiting for delivery from the vendor. Other variables that can impact the duration of a fixed-duration task include shipping, processing, cycle, review, and approval time, as well as lead time to order.
5. Using the effort estimate influenced by either the resource-driven or fixed-duration option, develop a duration estimate for each task. Be sure to document your assumptions.

Figure 8.7 presents a task-estimating model that uses the forecasting or parametric estimating technique, which is described in more detail next.

Guidelines for Developing Task Effort Estimates

The following guidelines should be considered when developing effort estimates:

- Compare the effort performed on previous similar projects.
- Develop standards that can be applied to similar work—for example, project team members typically have 60 percent of a day to work on project-related tasks.

Figure 8.7 Task Estimating Model

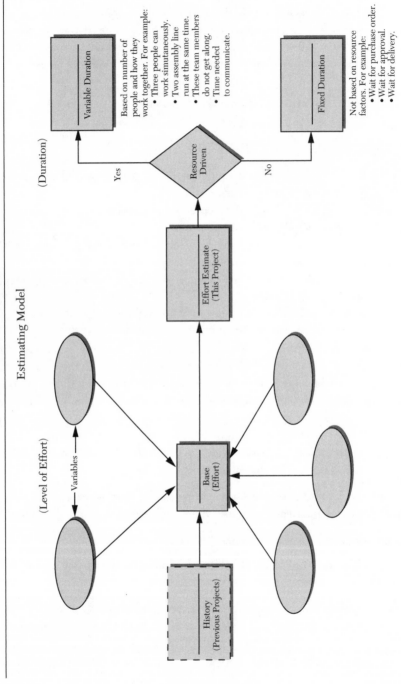

Estimating Model

(Level of Effort)

Variables

Base
(Effort)

History
(Previous Projects)

Effort Estimate
(This Project)

(Duration)

Resource
Driven

Yes

No

Variable Duration

Based on number of
people and how they
work together. For example:
- Three people can
  work simutaneously.
- Two assembly line
  run at the same time.
- These team members
  do not get along.
- Time needed
  to communicate.

Fixed Duration

Not based on resource
factors. For example:
- Wait for purchase order.
- Wait for approval.
- Wait for delivery.

- Consider the impact on the normal estimate by such variables as:
  —Product issues such as complexity and level of innovation
  —People issues such as expertise and learning curve
  —Project-specific issues such as location of project team and knowledge of the project client

For instance, a less experienced team member may require more effort to complete a task than a more experienced person, or a less complex product may require less effort to develop.

THE PROJECT NETWORK

The project network is constructed by determining the logical order in which tasks can be performed. Task interdependencies are typically portrayed in a graphic format known as a Project Network. The determination of task interdependencies is the last piece of information needed before a schedule can be produced.

This model utilizes task nodes and dependency arrows to depict relationships. As displayed in Figure 8.8, the Project Network is built with these symbols. The task node implies work effort exerted and a deliverable completed, and the dependency arrow shows task relationships from predecessors to successors.

Essentially, the Project Network can be created by writing each task's short description on a Post-it™, arranging the Post-its on a wall or a flipchart until they are in the correct order, and then connecting each of the tasks (Post-its) with dependency arrows, as described in the following section.

Figure 8.8   Symbols Used in Project Network

Task Node:
Contains an Activity and Its Duration

Dependency Arrow:
Shows Task Relationship from
Predecessor to Successor

The Project Networking Process

The process of creating a project network involves these four steps:

1. On a stick-back slip, write a description of each task at the lowest WBS level.
2. Identify starting tasks. Place them at the left side of a flipchart page.
3. Identify the immediate successors of each task by asking, "What task or tasks must wait for this task to finish before they can begin?" Place successor tasks to the right of their predecessors.
4. Connect predecessor tasks to successor tasks with dependency arrows.

Figure 8.9 is an example project network that portrays our sample project. It depicts those tasks that must occur in sequential order and those that can be performed simultaneously.

This project network diagram portrays the flow of deliverables and the flow of control from the start of the project to the end. It is a roadmap of how the work within the project will be performed.

Guidelines for Project Networking

A thorough analysis of the dependencies of one task to all the others is key to creating a realistic project plan network. For each task, answer the following three questions to ensure that you have done an accurate dependency analysis:

1. What task(s) must precede this task?
2. What task(s) could take place concurrently?
3. What tasks follow this task?

Figure 8.9   Sample Project Network

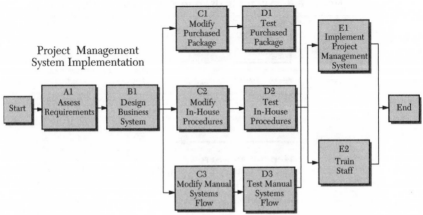

The *PMBOK* describes the types of dependencies. Mandatory dependencies are inherent in the nature of the work, which is usually physical, and are sometimes referred to as *hard logic*. Discretionary dependencies are twofold: *soft logic* dictates best practices, and *preferential logic* reflects special circumstances defined in the project.

After developing estimates and defining task interdependencies, you will be able to determine whether there is enough information to answer the following important questions:

- What is the duration of the entire project?
- When will tasks take place?
- How much scheduling flexibility do we have?
- What is the impact of a missed deadline (task delay)?
- How can we meet a mandated due date?

Critical path analysis provides the answers to these and many other questions.

THE CRITICAL PATH

The critical path is the longest duration of tasks in the project network. Defining the critical path is essential to project planning because a delay in any task on the critical path can delay the entire project. The critical path can be used for several purposes. If, at the beginning of the project, a shorter time frame is requested, critical path compression techniques can be used to enable the project to meet a more aggressive due date. A project can be managed by concentrating on critical path tasks.

The Process of Defining the Critical Path

The process of identifying the critical path employs the project network model described above and involves the following three steps:

1. Post each task's duration estimate in the node representing the task.
2. Add the duration estimates of all tasks along every path to identify the longest path, which determines the projected duration of the entire project (T_E). This longest path is called the critical path.
3. Connect critical-path predecessor tasks to critical-path successor tasks with bolder or different-colored dependency arrows. Denote the critical path with bolder or different-colored dependency arrows.

To the sample project networking model, Figure 8.10 adds the critical path. The critical path is shown with bolder arrows and boxes. They represent, in total, the longest series or path of duration in the project network.

The *PMBOK* describes critical path as "the series of activities which determines the earliest completion of the project." In Figure 8.10, note that the longest path takes 10 months to complete. Therefore, the duration of the example project, "Project Management System Implementation," is 10 months from the day that it starts.

Note also, in Figure 8.10, the noncritical path takes less time than the critical path. For example, the critical path segment of tasks C3 and D3 is estimated to be completed in five months. However, the noncritical path segment of tasks C2 and D2 is estimated to take only 2.5 weeks. The difference of 5 months and 2.5 months or in other words 2.5 months is the amount of float that the noncritical path has before it must absolutely be finished.

THE PROJECT SCHEDULE: GANTT CHART

Taking the data from the Project Network and placing the tasks on a schedule or Gantt Chart portrays a time scale.

Figure 8.10 Sample Project Network with Critical Path. The duration of the project, T_E, is equal to 10 months. Critical path includes tasks A1, B1, C3, D3, and E1.

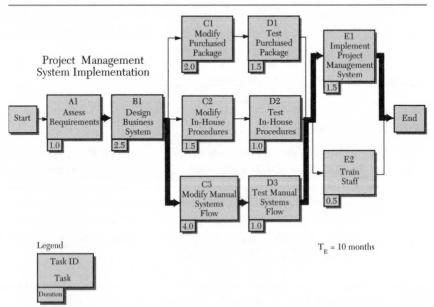

The Scheduling Process

To create the project schedule, follow these four steps:

1. Plot tasks onto a calendar known as a Gantt Chart, path by path, in the order in which they will be performed.
2. Indicate with upright (Δ) and inverted (∇) delta symbols where tasks start and end, respectively.
3. Add float and late finish deltas at the ends of noncritical paths.
4. Indicate interdependencies; using vertical lines, connect the end of the predecessor tasks to the start of the successor tasks.

Figure 8.11 is the Gantt Chart for our example project. Notice that the critical path is bolder than the others. Noncritical paths are shown with tasks starting and ending as soon as they can, relative to their dependencies on predecessor tasks. At the end of the noncritical *paths,* the amount of total float available to each path is shown in hatched lines.

In Figure 8.11, each of the predecessor activities must be 100 percent complete before the successor task(s) can start. This is called a finish-to-start relationship. There are many other variations of dependency. Note, for

Figure 8.11   Sample Project Gantt/Schedule Chart

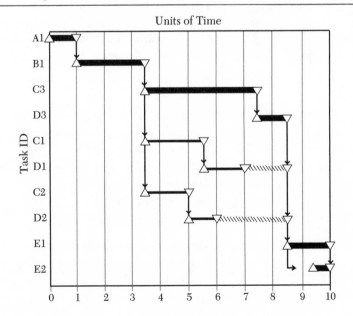

instance, that task E2 is scheduled to start and finish as late as possible. This task is scheduled in this way because training is involved, and it is not logical to train people before they can use the software that is the subject of their training.

Tasks A1, B1, C3, D3, E1, and E2 are on the Critical Path. These tasks have no float or buffer. Tasks C1 and D1 are on a noncritical path, which has 1½ months of float to share between the two tasks. Tasks C2 and D2 also share a noncritical path but in this situation have 2½ months to share between them.

THE PROJECT STAFFING PLAN

All resource assignments are meaningless if individual resources or resource pools have committed more time to one project or to other endeavors than they have available. The resource loading and leveling process determines the scheduling of a resource (or a pool of resources) to simultaneous tasks or projects. If resources are overcommitted, it is the responsibility of the manager of projects, coordinating with the functional manager, (1) to reschedule tasks, (2) to reprioritize work, or (3) to negotiate for additional time, resources, or downsizing of scope. The deliverable from this process is the *staffing plan*.

The Staffing Planning Process

The process of planning the staffing of a project essentially involves the following three steps:

1. Determine what percentage of time (effort) each project team member has committed to each task.
2. Calculate the total effort for any one project each project team member has committed during any one time window; include all the parallel tasks that have been scheduled in that time frame. A time window is the period of time during which no new tasks begin or end. When a new task begins or an old task ends, a new time window starts.
3. If any project team member has committed more effort than he or she has available to give to the project, perform resource leveling.

In this process, each project team member estimates the percentage of his or her time that must be contributed to each task. This can be done (1) on a task-by-task basis, with the team member guesstimating the percentage, or (2) by calculating the percentage as follows:

$$\frac{\text{Efforts estimate}}{\text{Duration estimate}} = \frac{\text{Efforts per calendar unit of time}}{\text{[or percent of time (effort) committed to the task]}}$$

This percentage for a specific source, Marie Smith (MS), is posted on the Gantt Chart. In Figure 8.12, which depicts a sample resource-loaded chart, MS, or Marie, has calculated the percentage of her effort that she can reasonably contribute to each of her tasks in the sample project. By calculating each time window when tasks begin and end, we can see where Marie has overcommitted herself. Let's say, for sake of argument, that Marie is available to work on this project 100 percent of her time and no more. Figure 8.12 shows that Marie is scheduled for 118 percent of her time from month 5 to month 6, and 133 percent of her time in the last half-month of the project. Obviously, this is not doable.

As shown in Figure 8.13, when resource loading is depicted on a histogram, overloads above the resource ceiling and gaps are easy to see. A blank histogram form is provided as Performance Support Tool 8.4 at the end of this chapter.

To resolve Marie's overcommitted windows of time, we can pursue various options, as shown in Table 8.1.

Figure 8.12   Sample Resource-Loaded Gantt Chart

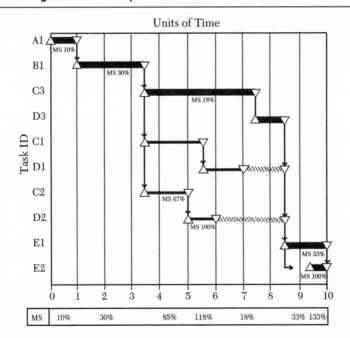

Figure 8.13   Sample Resource Histogram

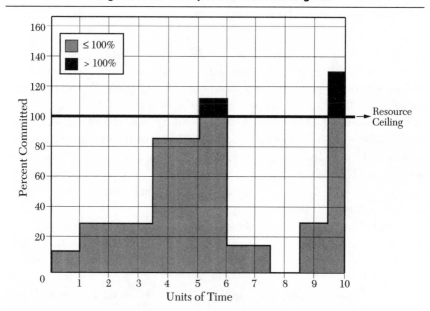

Table 8.1   Resource-Leveling Options

	Option	Caveat
1	Move task into the float, finding a window resolving the overloading . . .	being sure not to overload any other resource(s)
2	Extend duration of the task (within its available float) to decrease individual commitment . . .	see caveat for Option 1 and never beyond the Late Finish date
3	Allocate effort nonlinearly over the task . . .	keeping minimal commitment if they are to return later in the project
4	Off-load the effort to someone else who has available time . . .	and the right skill mix
5	Break dependencies, either starting sooner or ending later . . .	accepting the business risk
6	Add people, overtime, technology, and so on . . .	accepting the increase to the budget
7	Reduce scope or push out project end date . . .	if the client agrees

Note: The PMBOK refers to the limiting constraints (i.e., caveats) as resource leveling heuristics.

When this resource loading and resource leveling effort has been completed for every member of the project team, the resulting Gantt Chart is a staffing plan that can be accommodated by the team members who are working on the project.

THE PROJECT BUDGET

The project budget allocates costs for labor, equipment, supplies, and other relevant expense categories, to be spent over the duration of the project. Spreadsheets and cost graphs are helpful for tracking and reporting.

The Project Budgeting Process

To generate a project budget, follow these four steps:

1. Determine the *expense categories* that are relevant to your project.
2. Build a basic *(periodic) spreadsheet* by drawing information from:
   • Resource loading charts
   • The project schedule
   • Detailed task descriptions
3. Use the periodic spreadsheets to formulate a *cumulative spreadsheet.*
4. Build a line or bar *graph* based on periodic and/or cumulative project expenditures.

Innumerable potential categories of expense must be considered in the budgeting process. These include: labor, supplies, materials, equipment, travel, legal, software, consultants and contractors, land/real estate, training, and marketing/advertising to name a few. One method of calculating each expense is to even-load it equally over the relevant project period. Another method is to front-load or back-load the payments. This method is typically used when providing up-front payments for work to be performed or holding back final payment until the job is completed. The third method is to fix-load the expense as you expect to pay for it; for example, the equipment will be paid when it is delivered. These three methods of budget loading are shown in Figure 8.14 on page 258.

Performance Support Tools 8.5 through 8.7, at the end of this chapter, will help you compile budgeting information.

Budgeting Guidelines

• Resource loading charts as shown in Figure 8.12 help determine the labor budget. Multiply the charge-out rate for each of the individuals

Figure 8.14   Sample Project Budget Loading Options

	Units of Time				
	0	1	2	3	4
Option 1: Even Loading	Engineering 1250 Drafting 500	1250 500	1250 500	1250 500	
Option 2: Front/Back Loading	Consultant A 3000 Consultant B –	1500 250	500 750	1000	
Option 3: Fixed Loading	Equipment A 2000 Equipment B	1000	1500	2000 500	

by their allocation to the project. Add these together to generate the total labor budget, as shown in Figure 8.15.

- For planning, use the project schedule to spread every category of expense over the duration of the project. Include only those categories for which you will be held accountable. Then transcribe these expenses onto a periodic cost spreadsheet, as shown in Figure 8.15.

Figure 8.15   Sample Periodic Cost Spreadsheet

Total Budget $230K

P = Plan
A = Actual

Cost Categories		Cost by Period									
		1	2	3	4	5	6	7	8	9	10
Labor	P	$4,000	$8,000	$8,000	$12,000	$16,000	$21,000	$8,000	$6,000	$9,000	$10,000
	A										
Equipment	P	0	6,000	6,000	16,000	26,000	22,000	4,000	2,000	2,000	0
	A										
Supplies	P	3,000	2,000	2,000	7,000	12,000	8,000	4,000	2,000	2,000	2,000
	A										
Period Total		$7,000	$16,000	$16,000	$35,000	$54,000	$51,000	$16,000	$10,000	$13,000	$12,000

Figure 8.16   Sample Cumulative Cost Spreadsheet

Total Budget $230K

P = Plan
A = Actual

Cost Categories		Period to Date									
		1	2	3	4	5	6	7	8	9	10
Labor	P	$4,000	$12,000	$20,000	$32,000	$48,000	$69,000	$77,000	$83,000	$92,000	$102,000
	A										
Equipment	P	0	6,000	12,000	28,000	54,000	76,000	80,000	82,000	84,000	84,000
	A										
Supplies	P	3,000	5,000	7,000	14,000	26,000	34,000	38,000	40,000	42,000	44,000
	A										
Total		$7,000	$23,000	$39,000	$74,000	$128,000	$179,000	$195,000	$205,000	$218,000	$230,000

- For tracking, the plans are cumulative period-to-date. If you go over budget one month, you have an opportunity to bring the project back into budget the next month. A cumulative budget can be presented as a cumulative cost spreadsheet (Figure 8.16) or a cumulative cost line graph (Figure 8.17).

The *PMBOK* describes several techniques for estimating costs. Top-down estimating uses the actual costs of previous similar projects as the basis for the

Figure 8.17   Sample Cumulative Cost Line Graph

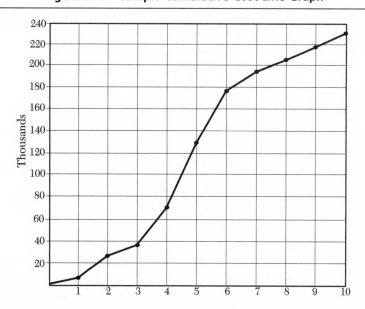

estimate. Bottom-up estimating uses detailed tasks in the WBS and rolls up estimates to the top level. Parametric modeling uses a statistical relationship between historical data and other variables, and adjusts for major differences.

CONCLUSION

This chapter presents the key tools that managers of projects should have in their toolkit and should use in project planning. Let's review them briefly.

The *work breakdown structure* represents all tasks that must be completed to finish the project. It is wise to involve team members and technical experts in the WBS effort to ensure completeness, accuracy, and buy-in. To ensure the highest level of accuracy and thoroughness, decompose the work to a point where the task can be described with a single verb, one person is designated as the task owner, and its outcome is a single deliverable.

REMEMBER   If it's not in the WBS, it's not in the project.

When assembling the project team, create a *skills inventory:* by identifying the skills necessary to complete all work in the project. Then match the necessary skills with the team members, using the *responsibility matrix.* Assign one—and *only one*—prime or task owner to each task. To perform a reasonability check on the responsibility matrix, make sure that, for each task: (1) someone has taken prime responsibility; (2) that accountable individual has the most experience, the highest skill level, and/or the greatest vested interest; (3) only one person is prime; and (4) all people assigned have the skills, the time, and the desire needed for this project.

REMEMBER   Availability is not a skill set.

To *estimate* effort, start with historical data when available, then calculate the impact of any variables relevant to the level of effort. To extrapolate effort estimates into duration, remember that variable-duration tasks are affected by the resources assigned to them; fixed-duration tasks are not. Document all the assumptions on which estimates are based.

REMEMBER   An estimate is the best guess that can be made at a moment in time, with the information available.

By examining task interdependencies, you can determine the logical order in which the work can be done, and can then portray those logical relationships on a *project network*. Some tasks must be performed sequentially; others can go on simultaneously.

REMEMBER   Using the Post-it technique is the best way for the team to come to a consensus on the relationships of tasks within the project network.

The *critical path* is the longest series in terms of duration of tasks in the project network—it is a chain of tasks with no float. After developing estimates, defining task interdependencies, and analyzing critical path data, you know what the duration of the entire project is or you can commit to the completion date of the project.

REMEMBER   Tasks are not on the critical path because they are the most important. They are there because they exist on the longest path relative to duration of tasks in the network, and that longest path has defined the time frame of the project. Therefore, if any task on the critical path slips, the completion date of the project will slip. That is what makes the path critical.

The *schedule,* or *Gantt Chart,* which is an interpretation of the network, portrays the order in which tasks are planned on a calendar. If it is necessary to shorten the duration of the project as a whole, the critical path must be shortened.

REMEMBER   All tasks are not major emergencies. Manage to the critical path and be flexible on the noncritical paths.

When preparing a *staffing plan,* calculating individual commitment is the most accurate method of generating resource-loading data. Resource-leveling techniques help smooth out overloads and gaps.

REMEMBER   No matter how committed people are, they cannot perform more work than they have time available to give to their job and to the project. People have lives, too.

To create a *project budget,* determine the expense categories that are relevant to your project and for which you are accountable. Use the schedule (Gantt Chart) to spread every expense category over the project's duration. Then portray these data in a way that shows not only how much money is to be spent in any one period of time but also the total cumulative expenditures, period-to-date, for each cost category.

REMEMBER   If staying within a project budget is one of the project's success criteria, be sure you have a voice in setting it.

You may not be building a railroad or attempting to get a new drug to market, but your project enterprise is important within your project-driven organization. Therefore, as the entrepreneur accountable for this project enterprise, you must plan it, organize it, communicate it, and collaborate with others about it. Successes do not happen in and of themselves. They happen because people make them happen. The planning tools in the toolkit will position you and your project for success.

PERFORMANCE SUPPORT TOOL 8.1

Work Breakdown Structure List Worksheet

Project Name:

Project Manager:

Date Prepared:

Task ID	Task Name	Task Owner	Deliverable

PMSI-Project Mentors encourage the use and reproduction of this form.

PERFORMANCE SUPPORT TOOL 8.2

Task Description Worksheet

Project Name:

Project Manager:

Date Prepared:

Task ID:

Task Name:

Task Owner:

Task Description:

Deliverable Description:

Success Criteria (for the deliverable):

Assumptions:

PMSI-Project Mentors encourage the use and reproduction of this form.

PERFORMANCE SUPPORT TOOL 8.3

Responsibility Matrix

Project Name:

Project Manager:

Team Members

Task ID	Task Name							

P = Prime; S = Support

PMSI-Project Mentors encourage the use and reproduction of this form.

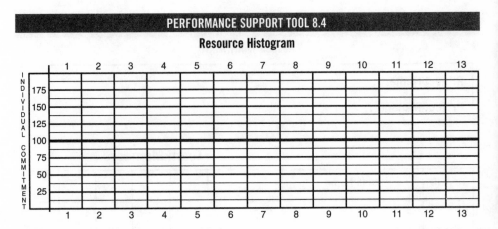

PMSI-Project Mentors encourage the use and reproduction of this form.

PERFORMANCE SUPPORT TOOL 8.5

Budget Worksheet

Project Name:

Project Manager:

Task:

Date Prepared:

Labor

Name/Category	Billing Rate	×	Estimated # of hours	=	Labor $	Specifics on Loading*
_____	$ _____	×	_____	=	$ _____	_____
_____	$ _____	×	_____	=	$ _____	_____
_____	$ _____	×	_____	=	$ _____	_____
_____	$ _____	×	_____	=	$ _____	_____
_____	$ _____	×	_____	=	$ _____	_____
_____	$ _____	×	_____	=	$ _____	_____
			Total Labor Budget	=	$ _____	_____

Other Expenses

Category	Specifics on Loading*	Other Expenses
_____	_____	_____
_____	_____	_____
_____	_____	_____
_____	_____	_____
_____	_____	_____
_____	_____	_____

*Front/back, even, or fixed loading

Total Other Expenses $ _____

Total Estimated Task Budget $ _____

PMSI-Project Mentors encourage the use and reproduction of this form.

PERFORMANCE SUPPORT TOOL 8.6

Task Estimating Worksheet

Task Name:

Duration Estimate:	Effort Estimate:
Duration Assumptions:	Effort Assumptions:

Labor

Resources Required	Effort per Resource	Cost per (Day, Week)	Total Cost/Resource

Other

Cost Estimates by Category	Cost per Unit	Quantity	Total Cost

PMSI-Project Mentors encourage the use and reproduction of this form.

Project Budget Form

Plan Budget $ _____

P = Plan   A = Actual

Cost Categories		1	2	3	4	5	6	7	8	9	10	11	12	13
	P													
	A													
	P													
	A													
	P													
	A													
	P													
	A													
	P													
	A													
	P													
	A													
	P													
	A													

PMSI-Project Mentors encourage the use and reproduction of this form.

Project Planning Assessment

General Questions	Response Answer each question in the space provided.
1. How much time do you spend planning a project up front?	
2. To what degree do you involve others (team members) in the planning process?	High _____ Medium _____ Low _____
3. At what point do you see the plan?	
Work Breakdown Structure	**Response** Answer each question in the space provided.
1. Do you develop a list of all tasks required to complete the project?	Yes_____ No_____
2. Does each task have a task owner?	Yes_____ No_____ Sometimes_____
3. Does each task have a defined deliverable?	Yes_____ No_____
4. How would you describe the level of detail?	_____ High-level tasks only _____ Medium detail _____ Fine detail
5. How often are tasks forgotten or left out during the initial planning? What is the impact when this happens?	Very often____ Sometimes ____ Seldom ____
Roles And Responsibilities	**Response** Answer each question in the space provided.
1. Are roles and responsibilities for each task clear?	Yes_____ No_____ Sometimes _____
2. Is task ownership accepted and carried out? Why or why not?	Yes_____ No_____ Sometimes _____

Estimating	**Response** Answer each question in the space provided. Where 1 to 10 are used, 1 = Lowest score and 10 = Highest score.
1. How strong is your ability to estimate project completion dates?	1 2 3 4 5 6 7 8 9 10
2. Project task durations?	1 2 3 4 5 6 7 8 9 10
3. Project costs?	1 2 3 4 5 6 7 8 9 10
4. To what degree do you have the information needed to produce effective estimates?	High _____ Medium _____ Low _____
Sequence and Critical Path	**Response** Answer each question in the space provided. Where 1 to 10 are used, 1 = Lowest score and 10 = Highest score.
1. How often do you and your project team work out task sequences and dependencies?	Very often____ Sometimes ____ Seldom ___
2. How often do you use project network (PERT) charts?	Very often____ Sometimes ____ Seldom ___
3. How meaningful are they?	1 2 3 4 5 6 7 8 9 10
4. How helpful are they?	1 2 3 4 5 6 7 8 9 10
5. To what degree are you aware of critical path?	High _____ Medium _____ Low _____
6. How often do you need to compress the critical path to meet a mandated due date?	Very often____ Sometimes ____ Seldom ___
7. How do you use critical path information?	
Schedules	**Response** Answer each question in the space provided. Where 1 to 10 are used, 1 = Lowest score and 10 = Highest score.
1. How often do you use Gantt (schedules) charts?	Very often____ Sometimes ____ Seldom ___
2. How meaningful are they?	1 2 3 4 5 6 7 8 9 10

3. How helpful are they?	1 2 3 4 5 6 7 8 9 10
4. How do you use them?	
Resource Loading	**Response** Answer each question in the space provided.
1. How often do you calculate resource loading for your projects?	Very often____ Sometimes ____ Seldom ___
2. Do you do this manually or do you use software?	Manually_____ Software _____
3. How often do you and your team members make an effort to level resource commitments?	Very often____ Sometimes ____ Seldom ___
4. How often do you consider that team members are working on multiple projects?	Very often____ Sometimes ____ Seldom ___
5. How many projects do people typically work on at one time?	
6. What is the impact of multiple project involvement on people? On projects?	
Budget	**Response** Answer each question in the space provided.
1. To what degree are you accountable for your project budget?	High _____ Medium _____ Low _____
2. If you are not fully accountable, who is?	
3. How much time and attention do you pay to budget issues during a project?	

CHAPTER 9

Execution Management: Monitoring, Tracking, and Controlling

Have you ever been in a hurry to get to a meeting and found yourself standing at the elevator and waiting impatiently for the next car to arrive? The wait seems interminable. As you become more anxious, your mind starts presenting alternatives. Take the stairs; the meeting room is only five flights above you. But if you take the stairs, you'll be hot, sweaty, and out of breath when you walk into the meeting. But when will the elevator come?

That is how people feel when they are working in a project environment. They are anxious about what is going on within the project. When will the project be done? Can the deadlines be met? Can we do anything to make things happen faster?

What floor is the elevator on now? Is it moving toward this floor or away from it? Is it being held on another floor for some reason? If I could answer those questions, I could decide whether to wait or take the stairs.

If you could be sure that the elevator has been hung up on another floor, you might quickly decide to take the stairs. If it was moving, even in the other direction, you could calculate how many floors it had to pass to reach the end and then return to pick you up. Knowing that, you could determine whether it would be faster to wait or to take the stairs. And if you knew that the elevator was coming in your direction, you would probably calm down and wait patiently for it to arrive.

Knowing the facts of a situation alleviates anxiety and offers the information needed to make an informed decision. In the project community, knowing that project baselines are being monitored, tracked, and managed, and being given status information on the project (is it headed our way or is there a hold-up?) relieve anxiety and give everyone involved an opportunity to make good business decisions.

--- **CHAPTER OVERVIEW** ---

Among other evils which being unarmed brings you, it causes you to be despised.

—Niccolo Macchiavelli, *The Prince*, 1532

Without a good project plan that is being monitored, tracked, and controlled, you are simply unarmed. Your project plan, the foundation of your project, must be kept up-to-date. It is your personal armor; it allows you to survive and prevail in the world of project management, which can be hostile and unpredictable. This chapter addresses *how* to keep your project plan up-to-date, and how to successfully monitor, track, and control your project.

Suppose, hypothetically, that your project plan is complete. It has been presented to, and approved by, the project client and senior management. Work on the project is about to commence. Now is the time for the manager of projects to ensure that the procedures for monitoring, tracking, and controlling the project are in place. Such procedures will address changes to the project plan and possibly to the project definition. It is time to define the manner in which the work will be controlled during the project's execution.

In performing project control, the manager of projects is gathering data about new assignments, work-in-progress and completed tasks up to an established cutoff date. These data are used to produce status reports on project performance. The manager of projects then conducts trend analyses and prepares forecasts that predict future performance on the project, based on historical data and performance to date.

These status and forecast reports are the bases for identifying problems in work execution and negotiating preventive or corrective actions. After the required preventive or corrective actions have been taken, reports incorporating those actions are used as the bases for preparing summary reports for senior management and for the project client. Thus, frequent updates give the manager of projects the information necessary to keep all concerned parties informed about the project's condition.

Data are collected concerning recently completed tasks as well as tasks presently under way. Status reports (historical in nature) are prepared and are used to forecast future performance on the project. These forecasts clarify any need for corrective or preventive actions negotiated among the manager of projects, the project client, the resource manager, and the project team members.

All of these activities are crucial to the success of the project.

In the project management discipline, *controlling* may be a misnomer. Many of us do not control our projects. At times, our projects seem to control us. More appropriate terminology might be *monitoring*, or *tracking*, or *managing* a project. Whatever the description, managers of projects must take steps to monitor the progress of plans, to track plans against actual results, and to make whatever business decisions are necessary to keep the project on target.

Controlling, or managing, the project is the process by which project actuals are collected, the project's status is analyzed, plans are updated, status reports are produced and published, and corrective actions are formulated and initiated. The purpose of this process is to track the progress of the project in order that proactive steps may be taken to identify and correct problems before they severely impact the successful completion of the project.

Surprises are unacceptable. Management and the project client want to be kept informed of potential problems and any corrective action, and they want to hear it from the manager of projects *first*.

This chapter focuses on collecting and analyzing data on the status of work in progress, forecasting the eventual outcome of the project, and preparing appropriate status reports. We will begin by outlining a seven-step *Control Process* model. Within this framework, we will analyze an alternate technique that does not look at activity per se but considers the results of activity, identified as quality deliverables. This technique is called *Managing Work Accomplishment*. This chapter offers Performance Support Tool 9.1, "Executive Project Progress Checklist." This checklist provides all executives a boilerplate questionnaire consisting of alternative questions to ask the manager of projects during each of the four phases of the project management life cycle. This Performance Support Tool is available for download at www.pmsi-pm.com.

Before reading the rest of this chapter, you may want to complete the Assessment Tool at the end of the chapter. This assessment will help you identify your organization's strengths and weaknesses in the execution and controlling of projects.

THE CONTROL PROCESS

The seven-step Control Process described in this chapter monitors and tracks project-related work to determine whether any significant deviations from plan have occurred. If deviations exist, methods for rectifying them must be applied as quickly as possible. These are the steps that we will be reviewing in detail:

Step 1: Freeze the plans.

Step 2: Collect actuals.

Step 3: Compare actuals to plans.

Step 4: If a variance does not exist outside the acceptable tolerance, go back to Step 2. If a variance exists, determine the cause and analyze the impact of the variance.

Step 5: If the impact is low, go back to Step 2. If the impact is medium to high, take corrective action.

Step 6: Perform a trend analysis and revise or replan/reforecast the project plan as necessary.

Step 7: Report the status and any revisions; then go back to Step 2 and begin the next cycle of collecting actuals. (See Figure 9.1.)

STEP 1

Freeze the schedule, resource, budget, and work accomplishment plans.

You can walk on water; but it is easier if it freezes first.

Approved-and-frozen plans are referred to as baselines. A baseline can be changed only when there is a significant impact to the end date, the cost, and/or the resource requirements of tasks. We say *significant* because one does not want to repeatedly change the baseline for small and possibly recoverable variances. It takes too much time and effort, and it makes the project appear out of control to the outside world.

It is important to retain the baseline. Two techniques are available:

1. Keep the baseline sacrosanct, never modifying it. Show the revised plan as a data element that is separate from the revised plan and from actuals as they are determined.
2. Show the baseline and the revision as one line item differentiated by a change in line style or color as compared to the actuals, which are shown as a separate data element.

Either way, the baseline is preserved.

The purpose for preserving the baseline is threefold:

1. To have a frame of reference from which ultimate success or failure can be measured.

Figure 9.1   Project Control Model

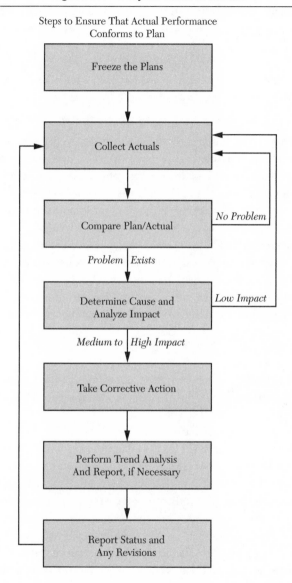

2. To ensure accountability. If team members are permitted to continually change the baseline, they create a moving target with no audit trail. Under these circumstances, it becomes extremely difficult to explain changes to the plan.
3. To accumulate data that can be analyzed so that team members and managers of projects can learn from their successes and mistakes and be more accurate the next time they plan a project.

There are two levels of changes to the baseline. The first level is a "revision"—a change in the baseline without changing the original parameters of project completion, staffing, and/or cost. In other words, revising the baseline does not mean that the ultimate project commitments have changed. The second level of change to a baseline is a replanning or reforecasting of the baseline. It indicates that the original commitments are not going to be met. This change is obviously more serious than a revision.

It is important to have all baseline change decisions linked to the functional groups that are impacted and to have everyone informed of prospective changes in a timely manner. In this way, affected parties will have the opportunity to give input and sufficient lead time to prepare accordingly.

Once the baselines are firmly established, tracking can begin.

STEP 2

Collect the actual project progress data, using hard data (numbers, dates, and so on) and soft data, such as changes in attitude, assumptions, and concerns.

The manager of a project must first consider what is to be analyzed; he or she knows that everything in the project cannot and should not be controlled. After choosing the categories of information to measure, the manager looks at specific data elements—those that will be used to evaluate hard or quantifiable status, and those that indicate potential soft or intangible concerns.

There are several ways to collect these data; we will explore them now. Drilling down on techniques to collect data, we offer a list of guidelines for preparing a data collection mechanism, and we suggest the recommended frequency of collecting data. Let's start by looking at the possible categories of data to analyze.

Categories of Data

The manager of projects must first decide and specify what to measure. The choice is based on what data will best help the manager evaluate the present results versus the plan, in order to prevent major problems in the future. There is not enough time to collect data on every possible variable, and the team would revolt if asked to provide information of that scale.

All data elements are not meaningful to the evaluation of the status of every project. Creating a management-by-exception routine makes it easier not only to evaluate status but also to report status later in the process. There are five key categories for evaluating project status: (1) performance, (2) cost, (3) schedule, (4) staffing, and (5) team attitudes. We also suggest several possible data elements to collect within each category. Our list is not all-inclusive. Be creative with the elements you choose, and expand the following list to meet your needs:

- *Performance.* Number of deliverables completed; quality standards met for each of the deliverables completed.
- *Cost.* Work hours charged, plus overtime, invoices, and paperwork for cumulative period-to-date expenditures versus committed funds.
- Labor and nonlabor expenditures for the period being reported shown cumulatively and/or period-to-date.
- *Schedule.* Start and completion dates, milestones met, status of critical-path activities, percentage completed.
- *Staffing.* Work hours used; ensuring that the right people are participating in the project.
- *Team attitudes.* Morale, productivity.

The last item on the list, team attitudes, is considered soft data—qualitative, not quantitative, data. Soft data are equally important to collect. Indicators of negative team attitudes may include: team members' badmouthing the project, their peers, or the manager of the project, or not showing up at team meetings; functional (resource) managers' pulling team members off the project and reassigning them to other tasks; project clients' continually changing their minds and refusing to commit to project requirements.

Mechanisms for Collecting Actuals

The various methods for collecting data include:

- *Team member interviews.* The manager of the project interviews all members of the project team to determine their status. He or she conducts one-on-one meetings, querying the members about the task(s) to which they are assigned. Although this seems like a lot of work, it is beneficial when attempting to collect soft data as well as hard data.

- *Task owner update.* The person who has the prime responsibility, often called the *task owner,* updates the project actuals for which he or she is accountable and submits these data to the manager of the project. The task owner also creates a status report and submits it to the manager of the project for consolidation.
- *Team member updates.* Each member of the project team submits his or her status. This can be accomplished through e-mail, personnel time reports, time logs, or automated job accounting systems. When this technique is used, it is important to make this task less burdensome by providing the team member with as much information as possible. This means designing these data collection vehicles as "turnaround documents" that include preprinted basic data so that the team members merely need to fill in the actuals, any changes, and an explanation of problems, if any.
- *Status review meetings.* During project team meetings, which are held periodically, all participating team members share information. The project team meets on a prescheduled basis and reviews tasks begun and completed during the designated period of time, and tasks to be started and/or completed during the next period of time. The entire team then has an opportunity to hear what is going on and to work collaboratively to resolve any potential problems. This forum, though time-consuming, helps build team morale.
- *Informal data gathering.* The manager of projects spends time circulating, observing, listening, and assessing. This is how he or she can best ascertain the soft data concerning the teams' attitudes and morale. By talking with people within their own territory, the manager of the project gains information that otherwise would not be available. This information may reveal small irritations that, once resolved, would change the buy-in and commitment of the project player and, through a ripple effect, the attitude of the entire team.

Designing a Data Collection Vehicle

Follow these guidelines to design a computer- or paper-based data collection template:

- *Create a format that is simple and easy to complete because the basic information is preprinted.* For example, for a schedule report, provide the task ID, the task description, the names of the people working on the task, and the status as of the most recent report. Then the person filling out the form need only complete the current status and future projections.

- *Be sure that all the information submitted is used, and ensure that team members see the information being used.* Nothing is more disheartening to a team member than being ordered to provide information and later finding out that it is not being used. One entire project team submitted the same time sheet, with the same tasks and the same hours, for six successive weeks, waiting for the manager of the project to notice that nothing had changed during that time. The team knew that the manager of projects was not using their data, and they resented having to prepare and submit the report.

- *Make sure that the team members understand what the data are going to be used for, and why they have to fill out the form.* People often view these status forms as tracking tools that indicate whether they are doing their jobs. They may worry about being fired if it appears they are not working eight full hours every day. These documents are not Big Brother's way of looking over the team. Be sure that they are not perceived as such.

- *Verify that "as of" dates are consistent.* Do not compare apples with oranges. Be sure the report has a consistent cutoff date and that all the information submitted is "as of" that date—not before it and not after it.

- *Consider the need for revalidation or recertification.* In other words, how hard do you want to work to verify that the actuals are correct? Would you have people post their time sheets on their bulletin board in their cubicle and randomly check that the time sheet has been filled out daily? Or would you ask a person who quality-assured a deliverable to sign a certification form? The answers to those questions depend on how badly you want the data to be absolutely accurate. If you have a government-billed job, you may *need* to recertify that the time sheets are filled out daily, without fail. Or if your job involves a nuclear power plant reactor, you may want to recertify that each and every deliverable has passed quality assurance.

Frequency of Data Collection

When deciding the frequency of data collection, consider the following:

- *Scope complexity, risk, duration, and criticality of the project.* The more sensitive the variable, the more frequently the data need to be collected.

- *Geographic distribution of the project team, number of interfaces with work groups, size of the project team, and management (or customer) requirements.* These pose a risk to accurate communication; therefore, data may need to be collected more frequently.
- *Quality and detail of the progress data, which are related to the update cycle.* The longer an update cycle, the less detail and quality that can be reported. Conversely, progress data collected too frequently will cause clerical overload.

Step 3

Compare actuals to plans, to reveal variances. This can be done by looking at the appropriate baseline and asking these questions:

- Is the project ahead of or behind schedule?
- Is the project over or under budget?
- Is the project using the staff time as planned?
- Is the deliverable meeting the quality expected?
- Is the morale of the project team members at a desirable level?

Table 9.1 lists typical control factors for each of the major project parameters: schedule, staffing, budget, deliverable (quality), and morale.

WARNING No variable, in and of itself, accurately portrays the true situation. A combination of all of these control factors, or of at least more than one gives a meaningful portrayal. For example, the budget may be underspent, which would appear to be good unless the project is behind schedule—the result of having fewer resources than planned working on the project. The projected analysis would be: To catch up, additional resources will have to be mobilized to work on the project. At that point, the project will no longer be under budget but will approach the actual amount—or perhaps will exceed the actual amount if paid overtime is required.

Setting Thresholds

The manager of a project must set thresholds within which to operate and must communicate those thresholds to all the project players. For instance, the budget variance may be set at ±10 percent. The task owner and the manager of the project can then maneuver within a range of 10 percent over or 10 percent under the planned budget, and maintain control. If the variance becomes larger than 10 percent, the task owner must submit a corrective

Table 9.1   Control Factors for Each Project Parameter

Category	Typical Control Factors
Schedule	Critical-path tasks not meeting deadline
	Tasks slipping—late start dates
	Tasks slipping—late finish dates (more important)
	Tasks delayed because of a slippage in preceding tasks
	Any high-risk tasks, and the tasks that precede those high-risk tasks
	Additional scope requests with extended deadlines that affect any of the above factors
	Meeting milestone dates
Staffing	A team member is either over- or underutilized
	More staff than planned are working on the project
	Staff are not available
	Staff are being pulled off the project
	Staff with wrong skill sets are working on the project
Budget	Over budget by x% or y$
	Under budget by x% or y$
	Changes in pricing due to inflation or unforeseen events
	Note: Being under budget can indicate just as big a problem as being over budget.
Deliverable	Does not meet quality standard of performance criteria
Morale	Engaged; committed; bought-in
	Energized
	Productivity low

action plan to the manager of the project, who is then required to report the situation to the powers-that-be.

The logic is: Any slight variance does not require attention or action. Task owners should be trusted to work within a tolerance or under a threshold of concern. This policy makes the task owner accountable but provides some room to maneuver without being called on the carpet for small or correctable variances. This approach engenders more buy-in from the task owners because they are given the professional courtesy of dealing with their problems before they become publicly visible.

If a variance is within the acceptable range or tolerance, no further action is required at this time. (Step 4 reviews how to determine the cause of a variance outside of the acceptable range or tolerance.)

STEP 4

If variance exists, determine the cause and analyze the impact on the project.

Typical Causes

When a variance exceeds the tolerance or threshold discussed previously, search carefully for what is causing it. Understanding its cause will help you assess whether the variance will have a short-term or long-term impact on the project. Typical causes of variances include:

- *Poorly defined objectives.* The original objectives, scope statement, and/or requirements definition were incorrect or incomplete. This typically means that the sphere of the project deliverable and the magnitude of the work required to create this deliverable were underestimated. As the project is evolving, the inadequacies of these up-front definitions are coming to light and causing variances.
- *An incomplete or ineffective plan.* The project plan was either created too quickly and included improper historical data, or was prepared by uninformed people. In either case, the original baseline is incorrect. Consequently, variances should not be a surprise. Incompleteness of the plan is the most common cause of variances; always consider this possibility first.
- *Inadequate communication.* The project players have not been keeping each other informed, or the manager of the project's coordination of the work among the project players has been faulty. This could show itself by people working from different premises and therefore spending time creating deliverables that do not fulfill the visions of other project players.
- *Poor estimates.* The estimates were wrong in the first place. Either the wrong people were consulted or the right people did not have enough information to provide accurate estimates.
- *Changes of scope.* Given more information and more time, the people who envisioned the project deliverable have changed their minds. They see it differently now, and they want the requirements/specifications changed, to accommodate their shift in vision.

- *Inadequate skills.* The people who have been assigned to the project do not have the technical or social skills that are needed to do the job. The original plan and estimates were probably based on an assumption that competent players would produce the project. Consequently, the variances have resulted from an incorrect assumption.
- *Political problems.* Political agendas and/or corporate power battles have reared their ugly heads. This situation is difficult, if not impossible, to predict. Fighting political battles takes time and diverts the attention of the project players. Slippages in baselines then become inevitable.

Analyze the impact of the variance on the project schedule, the project budget, the project team, and the product quality. Based on this analysis and the visible trends, forecast the schedule, budget, and quality of the completed project. The remaining sections of this Step 4 discuss in more detail how to analyze trends and how to forecast the project parameters.

Impact Assessment

So far, we have talked about managing projects by taking a snapshot at a moment in time, determining from the snapshot whether the project is in good shape or in bad shape, and attempting to create an action plan that will resolve any problems. Let's take a few minutes to consider how we take that information and project or extrapolate it to the ultimate completion date, effort requirements, and costs. This Step 4 focuses on tracking trends and forecasting the future, so we will initially review the various types of information that can be tracked using trend analysis and will then explain how to use the trend data to forecast the projected end of the project.

Categories of Information for Trend Analysis

The following types of data lend themselves to trend and projection analysis:

- *Schedule.* What activities are being completed ahead of schedule, on schedule, or behind schedule? Are critical-path tasks slipping? How about the noncritical-path activities? Are any noncritical paths becoming critical? What would be the final completion date of the project if a trend continued? The reforecasted schedule can be portrayed task-by-task, phase-by-phase, or as a date of completion.
- *Staffing (Resource Utilization).* Which resources are giving more effort, less effort, or the same effort as originally committed? Is there a

trend indicating that particular individuals or groups are not meeting their commitments? If this trend continues, what will be the impact on the schedule and/or budget? The reforecasted staffing plan needs to display person hours for a single person, a single skill, a functional group, or the total resources at completion.

- *Finances.* Is the amount of money being spent equal to, less than, or greater than planned? Is there a trend in any expense category? If so, what would projections be for this expense category and for the project as a whole if the trend continues? Remember to take into consideration staffing and schedule status. Reforecasted financial data can be portrayed as the dollars allocated to a task or expense category; or as capital assets or cash flow when dollars are committed or booked, or when they are invoiced or paid.

- *Scope.* Have there been many scope changes? If so, how many additional effort hours and dollars, and how much more duration time has been needed to accommodate these changes? Have plans been changed accordingly? Is there a trend in the quantity, sources, and/or magnitude of these changes? If this trend continues and the original baselines are not being changed accordingly, what are our projections for the completion date, staff requirements, and budget?

- *Unit Cost.* If a product is being produced and a unit cost per product has been estimated, is this unit cost still valid? If not, does the trend indicate that the unit cost is decreasing or increasing? If this trend continues, what will be the final unit cost for the product?

- *Contingency (Management Reserve).* Are the contingency funds (in dollars and in time) being expended? If so, is there a pattern to show where the funds are being spent? If this trend continues, will there be a need to request more contingency funds?

It may be useful to track trends in other categories, such as testing and vendor quality, to monitor issues such as defects found in the testing process, vendors who have failed to perform, and so on.

Data Elements Required

The following types of data are required to analyze trends and to report reforecasted projections:

- *Time Now.* Indicates the *as-of* date of this report; in other words, the data represent actuals up to and including this *as-of* date.
- *Plan.* Shows the original baseline of each individual item.

- *Actual.* Shows the most recent status to date. These data are acquired from the data collection system.
- *Variance to Date.* Calculated by subtracting actual from plan.
- *Estimate to Complete.* Indicates the amount required to complete. These data are estimated by the person(s) performing the work.
- *Forecast (Estimate at Completion).* Indicates the new plan for those items that are not finished. The forecast may be the same as the original plan or may be different. The difference may be greater than or less than the original plan. These data are derived via a mathematical calculation that takes the estimate for completion and adds it to the actual status at the *as-of* date.
- *Variance at Completion.* The difference between what was planned to be completed at the end of the project and what is projected to be completed according to the forecast.
- *Limit.* Establishes, for the forecast, a ceiling that cannot be exceeded without negotiation.

Representation of the Above Data

The trend/projection data can be shown as a line graph, as columnar charts, or in tabular (spreadsheet) formats, to name a few options.

Hints to Interpret These Data

1. If the staff or expenses trail is consistently less than planned, the schedule and the work accomplished are probably behind schedule.
2. When the expenditure of hours or dollars begins to increase, there should be a corresponding acceleration in both work accomplishment and schedule.
3. If the actual effort and/or dollar amount begins to go over plan, both the schedule and the work accomplishment should be *ahead* of plan.

Comparing a plan to an actual result as a snapshot in time does not yield a complete picture. It is important to have the manager of projects pay attention to trends being established from one reporting period to the next, and to project out (or forecast) what the final baselines would be at the completion of the project, if this trend were to continue.

If the impact on original parameters of schedule, staffing, budget, and quality is low, no further action is required at this time. If it is medium or high, proceed to Step 5.

Step 5

Take corrective action.

During the project, corrective action may be required to ensure that actual performance conforms to plan. The three corrective action options offered here are followed by a series of guidelines to use during the corrective action process. We will then explore some possible scenarios, posing such questions as: What would you do if the project schedule or the project budget has slipped? In the worst case, you would negotiate trade-offs, which are explained below. We will then consider five techniques for performing a reality check on the action plans.

Three Corrective Action Options

Depending on the significance of the variance (discussed in Step 3) and the impact (discussed in Step 4), one needs to consider the three options listed below. These options start with the one that is appropriate for a minimal variance and impact, and they progress to the one that addresses a significant variance and high-level impact.

1. Do nothing; wait for more information.
2. Make minor revisions to the project plan while staying within the original schedule, staffing, cost, and quality parameters.
3. Negotiate trade-offs and replan (or reforecast) by (1) applying additional resources, dollars, or time; (2) offering a reduced version of the end product; or (3) phasing commitments over a longer period of time.

Guidelines

It is wise to involve project team members in problem solving during the corrective action process. A small group with knowledge and experience relevant to a problem can often devise a better solution than an individual working alone. You *and* the team need to generate creative multiple corrective-action options before you decide which action to take. After you have developed alternative action plans, assess the impact of each solution and then recommend (or take) action on the solution(s) most appropriate for the situation. Be sure that you manage communication and expectations. Let those involved know what has changed and why.

What Would You Do If . . . ?

Table 9.2, expanding on the typical control factors listed in Table 9.1, includes the solutions if the project is not meeting its original parameters of schedule, staffing, or budget.

Trade-Offs

When it becomes necessary to negotiate trade-offs, follow these five guidelines:

1. *Reconfirm the project client's priorities.* Which of the triple constraints has the highest priority: schedule, resources, or quality? If schedule is the project client's highest priority, it would not be politically astute to attempt to renegotiate the completion date. Negotiate only that which is negotiable.
2. *Identify any reserves in time, dollars, other resources, and/or scope.* Was a "contingency fund" set aside to accommodate possible slippages in any of these areas? If the answer is *yes*, attempt to obtain some of those funds to offset the current shortfall.
3. *Assess the impact of making or not making changes.* Do not keep your rose-colored glasses on too long. Problems will not disappear magically. As someone once said, "You can hide the fire; but what are you going to do with the smoke?" Admitting that there is a problem and suggesting a solution, even if the solution is not popular, is better than waiting and surprising the powers-that-be.
4. *Present professional recommendations.* Be well prepared when making proposals or offering solutions. Have your facts down pat. Prepare strong arguments as to why your recommendation is the correct one. Present some alternative recommendations that you have evaluated, and explain why you have discarded them. Be firm. The people with whom you are attempting to negotiate trade-offs get paid to question your recommendations. They try to be sure that any trade-off, which usually means giving up something (money or functionality), is truly necessary.
5. *Think twice before adding more people to solve a project problem.* It has been proven that there is a law of diminishing returns when people are added to an ongoing project. New people have to be "brought up to speed." The increased interactions with them, and the efforts required to establish and maintain communication channels, may be counterproductive to the project.

Table 9.2   Control Factors and Solutions for Each Project Parameter

Category	Typical Control Factors	Recommended Solutions
Schedule	Critical-path tasks not meeting deadline Tasks slipping—late start dates Tasks slipping—late finish dates (more important) Tasks slipping because of a slippage in preceding tasks Any high-risk tasks, and the tasks that precede those high-risk tasks Additional scope requests with extended deadlines that affect any of the above factors Meeting milestone dates	Determine whether the project is behind schedule, compress the critical path. Use incentives for on-time completion. Negotiate for additional resources only if they will add productively to the ongoing efforts.
Staffing	A team member is either over- or underutilized More staff than planned are working on the project Staff are not available Staff are being pulled off the project Staff with wrong skill sets are working on the project	If the staffing actuals are not meeting the plan: • Negotiate with functional managers to be sure that team members are available and are contributing the time planned • Find replacement team members from within the organization or from outside • Provide training to existing team members, or go to the outside to get competent team members
Budget	Over budget by x% or y$ Under budget by x% or y$ Changes in pricing due to inflation or unforeseen events *Note:* Being under budget can indicate just as big a problem as being over budget.	If the project is over budget: • Look for ways to reduce costs without impacting the quality of the end product • Reduce end-product scope or requirements • Negotiate for increased funding

Table 9.2   Continued

Category	Typical Control Factors	Recommended Solutions
Deliverable	(1) Not meeting quality standard of performance criteria (2) Not completing the deliverable on time	(1a) Institute more frequent checkpoints so that defects are detected sooner and rework is minimized. (1b) Review standards to be sure they are quantitative, clearly stated and attainable. If not, rewrite the standards. (2) Refer to the solutions related to Schedule.
Morale	Not engaged, committed, bought-in Not energized Productivity if low	Talk one-on-one with anyone displaying poor attitude. Arrange an event to celebrate a success. Be sure everyone remembers the charter, the reason we're doing the project and their role.

Reality Check

After a solution is chosen or an action step has been identified, the person accountable for its success should perform a reality check on that solution or action step. Five criteria can be used to evaluate your choice. To employ these criteria, you must ask yourself some straightforward questions and answer them, without bias, as logically and honestly as possible.

Imagine the following scenario. You have identified the real problem, and you have generated alternatives. You have also made a choice—or have selected more than one choice—that you believe can be consolidated into a viable solution package. Your instinct now is to move ahead and implement that solution. Before you do, perform a reality check evaluation. This step will force you into critiquing objectively rather than subjectively, the choice(s) that you have made.

Use the following questions and guidelines to evaluate your choice(s). Look at the action plans that you have made, and ask yourself these questions.

1. *Is this choice going to achieve the result that you are looking for, or is it merely addressing the steps toward achieving that result?*

Are you addressing the work that needs to be performed, or the result that you hope to gain from that work? The objective here is to focus on the result. For example, Choice A might be: "I am going to hold a meeting with the team to resolve the conflict." Choice B might be: "Within 30 minutes from the time the meeting starts, the team will reach consensus on how to resolve the conflict. As consensus implies, anyone not agreeing with the solution will still abide by the wishes of the team." Choice A is how you plan to attack the problem but it does not state the result that you expect to accomplish.

Guideline: Prescribe the result, not the procedure, to attain the result.

2. *Have you thought this choice through to its final and ultimate implementation?*

Can this choice run the gauntlet and be implemented successfully? Begin with the solution that you've chosen, and ask: "Then what will happen if we go forward with implementation?" Continue to ask *"Then what"* for every answer you come up with, until you're satisfied that you have exhausted all potential impacts and roadblocks. Determine how you will proactively address any potential barriers that may arise. The rule of thumb is: If you can answer the then-what question seven times and the solution is still viable, it is acceptable for implementation.

As an example of this process, let's look at a sample solution to a problem and two then-what questions. Your potential solution is to go to the functional manager and obtain his or her authorization to commit an employee's time to a project. You ask yourself: Then what? Suppose the functional manager is unwilling to authorize the time needed from your team member. Then what? You may try to enlighten the functional manager about the employee's importance to the project, but suppose the functional manager is not convinced. Then what?

Guideline: The choice is only valid if you have thought through every then-what labyrinth and know your plan of action at each turn.

3. *Have you considered the possible negative ramifications of your choice?*

To answer this question, you need to search your mind for any and all possible consequences, positive or negative, from implementing this choice. Positive consequences, such as completing the project sooner, might encourage you to move forward with that choice. However, to complete the project sooner, the team might have to work weekends, which could result in their becoming exhausted and burned out. That possibility might dissuade you from applying that solution.

Guideline: Consider the ramifications of each solution, and implement only solutions that have palatable ramifications associated with them.

4. *Are you making choices for other people without their acceptance?*

You have a right to make choices for yourself. However, you do not have a right to make choices for other people. Even if you are their direct line supervisor, attempting to force people to accept a solution in which they were not involved may be counterproductive. Let them figure it out. For example, the solution may be to work weekends, as discussed previously. It may make perfect business sense; however, that is your choice, not the choice of everyone else on the team. Maybe Joe's son is graduating from college during that time frame, and Connie's family is flying in for the week. It might be smarter to position the solution as: "We need to get *x* amount of work done within the next three weeks. I need your help. However you choose to make it happen is up to you. You may decide to work weekends or you may prefer to work at home. It is up to you. If there is anything that I can do to help, let me know." Implied in this statement is that you respect them and would not presume to make decisions for them; but you are also a manager with a job that needs to get done, and you require their support.

Guideline: Don't make choices for other people. Rely on them to get the work done within the framework that you set.

5. *Is this choice conditioned on something over which you have no control?*

A brilliant solution is no good unless it can be implemented. And a solution is not implementable unless you have formal or informal authority over all the extraneous forces that might influence that solution. When you ask project team members to exert extra effort, you may or may not have the formal or informal authority required to "make" these people comply. Formal authority usually comes in the form of direct-line reporting relationships. Informal authority centers around the relationship that you have with these individuals. They should know that you wouldn't ask if it weren't important.

Guideline: Be sure that you are in control of implementing the selected choice, whether through formal or informal authority.

Step 6

Make revisions/reforecasts to the project plan.

Based on corrective actions and progress to date, adjust the project plan to ensure that it remains a viable roadmap for all project players. Here are some guidelines:

- *Restate reserves in time, money, or scope (deliverables).* The project players should be able to see what reserves are remaining.
- *Allow changes to be made by authorized personnel only.* Not every person has the right to change a plan. However, project players can change baselines within the float or slack. The task owners can make changes that are within their predefined tolerances or thresholds. The manager of the project can change the business scope that is within his or her management authority. However, no one should make changes without communicating them to everyone involved.
- *Consider the possible adverse effects of a plan change.* When making a change, think about every possible negative ramification that could occur within the project itself or among the circumstances outside of the project. As an example, the manager of the project has renegotiated the completion date to be later than what was planned. However, several key resources were scheduled to start another project immediately and may not be available. This will negatively impact the current project or, if the resources are allowed to remain on the current project, will cause a delay in the start of the new project.
- *Don't be afraid to change the plan when necessary.* Changing a project plan too frequently is not healthy for the project, the project players, or the reputation of the manager of the project. However, when it must be changed, everyone needs to bite the bullet and do what is right.
- *Study alternatives.* Work within the constraints given. Ask for trade-offs only when absolutely necessary. Don't come back to the well too often.
- *Document the approved change.* Be sure that the change has been put into writing and that all of the involved parties have seen the revision and/or replan. The documentation should be kept as an audit trail during the project and for the project close-out, so that everyone can learn from the lessons contained there.
- *Track the change.* Be sure that the change that is implemented has the anticipated effect and generates the expected recovery.

STEP 7

Report status and revisions.

This step analyzes report formats and content, to portray the current project status and any revisions/replans. Let's first look at the steps needed to establish a status-report process. Then we'll explore what a project status report should include, what format is appropriate, and, some guidelines for creating project status reports.

Status can be documented in complete reports, which present all progress data, or in exception reports. The "management by exception" approach is strongly recommended. This report pulls only the specific data that clearly and concisely indicate a positive or negative condition.

Establishing a Status Reporting Process

The status reporting process is relatively simple. First, analyze the information needs of the project players. Second, organize and schedule reports and meetings to address those needs. Third, distribute the reports and conduct the project review meetings in accordance with the schedule established earlier. For more information on how to develop a communications plan, see Chapter 10, "Communications Management."

Contents of Status Report

This outline is suggested for a status report:

I. **Executive Summary.** The first few paragraphs in a status report present the Executive Summary—a brief review of the information that will follow. In essence, the summary answers the following questions:
   - Is the project in good shape or bad shape?
   - If it is in bad shape, what is being done to fix the problem(s)?
   - How can the person reading the document assist with successfully implementing the fix?
II. **Status.** This consists of a description of what existed "as of" a specific date. For example:

   Schedule
   - Brief synopsis of completions or slippages since the previous report
   - Graphics such as a milestone or Gantt Chart
   - Explanation of variance outside of tolerance if any
   - Forecasted project completion

   Budget. Brief synopsis of the expenditures, by category, for this reporting period and for the cumulative period to date:
   - Line or bar graph
   - Explanation of variance over thresholds, if any
   - Forecasted final budget

NOTE Staffing and scope issues will come to light as a by-product of the previous two sections.

III. Goals for the Next Reporting Period.

- Pending events, anticipated completions, and milestones
- Graphic showing a 30- to 60-day forward view

IV. Potential Problems.

- Problems that are threatening the planned project's parameters of schedule, resources, cost, quality deliverable, and/or team morale
- Workaround plans for problems the manager of the project can fix
- Problems that are beyond the capability of the manager of the project and the help he or she needs to fix them

V. Recognition for Special Achievements and Demonstrated Excellence.

Formats

Various formats will best present the information discussed above. Graphics are easy to understand, and they rapidly pinpoint problems by showing periodic and cumulative progress during the evolution of the project. A tabular approach gives a more granular reading on the project status and presents more specific and detailed tangible information. These two formats can best portray hard data. An accompanying narrative can provide the explanation and justification for the hard data and a place to talk about soft data as well. Examples of these formats can be found in Chapter 8, "Project Planning," and Chapter 10, "Communications Management."

Guidelines for Designing a Project Status Report

- Keep them simple and easy to read.
- Adapt them to the needs and interests of the audience.
- Ask all project team members to use a consistent format.
- Be flexible; adjust your status reports to suit the message and the image you want to communicate.
- Be concise, to ensure that busy managers will read and understand your messages quickly.
- Use graphics whenever they will help to get the message across.
- Archive copies of status reports, to document the project's history.
- *The bottom line:* Provide the necessary information to the appropriate people in a timely manner.

MANAGING WORK ACCOMPLISHMENT

Steps 1 through 7 form a classic monitoring, tracking, and reporting process. However, instead of focusing on the time and dollars exerted (activity), some people may prefer to focus on the time and cost of creating the actual work or deliverables produced from the project. The next section offers a method by which the manager of the project monitors, tracks, and controls work accomplishment.

Managing by Milestones

A milestone is the planned completion of a significant event in the project. "Milestone" is not an appropriate term for the completion of every task in the project. In an information systems environment, examples of a milestone might be the completion of the business (macro) design or of a successful systems test. In construction, a milestone might be delivery of materials or the arrival of a specific craft on the job site. And in research and development, approval of the required funding, or completion of a prototype, might be considered a milestone.

The manager of a project may prefer to manage by focusing on milestones, as a way of knowing when major events are completed. There are two problems with that logic:

1. Milestones usually come few and far between. You will not want to wait until the completion of a major milestone to find out that progress has not been made as planned. At that point, it may be too late to take corrective action.
2. Milestones are events—moments in time. To be told that a milestone is complete is not adequate. What if the *correct* deliverables have not been produced, or the deliverables that have been produced do not meet predetermined quality standards?

The alternative to managing by milestones is to manage by "inch pebbles" and deliverables. Each method is explained here.

Managing by Inch Pebbles

Before a milestone can be reached, a series of smaller markers must be passed. It is wise to obtain status data at specified checkpoints prior to the milestone date. Let's call these checkpoints *inch pebbles*. The premise is one of short-interval scheduling. At reasonably short intervals, the project team is required to complete a predefined segment of the project. Here are some examples:

- The *information systems* team has a major milestone to complete: the business (or macro) design. The concept design is the first inch pebble; documenting the system flow is the second inch pebble; and, obtaining approval is the last and final inch pebble, indicating completion of the business or macro design.
- In a *construction project* that requires delivery of materials, the signing of the contract might be the first inch pebble. This would be followed by turnover of the specs to the supplier. Specified supplier review meetings would follow and would culminate in delivery of the materials to the receiving area, where they would be unloaded from the truck.
- *Research and development* might consider completion of the prototype a milestone; however, the completion of each subassembly should be designated as an inch pebble toward the completion of this milestone.

Did you notice that each inch pebble is described not just as a moment in time when something happened (or, more correctly, was supposed to happen), but as the production of a deliverable that would have some quality criteria by which that deliverable could be measured? Let's look at managing by deliverables.

MANAGING BY DELIVERABLES

Layne Alexander, a longtime partner of mine, used to say, "I can't manage by the 'baby blue eyes syndrome'—which is to look into someone's baby blue eyes and ask them how they're doing to complete a milestone—then to receive the answer, 'No problem.'" Hearing "no problem" is comforting, but we need tangible proof of accomplishment, and that proof is to see (or to have someone who is knowledgeable see) a deliverable. Furthermore, just *seeing* the deliverable is not enough. It is critical to be assured that the deliverable's acceptability has been evaluated against a predetermined standard of performance criteria.

It is highly recommended that we not only position these checkpoints (inch pebbles) during the evolution of work, to ensure that the milestone deadline will be met, but we also require that a deliverable be specified so that it will be quality-assured at its completion.

In the information systems project discussed in the previous section, to complete the business (or macro) design milestone, the second inch pebble was to describe the flow of the system. What does that really mean? What are the outputs or deliverables out of that effort? The deliverables might be to produce the flowcharts and descriptive narratives portraying the flow of all data through the manual *and* the automated parts of the system. Therefore, the deliverables are the flowcharts and narrative. Furthermore, the standard of performance is defined as: all data being processed through the manual *and* automated parts of the system and the documentation of any and all financial control routines.

Thus, defining deliverables and the quality assurance criteria on which those deliverables are measured provides a more solid base for measuring success. Table 9.3 lists the questions that must be answered when managing work accomplishment.

Managing by work accomplishment, in its simplest form, is managing by inch pebbles (short interval checkpoints) and by the completion of deliverables (or work) that have been accomplished and have met a preestablished

Table 9.3   Work Accomplishments Questions

When managing work accomplishment, these questions need to be answered:

1. Were the checkpoints (inch pebbles) completed? (Were the events that were due to be finished during the last reporting period actually finished?)
2. If *yes,* were the appropriate deliverables produced out of each of those check points?
3. If *yes,* did the deliverables meet the established standard of performance/quality criteria?

If the answer to all these questions is *yes,* work is being accomplished with the quality assured. You are on schedule.

If the answer to any of the above questions is *no,* there is a problem, and these are the questions that need to be answered:

4. When will the appropriate deliverables be produced?
5. What is the corrective action plan to fix the defects in the deliverables so that they meet the quality standards?
6. What is the work-around plan to complete the delayed inch pebble?

In other words, when will the project be back on schedule? How much money will it cost? And how many additional resources will be needed?

standard of performance quality criteria. This most basic approach to managing work accomplishment is called the *earned value technique.* If you are interested in more sophisticated techniques, research sources of information on earned value.

CONCLUSION

The amount of effort associated with monitoring, tracking, and managing a project depends, in part, on the state of the project. In both types of control—managing by activity and managing by work accomplishment—less effort is required if the project is in good condition and is being accomplished in accordance with plan. If the project is in trouble, the manager of projects and all the project players will need to exert more effort, in the form of formal control and informal control. The monthly effort associated with informal control can be measured in minutes per day. Effort associated with formal control is measured in hours per month. A concentration of hours occurs shortly after the close of the formal reporting period. In reality, informal control may require as much—or more—effort as formal control, but the effort is spread out over the entire period.

The manager of projects can determine the frequency of informal control, which will depend on the time constraints and the general condition of the project. In most cases, informal control will occur on a daily or almost daily basis. The frequency of formal control is determined by management and the client, who, together, dictate the intervals between formal status reports they expect to receive. In most cases, the formal control period is each month or each accounting period, but in situations that occur either at critical junctions in the project or during high-risk periods, formal control is performed on a weekly basis.

The manager of projects compares the status and trend/forecast analysis reports to the mental image of the project condition formed during informal control. The reports and the image should be consistent with each other. There should be no surprises in the formal status and forecast analysis reports. If there is a surprise, it indicates to the manager of projects that the frequency of informal control needs to be increased. A successful manager of projects will then adjust the frequency of informal control when and as needed.

To determine the relative effectiveness of formal and informal control, several assumptions are needed. Let's consider a case in which the organization performs formal control on a monthly basis. In addition, the manager of projects, who has a wide range of responsibilities, cannot perform informal control. Assume that these broad responsibilities make it difficult for project team members to get the manager of projects' attention other than during formal interactions. To further complicate matters, assume that the team is geographically dispersed. Several members and the manager of projects are at headquarters, but another group resides at a remote facility over 400 miles away.

A problem in performing project work occurs on the sixth working day of the period. The project team member experiencing this problem has previously been frustrated in his or her attempts to contact the manager of projects, and the manager of projects does not take the initiative to contact the team member. Therefore, no attempt is made to communicate directly and immediately with the manager of projects. Under the formal control scenario, the manager of projects learns of the problem in the status report for the current period, which (optimistically) is prepared on the fifth working day of the next period. In that case, somewhere between 27 and 30 calendar days have passed between the onset of the problem and the manager of projects' awareness of it. During that period, if the manager of projects is lucky, the problem has not escalated; on the other hand, the situation may have become considerably worse. The team member has been trying to solve the problem but lacks the authority and resources to do so. Now that the problem has finally been brought to the attention of the manager of projects, it will be dealt with but will require more money and resources to solve.

Under informal control, during an impromptu phone call to the team member, the manager of projects would have learned of the problem within one to three days after the team member discovered it. The manager of projects could have immediately effected some authority and resources to solve the problem. Because the problem had minimal time to ripen, it required less money and fewer resources to solve. The impact of the problem on the end date, and the cost at completion of the project, will be less. And the organization is better off because the problem has been solved in less time, at a lower cost, and with significantly less frustration.

In summary, performing formal and informal control is not an either or situation. Both are required if the project is to be managed effectively. However, it is useful to remember that they serve different purposes. Problems surface quickly with informal control, which affords the opportunity to deal with them before they ripen and become larger. Formal control checks the adequacy of informal control and confirms what the manager of projects already knows about the health of the project. To be successful, a manager of projects must do both informal and formal control—and do them well.

Performance Support Tool 9.1, provides executives with a series of generic questions that they need to ask the Manager of the Project for each of the four phases of the project management life cycle.

In managing projects, be guided by this time-tested truth: Avoid these project control pitfalls: (1) monitoring data that's easy to gather, rather than data that are important; (2) focusing only on objective, quantifiable measures, at the expense of the soft data; (3) collecting everything, with no real intention of using it; and, (4) measuring activity rather than results.

PERFORMANCE SUPPORT TOOL 9.1
Executive Project Progress Checklist

To get what you expect; you must inspect. As an executive in a project-driven organization, you need to be assertive in determining how the project is progressing, and proactive in directing the project from your level. To accomplish this, your job, as an executive, is to inspect what is going on in a project so that you can be assured that you will get what you need and expect.

To perform this inspection at your level, you must ask the right questions of the manager of the project and the project team. You probably have lots of questions—maybe too many—to ask. Are they the right questions? Are you sure you're asking them in the right way? This Performance Support Tool offers a manageable checklist of a select number of questions. They will keep you adequately informed so that you can make the appropriate business decisions concerning the project.

Let's first consider the series of *questions that need to be asked.* Then we will consider the forum you should use to present these questions.

The Executive Project Progress Checklist consists of 22 questions. This is just about the right number. If you ask fewer questions, you may not be ferreting out the amount of information that you need for a proper assessment of the real status of the project. If you ask significantly more questions, you will probably overwhelm the manager of the project *and* the team; consequently, you will not receive credible, in-depth answers. In any event, 30 questions is the maximum number you should include in your own Executive Project Progress Checklist.

The 22 questions listed here are organized around the four phases of the project life cycle: (1) Initiation and Definition, (2) Planning, (3) Execution and Control, and (4) Closeout. Let's review each question and then consider the appropriate time and place to pose the Checklist.

QUESTIONS TO BE ASKED BY EXECUTIVES

INITIATION AND DEFINITION

1. Was there a business case with a compelling business justification?
2. Were all appropriate people involved in the creation of the business case?
3. Did the appropriate level of management approve the business case?
4. Are all the cross-functional departments prepared to commit resources (labor, equipment, and/or materials) to the endeavor?
5. Is the deliverable or output from the project defined in clear and quantifiable terms?
6. Were relevant risks considered before the project was approved?

PLANNING

7. Did everyone on the planning team review the business case? Did they understand it? Did they buy into it?
8. Is the plan an integrated solution that considers all the tasks and effort of team members involved in cross-functional areas?

9. Has the plan balanced the triple constraint of time (schedule), resources (cost), and performance (quality)? Has management announced which of the three triple constraints is the most important variable for this unique project?

10. Is a standard of performance/quality criteria defined for each deliverable out of each task on the work breakdown structure? Is the task owner checking to see that this quality criterion is being met? The premise is that if the deliverable of each task meets the quality requirement, it must follow that the ultimate deliverable of the project will also meet the quality commitment as defined in question 5.

11. Have major milestones been established to be used for executive-level reporting?

12. Has the project been planned to the appropriate level of detail for the next upcoming planning horizon and for future planning horizons?

EXECUTION AND CONTROL

13. At the beginning of this phase, is a change control process in place? During this phase, is the change control process being followed, and are time, resource, and/or cost impacts resulting from changes of scope being approved before effort is expended?

14. Are resources being applied to the project tasks as planned? In other words, are the resources working on the tasks, as promised?

15. Are all involved cross-functional departments reporting their status on schedule and with integrity?

16. Are variances to plan being addressed and resolved? Are reforecasted plans being communicated to the project client, and to management, immediately? Is management rewarding honesty?

17. Are events being arranged to encourage cross-functional team communication and ongoing commitment?

18. Are the risk prevention and the risk response/contingency plans being tracked and managed?

19. Are issues being dated and tracked? Are these issues being resolved as planned?

CLOSE-OUT

20. Were all participants given an opportunity to celebrate? Were all individuals who made special contributions recognized?

21. Was the project professionally closed? Were resources reassigned and did the product/process go into production? Were any enhancements or modifications initiated as a new project under a new project number?

22. Were any lessons learned? Were they documented and archived for use by similar future projects?

WHEN AND HOW TO ASK THESE QUESTIONS

Project management documentation is generated by the project team for senior management on a recurring basis at the end of each cyclical reporting period—at the end of every week, month, or quarter, as the executive requests. Specific project-related deliverables are produced during each phase of the project life cycle. As an executive, you can use a couple of techniques to review the documentation and the deliverables, using the 22 questions listed.

One approach is to conduct one-on-one meetings with managers of projects to review the state of their projects. Depending on the phase of the project, the executive uses the list of questions above as the focal point of discussion. As you review the project documentation appropriate to the phase of the project, you can obtain an honest evaluation of the status of the project, and the quality of the deliverables being produced, by asking the questions on the checklist.

An alternate approach is to call periodic project review meetings orchestrated to accentuate the positive aspects of project performance, and to unearth problem areas to which you, the executive, can offer help and solutions. Each month, you need to set aside several hours for project management reviews. They should be attended by the entire management team—the head of the organization performing the projects, the managers of the resource pools engaged in the project work, and the line management, as well as the manager of the project and the project team. The projects to be reviewed are randomly selected for presentation. Thus, all managers of projects have a chance to present their efforts and accomplishments to senior management. This approach also puts all managers of projects on notice. They need to stay in touch with what is going on in their projects because, any day, they may be asked to make such a presentation. A word of caution: To avoid excess time, effort, and expense, don't ask for elaborate graphic displays in these presentations.

Depending on which technique is used, the manager of the project and/or the team knows ahead of time the key questions that will be asked. Therefore, the manager of the project and the team will most likely concentrate on being sure that each of the questions can be answered in as positive a light as possible.

In summary, all executives need to demonstrate support for the use of project management in their organizations by inspecting what is happening and by clarifying what they expect. The Executive Project Progress Checklist will prove to be a valuable tool.

ASSESSMENT TOOL

Execution and Control Assessment

Tracking	Response Answer each question in the space provided.
1. To what degree can you control your projects overall?	High _____ Medium _____ Low _____
Time?	High _____ Medium _____ Low _____
Scope?	High _____ Medium _____ Low _____
Budget?	High _____ Medium _____ Low _____
Resources?	High _____ Medium _____ Low _____
2. How often are you able to accelerate projects if required by business conditions?	Very often____ Sometimes ____ Seldom ____
3. What mechanisms do you use to keep track of what everyone is doing?	
4. What methods do you use to track?	
5. Who asks for what information during the project?	
6. To what degree does standardization exist relative to tracking or reporting status?	High _____ Medium _____ Low _____
7. What information do you track so that you can manage the project?	
8. What information do you track because others ask you to?	
Status Reporting	**Response** Answer each question in the space provided. Where 1 to 10 are used, 1 = Lowest score and 10 = Highest score.
1. To whom do you report on the status of a project? How often? Using what format? Memo? Meeting? E-mail?	_____ _____ _____ _____

2. How well received are your status reports? Based on what criteria?	1 2 3 4 5 6 7 8 9 10
3. What categories of information do you include in your status reports?	
4. What should be reported?	
Change Management	**Response** Answer each question in the space provided. Where 1 to 10 are used, 1 = Lowest score and 10 = Highest score.
1. How frequently does the scope of a project change?	Very often____ Sometimes ____ Seldom ____
2. How severe is the impact of change on project cost?	1 2 3 4 5 6 7 8 9 10
3. Who requests changes?	
4. How are changes documented?	
5. How are changes approved?	
6. Who approves changes?	
7. If another project interrupts yours, to what degree do you typically understand the reasons?	High _____ Medium _____ Low _____

CHAPTER 10

Communications Management

A good friend of mine tells the following story about when he became the coach for a baseball team in the Teener League. He had been coaching Little League and was excited that he was to be coaching REAL BASEBALL: the field was big-league size, the teams used official rules, the coaches taught defenses, offenses, and signals—everything was real! Here is his story.

         o   o   o

As I organized the team, I realized that we would need a signal system that was simple enough to be understood by these young players. I developed a communication plan. I placed myself at third base—as the third-base coach—where all the youngsters could see me. The young people were told: If they were on base or at bat, they were to watch me for a signal for the next play.

When I touched my leg, the runner would steal. When I touched my hand, the batter was to take the next pitch. All the signs were tied to similar descriptive or suggestive actions. The signal to read the next signal was my touching my head—that is, think!

At practice, we rehearsed the signs; before each game, we held another quick review. At each of my signals, the players would easily call out the correct action.

However, in the game, everything went wrong. Runners were stopping halfway between first and second. Players were swinging at 3-and-0 pitches. It was horrible! My communication contained a flaw, and it was affecting the team's performance and morale.

In the third inning of the fourth game, it hit me. I was sending messages, but they weren't being received. I summoned my players to the dugout between innings and instituted a new signal: The player involved in the impending play was to touch his hat twice when he saw the signal

I had sent. If I did not get the message that my signal had been received, I knew that I needed to get the player's attention so I could send a clearer signal.

* * *

These players were like any project team. The missed messages were reflected in their production, their pride, and their willingness to be part of the team. It was the coach's responsibility to have them receive and acknowledge the messages that he sent.

Your team is in the same hectic world as the teenage baseball players. Messages come to them from all sides. You must know whether they are receiving your messages and are interpreting them correctly.

The coach's team won every game after he changed his communication system. There were no more misunderstandings about stealing second or about any other strategies. The narrative offers a lesson: Verify that your messages have been received and understood.

CHAPTER OVERVIEW

If you were interviewing an applicant for a job as a manager of projects, what critical competency would you seek in that person? Would you hope to find the best resource loader and leveler of life? Doubtful. An effective "influencer"? Getting closer, but is that a core competency? Your most important need would probably be: The candidate must be a capable communicator. The ability to share information, both in writing and verbally, would stand out as the overall top skill required by a manager of projects.

Communication is paramount because the success or the failure of a project often reflects the success or failure of the communications among all the project players. Imagine, for example, that a project team member says that the team has reached 90 percent completion of a particular work package. What does "90 percent" mean? Has the team spent 90 percent of the funds allocated to that task? Or has 90 percent of the allotted time elapsed? If so, will the remaining 10 percent end the task, on budget and on schedule? Or has 90 percent of the expected deliverables been completed? Any misinterpretation of the team member's intended meaning of the percentage completed could result in miscommunication between the manager of the project and the team members. Managers of projects must be sure that all team members, and the client, are on the same page with regard to the terms that are used throughout the project. More generally, the manager of projects must ensure, to the best of his or her ability, that communication is facilitated, orchestrated, and managed.

Even if an applicant for the job of manager of projects possesses excellent communications skills and accepts the job, he or she cannot be successful without a well-orchestrated communications infrastructure. This chapter discusses what a communications infrastructure is, and how to build a communications plan to facilitate such an infrastructure.

Three Performance Support Tools accompany this chapter. They are: Performance Support Tool 10.1, "Meeting Agenda Planning Sheet"; Performance Support Tool 10.2, "Action Item List"; and Performance Support Tool 10.3, "The Communication Plan Worksheet." These Performance Support Tools are available for download at www.pmsi-pm.com.

A COMMUNICATIONS INFRASTRUCTURE

Ensuring that communications will be successful requires an infrastructure that provides a common platform and a consistent process of communication. This infrastructure serves a variety of purposes:

- It helps the project players keep in mind the common goal or vision that has been created in the form of a project charter or project definition.
- It aids project players in staying on track by being sure that all the players are in possession of the project plan and are adhering to agreed-on baselines.
- It broadcasts the standard approaches and methods of conducting the project and producing the end product or deliverable.
- It facilitates change management by informing all impacted parties of requested changes so that they can respond with the anticipated work effort required to accommodate the change.
- It makes available a central repository of information concerning all the tasks that need to be performed and all the deliverables that are to be created through those tasks.
- It pinpoints all the stakeholders who need to be involved in the project management process so that all the project players know where to get, and from whom to request, information.
- It helps manage the expectations of the project clients and the key managers, thereby avoiding any negative impressions—of the projects'

progress and of the project team—that might result if there was an absence of information.

Envision the manager of projects as the hub of a wheel. Around the hub are spokes representing the various communications linkages that must be established between: (1) the manager of projects and the project client; (2) the manager of projects and the project team; and (3) the manager of projects and the other stakeholders in the project, including vendors and third-party suppliers (see Figure 10.1).

These are two-way channels of communication. The manager of projects must remember that sending *out* information, in the form of status reports or memos, is only part of his or her job. The really important part of the process requires receiving information from all the project players. Inbound communication can be structured in the form of filled-out forms or updated/automated scheduling programs. Really meaningful communication is one-on-one and, often, unstructured: Someone drops by a colleague's cubicle, or makes a phone call, or goes out to lunch. If project players are located at a remote site, the manager of projects must work harder at establishing and maintaining that communications link.

Figure 10.1   Manager of Projects as the Center of the Communications Infrastructure

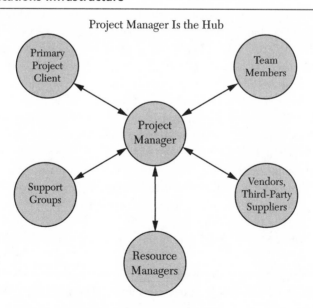

Barriers to Communication

To build a strong communications infrastructure, you need to be aware of the following barriers to communication and devise ways to overcome them:

- Today's technology is conducive to information overload—too much, from too many sources, all urgent. There is not enough time to read everything and respond appropriately.
- Information is either too detailed or too general for readers to understand it and respond appropriately.
- The purpose or, more importantly, the action required by the receiver of the message is often unclear.
- Because much of our communication is one-way—from the sender to the receiver via e-mail, voice mail, and memo—we are very reliant on the receiver's individual interpretation, which may or may not be what the writer meant.
- Each discipline has its own lexicon of terms and acronyms. Because these words and phrases are often undefined in written communications, they deliver unclear or misinterpreted messages.
- People use different styles to communicate. Some people employ a very homey, casual tone, expressing themselves in the familiar first-person "us" and "we." Others use a more formal, arm's-length approach, using only the third-person "they" or "one." When a sender of a message attempts to be more professional, the message may sound officious. If the writer works hard at being friendly, the message may be interpreted as flip or disrespectful. As hard as a sender may try to make a message objective, his or her mood and what has gone well or poorly during the day tends to creep into the tone of even the most important communications.
- Because of the volume of messages, the receiver may not get around to reading/listening to the messages and thus to responding in a timely manner. This can insult or put off the sender of the message.
- In an attempt to hurry, senders of messages (especially e-mailers) often use incomplete sentences, and the receiver may or may not interpret them correctly. Users of e-mail, bent on quick delivery, may misspell words or not think through the appropriateness of what they are writing. The faults in the message may be distracting to the recipient.
- The last barrier to good communication in a project-driven organization is the highest hurdle of all: *assumptions.* Every sender of a message has made certain assumptions about what the receiver already knows or feels or thinks about the subject. The receiver makes similar

assumptions about what the sender knows, feels, or thinks. These assumptions can often be incorrect and cause serious misunderstandings.

To overcome these barriers, it is essential that managers of projects build a strong communications infrastructure, beginning with the establishment of communication protocols.

Communication Protocols

A communications infrastructure consists of documented protocols describing what belongs in a communications plan, what needs to be done to ensure that messages are received and understood, an escalation process in case there is disagreement, and a procedure for continuously improving the protocols.

Communication protocols define who is to communicate with whom, in what time frame, by what medium or mode. These protocols start out by identifying the stakeholders in a specific phase of the project, and the appropriate channels of communication. New protocols, each with its own communications plan, are determined for every phase of the project management life cycle, including initiation and definition, planning, execution and control, and closeout.

Communication protocols include the purpose of the communication, the people who need to communicate with each other, templates or forms that need to be filled out, and common elements of information that need to be communicated. If there is a delegation of authority or a level of accountability, the protocol needs to articulate that fact.

Let's walk through a communication sequence initiated by a request for a change in the scope of a deliverable. Let's suppose that the project deliverable was to be blue, but now the project client wants it to be brown. The purpose of the communication is to request, and receive in return, an evaluation of the time and dollars needed to accommodate this change. The person requesting the change must communicate with the manager of the project and with the people on the project team who will be asked to determine the impact of the change on the current project plan. A template that asks for (1) specifics of any changes, and (2) criteria for approving the work required to accomplish any changes, should be readily available.

After the form has been completed, how should the recipient of the message confirm receipt? A communication protocol deals with how to resolve miscommunication. It includes a *feedback loop* that will confirm when a message has been received and understood. In the above example, the protocol will indicate that, after the project team members have evaluated the impact of the change of the color from blue to brown and have informed the requester of the impact on time and cost, a communication feedback loop will allow the project client to approve the additional time, effort, and cost needed to make the change. The project team members must not perform any change-related work until they receive this official approval. (Recall how the baseball team signaled back to the coach that his instructions were understood.) If the receiver of the information does not accept or is unwilling to follow the direction, he or she must move the plea to a court of appeal.

The communication protocol allows an *escalation process* to be used when disagreements occur. In this process, a specific person is designated as an arbitrator or a mediator during the initial phases of the project. When an unresolved issue emerges, the contenders bring the issue to this arbitrator via an escalation process. In our color-change example, what happens if the requester does not believe that changing the color from blue to brown will take three months and will cost $100,000, as the project team has estimated? Whom can the project client ask to arbitrate or mediate this difference of opinion? A court of appeals process is warranted in many types of communications. First, the requester discusses the disagreement with the project team, to confirm that the requester understands the basis on which the time and cost impacts have been determined. Given the facts and rationale, the requester may accept the decision gracefully. However, if he or she does not accept the numbers, it should be the requester's prerogative to carry the questions to a higher body for resolution. The arbitrator then hears both sides and makes a final decision by which both sides must abide.

Like any part of the project management process, communication protocols must be "living" documents that are reviewed and updated on a regular and frequent basis. The communications infrastructure itself requires *a continuous improvement process*. The following questions need to be answered if the communications infrastructure is to be effective:

- Are all the routine communications necessary? If not, cancel those that are superfluous. Consider the old technique of ceasing to send out a seemingly useless report. If no one complains, cancel its production and distribution.
- Are the communications channels and timetables being adhered to? If not, add or delete people from the distribution list and/or change the frequency of the communication. For example, if a weekly-status phone conference is too frequent, change it to biweekly. If a compliance problem arises, find a way to encourage people to honor the communication protocols. Distributing a report that lists only the people who have met

the quality or timetable specified within the plan can elicit some positive results—especially if this report goes to the relevant bosses.
- Does the template require more information than is necessary for all
the situations? If so, designate some portions of the template as
mandatory and other sections as optional.

Methods and Modes of Communication

When designing a communications infrastructure, consider the myriad communication techniques that are available. As shown in Figure 10.2, these
modes of communication range from a "rich" or more personal medium, such
as face-to-face meetings, to a "lean" communication vehicle, such as a project newsletter.

"Rich" modes of communication are person-to-person, allow interaction,
and permit a stream of consciousness. Examples of "rich" modes of communication are: face-to-face meetings (one-on-one or in groups), telephone,
teleconference or videoconference, and chat rooms.

"Lean" modes of communication include written documents such as reports,
memos, faxes, voice mails, and newsletters. A "lean" mode of communication is
a one-way communication. It broadcasts to the receiver information that requires either no response or a particular action on the part of the receiver.

Figure 10.2   Richness of Communication Channels

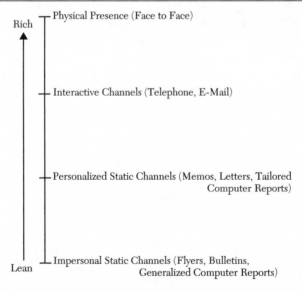

Rich — Physical Presence (Face to Face)

Interactive Channels (Telephone, E-Mail)

Personalized Static Channels (Memos, Letters, Tailored
Computer Reports)

Lean — Impersonal Static Channels (Flyers, Bulletins,
Generalized Computer Reports)

In the continuum between totally "rich" modes of communication and "lean" modes of communication are variations such as e-mail and project Web sites, which do not mandate interaction but accommodate a two-way dialogue as needed.

Technology has afforded us ways to accommodate, for a cheap price, a "rich" mode of communication for project players at different geographic locations. Setting up a teleconference is cheaper than bringing everyone into the home office, although it does not allow the same level of personal interaction.

The next question is: When are "rich" modes and "lean" modes of communication appropriate? The answer is relatively simple. When the communication is routine, such as sharing a roster of the players on the project team, including their phone numbers and e-mail addresses, a "lean" mode of communication is satisfactory. The purpose of the communication is to share information and provide documentation for reference purposes. Therefore, personal interaction is not necessary and would not be appropriate. However, if the manager of projects wishes to distribute a weekly Status and Variance Report, or a similar nonroutine form of communication that requires dialogue, a lean mode would be inappropriate. This type of communication requires a "rich" mode of communication—a formal face-to-face review meeting, or a one-on-one phone conversation between the manager of projects and each of the affected project players.

In summary, it is important, when building communication protocols, to pick and choose the mode of communication carefully. If the communication is nonroutine, pick one of the "rich" modes, to facilitate the interaction and personal buy-in necessary to solve a problem or reach a consensus. If the communication is routine and merely informs the recipients, a "lean" mode of communication will work just fine. Employing technological alternatives such as e-mail and project Web sites allows both semi-"rich" and semi-"lean" communications via one medium. Figure 10.3 displays an analysis of modes of communication.

Helpful Hints to Better Communication

Whatever method or mode of communication you use, the following six tips will help you communicate better:

1. *Each team has its own personality or style.* Some teams tend to be fraternal and social; others are more distant and official. The size, demographics, and makeup of the project team, relative to represented functional areas,

Figure 10.3   Analysis of Communication Channels

	Routine	Nonroutine
Rich	**Communication Failure** Data glut. Rich channel used for routine messages. Excess cues cause confusion and surplus meaning.	**Effective Communication** Communication Success because rich media match nonroutine messages.
Lean	**Effective Communication** Communication Success because channels low in richness match routine messages.	**Communication Failure** Data starvation. Lean channels used for nonroutine messages. Too few cues to capture messages' complexity.

create the difference in its style. Tailor your communication plan to the style and preferences of your team. If your team has a fraternal bond, spend extra money, if needed, to bring team members together and allow them an opportunity to use a "rich" mode of communication. If they are overburdened and every minute is precious to them, orchestrate the simplest and most streamlined "lean" modes of communication.

2. *Establish a pattern of communication.* Be consistent. When people get into a habit of attending a meeting or completing a report, they will respond. Like taking vitamins, when a meeting becomes a habit, one doesn't think of it as a burden; it becomes a necessary part of life. So it is with communications. Keep the pattern familiar. Don't change the time or the required content of communications. Don't cancel an audio conference at a whim. Let people make time-to-communicate part of their personal schedules.

3. *Involve only those people who need to be involved.* Don't have everyone come to a meeting if the agenda pertains to only part of the team. Don't put everyone on the e-mail distribution list, thus adding unnecessarily to an already overwhelming number of messages. Sorting and extracting can be a difficult task, but too much communication, as well as too little, can be a cause for failure.

4. *Consider how to follow up on the communication that is being dispersed.* Remember that you must inspect what you expect. Emphasize due dates and any deliverables required from each action item. Arrange a way to determine whether people actually are reading their messages and, more

importantly, are performing the required action. This can be the most difficult part of the communications loop. Verify not just that the recipients have received the message but that they understand it and will do what is needed in the time frame required. Be sure to build this feedback loop into your communications plan.

5. *Create a common repository.* Designate one place for storing all the communication protocols and the actual communications that have been distributed. This common repository is a knowledge-based system that provides an audit trail back to any past communication, and a historical database to be used during project closeout and, ultimately, when planning the next similar project. Hold project team members accountable (with consequences) for updating and accessing this knowledge-based system. If there are no consequences, experience has shown that the system will never be maintained.

6. *Identify a communications center.* Assign a "point person" for each communications plan within the communications infrastructure. This person is to make sure that: (a) all the channels of communication are included in each communications plan; (b) the timetables are met; (c) feedback loops are in place; and (d) the communication protocols are reviewed and revised as necessary.

BUILDING A COMMUNICATIONS PLAN

The project was nearing completion. Forms to support the new system had been designed, approved, and sent to the printer. Instruction booklets had been printed, training sessions were scheduled, and a conversion date had been announced. The new forms featured a creative three-fold design and were unusually expensive to print. Management was particularly pleased with the innovative new forms, which were expected to facilitate use of the new system.

Then came the shock. The forms were rejected by people in a department that no one had thought to consult. These people were in charge of storing active forms. The innovative three-fold design was sensitive to humidity. Humidity would cause the form to separate, and a separated form could not go through the printer. Options: The storeroom would need to construct a humidity-free storage area, or the forms would have to be redesigned. The solution? Stop the presses and return to the drawing board for an expensive redesign and reprinting.

Managers of projects often complain that one of their biggest problems stems from miscommunication—not getting input from the correct parties, or not providing output to those who need to know. This problem is often caused by an inadequate effort to produce, disseminate, and adhere to a communications plan for the project.

A communications infrastructure includes a total plan for project communications. In this section, we discuss how to create a communications plan, how to prepare meaningful reports, and how to plan for productive meetings, both for the project team and for senior management.

Content

A communications plan includes what, why, and how communications will occur with every person, department, or organization that is linked to the project in any way, and when those communications should be distributed. Let's look first at the *who, what, why,* and *how.* Later in the chapter, we'll address the frequency of distribution—the *when.*

Who

A good starting point for identifying who should be included in the communications plan is an *organization chart.* First, identify all the groups and departments that will contribute to the project. They might include:

- The project manager's own department or work group
- Functional departments and key contacts that have the expertise needed to complete the project
- The project client organization
- Those who will be impacted by work on the project or by its end result, such as various levels of senior management
- Contractors, subcontractors, and vendors
- Strategic partners or joint venture firms
- Other external groups—regulatory agencies, financial corporations, or community organizations—as needed

Then create a list of individuals who belong on the project distribution list—the actual people with whom the project will need to communicate.

NOTE If your project client is an external customer, you may need to do this analysis twice: once for your own organization, and then for the customer's organization.

What

Ask what role, relative to the project, is appropriate for each person on the distribution list. Consider these active roles:

- *Owner:* The person who will assume accountability for communicating the completion of a task on the work breakdown structure, or for monitoring a process such as risk or change control
- *Support:* The person(s) who will communicate time and effort to assist the owner
- *Reviewer:* The person(s) who will review and give feedback and/or authorization to proceed
- *Decision maker:* The person(s) who has the authority to make choices and judgments and must communicate them to all appropriate parties
- *Arbitrator:* The person who can manage a dispute and declare and communicate a final solution during the escalation process
- *Adviser:* A person who has expertise and can be called in to give suggestions and guidance.

Don't become so narrowly focused that you think only of people who are doing actual work on the project. Many other stakeholders should be included in the communications plan. Some people need only to be aware of what is going on within the project. Their project updates can be distributed simply as "For Your Information" (FYI). Others need to provide input from their functional group, or to participate in project-phase gate meetings. Think of anyone and everyone who needs to feel part of this project community.

Why

Next, define the goal of communications for each and every situation and each and every person. Do you need information, or a decision, from this person? Will you need this person's time and effort? Will these people be involved in solving problems during the project? Do they have the authority to make these decisions and sign off?

Data are not information. If you provide people with a lot of text or a jumble of numbers, you are giving them data that may be meaningless to them. To ensure that you are offering meaningful information, think carefully about what data to provide. Tailor each communication to the recipients by:

1. Extracting only the data that are important to them
2. Sorting the data in the most meaningful order
3. Laying the data out, or arranging them on the paper or screen, or in the agenda, in a way that gets the message across successfully

For example, in a status report for project team members, each member would probably like to see only the data that pertain to the tasks on which he or she is working. In other words, team members don't want to see all the tasks within the entire work breakdown structure. They might want to see the data sorted so that tasks on the critical path are followed by tasks on the highest-risk paths, and then by tasks that are on paths with substantial amounts of float. In addition, each project team member might like to see the tasks that precede his or her assignments, and learn who is handing off what deliverables, and when. A team member might also want to see the tasks that follow his or her contribution, in order to get a picture of who will be using the deliverables and when that person expects to receive them. When they have been extracted, sorted, and laid out in a meaningful way, the data will become *information* for the project team members.

REMEMBER   Communication is a two-way street. It consists of not only what these people owe you but what types of communication you owe them in return. Do you simply need to keep someone informed, or do you owe him or her deliverables and/or support?

How

Ask what form of communication you will use with each person in your plan. Will it be meetings (group and/or individual), phone calls, written status reports, e-mail, or some combination of these? Let's look at some examples.

Types of Communication

The two major types of communication are: written (or computer-presented) communication and face-to-face communication. Because meetings are often the bane of a team's existence, let's take time to explore formal meetings that the manager of the project holds with the team and with senior management. After we consider how to best conduct these formal meetings, we'll talk about the importance of informal one-on-one conversations.

Written and Computer-Presented Information

If you are going to use written communications, define the content, level of detail, and format for your reports. You must adjust your status reports to the needs of each audience. Senior management will require different content, level of detail, and format than will the project team, for example. It has been proven that team members prefer a more linear form of communications at a lower level of detail. For a team member, the status report comparing the plan against the actual output would be formatted to include a list of the tasks for which the team member is responsible (1) within the current

Figure 10.4   Report Composition

	Top Management	Team Members
Levels of Detail	Less detail More graphic information tool	Greater detail Lists Action tool
Timing	Less frequently (minimum monthly)	More frequently (minimum weekly)
Content	Just the overview problem identification and recommendations	Overview and sections that impact it

time window and (2) projected out for the next 60 to 90 days (the planning horizon). The data associated with each task would consist of: when it started or is expected to start, when it finished or is expected to finish, and, in the comments column, the reasons for any slippages. On the other hand, as shown in Figure 10.4, studies show that senior management prefers to see a more graphic presentation of the data at a higher level of detail. This can take the form of a schedule Gantt Chart, a cost-line graph, or a resource utilization histogram. Information can also be shown in pie charts, columnar charts, and network diagrams. There are endless ways to arrange data in a simple and easy graphic representation. Several of these are shown in Chapter 8, "Project Planning."

Work out the format in advance, so you're sure that your written communications will hit the mark. Reports or written documents are the most widely used means of communicating within a project team. A meeting that allows the project community to communicate face-to-face is often a close second.

Meetings

If you are planning to include meetings in your communications plan, devise a meeting management protocol that includes:

- Who will attend
- Whether everyone must attend, or just the core team, or just those who are involved in the current agenda items
- How often meetings will be held
- Where and when the meetings will be scheduled
- Who will be responsible for the agenda
- Who will record the minutes and see that they are distributed—if the minutes are not taken "real-time" during the meeting. Taking minutes online, or in real time, is accomplished by a designated scribe who keys the minutes into a computer during the meeting. This text can be projected on a screen as the minutes are being captured.
- Who will perform other logistical tasks, such as scheduling a meeting room

Let's look at some recommended guidelines for holding two specific types of meetings: a project team review meeting and a senior management review meeting.

Project Team Review Meeting

Before a meeting of the team is called to review the project, the following guidelines should be considered and completed (if applicable):

1. *Arrange a convenient meeting place.* Choose a place away from telephones and interruptions (ban the use of cell phones). In a neutral location that is equally accessible by all parties, no one will feel intimidated.
2. *Be specific in selecting attendees.* Select only those who need to be involved. The rest can be invited but not required to attend.
3. *Find out whether all key participants can attend.* If a key player cannot attend, explore whether a replacement might be authorized to make decisions in the key player's absence. If not, postpone the meeting.
4. *Give plenty of notice.* Team members need to put these meetings on their calendar well in advance and give them priority. No conflicting appointments should be scheduled.
5. *State the agenda explicitly.* For each agenda item, state the purpose of the topic, the expected end result, and the person who will be leading the discussion. Agenda items tend to have one of four potential purposes, as given in the following P-C-S-D model:
   - **P**lanning. The purpose is to look ahead and organize what the team is going to do in the future.

- **C**ommunication. The purpose is only FYI. No discussion is required, nor will discussion be encouraged.
- **S**olving Problems. The purpose is to have the group identify problems, brainstorm solutions, and identify actions and their related pros and cons. Because this is a problem-solving effort, the participants should think through this problem-solving process before the meeting convenes, and be prepared to contribute.
- **D**eciding. This type of topic requires a conclusion. Participants must be ready to discuss and evaluate possible solutions, and to select the best course of action. For each participant, foresight is required—including going, in advance, to the decision maker in his or her functional areas and determining whether there are any constraints on the decision to be made. See the P-C-S-D model in Performance Support Tool 10.1, "Meeting Agenda Planning Sheet," at the end of this chapter.

6. *Limit the number of agenda items.* Attempt to cover only the number of items that can reasonably be handled in the scheduled time. Do the math. Scheduling 10 agenda items in a 60-minute time frame, for example, would allow only six minutes for each item to be presented and discussed.

7. *Budget your time carefully.* Establish an expected limit, for yourself and for the attendees, as to the amount of time that will be invested in each topic. This pre-sets a sense of urgency to complete each topic so that the meeting can move on and deal with all topics more or less equally.

8. *Select a minutes taker.* As the facilitator, you cannot lead the meeting *and* keep good notes. Someone else must be asked to perform this task. Be kind. Circulate this job so that everyone gets a turn.

9. *Cover the most important topics early.* It is a known fact that attention wanes after a short period of time. Discuss the most important items at the start of the meeting, while the group is still fresh and focused.

10. *Insert buffer time into the schedule, early in the meeting and at several other points in the agenda.* Buffer time is most effective early in the meeting, when people are just getting settled and have a tendency to be more vocal. Be sure some buffer time is allowed for verbal contributions that are longer than expected.

11. *Preview the agenda with your client (boss) and ask for feedback.* Do not put on the agenda anything that is inappropriate or politically sensitive in the opinion of your boss or your project client.

12. *Dry-run the high-risk speakers.* If you are asking others to deliver part of the presentation, ask them for either a dress rehearsal in front of you or, at least, have them talk through their speech before the meeting. (Someone once told me that we should dry-run not only our high-risk speakers but *all* of our speakers, at least once.)

During the meeting, adhere to these seven rules:

1. *Start on time.* Time is precious, and businesspeople resent wasting their time waiting for latecomers to show up. In addition, you have a tight agenda. The stopping time of the meeting should not change. The participants will bolt out of the meeting at the published end time whether the topics have been covered or not. Start on time so that you have a chance to address all the agenda topics within the stated time frame.

2. *Be the first person to speak.* To set the proper tone, start with an overview of the agenda or a short introduction of the objectives or purpose of the meeting. Put yourself in control, and alert the attendees to your objectives and your major concerns. Follow the time-tested Speaker's Golden Rule: "Tell 'em what you are going to tell 'em, tell 'em, and then tell 'em what you told 'em."

3. *Nominate a scribe.* The job of the scribe is to keep a list of open, unresolved issues and to be the timekeeper.

4. *Adhere to the agenda and the purpose of each agenda item.* Allow the agenda to be the policeman rather than you. Make it clear that it is the agenda that says "We must move on." Avoid the inference that you insist irrelevant discussion must stop. The agenda items are specific as to the topic, the purpose, and the time frame; therefore, no unnecessary tangents occur.

5. *Document action item(s).* Assign responsibility for action item(s). Devise a follow-up plan to ensure that the action is being performed and is having the appropriate and expected effect. (See the model Action Item List in Performance Support Tool 10.2.) The Action Item List consists of a description of actions that need to be taken; who requested a particular action; to whom the action is due; and when and if this is an open item—one left over from the last project team review meeting that was held.

6. *Don't lose control of the meeting.* Keep the attendees focused on the agenda. Manage the time and the direction of the dialogue, and, most importantly, do not allow anyone to take over the meeting. If you can't keep control of a meeting, how do you expect the project team members to believe that you can control the project?

7. *Don't overrun your allotted time.* People have made a commitment to attend your meeting for the duration on their schedule. They have planned psychologically to allot that much time out of their workday. Some people have another meeting to attend. Others just need to get back to their desks and get some work done.

Now that we have looked at how to prepare for and conduct the meeting, the next question is: What should we talk about during the meeting? Table 10.1 suggests an agenda for a meeting during which the project team members will review the status of the project and look to the future.

Within this agenda, you will want to give project team members some advance notice about what might be asked during the meeting. Here are some questions that the team can anticipate being asked:

Do you foresee any problems coming up in the future?

Are your resources being threatened—that is, are people being pulled off the project?

What is the level of productivity for you and your team? What is hindering productivity? What are you doing about the situation?

What are you doing about persistent problems?

What do you need in order to do your job more effectively?

Are you planning ahead for key deliverables, documentation?

Now that we have looked at how to conduct a project team review meeting, let's look at another type of meeting that the manager of projects conducts: the Senior Management Review Meeting.

Table 10.1   Project Team Review Meeting Agenda

I. Major accomplishments since the last review.

II. Schedule status (actual vs. plan), including any slippages that will make the project come in late.

III. Financial status (actual vs. plan), including a clear explanation of variances that are over or under the agreed-on thresholds.

IV. Major issues (problems) and action plans that require mitigating, including requests for specific help from the project client or boss, if appropriate.

V. Plans for the next period (i.e., week or month).

VI. Special topics (usually expected further in the future).

VII. Review of action items established during this meeting; the agreed-on prime person who will be held accountable, and the due date for each item.

VIII. Confirmation of time and place for the next meeting.

Senior Management Review Meeting

Status for senior management is generated at the end of each cyclical reporting period. To receive and review this information, senior management has a number of options. A one-on-one meeting can be scheduled with an individual manager, to discuss the state of his or her projects. A special meeting of the entire project team can be called when senior management has concerns about a negative status of any project. During these meetings, action items are created either to investigate special situations or to implement corrective strategies relative to projects that are experiencing problems. These two alternatives tend to accentuate the negative aspect of the project. They focus on problems. (See Performance Support Tool 10.2 for a template for listing action items.)

In support of project management, which is the key to success in a project-driven organization, senior management needs to call periodic project reviews orchestrated to accent the positive aspects of project performance as well as to unearth problem areas in which management can offer help and solutions. Each month, the organization's management team should set aside several hours for a management review. The review should be attended by the entire management team: the head of the organization performing the projects, managers of the resource pools engaged in the project work, and the line management above the level of manager of projects. Projects are randomly selected for the review: (1) so that all managers of projects have a chance to present their efforts to senior management, and (2) to keep all managers of projects aware that, on any day, they may be asked to make such a presentation.

A typical review should consume less than 30 minutes and should be highly structured. Senior management will expect the same ground to be covered in every review. Six topics that might be covered in the review are shown in Table 10.2.

WARNING   To avoid excessive expense, don't introduce elaborate graphic displays in your presentations.

Informal One-on-One Conversations

So far, we have talked about formal protocols relative to communications management within a project-driven organization. To be successful, we also need to extend ourselves and communicate within a more informal mode. This section deals with truly informal and more personal conversations with members of the organization's project community.

Table 10.2   Senior Management Review Meeting Agenda

I.	Project Introduction: Summarizes the project objectives and the composition of the project team.
II.	Accomplishments: Highlights positive events and contributions to the project since the last management review.
III.	Subjective Assessment: Gives the manager of the project's assessment of the state of the project and the degree of client satisfaction with the job.
IV.	Status: Presents a high-level project management display of the schedule, cost, resource, and work accomplishment status.
V.	Presents each problem being faced by the team, and includes a worst-case scenario, the action required to fix the problem, and the approvals required to implement the solution.
VI.	Outstanding Decisions: Enumerates decisions owed to the manager of the project by senior management and the project client, as well as the consequences of a delay in receiving these decisions.

The term "Management by Wandering Around" was coined by Thomas J. Peters and Robert H. Waterman, Jr., in *In Search of Excellence: Lessons from America's Best-Run Companies*. To maintain informed and informal communication, the technique of "walking the halls" or going out into the field can be most effective and can deliver several benefits:

- You learn a lot more than you will ever learn seated at your desk.
- You meet people in their own work environment. Here, they may be more open and honest than if they were in your office or in a conference room where there are other project players.
- You become highly visible to all project players, not just your subordinates. You become viewed as a team member and have a better chance of building relationships.
- Your team will be delighted to explain their latest successful efforts. Nothing begets success like success. The more you make team members feel good about their accomplishments, the more they will try to accomplish.
- You learn of brewing problems faster than if you wait for them to appear on a status report or to be brought up in a meeting.
- You develop a sixth sense for what is normal within the team and can be more proactive in discerning potential problems.

One caution: As you wander around, resist the urge to micromanage. Do not start giving directions on the spot; the decisions involved are the responsibility of someone else on the project team. If you micromanage, you may undermine a person of prime accountability that you yourself established. You also will send mixed messages as to whom the project team members are to follow.

If circumstances and your schedule allow, perform informal control daily (or almost daily). You need interaction with your team members, and as you gain increased awareness of a project's current condition, you can identify items that need immediate attention. In addition, you will gain a mental image of the project's status and can compare this image with the formal, documented data that are coming across your desk.

As you interact with your project team, give all members an opportunity to ask questions and present problems. As you work with your team members, solicit potential solutions to current problems, evaluate them with the team, and take the necessary action. Your informal communication should increase mutual accessibility between you and your team. Your accessibility is the key to informal control. If you are inaccessible, you will not learn of issues that are in need of attention. The project may very well suffer if you do not manage your team by "wandering around." Making time for this type of informal communication helps you to carry the image of the project's current condition into the formal communication process.

Frequency

What should be the planned frequency for communication? How often do you expect to be in touch? Some individuals will need or request more frequent communication than others. Studies have shown that individual team members require information more often and that the project client and the management team as a unit require it less frequently. In addition to regularly scheduled communications, such as the end-of-quarter financial reconciliation, consider having meetings or calling for reports when key project milestones or other checkpoints are reached. The meeting plan should be part of the project plan, and the time to create, distribute, and review project reports should also be included. This is done so that everyone knows what targets are expected of him or her, and when they must be completed.

The Communication Plan Template

Performance Support Tool 10.3 is an example of a communication plan worksheet. This worksheet consists of four labeled columns. The far-left column, labeled "Who," lists the key stakeholders who will need to receive or to give information about the project. They include the senior management, the project client, the manager of projects, the team members, and the involved resource managers, to name a few. The next column, labeled "What," will indicate the information that this stakeholder needs to receive. The "When" column, in other words; weekly, monthly, quarterly, and so on. On the far right, the "How" column advises what medium will be used for delivery to the stakeholder (e.g., memo or e-mail).

Here are five guidelines to follow when you must generate a communications plan:

1. As with other elements of a project plan, you'll achieve the most thorough and complete result by involving key members of your project team in the process.
2. Working with each member of your team, develop a communications plan that defines your mutual working relationship: how and when communications will take place, and how you'll work together to solve problems. Devising a strategy with each person helps ensure that nothing will fall through the cracks, and protects against "ruffled feathers" among people who feel they have been forgotten.
3. Attempt to have the same information communicated in several different modes, so that, regardless of each person's preferred mode of communications, the information will be available in that mode. For example, some people just don't relate to e-mail. They need to have information sent to them as hard copy or recorded as voice mail.
4. Begin developing your communications plan as soon as you take on a new project. Update it as needed. Project players often change in a project-driven organization. Be sure that you take note of any changes, and develop new communications strategies that are appropriate to the new person.
5. Be considerate toward newcomers or replacements on the project team. Often, they are not given past communications that will bring them up to speed; therefore, they are unable to contribute as quickly as they might.

CONCLUSION

Successful communication does not occur without work. It is the job of all managers of projects to design and implement a communications infrastructure that contains protocols for every type of communication that might occur from the beginning of the project until the end.

These protocols will define the purpose of the communication, the senders and receivers of the messages, the preferred mode of communication, and any relevant support tools—templates, forms, models, checklists, questionnaires, time frames, accountability/authority, and follow-up feedback-tracking mechanisms.

When you decide on the preferred mode of communication, keep in mind that there are multiple modes to facilitate communication. Choose the most appropriate mode, not necessarily the easiest or most accessible. "Lean" modes, such as memos and reports, are appropriate for routine communications requiring no interaction. "Rich" modes, such as phone conversations and one-on-one meetings, are more productive for nonroutine exchanges that need discussion and consensus. Informal one-on-one conversations can offer much information that is helpful in managing a project.

In conclusion, the communications plan does require additional effort, but it has many benefits. You'll have fewer problems, mistakes, and misconceptions. You're likely to reduce the number of wrenches thrown at the project midstream because people were not informed. But perhaps the strongest benefits are on the people side of the equation. You're likely to achieve greater buy-in to the project. You may even reduce the impact of difficult people because they have the information that they need to do their jobs, and they feel included in the process. Communication is one of the critical components of a successful project. As managers of projects, we cannot assign this effort to chance or owe a communications infrastructure to our project players.

Like the baseball coach, we give the signals to the team on the field. We need to be sure that everyone on the team understands how to read those signals. We need to separate signals that are truly urgent and important from signals that can be ignored because they are just informational or are no longer current. We also must create a feedback mechanism to be sure that each team member has received the signal, has understood it, and is willing and able to follow it.

PERFORMANCE SUPPORT TOOL 10.1

Meeting Agenda Planning Sheet

Project Name:

Project Manager:

Meeting Agenda Planning Sheet
For meeting on:

ID	Agenda Item Description	Presenter	Desired Outcome(s)	Purpose* P•C•S•D	Planned Duration	✓ if from last Mtg.

* Key: P = Planning   C = Communications   S = Solving Problems   D = Deciding

Action Item List

Project Name:

Project Manager:

Action Item List

Meeting date:

Name:

ID	Description of Action	Requested By	Deliverable	Due To	Due Date	✓ if from last Mtg.

PERFORMANCE SUPPORT TOOL 10.3

The Communication Plan Worksheet

Who (Project Community Members)	What (Kind of Information)	When (Frequency Needed)	How (Communication Method)
1. Senior Management			
2. Project Client			
3. Manager of Projects			
4. Team Members			
5. Resource Managers			
6.			

CHAPTER 11

Risk Management

The following is a true story about how much risk I am willing to take in front of 200 people. Several years ago, I was going to give a speech at the Project Management Institute's Annual Symposium. As a speaker, I always like to start my presentations with a short, typically theatrical opening that clearly conveys the theme of the speech and intrigues the audience to want to hear more. My speech was to be on risk, and my objective was to demonstrate how much potential risk people are willing to take before they realize that they need to plan for and manage the risk.

I asked Bob, a colleague whom I had known for years, to play along with me. As the session began, I pretended to pick Bob arbitrarily out of the audience. I explained to Bob and the audience that I was going to stand in front of Bob, put my arms out to my sides, become as stiff as I could, and fall back into Bob's arms. Then I would take a step forward (away from Bob) and fall back again into Bob's arms. Each time I moved farther away and the risk that Bob would drop me became greater, I would ask the audience to help me decide whether to take the risk.

I had identified the risk. If I moved too far away from Bob, he might drop me, and I would be lying on the floor in front of an audience of 200 people. The good news is: Bob is a tall and strong man.

The first thing I did was to determine the degree of risk I was taking. I asked Bob the following questions in front of the audience:

"Bob, do you have any back or physical problems that would prevent you from catching me?"

"Bob, do you have anything against short, blond girls [which describes me]?"

"Bob, do you freeze up in front of an audience?"

Bob answered *No* to all of these questions, so the probability that he would drop me was reasonably low. However, I also performed a risk assessment of the impact if he *did* drop me. I identified the risk, and I determined the probability that the risk might occur, and the impact if it did occur. (The impact if he dropped me would be extremely high.)

Then Bob and I started the experiment. I stood in front of Bob with my arms out and my body stiff. I asked the audience whether they thought I should take the risk. When they said yes, I asked Bob if he were ready to catch me. When he said Yes, I promptly fell back into his arms. Then I stood back up, moved a giant step forward, and started the process all over again. As you might imagine, the audience was enthusiastically encouraging when I was closer to Bob; but as I got farther away, more and more people strongly discouraged me from doing it again. Even Bob's confirmation that he was ready to catch me was growing less and less reassuring.

At a certain point, I did lose my nerve and stopped the experiment. Then the audience, Bob, and I talked about how our projects have risks that could embarrass us and possibly hurt us, and how we need to position a risk management process as part of the project management discipline.

CHAPTER OVERVIEW

Risk management is one of the most difficult kinds of planning. After all, risk management is planning for the "expected unexpected"—those events that could happen and have happened, but may not occur in a particular project. Risks, by definition, are unplanned and unexpected discrete events that can affect our projects for better or worse.

The risk management effort is often overlooked because we do not regard it as a distinct process. We just barrel ahead and later smack our forehead and ask, "Why didn't I think of that?" At that point, if we haven't made an effort to at least examine potential risk before the project begins, we have little or no defense.

There are various barriers to risk management. A few of these, along with strategies for overcoming them, are as follows:

- Attempting to perform risk management in a culture that penalizes discussion of risk.
  Strategy: Discuss risk openly with staff, at frequent intervals. Reward honest discussion of risk and of an effective risk management process.
- Scheduling urgency that makes project players feel they don't have time to deal with risk management.

Strategy: The project client may have underestimated the risk inherent in the project. Paint a worst-case scenario and use it to leverage some time for the risk management process.

- Lack of historical information from which to identify risks or to find out what solutions worked in previous projects.
Strategy: Even if there is no documented history, combined individual experiences can be very useful.

Other barriers to good risk management include: product/project complexity, product/project uncertainty, unclear scope/deliverables/requirements, lack of knowledge of clients' priorities, inability to identify risks, and general client reluctance to spend time on risk management. To position risk management for success, these barriers need to be surmounted. Performance Support Tool 11.1, "Barriers to Good Risk Management," at the end of this chapter, will be helpful. Check off the barriers that currently exist in your world, and prepare strategies to overcome them. Do your best to overcome these barriers with the formal and informal authority that you have.

The management of potential risks consists of four distinct efforts. The first three are tactical: (1) risk assessment, (2) risk abatement planning, and (3) risk monitoring, reporting, and managing. The fourth effort, risk planning, is strategic and comes chronologically before the tactical efforts. Risk planning involves a pre-project look at how we approach risk management. As an organization, we decide how much rigor we will apply to managing risk, how risk-tolerant we are, and how we will deal with risks that occur.

In the tactical risk management process, risks are identified and assessed in terms of their probability of occurrence and their impact on a project if they were to occur. If a risk is assessed as needing further risk management, the risk is subjected to a risk abatement planning effort, during which a variety of techniques are used to accommodate, to avoid, and/or to respond to the risk. After the abatement planning process, an individual monitoring, tracking, and reporting effort is made, just for the management of risks.

The risk management phase of project management overlaps the project planning and project control/execution management phases. As demonstrated schematically in Figure 11.1, risk assessment and risk abatement planning are conducted in conjunction with the planning phase, and management of the risk abatement plans is performed during the control/execution management phase.

In this chapter, we look first at the three-part tactical risk management process. We then consider pre-project positioning (risk planning), which involves the identification of strategic policies, procedures, and thresholds that need to be in place before the risk management process can begin. The four

Figure 11.1   Risk Management Mapped against the Project Management Model

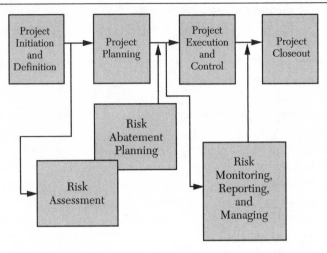

Performance Support Tools at the end of the chapter will help you implement a risk management program in your organization.

This chapter offers five Performance Support Tools for your use. Performance Support Tool 11.1 is a list of barriers to good risk management along with suggested strategies to overcome those barriers. Performance Support Tool 11.2 are examples of Project Risks relating to schedule, budget, scope/quality and resources which will help in the Risk Identification effort. A Risk Report is presented in Performance Support Tool 11.3 to be used to report status of risks during Risk Monitoring, Tracking, and Managing. Performance Support Tool 11.4 is an implementation plan titled "Strategies for Back on the Job." And finally, Performance Support Tool 11.5 provides a worksheet on which you can identify, assess, and plan for each risk found during the Risk Identification effort. These Performance Support Tools are available for download at www.pmsi-pm.com.

Before reading further, refer to the three questions on the Risk Assessment Questionnaire at the end of the chapter.

THE TACTICAL RISK MANAGEMENT PROCESS

As shown in Figure 11.2, the tactical risk management process consists of three efforts: (1) risk assessment, (2) risk abatement planning, and (3) risk monitoring, reporting, and managing. Let's define each of those stages and then delve into each of these efforts in more detail.

Risk assessment isolates the areas of major jeopardy within a project. During this effort, the risks are identified and the areas of high risk are analyzed to determine those that have a high probability of occurring and those that will have the highest potential impact on a project. Simply identifying assessed risks, documenting them, and presenting them to management is, however, only the first part of the process. These risks cannot be simply filed away. Identifying and assessing risks is pointless if the risks are not then carefully and proactively managed. The risks that get through the risk assessment filter move on to the risk abatement planning effort.

Risk abatement planning determines what can be done to accommodate and/or avoid the occurrence of high risk. If the accommodation plans and the avoidance/preventive plans have not been successful, and risk occurs, another step must be taken to respond. Risk abatement planning looks proactively, as well as reactively, at dealing with high risk.

Risk monitoring, reporting, and managing is the ongoing effort, once the project begins, of implementing the preventive risk abatement plans discussed above and monitoring trigger points that indicate a need to put a reactive response plan into motion.

Let's look at each of those risk management efforts.

Figure 11.2   The Three Risk Management Efforts

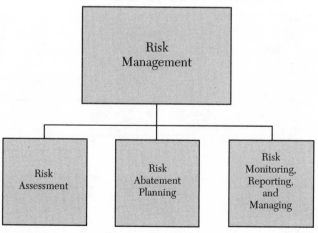

Risk Assessment

As Figure 11.3 shows, risk assessment has three steps: (1) risk identification, (2) probability assessment, and (3) impact assessment. Risk identification isolates the risks associated with a project. Probability assessment determines the likelihood that the risk will occur during the evolution of the project. Impact assessment anticipates the impact on the project if the risk were to occur. Ultimately, the assessment of probability and impact will help you decide the worth of proceeding to the risk abatement planning effort.

Risk Identification

Risk identification points out situations that could affect the project negatively. Four techniques are used to identify areas of risk:

1. Return to the assumptions that were defined during the initiation and definition and the planning phases of the project. (See Chapter 7,

Figure 11.3   Risk Assessment Components

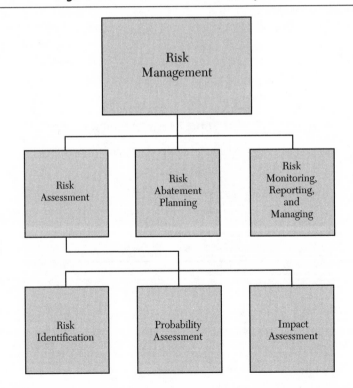

"Portfolio Management," and Chapter 8, "Project Planning.") Consider ramifications to the project if any assumption proves invalid. For example, if you assumed that you would contract with a reliable vendor, how would the project be affected if that vendor proved to be unreliable?

2. Review every task on the work breakdown structure (WBS), every assignment on the staffing plan, every requirement of the end deliverable, and every category of expense in the project budget. Do any of these contain hidden risk? For example, if training the staff to use a new technology has been estimated to take two weeks, what will happen if the technology turns out to be more complicated than expected and the class needs to be longer? What if all of the people who need to be trained are not available in that specific two-week time frame? What if the number of people to be trained is greater than anticipated? These could all be areas of high risk.

3. Revisit the risk management log of similar past projects to determine whether any risks that occurred in previous projects might occur in this project. For example, the project client for this project might have a reputation for changing the scope of the project. Continual change of scope is a potential risk.

4. Bring together a group of project players who have worked on projects similar to this one. Congregate in a room and brainstorm every possible thing that could go wrong in your project. Even if some of the possible risks described seem outlandish, ignore nothing. If you cannot get everyone into the room, as the manager of the project, you should talk one-on-one with all of the identified subject-matter experts. Bear in mind, however, that having all the players in one room may generate ideas that would be lost in individual interviews.

Almost any group idea-generating tool or model will work here. The objective is to focus on any possible risk events that have not been scheduled into the project. The factor that is most critical to the success of this step is discovery of as many potential threats and opportunities concerning the project as possible.

The output of this step is a list of risks. This list should not be prioritized or contain valuations or fixes. The risks may be categorized into functional areas—if the testing group came up with its list of risks, and the engineers developed their list, each list could be kept separate, by function. If your team has used the WBS as a focal point for the discovery of risks, then each risk might be cross-referenced to a WBS identifier or root-cause task.

Many types of risk can impact a project; specific risks tend to vary with the project and the industry. The three generic categories are (1) business risk, (2) product risk, and (3) project risk. A few risks, primarily in the business and product categories, are evident at the time a project is proposed, and before it is selected and approved. Other risks become evident when the scope document is first prepared. Still others become evident as the project is planned. Examples of the three generic categories of risk follow.

Business risks are risks to the organization itself and can include these possibilities:

- The project is intended to alter the manner in which the organization operates (fundamental business processes). For example, an organization that has had a centralized information systems function is now converting to a decentralized approach in which all divisions will have their own computing facility and staff. This type of reorganization faces a high risk that the staff may not accept the new organization and may revolt against the process.
- The product or process being created requires a change in the culture of the organization. For example, the entire organization is changing from a transaction-driven business to a project-driven business; therefore, rather than the processing of transactions such as insurance claims which once drove the business, now projects such as automating claims processing are most important to the success of the business.
- A new commercial, industrial, or consumer product-development project is creating a product that will be entering into new markets in which the organization lacks experience or familiarity. For example, when an organization that is experienced in industrial product marketing undertakes the development and introduction of a consumer product, the organization is putting itself at risk.

Product risks arise because of the nature or substance of the product or service. These may include:

- Potential acceptance by the marketplace of a new technology that is incorporated into the product
- The timing of the product or service introduction. Being too early or too late can cause risk.
- Pricing of the project or service

Other types of product risks are too numerous to catalog. Keep in mind that product risks involve lack of acceptance of the product, not failure of the technology. If the technology fails, the product will not arrive at the market. This is a project risk, not a product risk.

Business and product risks must be evaluated in the portfolio management process. A preliminary review of the amount of risk an organization can assume may dictate that the project not be approved. If the project is approved, careful planning must allow for monitoring the business and/or product risks that may put the project in jeopardy.

As an example, let's say a decision has been made: We must increase our market share within the market segment of 18-to-35-year-olds. We are mandated to increase our net revenue within a certain time frame. This is a project we can normally do, without the extra pressure of time and volume. We will probably add to this project certain tasks that we would not ordinarily do. We might add a potential customer survey; we might want to watch estimated household earnings in this group; we might monitor competitors' activities and promotions in this area; or we might examine present distribution activities to see whether our needs can be accommodated. These additional tasks are now part of the project. They require careful monitoring because if any task deliverable fails to meet desired thresholds, we may be unable to meet the goal of increased profit. The bottom line is: Our project is now too risky.

Project risks revolve around schedule, staffing, budget, and scope, as summarized in Performance Support Tool 11.2, "Examples of Project Risks," at the end of this chapter. These are the risks that managers of projects are likely to be addressing during the risk identification effort.

Areas of high risk regarding the *schedule* include:

- Tasks on critical paths that have no float to accommodate risk occurrence
- Tasks that are dependent on several predecessors
- Tasks that have little float and thus no room for maneuvering
- Optimistically estimated tasks that are already tightly scheduled
- Tasks reliant on external dependencies, such as vendor shipments, over which the manager of the project has minimal control
- Major milestones for which on-time completion is crucial
- Unforeseen tasks

Areas of high risk regarding *staffing* include:

- Tasks assigned to one individual, who will pull the linchpin out of the project if he or she leaves
- Tasks involving many people, who may not communicate clearly to one another and therefore cause quality problems
- Tasks utilizing scarce resources that may be pulled off and reassigned to higher-priority projects

- Underskilled or unqualified team members who will not do the task correctly and will drain productivity from more qualified team members who must help or fix their mistakes
- Illness and/or turnover that will cause a delay until recovery occurs or a new person is found

Areas of high risk regarding *budget* include:

- Uncertainty of corporate budgeting in hard economic times. This can mean a hit to any and all projects under way.
- Shifts in corporate budget priorities that siphon money from one project and award it to a higher-priority project
- Uncertain resource costs that were either unavailable at the time of budgeting or have changed

Areas of high risk regarding *scope* include:

- Uncertainty of new product development because there is no history on which to rely
- Dynamics of product requirements that change at the will of the project client
- Lack of tools and techniques, in the form of equipment or technology or in the form of processes and procedures
- A large number of defects, which creates a snowball effect on tasks downstream and ultimately yields an unacceptable end product

This chapter focuses on project risks. In that regard, it is very important to understand a critical concept that some readers may find difficult to accept. A risk is a potential future event. Both words, *potential* and *future,* are important. After the fact, it's easy to say something happened. But, between now and then, we have a potential risk event that might occur in the future. If it is going to happen and we know it, it is not a risk but an issue we must deal with. For example, if resources are going to be pulled from your project because that is the nature of your organization, then it is not a risk; it will happen, and no amount of whining will prevent it. If that condition exists, it must be dealt with in the original plan. However, if it is possible that a particular resource might be pulled during a critical task and that losing that particular resource at that time will affect the succeeding tasks, then it is a risk to the project, and we can address it with a risk management process.

Figure 11.4 is a worksheet that supports the risk assessment and risk abatement planning within the risk management process. Box 1 refers to a high-risk situation. In this box, you write the event that will cause the risk to

Figure 11.4   Risk Worksheet

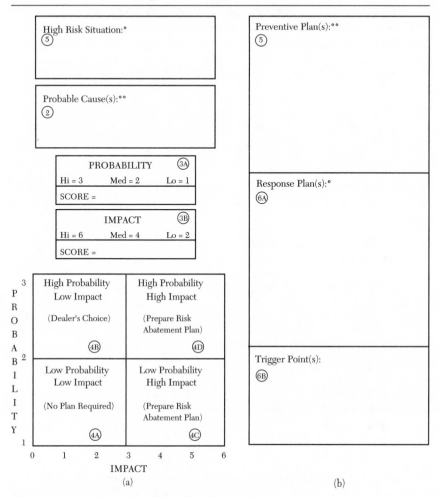

(a)

(b)

*The Response Plan responds to the risk situation.
**The Preventive Plan responds to the probable cause(s).

occur. To fill in this box and to identify areas of high risk, these questions must be asked and answered:

- What are the things that can go wrong on this project?
- What has gone wrong in the past and how did it impact the project?
- What other things could happen that would jeopardize the desired project outcome?

Box 2 of Figure 11.4 refers to probable cause(s). In this box, you write all the situations that could possibly cause the high-risk event to occur.

Consider the following two examples, as if you were filling out the risk worksheet shown in Figure 11.4.

Example 1   Risk: Equipment may not be delivered on time.

Causes:

1. Our specs were not clear enough.
2. The vendor caters to other clients.
3. The vendor is incompetent.

Example 2   Risk: A key player will quit the project at a critical time.

Causes:

1. The player gets a better salary.
2. The player perceives a better career path.

Now that we have identified and documented the high-risk situation and its associated causes, let's look at how to assess the risk and determine whether it warrants a risk abatement plan. We'll start with a probability assessment.

Probability Assessment

The second major step of the risk assessment is *probability assessment*. Box 3 in Figure 11.4 presents a probability index. Each risk that has been identified must be examined, and the probability that the risk will materialize must be determined. It is difficult to quantify some of these probabilities. To serve the needs of most organizations, it is sufficient to classify the probabilities as being high, moderate, or low, which might equate them to the following ranges: low, 0 to 20 percent; moderate, 20 to 30 percent; and high, 30 to 50 percent. The maximum probability of risk is 50 percent because events with a likelihood of greater than 50 percent are considered givens that should be reflected in the project plan. If the probability of a risk's materializing is greater than 50 percent, the plan should reflect the risk, since it is more likely that the event will be encountered. It is important to consider this threshold in your strategic risk-planning effort, which is discussed later in this chapter.

For risk assessment to produce a balanced view, the probability assessment should include opportunities. An opportunity is the potential to complete a project under more favorable circumstances than expected, because a risk that was built into the plan does not materialize. Opportunity is the reciprocal of risk. If a risk has a 70 percent chance of materializing, it is included in the plan, and the risk assessment identifies a 30 percent opportunity to reduce the conservative cost or shorten the schedule of the project.

The above approach to probability assessment is very conservative. In forecasting the potential risks of their projects, some organizations may wish to take a less cautious approach. For example, the line between risks and opportunities may be drawn at a percentage greater than 50 percent. Drawing the line at 75 percent results in a project that is subject to much greater risk and offers fewer opportunities to be gained during project performance. On the other hand, ultraconservatism might incline the organization to draw the line between risk and opportunity at 25 percent. The resulting plan would be relatively risk-free and flush with opportunities to shorten the schedule and/or to reduce the project cost. However, the plan's higher budget and longer schedule may make the project more difficult to justify economically.

In the worksheet shown in Figure 11.4, we have chosen a middle-path approach to quantifying probability and impact. This worksheet simply gives scores of 1 to low probability, 2 to medium probability, and 3 to high probability. Let's consider our earlier examples again, using this scale.

Example 1   Risk: Equipment may not be delivered on time.

Causes:

1. Our specs were not clear enough.
2. The vendor caters to other clients.
3. The vendor is incompetent.

In this scenario, let's assume that the vendor in question is new to your organization, and you chose this company because it came in with the lowest bid. At this point, you can consider the probability of risk to be medium-to-high. In Box 3A, you can score this risk 2.5.

Example 2   Risk: A key player will quit the project at a critical time.

Causes:

1. The player gets a better salary.
2. The player perceives a better career path.

In this scenario, let's assume that the key player comes from a department in which a functional manager strongly supports your project and project management. Thus, you would score this risk as a low probability. In Box 3A, you can give it a score of 1.

Impact Assessment

The third step in risk assessment, after risk identification and probability assessment, is impact assessment. In this step, each risk is evaluated to determine its potential impact on the project's or product's quality, cost, and/or completion date. The impact can be evaluated as high, medium, or low, or given a percentage score. In Box 3B in Figure 11.4, we have weighted impact more heavily than probability by using a scale of 1 to 6 rather than 1 to 3. This is because the ramification to the project if the risk were to occur puts the project in greater jeopardy than does the probability if it were to occur. The purpose is to indicate that the impact variable is more important than is the probability variable. Let's look again at our examples, using this new scale.

Example 1   Risk: Equipment may not be delivered on time.

Causes:

1. Our specs were not clear enough.
2. The vendor caters to other clients.
3. The vendor is incompetent.

In this scenario, let's assume that the delivery of the equipment is on the critical path. If the equipment is not delivered on time, the critical path will slip. Therefore, in Box 3B, we will score the impact of this risk as 6.

Example 2   Risk: A key player will quit the project at a critical time.

Causes:

1. The player gets a better salary.
2. The player perceives a better career path.

In this case, the risk derives from the departure of the key player at a critical time in the project. Thus, this risk deserves a high-impact score. Give it a 5 in Box 3B.

Analyzing Probability and Impact

In Figure 11.4, Box 4 contains the probability/impact grid of the risk worksheet. The process of analyzing probability and impact requires plotting the coordinate where the probability and impact scores meet, and determining in which quadrant the coordinate falls.

The implications of locating probability/impact determinants in each of the four quadrants presented:

- *Lower left quadrant.* If the situation ranks as low probability and low impact (Box 4A), you need not do anything more. In the unlikely event that the situation occurs, it will have minimal impact, and the project team can deal with it at that time. No risk abatement plans are necessary.

- *Upper left quadrant.* If there is high probability and low impact (Box 4B), the dealer or the manager of projects chooses whether to move into the risk abatement planning process. Creating a risk abatement plan is not essential, but, because of the high probability, the manager of the project may want to put such a plan in place.
- *Lower right quadrant.* If the probability is low but the impact is high (Box 4C), as we have determined in Example 2 (in which the key player might quit—a probability score of 1 and an impact of 5), a risk abatement plan should be developed. Although probability is not high, if the risk were to occur, it would have a significant negative impact on the project, and a plan must be in place to deal with it.
- *Upper right quadrant.* If the probability is high and the impact is high (Box 4D), as we found in Example 1 (in which the equipment vendor might not ship on time, a probability score of 2.5 and impact of 6), it is recommended that a risk abatement plan be developed. The risk event has a high degree of probability and it will have a dramatic impact on the project, and you had better plan for it.

Now that we have filtered out the risks that do not require risk abatement planning and are left with only those risks that indicate a need for further attention, we can move forward to the next effort: risk abatement planning.

Risk Abatement Planning

Upon determining that a risk may occur and that it may have an impact on the project, risk abatement planning is performed. As shown in Figure 11.5, there are three types of risk abatement planning: (1) accommodation planning, (2) avoidance planning, and (3) response planning.

Let's explore each method of risk abatement planning. Then we will look at the review-and-approval process that must follow any such method.

Accommodation Planning

Accommodation planning can be accomplished in two ways: (1) by presenting a worst-case scenario plan in addition to the expected plan; or (2) by establishing contingency funds in time, and/or in dollars, to be drawn on when a high-risk situation occurs.

Worst-Case Scenario.   One method of accommodation planning is to present a worst-case-scenario plan in addition to, or in place of, the expected plan. Using the project plan, the task(s) affected by the risk or opportunity are

Figure 11.5   Risk Abatement Components

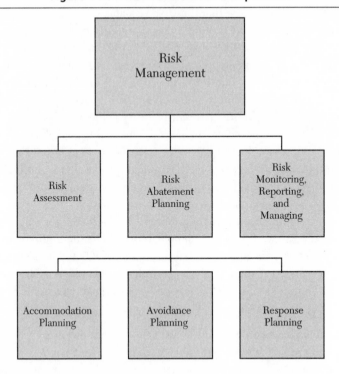

reestimated to include the effect of the risk or opportunity. The worst-case scenario plan can be looked on as a warning of the consequences of late completion, an overspent budget, and/or the poor-quality product that might result if the identified risks were to occur.

With this approach, the project is managed against the original and most likely plan. However, each high risk that actually occurs is recorded and compared to the worst-case scenario as a portent of a need to reforecast the schedule, staffing, and/or budget.

Specifically, the worst-case schedule might indicate new deadlines for high-risk tasks, to accommodate potential slippage. This also involves scheduling, later in the project, tasks that can be postponed or canceled if necessary, and conservatively estimating the duration of tasks on the critical path. The worst-case resource plan would reassign strong people to high-risk tasks and critical-path tasks. It might assign a person, if only minimally, as a backup on any tasks in which the loss of a team member would be damaging, even though this additional resource would require an increased budget. An ultraconservative manager of projects would replace the original expected plan with the worst-case scenario plan.

Let's apply worst-case accommodation planning to our examples.

Example 1   Risk: Equipment may not be delivered on time.

Causes:

1. Our specs were not clear enough.
2. The vendor caters to other clients.
3. The vendor is incompetent.

In the worst-case scenario plan, several steps should be taken to plan ahead for a late delivery. Extra time should be added to the duration of the task, just in case there is a late delivery. Dollars should be added to the budget, to pay the vendor an incentive. Staff should be made available to work with the vendor on the installation task, which is the next effort on the critical path.

Example 2   Risk: A key player will quit the project at a critical time.

Causes:

1. The player gets a better salary.
2. The player perceives a better career path.

Several changes might be made within the project plan, to accommodate this eventuality; for example, extra time may be scheduled to train a replacement. The most experienced person assigned to the project is also the highest paid person thus increasing the project budget. Two people are put on this task. In case one person leaves the other person can pick up the workload.

Negotiating Contingency Funds in Time and in Dollars.   Contingency funds are to be drawn on when a high-risk situation occurs. Contingency funds can be calculated by reestimating the time, staffing, cost, and scope of each task associated with the high-risk situation. The cost of each of these potential new project parameters is totaled to establish the amount of the contingency fund. If you lack time enough to perform a risk-by-risk and line-item-by-line-item evaluation, you can ballpark the additional funds that might be needed. In our two examples, a total contingency for all possible risks would be established, not a contingency for each individual risk.

Contingency funds in dollars are common in many industries. Ten to 15 percent is typically added to the budget to accommodate unknowns, uncertainties, and areas of high risk. Contingency funds to allow extra time are not so typical. However, because planners may be equally uncertain when estimating time or dollars, a 10 to 15 percent contingency fund of time can be allocated at the end of every phase of a product development life cycle.

Ten to 15 percent contingency funding is a rule of thumb. Bear in mind, however, that if the project has already been done many times and a project history is available, a lower percentage may suffice. On the other hand, if the project is new or state-of-the-art and has technological overtones, a higher percentage may be required. After acquiring some project history, each organization will establish its own metric for contingency fund calculation.

WARNING This contingency fund is not to be used for changes of scope. Changes of scope are funded separately, through the change control process. However, for unexpected events that require more money; the contingency fund can be used, with proper authorization.

Avoidance Planning

Avoidance planning involves creating preventive plans. These plans are approaches, either inside or outside the project plan, that would prevent a high-risk situation from occurring. Risk prevention consists of a series of actions that are taken to avoid having risks materialize. Some risk prevention efforts become additional tasks in the project plan. Other risk prevention actions are taken outside the context of the project. Each preventive measure is mapped to a corresponding cause. In Figure 11.4, preventive plans (Box 5) respond to probable causes, whereas response plans (Box 6, discussed below) respond to actual risk situations.

Let's apply avoidance planning to our two examples.

Example 1   Risk: Equipment may not be delivered on time.

Causes:

1. Our specs were not clear enough.
2. The vendor caters to other clients.
3. The vendor is incompetent.

Several preventive measures can be created for this risk event, each mapped to its corresponding cause:

- Create tight and accurate specifications.
- Make contracts strong enough to motivate the vendor to meet the ship dates. Offer bonuses, progress payments, or penalties. Encourage the vendor with future business.

- Conduct a thorough vendor selection process. Monitor progress carefully, and adjust before it becomes a problem.

Example 2   Risk: A key player will quit the project at a critical time.

Causes:

1. The player gets a better salary.
2. The player perceives a better career path.

What can you do to prevent a key player from quitting? The following preventive measures are also mapped to corresponding causes:

- Motivate with a bonus at the end of the project.
- Provide as much intellectual challenge and personal career growth as possible.
- Legally contract with the key player to remain to the end of the project.

Accommodation and avoidance-planning approaches to risk abatement planning are displayed in Figure 11.6. The third approach is response planning.

Response Planning

Response planning is a classic *what if* analysis. A response to each risk or opportunity is planned so that, when and if it materializes, an immediate reaction is possible. This minimizes the amount of time that will elapse from when the risk occurs to when corrective action is taken. It also allows a maximum advantage to be realized from each opportunity, when and if it materializes.

Response plans anticipate situations as precisely as possible. They envision the high risk actually occurring, and they identify what actions would need to ensue as a consequence. This prophesying is sometimes just best-guessing a solution. In most cases, similar situations have occurred, and a project team member recalls what was done to respond successfully.

As in accommodation and avoidance planning, the original project plan is used in response planning. Workaround plans are evaluated, and several alternative responses to the risk or opportunity are selected. Again, as noted in Box 6A of Figure 11.4, response plans address actual risk situations, not probable causes.

NOTE   The nature of some risks may severely alter the viability of the project by delaying its completion too long, causing it to go too far over budget, or producing a totally unacceptable end product. If a risk of this magnitude is identified, it is appropriate to have a planned response that

Figure 11.6   Accommodation and Avoidance Techniques of Risk Abatement Planning

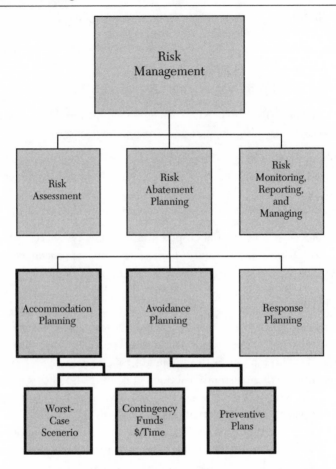

includes consideration of terminating the project in the event that this risk materializes.

Let's apply to our examples the response planning approach to risk abatement.

Example 1   Risk: Equipment may not be delivered on time.

Causes:

1. Our specs were not clear enough.
2. The vendor caters to other clients.
3. The vendor is incompetent.

Several response plans can be created for this risk. One plan would be to contract with a carrier service that costs more but can get the delayed shipment delivered fast. The original contract would specify that the vendor must pay for this shipment. A back-up plan is to start a dialogue with another vendor who can produce the same equipment and, for premium dollars, can produce it fast. Another is to go to the vendor's location and meet with the management, impressing on them the importance of the job, and possibly offering them a bonus to expedite the work.

Example 2   Risk: A key player will quit the project at a critical time.

Causes:

1. The player gets a better salary.
2. The player perceives a better career path.

In this scenario, consider these response plans. A substitute who can assume this role is groomed. Negotiations are undertaken with a functional/resource manager who would designate a backup person if needed. A relationship is cultivated with a consulting firm that contracts out people who have this special expertise.

In Figure 11.4, Box 6B in the risk worksheet allows space to list trigger points. A trigger point is the moment when the response plan is to be activated. This is the time when the team admits that the high-risk situation has materialized, and it is time to respond. Let's define an appropriate trigger point for each of our two examples.

Example 1   Risk: Equipment may not be delivered on time.

Don't wait until the vendor's shipment does not show up at the dock, and then figure out that you have a problem. If the vendor hasn't put the shipment on the road 30 days before the delivery is due, it may be time to set the response plan into action.

Example 2   Risk: A key player will quit the project at a critical time.

It is more difficult to recognize a trigger point in this situation, unless the key player actually comes into your office and quits. However, you can watch for indicators: long lunchhours, new suits, negative comments about the job and the company, and reading *The Wall Street Journal* want-ads at his or her desk.

Review and Approval

To bring the risk abatement planning effort to closure, each of the deliverables must be reviewed, approved, and positioned for use when the project gets under way. Let's take a look at each of the four possible deliverables produced in the risk abatement planning effort.

Worst-Case Scenario.   The manager of the project needs to make all appropriate project players aware that a worst-case scenario plan has been created, and must acquaint them with how it is going to be used. [See Figure 11.7(a).] In the most conservative situations, the worst-case scenario plan will become the active plan that the project team will use. The project will be managed against all the parameters that will accommodate the risks. In other cases, the worst-case scenario plan will merely be presented to put management on notice as to what can be expected if all of these risks occur. The objective is to make management aware of the possible downside. We are saying: "Using the worst-case

Figure 11.7   Risk Abatement Planning Review and Approval

Gain Awareness of
Worst-Case Scenario
and How It
Should Be Used

(a)

Obtain
Approval
of
Contingency Funds

(b)

Inform of
Preventive
Measures
and Impact

(c)

Get Authorization
to Activate
Response Plans
at Trigger Points

(d)

scenario as our benchmark, we will inform you of any changes that may ultimately affect the project's time, cost, and/or quality."

Contingency Funds.   Management and the managers of the project agree on and approve a sum of money (and a total of time) to be set aside as a contingency for the project, as shown in Figure 11.7(b). Agreement must be reached that the manager of the project can use this money to deal with risks and unforeseen occurrences, as required.

Preventive Plans.   Every person affected by the preventive plans is informed of what he or she must do to keep the risk from occurring. [See Figure 11.7(c).]

Response Plans.   The manager of the project obtains authorization so that he or she can immediately activate the response plan when the trigger point occurs, as shown in Figure 11.7(d). This precludes the need for the manager of the project to ask for permission to respond to the risk once it has occurred. There is one exception to this rule: If the response to a particular risk is the termination of the project, this response should be carefully reviewed with management, and an estimate of sunk costs at the time of the decision should be presented.

Risk Monitoring, Reporting, and Managing

Throughout the execution of the project, risk monitoring and opportunity harvesting occur. This is a continuous process; it starts when the plan is approved and culminates at the completion of the project. This process includes the steps of monitoring, reporting, and responding/taking action, as shown in Figure 11.8.

In the monitoring task, each risk or opportunity is periodically reviewed to determine whether the probability and/or potential impact have changed significantly. It is then described in a report, and any relevant action is taken, including either preserving or eliminating the associated risk abatement plan. Every risk or opportunity has a point in time beyond which it is no longer a factor in the project. At that time, the risk or opportunity can be eliminated from the risk abatement plan. When the risk or opportunity impact is originally assessed, a date by which the risk/opportunity might materialize or be eliminated is forecast. This date is used in the risk monitoring process. As the targeted date approaches, the frequency with which the risk or opportunity is monitored should increase. This allows the fastest possible response when action is required. Risk monitoring is presented schematically in Figure 11.9.

Figure 11.8   Risk Monitoring, Reporting, and Managing

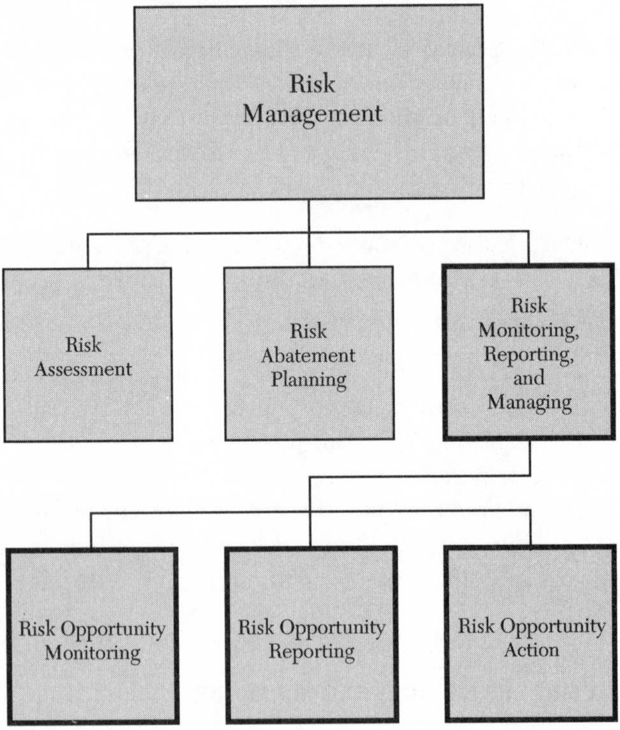

After monitoring, the next component of risk management is risk/opportunity reporting. In this part of the process, the manager of the project informs senior management, and/or the client, of changes in the risks and opportunities associated with the project. Routine periodic reporting updates the risk assessment and presents the current profile of risks and opportunities—past, present, and future. For a suitable risk report format, refer to Performance Support Tool 11.3, "Risk Report," at the end of this chapter.

NOTE On the Risk Report, a Risk Owner has been identified. This is the person who will be responsible for monitoring, tracking, and managing this specific risk. He or she is chosen because they are closest to the risk and can determine better than anyone else whether or not the risk will occur and whether the response plan should be put into motion.

The final element of risk management is *managing the risk*. This is an effort to minimize the impact of a risk once it has materialized, or to take

Figure 11.9   Risk Monitoring

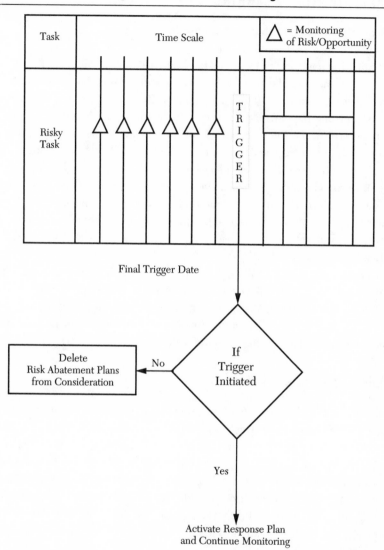

maximum advantage of an opportunity once it presents itself. In this effort, the planned responses to risks and opportunities are implemented. If a risk or opportunity is encountered and it has no planned response, the process includes planning the response, obtaining the required approvals for the response, and taking action once this response has been approved.

STRATEGIC RISK PLANNING

Well before the project starts, the manager of the project needs to look carefully at the heat of the battle that lies ahead. The manager must visualize strategies for handling risks, identify the tactical areas that are most sensitive to risk, and consider how to deal with them. This is never a popular process, but it is a reality of managing projects. It is vastly preferable to waiting until something happens and dealing with it by pointing fingers, calling for more resources, working ungodly hours, ordering do-overs, explaining reduced profits, holding someone's feet to the fire, and witnessing other forms of corporate torture. This part of risk management involves developing policies and procedures to deal with the entire risk process. Risk planning dictates that before the first project dollars are spent, decisions are made concerning the handling of risk areas and risk events. This process uncovers important information that is used later, when the risks that are found are tactically analyzed.

Risk planning means looking at a project and applying proactive perspectives on how to handle risks from an administrative standpoint. Included are such tasks as establishing project rationale, setting the tone, archiving a project's history, assessing thresholds, introducing an escalation process, planning horizons, and accepting accountability.

Establishing Project Rationale

As you analyze risk, always keep in mind the reason for the initiation of the project. Is it based on getting a deliverable into the marketplace? Is it designed in such a way that it can be upgraded later? Is it a matter of making absolutely sure the deliverable performs? (The pharmaceutical industry comes to mind here.) Or is it a deliverable that must meet cost guidelines, as in a fixed-price bid by a solution provider for an outside customer? The manager of the project must know the reason a deliverable is being created. Knowing this, he or she can help to plan for risk management by focusing on the constraint(s) of the end product.

Setting the Tone

All risk management processes must be presented to the project team as soon as, or before, the project actually starts. Let the team members know what is expected of them in the event of any business, product, or project risk. Team members are the single best source of risk discovery. The managers of the projects should provide leadership to the team and demonstrate the processes and tools to be used. The team should know that there is no "Shoot the messenger" attitude, and every risk that is exposed will be given its due under the risk management process. The team should know that upper management expects the manager of projects to report data, variance, progress, and changes in risk situations.

Archiving a Project's History

As in all other aspects of the project management endeavor, keeping and referencing historical project data are vital to the risk management process. Two questions need to be answered: (1) Have data concerning previous risks that have occurred and what was done to deal with them, either successfully or unsuccessfully, been kept? (2) Will managers of projects be required to review the archived history concerning risks? The more rigorous or formal the requirements for structure, the likelier the answer to both questions will be *Yes*.

Assessing Thresholds

The discussion of probability assessment, earlier in this chapter, refers to establishing acceptable thresholds for probability and impact. One option is to define these two parameters as simply high, medium, and low. Another is to rate each of the parameters via a scoring system. The system applied to our worksheet scores probability 1, 2, or 3, and impacts any number from 1 through 6. A more sophisticated alternative is to assign a percentage to each of the two variables. For example, as suggested above, the top of the probability range could be 50 percent. If the probability is considered greater than 50 percent, it is no longer a risk but a given and, as a given, should be part of the *project plan*, not simply the *risk abatement plan*. This part of the strategic risk plan process will define the thresholds that determine which events are considered risks and which are considered givens.

Introducing an Escalation Process

Escalation usually addresses a single risk (or opportunity) that has materialized and how it needs to be reported to the appropriate senior management or client. It is my recommendation that escalation should occur at the first practical moment after the risk or opportunity has materialized. Of critical concern here is ensuring that management and/or the project client is informed of the significant event by the manager of the project, rather than by some other source. It is essential that management and the client be informed before others—who might ask questions of management or the project client—learn of the significant event.

Planning Horizons

Risks, like all the other parts of the planning process, follow a rolling-wave pattern. At the end of every phase of the product development life cycle, the risks that have or have not occurred will be evaluated. The risk events that have not occurred will be deleted from the risk list. The risk events that have occurred will be documented, and their impact on the project completion date, budget, and quality of the product will be considered in light of the worst-case scenario. If there are major ramifications, either positive or negative, the impact will be communicated to the project client and to management. The manager of the project will also assess how much of the contingency fund has been used. If needed, the manager of the project may negotiate more contingency funds. In addition, the manager of the project and the project team will look forward to the next phase. They will review the identified risk list, delete any risks that are no longer valid, and add any new risks that warrant consideration. Then the team will reconfirm that preventive plans are in place for both the old and the new risks identified. They will review the response plans and associated trigger points, and will ready themselves to act if necessary. And, they will create new risk—response plans for the new risks that have been isolated. In other words, at the end of a planning horizon, the team looks at how events in the previous phase might affect the remainder of the project, and then plans, in detail, what is coming up in the next phase.

Risk planning guides us, as managers of projects, in establishing a more rigorous risk management approach. This implies that some formality is given to risk management. We have the ability to add to or lessen that formality. Risk management can range from informally setting aside meeting time to go over what-ifs as a project team, to establishing an oversight board and giving it certain authorizations and formal risk measurements. The manager of the project must gain an understanding of corporate expectations on the risk side of the project management chores. In fact, in a growing number of instances, upper management will be looking to managers of projects for leadership as to which risk management tools and processes can be used.

Accepting Accountability

This policy considers who should be accountable for managing risk, once it is identified and a risk abatement plan is formulated. Should it be the manager of the project? Should various risk owners be given individual risks to "manage"? The second alternative means that the risk owner would be accountable for ensuring that the preventive plan is in place. He or she would also track how fast the contingency funds are being depleted to accommodate the risk when and as needed. In addition, he or she would ensure that the trigger is being monitored and that the response plan is being activated when appropriate. To move one more step toward formality, should a Risk Management Committee be formed and take control of interventions relative to management of risks? These strategic decisions need to be made in a risk-planning effort *before* the project begins.

CONCLUSION

The management of potential risks consists of four distinct efforts. Risk assessment, risk abatement planning, and risk monitoring/reporting/managing are the three tactical efforts. The fourth effort, risk planning, is strategic and involves a preproject assessment of the manner in which risk management will be approached.

In the tactical risk management process, risks are identified and assessed relative to their probability of occurring and their impact on the project if they were to occur. If a risk is assessed as being worthy of further risk management, the risk goes through a risk abatement planning effort during which a variety of techniques are used to accommodate, avoid, and/or respond to the risk. The risk abatement planning process is followed by a risk monitoring, tracking, and reporting effort.

At the end of this chapter, Performance Support Tool 11.2, "Examples of Project Risks," lists numerous types of risks that can be encountered in scheduling, budgeting, scope, and resource alignment. A few risks, primarily in the business and product categories, are evident when the project is proposed and before it is selected and approved. Others become evident at the time the scope document is first prepared. Still others become evident as the project is planned. Some risks do not become evident until we plan for the next phase of the project. Risks that are not identified as part of the first risk assessment effort should nonetheless be identified and subjected to the risk abatement planning process. Unfortunately, some risks are never identified until they occur. Even though these aren't caught until it is too late to do anything but react, we still need to document them—and our responses to them—so that this experience is archived for future use.

Risk is viewed differently, depending on whether you are a team member, a manager of small projects, or a manager of large projects. A team member considers those risks that impact him or her. A manager of small projects considers all the project risks often in an informal manner, and a manager of large projects considers all the project risks in a more formal way. For example, the manager of small projects asks team members to identify the risks to their tasks at every status review meeting. To review the risk management process, the manager of large projects would hold a dedicated risk management meeting at the beginning of every major phase of the project.

To find out more about incorporating risk management into the project work of team members, the manager of small projects, and the manager of large projects, see Performance Support Tool 11.4, "Strategies for Back on the Job," at the end of this chapter. In addition, think about how much tolerance you personally have, and how much tolerance your organization has, toward taking risks. If your organization is risk-averse, I suggest that *you* become risk-averse. If the environment in which you work is risk-tolerant, you need to follow suit. Once you come to terms with the degree of risk you are willing to take, apply what you have learned from this chapter to identify, plan, and manage risks.

PERFORMANCE SUPPORT TOOL 11.1
Barriers to Good Risk Management

BARRIERS	STRATEGIES FOR OVERCOMING BARRIERS
Culture that penalizes discussion of risk	Discuss risk openly with staff at frequent intervals. Reward honest discussion of risk and effective risk-abatement plan development.
Product/project complexity	Develop detailed WBS and schedule for first planning horizon, and focus on risks within this phase. Identify the complexity itself as a risk.
Schedule urgency	The project client may have underestimated the risk inherent in the project. Paint a worst-case scenario and use it to leverage some time for the risk management process.
Product/project uncertainty	Focus on the purpose of the project with the owner or client. Examine alternative objectives to be pursued.
Unclear scope/deliverables/requirements	Make necessary assumptions to come up with a clearer scope/deliverables/requirements, and get client's sign-off. Never proceed with a project plan without a clear objective.
Lack of knowledge of client's priorities	Identify risks to scope, budget, staffing, and schedule, assuming each is important. Pose different scenarios and get client's feedback.
Inability to assemble team in one location	Talk to strategic team members one-on-one, if necessary, to help you identify risks. Follow up verbal communication with a written risk worksheet.
Lack of historical information	Even if there is no documented history, combined individual experiences can be very useful.
Client/sponsor reluctance to spend time on risk management in general	The client/sponsor may have underestimated the risk inherent in the project. Paint a worst-case scenario based on actual past history, and use it to leverage some time for risk management.

PERFORMANCE SUPPORT TOOL 11.2

Examples of Project Risks

Schedule

- Delays due to regulatory approvals, sign-off
- Dependence on external team members, vendors
- Lack of realistic schedule developed to appropriate level of detail
- "Best case" estimating
- Uncertain duration estimates due to lack of experience or history
- Directed (mandated) completion date
- Overuse of "fast-track" ALAP (as late as possible) start (just-in-time scheduling)
- Late delivery

Scope/Quality

- Several clients with competing or multiple objectives/priorities
- Unclear objective
- Inconsistent objectives
- Frequent scope changes
- Unrealistic sponsor expectations
- Inconsistent expectations
- Project complexity
- Concurrent development of components followed by integration
- Scope increase, without increase in schedule or budget
- Early in the process
- Incomplete designs
- Requirements "creep"
- Sheer size and complexity—possible incomplete task list

Budget

- Funding delays
- Inappropriate procurement strategy leading to cost overruns
- Contracts without cost controls (e.g., no earned value)
- Uncertain cost estimates related to lack of experience or history
- Budget cuts potential
- Fixed-price contracts with incomplete design (change orders abound!)
- Unrealistically low cost expectations and constraints
- Fixed-price contracts on developmental projects

Resources

- Lack of clear team structure and communication plan
- Key players without backup
- Key players with other commitments

- Underqualified people
- Lack of availability of appropriately skilled outside vendors
- Lack of management support for project structure, especially in a matrix environment
- Lack of commitment from other department heads
- Lack of commitment from sponsor
- Client not available for reviews
- End users not committed to success

PERFORMANCE SUPPORT TOOL 11.3

Risk Report

Initiator:	**Risk Owner**
Initiated:	**Report Date:**
Telephone:	

1. WBS Line Item:

   WBS Title:

2. Risk Description:

3. Project Impact:

4. Response Plan Implemented:

5. Status:

6. Closure Criteria:

7. Closure Signatures

_____   _____   _____
Initiator   Risk Owner   Manager of Project

PERFORMANCE SUPPORT TOOL 11.4
Strategies for Back on the Job

Risk Management Steps	If You Are a Team Member	If you Manage Small Projects	If You Manage Large Projects
Risk Assessment (identification)	Communicate honestly about risk.	Establish conditions for honest and frequent communication on risk.	Establish the conditions for honest and frequent communication on risk.
	Ask the manager of the project what the project cost, schedule, and quality parameters are.	Ask your project client what the driving project parameters are.	Ask your project client what the driving project parameters are.
	Identify the risks to project tasks, especially those that affect the project parameters.	At every status meeting, ask team members to identify the risks to their tasks, especially those that affect the project parameters.	Hold a dedicated risk management meeting at the beginning of every major phase of the project, particularly if you bring in new team members.
	Make sure you have a solid risk management project plan.	Make sure you have a solid project risk management plan.	Identify risks systematically (project management, deliverable, organizational, external).
			Make sure you have a solid risk management plan.
Risk Assessment (probability/impact analysis)	Make a judgment about which risks are more than 50 percent likely and where the impact will threaten the project client's driving project parameters.	Determine informally with your team if the probability and impact are high enough to threaten the project plan. Try to use risk event value to weight the risks relative to each other so you can focus on the most important tasks.	Select a method to quantify risks.
			Identify the top 10 to 15 risks and weight them by risk event value.

Risk Management Steps	If You Are a Team Member	If you Manage Small Projects	If You Manage Large Projects
Risk Abatement Planning	Document preventive and response plans and get approval from your manager of projects. Identify metrics that are measurable and predictive for response planning and technical performance measurement.	Identify the risk owner for each risk, and have the owners document the risk management plans on a risk management worksheet. Get plan approval from your project client.	Develop preventive, accommodative, and responsive plans for these risks, as appropriate, and get approval from your project client. Identify the risk owners and have them document the risk management plans on a risk management worksheet.
Risk Monitoring, Reporting, and Managing	Notify your project manager if the trigger events occur, and get approval to activate response plans. Document all risk events and your responses.	Notify your project client and your team if the trigger events occur, and get approval to activate response plans. Document all risk events and your responses.	Notify your project client and your team if the trigger events occur, and get approval to activate response plans. Identify a date for revisiting the risk management plan. Document all risk events and your responses.

PERFORMANCE SUPPORT TOOL 11.5

Risk Abatement Planning

High Risk Situation:*
(1)

Probable Cause(s):**
(2)

PROBABILITY		(3A)
Hi = 3 Med = 2 Lo = 1		
SCORE =		

IMPACT		(3B)
Hi = 6 Med = 4 Lo = 2		
SCORE =		

3	**High Probability Low Impact** (Dealer's Choice) (4B)	**High Probability High Impact** (Prepare Risk Abatement Plan) (4D)
2	**Low Probability Low Impact** (No Plan Required) (4A)	**Low Probability High Impact** (Prepare Risk Abatement Plan) (4C)
1		

P R O B A B I L I T Y

0   1   2   3   4   5   6

IMPACT

(a)

Preventive Plan(s):**
(5)

Response Plan(s):*
(6A)

Trigger Point(s):
(6B)

(b)

ASSESSMENT TOOL

Risk Assessment

General Questions	Response
	Answer each question in the space provided.
1. To what degree do you assess risks?	High _____ Medium _____ Low _____
2. To what degree do you develop contingency plans?	High _____ Medium _____ Low _____
3. How often do you produce best/worst case schedules and resource analysis?	

CHAPTER 12

Closeout Management

The project is over. As the manager of the project, I've scheduled a super party. We're going to have wine and cheese. I've rented a room in a nearby restaurant. Significant others are invited.

The plan is for all of the project team, the project client, and specific stakeholders to leave the office at four o'clock and head for the restaurant. We'll all stand around and talk for about an hour. Then I'll present a toast to thank everyone for his or her help and support. And if it goes as other closeout parties have gone, everyone will start heading for home as soon as the toast is over.

Of course, I don't want to say anything about the bad things that happened during the project. Every project has its failures. In fact, we did some things wrong on this project that we did wrong on the last project too. I wonder why we can't ever learn. No matter. I'll make reference only to the good things that happened. We did get the project done, and that is something to celebrate.

I've done lots of these wine and cheese parties after projects, and they never seem to be very satisfying. People don't seem to be excited about coming. They almost act like it is a chore. I'd like to give some kind of rewards or recognition, but once I give it to one person, I need to make up reasons to give something to everyone because I don't dare leave anyone out.

I wish there was a more professional way to bring closure to a project. A way in which we could get together as a group and hash out what went right and went wrong, and be able to learn from our successes and failures for the next time. But a meeting like that would turn into an attack session in which everyone would be trying to put blame on everyone else. That would be less than productive, so I guess I'll forget that idea.

Well, it's four o'clock. Let's go. It's only a couple of hours, and it will soon be over.

CHAPTER OVERVIEW

Closeout is the last major phase in the project life cycle. The process is generally referred to as post-project review. Closeout includes the steps that the project client, the manager of the project, and the team will take to collect the final actual data, to evaluate the project, and to archive the project information. When this step is finished, the project is officially over, and the team is officially released to move on to other projects. Figure 12.1 is the model that portrays the close-out phase.

The purpose of the post-project review is to look back at the just-completed project and identify what was done well and what was not done well. This is not just the wine and cheese party. A celebration is certainly appropriate, but the closeout effort itself is a professional review of the successes and failures of the project. The closeout is not a bashing, nor is it an attempt to lay blame on anyone. Its purpose is to have the project team, and any other people who were involved in the project, spend time reevaluating what went on during the project, and to glean what they can. This reevaluation is done so that people can learn from the effort and can grow and become better at their jobs. The process supports a philosophy of continuous improvement. The lessons learned need to be documented and made available so that people who may be working on similar projects in the future can take advantage of this team's experiences.

This phase of the project life cycle is often forgotten—or avoided. The countless reasons for avoiding it include:

1. It often takes time and effort that are not budgeted. In some (if not most) project schedules, time is allocated to finish the project and complete the deliverable, but not to go back and ferret out the good and the bad.
2. The people involved in the project have headed off, or are anxious to head off, to other jobs. If the project ran beyond the original time estimate, team members may be late for their next assignment.
3. Project team members are afraid that if they made a mistake during the project, they will be embarrassed or their reputation will be sullied if the project work is reviewed.

A decision to avoid the post-project review is not prudent. At the end of the project, the project team and any involved project players must conduct a formal evaluation in order to learn from what went on and to pass on those lessons to other people who will one day be in their shoes. It is highly recommended that post-project reviews be conducted at the end of every project.

Figure 12.1   Closeout Model

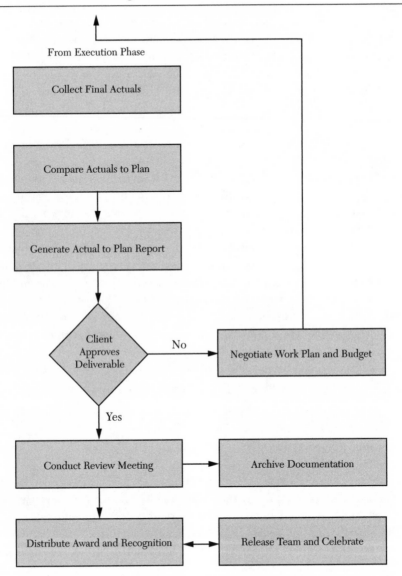

For projects of long duration, it is wise to conduct a closeout effort at the end of every phase of the product development life cycle. This allows the exercise to be done when the lessons learned are still fresh in everyone's mind, and it encourages the team to apply those lessons to upcoming phases of the project.

This chapter explores the closeout process and discusses preparation for the review, the required closeout steps, the appropriate questions to ask during the process, and how to identify and archive the lessons learned. Performance Support Tool 12.1, "Project Closeout Questionnaire," is an important element of this chapter. It offers a list of questions that must be answered during the post-project review. The questions can be distributed as a questionnaire or discussed in a review meeting. The information gleaned from this exercise should be codified and archived for future reference. This and all other Performance Support and Assessment Tools referenced in this book are available for download at www.pmsi-pm.com.

We begin by differentiating between the post-project review that should be done immediately after the project is completed, and a second review that should be conducted later, to determine whether the project's end-product is meeting its business goals.

Before reading further, complete the Assessment Tool at the end of this chapter to determine your perception of the maturity of your organization regarding Project Closeout.

THE SHORT-TERM AND LONG-TERM POST-PROJECT REVIEW

Traditionally, two separate efforts constitute a post-project review. The first effort is conducted shortly after the project is completed. Its purposes are: to secure acceptance of the end-deliverable by the project client, and to discuss with the project team the project lessons learned (ideally, while they are still fresh in mind). The second review is an evaluation of the product or service that was accomplished by the project, and how it is performing. This review is done several weeks or months after the project has been completed, to allow enough time for the users of the product or service to adequately evaluate its performance. Why wait for several weeks or months to perform the second review? Here are three reasons:

1. Possible defects aren't always detected immediately after implementation.

2. The operational client (the person using the product or service) needs time to get beyond the cultural shock of using something new or doing something differently. It has been proven that, no matter how good the end-product is, the people using it will find problems with it just because it is new to them. Waiting an appropriate period of time allows the subjective response to fade. End-users will then be more objective in their evaluations.

3. Any effort to modify or enhance the product or service must be regarded as a new project, which would be subject to new portfolio management and project planning processes. If there is no interim waiting period, project players may regard any modifications or enhancements as mere continuations of the original project, which do not necessitate new funding. The waiting period also allows the product or service to be shaken out so that as many change requests as possible can be packaged in one project, rather than attempting to justify a whole series of new projects.

This chapter concentrates on the short-term post-project review process—seeing whether the end-product has met the requirements/specifications, and exploring what can be learned from the project process. To be prepared, at the end of the project, to conduct this post-project review, the manager of the project and the key stakeholders must reach consensus about what will be evaluated. Here, we will look at what needs to be done at the beginning of the project so that we are ready for the closeout.

To Be Ready for the End, Prepare at the Beginning

During the review of the project, all the involved project players will respond to a list of questions. The answers to these questions represent the lessons that have been learned during the evolution of the project. These questions delve into not only what happened as the project progressed but what any or all project team members would do differently if they had to do the project over again. The lessons learned will provide insight into the specifics of what occurred during the project and will offer guidance for how to plan, organize, and manage future similar projects.

Although we respond to these questions during the last phase of the project life cycle, the review questionnaire must be considered and prepared at the beginning of the project so that:

1. All project players are aware of how the project will be evaluated at the end of the effort.
2. The project players who control data, files, documents, and logs are informed of what they are being asked to compile and maintain. All project players are compiling the needed documentation from the moment the project begins. The documentation will then be ready when the project moves into the closeout phase, so people will not need to spend time racing around collecting the data that are necessary for review.

3. The appropriate documentation will not be lost by the end of the project.

4. Project players can modify the questionnaire to accommodate their own unique project and group of people.

What needs to be done at the beginning of the project to prepare everyone for the closeout at the end?

The team needs to modify the Project Closeout Questionnaire (provided as Performance Support Tool 12.1, at the end of this chapter) according to the needs of the project and the organization. Each member of the team must read the list carefully and note any areas in which modifications seem appropriate. Several types of modifications might be necessary, such as:

1. The terminology may be different for this team/project, so the lexicon of terms may need to be revised.

2. Because all of the steps in the process may not be relevant, some may be deleted and others may need to be added.

3. The project team members who are accountable for the various steps in the process may vary, depending on the project.

4. The type of information that is required, and the means by which it is collected, may change from project to project.

5. The technique for getting responses to the questionnaire may differ, depending on how far apart geographically the project players are.

6. The location of the archived information should remain the same, but the format for presenting the output may change.

After the content of the questionnaire is solidified, the revised version must be distributed to all the project players. This makes them aware of the questions they will be expected to answer after the completion of the project. Instructions on how to accumulate and maintain the necessary data must also be disseminated. Project players might be encouraged to prepare a log book, preferably online, in which they can keep a running diary of the answers to these questions.

REMEMBER One must inspect what they expect. The manager of the project must periodically ask to see the logs, the compiled reports, the spreadsheets; or whatever other mechanisms have been chosen to accumulate the information that will be needed at the end of the project.

Given a basic understanding of the short-term post-project review and of how to prepare, at the beginning of the project, for orderly accumulation of the data that will be needed at the end, let's examine the steps in the closeout phase.

Steps in the Post-Project Review Process

The eight steps in this process are listed in the model of the post-project review process presented in Table 12.1.

As we look at each step in detail, we will consider what needs to be done, who is accountable, and the benefits to the closeout process.

Step 1: Collect Final Actuals

The manager of the project collects final actual data ("actuals") from the team. This process often requires persistence, especially if, as often occurs, the project team members have disbanded and are working on other projects while this project is still under way. Team members may feel that they no longer report to the manager of the project.

Actuals can come from any or all of the following sources:

- *Accounting.* In most organizations, the finance department—as part of its normal business operations—will have been keeping records relative to the payroll of project players, out-of-pocket expenses for purchase of equipment, payments to subcontractors, travel costs, and other necessary outlays.

Table 12.1   Steps in the Post-Project Review Process

Step	Activity	Prime Responsibility	Support Responsibility
1	Collect final actuals.	Manager of project	Project team
2	Compare final actuals to plan.	Manager of project	
3	Generate final actual versus plan documentation.	Manager of project	
4	Approve final deliverable (decision point).	Project client	
5a	Conduct post-project review meeting.	Manager of project	Project team
5b	Negotiate final work plan and budget.	Manager of project	Project client
6	Distribute awards and recognition.	Manager of project	Project team
7	Archive project documentation.	Manager of project	
8	Release team and celebrate.	Manager of project	Project team and others

- *The team.* All involved project players will have been instructed to keep a log that is linked to the list of closeout questions, and any and all documentation that supports either a positive or a negative lesson learned.
- *The project plan.* The project plan is the tangible, touchable proof that compares what was planned and what actually occurred. Project plans consist of the schedule, the staffing plan, the budget, the risk management plan, the issues log, the work accomplishment plan, and any other plans that the manager of the project may have created.
- *The change log.* The change log documents the history of any changes to the scope of the product or service, the amount of time invested in deciding whether to perform the change, the decision on whether to approve and fund the change, and the amount of time and/or money required to make the change.

The manager of the project must validate the final actuals for accuracy and review all the data for reasonability. He or she could not possibly know whether all of the information is absolutely correct, but the actuals should be close enough to reveal anything that does not ring true. When something does not make sense, the manager of the project needs to question the source. If the data are not valid and there is no way to reconstruct their origins, they should be eliminated from the evaluation.

Benefit Because the project is not declared complete until all final data have been submitted, the team members are motivated to finish this step in the closeout process so that they can be officially released to other projects and functional/departmental work.

Step 2: Compare Final Actuals to Plan

The manager of the project reviews all of the final data collected in Step 1, compares them to the plan to determine final variances, matches the actual quality of the deliverable(s) against the specifications/requirements, and reviews the project process.

When actual variances are compared to the plan, there are only three possible outcomes:

1. We did better than planned.
2. We did worse than planned.
3. We did exactly what was planned.

This comparison involves the last negotiated plan as well as the original baseline. The comparison to the last negotiated plan shows how the outside world will evaluate our success or failure. The comparison to the original plan will offer insight into what changed from the original plan and what we can learn so that we can plan better in the future.

WARNING   If everything meets the plan, something is wrong. No project, no manager of a project, no project team is that good; this outcome does not pass a reasonability check. The manager of the project should go back and recheck the validity of the data.

Benefit   This step helps the manager of the project to develop the final actual-versus-plan documentation and to prepare for the final project review.

Step 3: Generate Final Actual versus Plan Documentation

The manager of the project uses the final actuals to complete the actual-versus-plan documents. These documents will be distributed to all the stakeholders for use as part of their formal evaluation. The information that must be compiled for this report can be organized in the following model outline:

I. Background of the Project

Includes project ID number, designated project client or champion, names of all project players and their departments, project charter or statement of work, and project's priority position. This is the same data that was entered into the project database during the registration process of the Portfolio Management systems discussed in Chapter 7.

II. Product

Answers whether the product did/did not meet expectations and what changes were/were not made to the specifications/requirements

III. Project

Offers documentation of the comparison of the actual against the plan and sets the stage for further exploration of the variances that were analyzed in Step 2

Benefit   The stakeholders have the complete data needed to conduct their project evaluation, which ensures that appropriate and consistent information will be considered.

We now approach the point of decision concerning the approval of the end-product. Only after Step 4 is completed can we move on to an evaluation of the project process. Let's look first at the evaluation of the product.

Step 4: Approve Final Deliverable

The project client approves the final deliverable. This critical step represents a formal sign-off and acceptance of the project deliverable and signals that the project work is complete. (Keep in mind that analysis of the project process remains to be done.)

> **Benefit** This step creates an official end-point for the project work and requires the project client to accept or reject the deliverable. The acceptance or rejection of the end-product is objective; it is based on quantifiable performance criteria. If management and/or the project client has participated in scope-change management and phase reviews throughout the evolution of the project, rejection of the deliverable at this point should be rare.

This is a decision step, not an action step. If the project client does not accept the deliverable, the manager of the project and the project client must address that situation in the manner described in Step 5(a) below. If the project client accepts the deliverable, the post-project review of the project process begins. [See Step 5(b).] Let's look first at a scenario in which the project client rejects the deliverable.

Step 5(a): Negotiate Final Work Plan and Budget

If the project client rejects the deliverable, the manager of the project and the project client negotiate a new project plan and budget to complete the needed work. If the project client rejects the deliverable because it lacks features that were not included in the latest approved scope, the manager of the project can appeal the decision to management and lobby for additional funds and time to begin a new project that will satisfy these new requirements. In other words, if the client rejects the deliverable because he or she wants features not specified in the latest scope statement, the manager of the project can appropriately require a new business case for delivery of the additional features. If the project client rejects the deliverable because it fails to pass the agreed-on completion and performance criteria, the manager of the project has little recourse and must extend the project until the deliverable passes muster. After completion of the remaining work, the post-project review starts again at Step 1.

> **Benefit** This step requires the manager of the project and the project client to agree on a project plan for the remaining work. Without

an agreement, work cannot proceed. Because all the parties benefit from completing the project as soon as possible, the project client and the manager of the project have a strong incentive to collaborate on a solution.

Now that we have addressed the post-project review of the product and have an accepted product/service, we move on to the review of the project process.

Step 5(b): Conduct Post-Project Review Meeting

The manager of the project and the project team convene a post-project review meeting with the appropriate stakeholders. This step allows all parties to evaluate the project and to capture lessons that can be applied to future projects. (Specific questions are summarized in the next section, "The Right Questions to Ask," and are included in Performance Support Tool 12.1 at the end of this chapter.)

The agenda for the post-project review meeting can be tailored from the following model:

I. Background of the Project
Presents the same information as in the final document produced in Step 3: the project ID number; the designated project client or champion; the names of all project players and their departments; the project charter or the statement of work; and the project's priority position

II. Comparison of Plan versus Actual Data
Presents all of the information compiled in Step 3, plus any modifications that have resulted from the manager of the project's reasonability check

III. Analysis of the Project Closeout Questionnaire
Discusses the content of the Performance Support Tool included at the end of this chapter

IV. Rewards and Recognition
Follows the process described in Step 6. (following)

V. Next Steps
Explores how lessons learned will be finalized and documented, and where they will be archived for future reference

This post-project review meeting should be conducted like all other meetings, while observing the following guidelines, which are unique to this specific meeting:

- Be sensitive to people's time. Most of the participants either have moved on or are anxious to close this project experience and move on to the next job.
- Publish the agenda in advance. Everyone must be prepared to discuss each of the questions and offer insights succinctly and tactfully. The project team will have had the questionnaire since the beginning of the project; so they should be able to prepare without too much difficulty. Remind them to think through their answers in advance, so as not to waste the group's time.
- Establish a clear purpose; the meeting should be a positive experience that makes the attendees better and smarter the next time. To ensure that the meeting does not become an attack-and-blame session, the facilitator should maintain a positive tone of continuous improvement and lessons learned. Insist on objectivity.
- Meticulously record any actions or practices worth repeating or avoiding, and anything that should be done in the future to achieve even greater success. If the lessons learned are brought out on the table but are not captured for future generations, the effort is worthless.
- Describe where it will be archived and how it can be accessed in the future by this team and other teams so that everyone understands that the information being compiled during the meeting will actually be used.

Benefit   This step allows the project to be evaluated as a holistic endeavor by all appropriate stakeholders. If a project comes in on time, on budget, and per quality specifications but lacks a satisfied project client or a group of team members who are willing to work again with the manager of the project, today's business community will not consider that project successful. This step allows all the data, hard and soft, to enter into the evaluation.

Step 6: Distribute Awards and Recognition

The manager of the project distributes awards to the project team members. This is his or her opportunity to thank and acknowledge all the team members for their participation and to bestow specific awards on team members who deserve special recognition. The manager of the project should develop clear, objective criteria for bestowing special awards.

Managers of projects should give recognition to project team members who have made a difference in the success of the venture, not simply to folks they like. It is not necessary to give an award or recognition to everyone. Inventing some reason to reward every project player becomes fairly transparent and will not gain favor for the manager of the project. The correct political solution is to give a group award/recognition to everyone on the team, listed in alphabetical order, and also to give specific awards/recognition to team members who truly deserve accolades.

Benefit   The team will appreciate the manager of the project's recognition of the human side of the project. Managers of projects who succeed in removing barriers for their team, and who motivate through acknowledgment and insistence on high standards, will be more successful in recruiting resources for future projects.

Step 7: Archive Project Documentation

The manager of the project archives the project documentation in a designated location that is accessible to appropriate people for future planning purposes. The manager of the project can archive selected project data onto a server or Intranet for quick reference. Hard-copy documentation must also be stored in an accessible place.

NOTE   In electronic or hard-copy media, the manager of the project archives the WBS in a "template library" so that it can also be used for future projects.

Benefit   If the data are available and put to good use, the organization can avoid making the same mistakes over and over.

Step 8: Release the Team and Celebrate

When the manager of the project officially releases the team members from the project, this step marks the formal close of the project management process for the project. Team members no longer have any obligation to the project and are officially available for other project work. This step should always include that wine and cheese party or an appropriate celebration of the work accomplished.

Benefit   Everyone knows the project is over. Team members have been acknowledged for their work. The celebration gives everyone who has been involved in the project formal closure and a chance to bask in a sense of accomplishment. This ending builds morale for future projects.

Now let's return to the questionnaire discussed in Step 5(b) and learn more about its content.

THE RIGHT QUESTIONS TO ASK

The post-project review questionnaire consists of three parts. Questions need to be asked about (1) the **product** and its development; (2) the **process** issues related to procedures and systems; and (3) the **people/politics** issues that deal with human or sociological considerations. (Performance Support Tool 12.1, at the end of this chapter, presents the entire questionnaire.)

Part I: Product

To get a good sense of how the product turned out and how its specification and design were developed, answer the questions listed below. This part of the questionnaire addresses the deliverables, requirements, and design issues. Here is a brief explanation of each of those sections:

Deliverables. Explores whether the product/service met specifications/requirements.

What worked? What didn't work? What would we do differently?

Requirements. Consider the techniques that were used to define the requirements.

What worked? What didn't work? What would we do differently?

Design Issues. Delves into both the process used to deal with design changes and the methodology used to produce the design in the first place.

What worked? What didn't work? What would we do differently?

Part II: Project

To analyze the project baselines plan against actual, answer the questions below. This section addresses schedule, resource, and budget:

Schedule. Considers basis on which the project deadlines and the phase deadlines were planned. Determines whether the entire project and the project phases finished on schedule. If they did not, what was done to bring the project back on schedule?

What worked? What didn't work? What would we do differently?

Resources. Analyzes the personnel mix involved in the project: full versus part-time, management versus staff, total numbers contributing and so on.

What worked? What didn't work? What would we do differently?

Budget. Considers basis on which the project budget was planned. Determines whether the project came in on or under budget. If it did not, what was done to bring the project back on budget?

What worked? What didn't work? What would we do differently?

Part III: Processes

To obtain feedback on the processes used during the evolution of the project, answer the questions below. This part of the questionnaire looks at history metrics, communication infrastructure, change control, project management tools, risk management, and execution management:

History Metrics. Considers the history of previous projects and current history relative to such basic project parameters as schedule, staffing, budget, and quality and how that will be passed on to the next generation.

What worked? What didn't work? What would we do differently?

Communication Infrastructure. Addresses the communication techniques among the team and between the team and upper management.

What worked? What didn't work? What would we do differently?

Change Control. Examines the process used to manage changes to the scope or requirements of the product.

What worked? What didn't work? What would we do differently?

Project Management Tools. Focuses on the automated tools that were used to track the plan against the actual and to produce reports for stakeholders.

What worked? What didn't work? What would we do differently?

Risk Management. Explores the risk management process as well as how response plans were used.

What worked? What didn't work? What would we do differently?

Execution Management. Explores how actuals were captured, how variances were isolated, and how baselines were replanned and, if necessary, reforecasted.

What worked? What didn't work? What would we do differently?

Part IV. People/Politics

To evaluate the human considerations in order to get feedback on team dynamics, answer the questions below. These questions deal with organization, client interaction, accountability, the project team interactions, cross-functional teams, and managing relationships:

Organization. Examines the breadth and commitment of functional areas that were involved in the project.

What worked? What didn't work? What would we do differently?

Client Interactions. Searches for insights to the best relationship with project clients: considers how many clients are being serviced, when they were brought into the project, and how interaction with them was orchestrated.

What worked? What didn't work? What would we do differently?

Accountability. Delves into concerns of responsibility, accountability, and authority with the project team.

What worked? What didn't work? What would we do differently?

Project Team Interactions. Looks at the skills (or lack thereof), the behaviors, the amount of overtime required, and the turnover of this unique project team.

What worked? What didn't work? What would we do differently?

Cross-Functional Teams. Deals with the makeup of the group, size of the team and leadership of the team.

What worked? What didn't work? What would we do differently?

Managing Relationships. Views the interaction among the manager of projects and all the other project players.

What worked? What didn't work? What would we do differently?

What worked? What didn't work? What would we do differently the next time? That is the mantra of the closeout effort. It must be asked every time.

CONCLUSION

In addition to being the last major phase in the project life cycle, project closeout provides a systematic review of the product, process, and people. It is the basis of continuous improvement within the project discipline. However tempted you may be to ignore this vital effort and get on with your next project, the time you invest in focusing on project closeout will contribute enormously to the success of your future projects.

Prepare for closeout at the beginning of the project by determining the questions that will be asked at the end. Do not let crises prevent collection of the necessary data throughout the entire project. Do not cancel the post-project review phase of the project for any reason. This effort is crucial to the future success of individual projects and of the project management discipline.

PERFORMANCE SUPPORT TOOL 12.1

Project Closeout Questionnaire

This Support Tool lists the types of questions that need to be asked during the post-project review. The answers to these questions have evolved from the lessons learned during the evolution of this project. Review this list and modify it to reflect the terminology used within your organization and to fit the type of project that is being evaluated.

Solidify the Questionnaire during the planning phase of the project and inform all the involved project players of the questions they will be expected to answer after the project is completed. Consider preparing a log book, preferably online, in which the project players can keep a running diary of the answers to these questions.

The post-project review must be conducted at the end of every project. For projects of long duration, it is wise to conduct a review at the end of every phase of the product development life cycle, when lessons learned are still fresh in everyone's mind and can be applied to upcoming phases of the project.

Lessons learned not only provide insight into what occurred during the project but also offer guidance on how to plan, organize, and manage similar future projects. Categorize the responses in a way that will make the information easily accessible to people who would like to learn from the lessons and experiences of your project.

PRODUCT-RELATED VARIABLES

Deliverables

- What product or service was produced?
- What were the quantifiable success criteria on which the product or service was to be measured?
- When the project was complete, did the project deliverable meet success criteria without additional work? If additional work was required, describe it. Why was the additional work needed?
- Did the product or service produced meet the business need that justified the project?

Requirements

- In what way were requirements initially gathered?
- Did the requirements, as specified, meet the client's business needs?
- From whom were the requirements gathered? Were these the right people? In other words, were the operational clients and the strategic clients considered as well?
- Was there a methodology used for defining requirements used? Explain how it was used and the lessons learned.
- How were the requirements documented?
- How detailed did the requirement document become? Was it sufficient to prevent unnecessary work? Who was involved in specifying, collecting, and documenting the requirements?
- Were any particular techniques for defining requirements (especially quantitative techniques) used? Were they successful?

- How were the requirements documented and communicated to the project client, to the team, and to other stakeholders?
- What recommendations would you make for future projects regarding (a) how requirements were gathered, (b) from whom requirements were gathered, (c) the level of detail of the requirements, (d) how requirements were documented and communicated.

Design Issues

- Were there design changes? How many? Was there a differentiation as to small, medium, and large design changes?
- What were the guidelines for decisions on which design changes to approve and which ones to reject? How and when were these guidelines developed?
- What formal design methodologies were employed, if any? How did they work?
- Would you recommend this same design methodology for future projects? Why or why not? How could this (or another) methodology be better managed in future projects?
- How was usage of the methodology enforced? Would alternative enforcement techniques work better in future projects?
- How were design changes documented and communicated to stakeholders?
- What recommendations would you make for future projects regarding (a) guidelines for approval of design changes, (b) formal design methodologies used, (c) enforcement regarding the use of formal methodologies, (d) documentation and communication of design changes?

PROJECT-RELATED VARIABLES

Organization

- How many organizational units were involved in the overall project? Specify their names, their location(s), their functions within the organizational unit, roles in the project and contributions to the project.

Schedule

- What was the planned completion date of the project? Based on what constraints?
- What was the planned completion of each product development phase and/or key milestones? Based on what assumptions?
- How close to the scheduled completion date was the project actually completed? Was the schedule fixed?
- What factors enabled the team to stay on schedule? What factors caused delays?
- Was the WBS developed down to a level of detail that was appropriate for driving an accurate schedule?
- Were task estimates based on an effort and duration estimating model? Were updates ongoing? Were they based on new knowledge and project changes?
- Did the team effectively use a variety of dependency relationship types to optimize the schedule? If so, how did the team develop the dependency model?
- Was the baseline updated when schedule delays made the original plan unachievable? If so, was a record of baseline changes kept?

- How were schedule changes documented and communicated?
- What recommendations would you make for future projects on (a) developing an effective WBS, (b) task estimating processes and models, (c) use of task dependencies to generate the schedule, (d) setting and updating the schedule baseline, (f) documenting and communicating schedule changes?

Staffing

- How many individual team members and other stakeholders were involved? How did the numbers of full-time team members compare to the number of part-time team members? How did the numbers of resource managers compare to the number of supporting team members and other stakeholders?
- How was the responsibility for resource allocation determined and controlled?

Budget

- How close was the actual budget to the planned budget? Was the budget fixed?
- What factors enabled the team to stay within budget? What factors caused overruns?
- Did the manager of the project, and the full team, use accurate cost rates?
- Did the manager of the project identify and use all appropriate cost categories?
- Was the WBS developed in sufficient detail to provide accurate cost estimates?
- Was an estimating model used? If so, how effective was it in generating accurate budget estimates?
- Was the budget updated based on new knowledge and project changes?
- Was the baseline budget reforecast when project changes made the original budget unachievable?
- How were budget changes documented and communicated?
- On future projects, what recommendations would you make (a) developing an effective WBS for better budgeting, (b) cost estimating processes and models, (c) setting and updating the baseline, and (d) documenting and communicating the budget?

PROCESS-RELATED QUESTIONS

History Metrics

- In what ways did the project draw on experience from similar past projects? What were the sources of that history? How valid did you find that history? If invalid, how did you discern what was invalid and how did you compensate for the invalidity?
- For future records, by what percentage or absolute figure did overall project performance vary from initial estimates: budget, quality, schedule, and resources?

Communication Infrastructure

- How was communication across multiple locations and work groups accomplished?
- Were the majority of project team members aware of the full scope of the project and its various components? If not, did that have a negative impact on the success of the project? How could scope have been better communicated to the project team members?
- Were there ways in which intraproject communication could have been enhanced?

- How were the results communicated to upper management? Was the communication adequate? How could it have been improved?

Change Control

- Were the project deliverables and their success criteria sufficiently detailed to provide a basis for a formal change control process?
- Were requirements ever frozen? If so, when? Was the freezing of requirements effective in controlling scope changes? If not, why not?
- Was there a change control process? Describe it.
- Did stakeholders use the process? Describe how the process was adapted to motivate the cooperation of stakeholders.
- Who monitored and controlled the process?
- How was the impact of each change evaluated?
- What were the thresholds that triggered different authorization requirements to approve or disapprove changes?
- How were the change and the impact of the change communicated to relevant individuals/departments?
- For future projects, what recommendations would you make regarding (a) specification of project requirements and success criteria, (b) timing and effectiveness of freezing project requirements, (c) type of change control process, (d) control and monitoring of the change control process, (e) how the impact of change was evaluated, and (f) documentation and communication of changes to stakeholders?

Project Management Tools

- What project management scheduling product was used? Was it designed specifically for managing projects, or was other software used which was retrofitted for that purpose? How was the product chosen and by whom? What were the strengths and weaknesses of that product?
- Would you use that product again for another project? If you were to pick another package, what would you be looking for?
- What outputs from the project management scheduling product helped you the most with communicating with the project client? With management? With team members?

Risk Management

- Was there a formal risk analysis performed? When was it performed, and by whom? How (if at all) did the risk assessment influence the original plans of time, resource requirements, and budget?
- Was there a risk abatement planning process conducted? If so, how and by whom? What response plans had to be implemented during the project, and in what circumstances? What events occurred that did not have a response plan in place? What should the response plan have been? For future projects, how might the risk abatement planning process be improved?

- Did the structure or goals of the parent organization change during the project? If so, how did the changes affect the project? What approaches were used (or could have been used) to maintain equilibrium and continuity?
- What recommendations would you make for future projects regarding (a) the use of formal risk assessment, (b) the application of formal risk assessment data to the schedule and budget, (c) the development and use of response plans, and (d) the management of changes in the structure or goals of the parent organization to maintain project stability?

Execution

- How were scope and quality controlled? Did the business case require specific thresholds to assist the manager of the project in assessing the severity of variances? What data were collected? When, and from whom? What problems were encountered when tracking and controlling project scope and quality?
- How was budget (both dollars and effort hours) controlled? Did the business case specify specific thresholds to assist the manager of the project in assessing the severity of variances? What budget data were collected? When, and from whom? What problems were encountered when tracking and controlling the project budget?
- How was the schedule controlled? Did the business case state specific thresholds to assist the manager of the project in assessing the severity of variances? What schedule data were collected? When and from whom? What problems were encountered when tracking and controlling the project schedule?
- How were variances from plan, if any, recorded? When variances exceeded the thresholds specified in the business case, how were they handled?
- Were the baseline(s) reforecast during the project? How were baseline changes documented and communicated to stakeholders?
- For future projects, what recommendations would you make regarding (a) getting guidance on acceptable variances in scope, quality, schedule, and budget in the business case, (b) the timing and methods of collecting data, (c) managing variances that exceed client thresholds, and (d) managing baseline changes?

General Questions

- Did the team make any technological discoveries or process or development innovations that should be applied to future projects?
- Did the manager of the project, or the project team, discover any project management techniques or processes that should be applied to future projects?

PEOPLE/POLITICS-RELATED QUESTIONS

Client Interaction

- Was there a defined project client? Was there more than one project client, and if so, how did this affect the project? Were other project clients discovered after the project got underway? Could that up-front omission have been avoided? If so, how?
- How was the client interface handled (e.g., single contact point, regularly scheduled meetings, client part of the cross-functional team)?

- Based on experience from this project (and other projects), what would be the optimal arrangement for structuring client interaction?

Accountability and Resource Responsibility

- Was one person accountable for the project? If so, who was that person, and from what functional organization did that person come? What responsibilities did this person have? For what responsibilities was that person accountable? What levels of authority did that person have? What made that person able to manage the project successfully? What prevented that person from managing the project successfully?
- If the project were to be done over again, what changes should be made in the source from which this person was pulled or in how the role and responsibility of this person are positioned?

Project Team Interaction

- How well did the core team work together? Did the core team members collaborate and support each other? If not, what were the barriers to full collaboration?
- Did the project have the right people with the right skill sets?
- Were there conflicts among team members? If so, what were they? What conflict resolution process was used? Was it accepted as fair by the team?
- What were the interpersonal skills and behaviors that contributed to the success of the project? How were these skills developed and/or reinforced during the project? What were the interpersonal behaviors that were detrimental to the success of the project? How were these behaviors addressed so that their negative effects were minimized?
- How were decisions made within the group? How could that decision-making process be improved for future projects?
- Was overtime required of the project team? Was the overtime excessive? In future projects, would there be a way to reduce the overtime required and/or to position overtime in such a way as not to cause negative reactions and possible burnout?
- Was there turnover in the project? Was it planned or unplanned? Who left the project and under what circumstances? Which types of turnover had the most negative effect on the project? Why? Are there any approaches that would combat turnover and/or negative impacts of turnover?
- What recommendations would you make for future projects regarding (a) creating a collaborative team, (b) matching skill sets with the team assignments, (c) managing conflict within the team, (d) developing and reinforcing positive interpersonal behaviors within the team, (e) using an effective decision-making process, (f) managing and reducing overtime, and (g) managing and reducing turnover?

Cross-Functional Teams

- What was the cross-functional team's makeup? Was there a core team plus extended teams? If so, how were the roles and responsibilities assigned?
- Was the makeup of the team constant throughout the project, or did it change? If there were changes, what impact did they have on the project? Would there have been a way to minimize the changes and/or the impact of the changes—and if so, how?

- What was the average number of people on the team? Were there too many? How could the size of the team be limited?
- Did a single person lead the team, or did the leadership rotate? If a single person led the team, what made him or her a successful or unsuccessful leader? What additional characteristics would help the manager of the project to be more successful?
- If the leadership rotated, what were the criteria for choosing the new leader? How often did the leadership rotate? If team leadership were to rotate on future projects, how, if at all, could it be orchestrated to be more efficient and effective?
- Was the team rewarded for good performance? If so, how?
- How were team roles and responsibilities documented and communicated among the team members and to stakeholders?
- What recommendations would you make for future projects on these topics: (a) organizing a cross-functional team, (b) managing team changes, (c) maintaining the optimal number of people on the team, (d) choosing and rotating leadership, and (e) rewarding teams for good performance?

Managing Relationships

- How well did the manager of the project and the team identify the major stakeholders at the beginning of the project?
- Was there a communication plan for the stakeholders? How effective was it?
- How effectively did the manager of the project and the team work with the project client?
- How well did the manager of the project and the team work with third-party suppliers? Would they want to contract with the organization in the future?
- What recommendations would you make for future projects regarding (a) identifying stakeholders, (b) developing an effective communication plan, (c) working with the project client, and (d) working with third-party suppliers?

General Questions

- Would the team want to work with the manager of the project again?
- Would the team want to work with each other again?

SUMMARY QUESTIONS

For each of the following issues, summarize what made the project successful:

- Design strategy,
- Choice and mix of representation from functional areas,
- Acquiring and maintaining management support,
- Communication with the project client, the project team and the stakeholders, and
- Management of changes.

ASSESSMENT TOOL

Close-Out Assessment

Post-Project Review	Response Answer each question in the space provided. Where 1 to 10 are used, 1 = Lowest score and 10 = Highest score.
1. What event(s) or communication(s) indicate the end of a project?	
2. How often do you hold a post-project review meeting for a project? What is discussed?	Very often____ Sometimes ____ Seldom ____
3. Of what value is a post-project review meeting to you personally? To other participants? To the company?	1 2 3 4 5 6 7 8 9 10 1 2 3 4 5 6 7 8 9 10 1 2 3 4 5 6 7 8 9 10
4. To what degree does anything change as a result?	High _____ Medium _____ Low _____
Documentation	**Response** Answer each question in the space provided.
1. How are projects documented?	
2. Which documentation is most helpful?	
3. Do historical records of past projects exist?	Yes_____ No_____
4. Where is this history located?	
5. How do you use it?	
6. What do you think should be saved in a project history file?	
7. How does key learning get passed on from one project to another?	
8. How is software used for documentation?	

PART IV

POLITICS

CHAPTER 13

Fitting Project Management into the Corporate Culture

Tillie is a team member of a very exciting, high-visibility project in the organization. She is extremely pleased to have been chosen for the team and is ready to give it her all. However, yesterday was the worst day of Tillie's life; she got caught in a battle between her resource/functional manager, Fred, and the manager of her project, Petra.

Tillie's resource manager is a vice president. He is extremely well respected and has, until now, favored Tillie by helping her move forward in her career. Petra is a new personality for Tillie. She does not know her well. She understands that Petra is an excellent manager of projects and has led several very successful projects within the organization.

But back to Tillie's terrible day, when she got caught between her two managers.

Petra needs the project to start immediately. And she needs Tillie to start working on the project *now*. Tillie is assigned to interview all top-level managers and list their desires for the new management process that will be put in place. For Tillie, this is a wonderful opportunity to meet and talk to all the top managers. It gives her exposure to the top brass, and it expands her knowledge of the entire organization.

There is one big problem. Her boss, Fred, doesn't want to release her from her current operational duties to contribute to the project. Fred is trying to be practical. Tillie is the best person in his department. Why should he release her to a project that offers little direct return to his department?

Yesterday, Petra came to talk to Fred and tried to persuade him to let Tillie work on the project. Both managers held their positions; neither wanted to budge. And Tillie didn't want to contradict her boss in front of Petra, nor did she want to miss the chance to work on the project.

The meeting ended in a stalemate. Tillie could not orchestrate a solution that would allow her to work on the project. She keeps asking herself these questions: Why aren't projects seen as vital enough to be equated with operational work? What does one do when one has two bosses? Shouldn't there be an organizational structure that officially accommodates projects *and* the functional parts of the business?

CHAPTER OVERVIEW

An organizational climate—the tone or atmosphere that permeates a company—can be positive or negative. The organizational climate in a project-driven organization may be negative because of incompetent leadership styles, poor time management, inadequate or nonexistent reward systems, undeveloped written communication skills, and poor human resources planning or training programs, to name a few.

A very simple problem, but one not easily pinpointed, perpetuates a negative organization climate: the presence of an organization structure that does not fit into the culture. A chain of command that does not support the organization's strategy, does not comply with the business strategy of the corporation, or does not perpetuate a successful communication infrastructure of roles and responsibilities will be unsuccessful.

In Figure 13.1, three possible project organization structures are envisioned on a continuum, from less project-oriented to more project-oriented. Note the influence of each structure on decision making; a traditional functional influence becomes a project-driven point of view.

- At the start of the continuum is the *classic functional or hierarchical structure* in which the operating organization undertakes a project that has boundaries within that functional area. This structure has limiting constraints and therefore is not employed frequently.
- As a business moves from a transactional orientation to a project orientation, it becomes necessary to involve various subject-matter experts from different functional areas. A project team is formed to accomplish a specific business objective. This is called a *matrixed structure*. However, the commitment of the project players in a matrixed organization is typically part-time. When project team members—and possibly the manager of the project—are pulled between project responsibilities

Figure 13.1   The Continuum of Organizational Structures

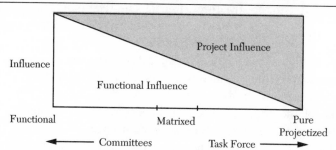

Source: Joan Knutson, *How to Be a Successful Project Manager* (2nd ed.), American Management Association, 1988.

and the operational responsibilities of their functional unit, they may not be totally productive in either effort.

- At the other end of the continuum is a *pure projectized structure*. The managers of projects and the project team members are dedicated full-time to the project. The pure projectized team may be located in one place so that they can communicate more easily. Their effort then becomes more dedicated, and their productivity is higher.

A choice of the appropriate organization structure depends on the type of project. Developing a proposal might best be served by a dedicated task force (pure projectized approach), whereas designing and implementing a software product might successfully employ the matrix method, in which different subject matter experts are pulled from different functional groups.

Different structures might be utilized during various phases of a project. For example, a functional or traditional hierarchical organization structure might best serve the design phase, but the development effort may achieve its best result by using a strong matrix with a centralized project office to coordinate the effort.

This chapter is divided into two sections. First, we explore the various project-driven organization structures. Later, we consider how a top management group, the Project Steering Committee, can best support a project-driven organization.

The section on the various organization structures explores how traditional, functional structures, which have supported transaction-oriented businesses, evolve into project-driven organizations. Then we look at each of the various project structures: functional, matrix, and pure projectized. As we consider each variation, the perceived benefits and disadvantages will be weighed relative to the structures. To complete the discussion of structures, we look at how the project office came into existence. The project office will be discussed in more depth in Chapter 14.

As you read about each type of organization structure, compare it to your organization. You will recognize that there is no pure form. Many organizations have utilized each of the options in varying situations, depending on the nature of the project, the required end result, and the unique politics. Accept the fact that each structure has some strong advantages and some offsetting and inherent disadvantages. Diligence is needed when considering which organizational type should be used and when it can be appropriately introduced.

We then look at the role of the Project Steering Committee in dealing with individual projects, identifying problems, providing solutions, and making the project management discipline stronger and more widely accepted throughout the enterprise.

PROJECT-DRIVEN ORGANIZATION STRUCTURES

As explored in Chapter 1, organizations have gradually evolved from the traditional hierarchical structure to a project-driven, cross-functional team structure. Let's look at how organization structures support projects.

Various Project Structures

The types of structures examined in this section are: the functional project organization, the matrixed organization, and the pure projectized organization. Most projects cannot be performed within the confines of the functional department. They require an organization structure that supports interdepartment involvement of team members with widely varied disciplines. The options for structuring projects within this more expansive project-driven organization are the matrixed and the pure projectized structures. We will explore the advantages and disadvantages of each type.

Functional Project Organization

The history of this approach dates from the beginning of the world of business, when the head of a company/agency delegated accountability and authority to various functional areas. As shown in Figure 13.2, traditionally, a hierarchically structured organization is shaped like a pyramid and has vertical lines of reporting.

Figure 13.2   Traditional Organizational Chart

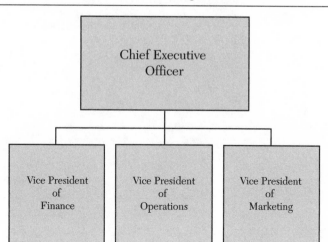

The pyramid is comprised of discrete departments or units under the head of the organization, the president of the company, or the director of the agency. Classic units are Finance, Operations, and Marketing to name a few. Most of these units have definite operational roles within the business. For example, Operations has the job of producing or processing products or services that generate bottom-line profits. Other units have a staff function that does not directly affect the bottom-line profit. For example, Finance is accountable for tracking and processing funds into and out of the organization. Both functions are recurring, repetitive efforts that are not projectized (i.e., do not have a discrete beginning and an ending that produces a discrete deliverable).

In the functional or decentralized approach to running projects, a project is run within a department or division of the organization. In Figure 13.3, employees B and C have been designated to work on project ABC. This one project is consolidated within this one area of the business.

The manager of projects may come from either of two different sources. The functional manager personally takes responsibility for running the project, in addition to his or her other operational duties. Or, the functional manager delegates the accountability for coordinating the project to one of the people in his or her organization, on either a full-time or part-time basis.

This alternative may cause redundancy and inefficiency. For example, many insurance companies are decentralized. Their organization structure includes branch offices, regional offices, and a headquarters. Suppose the marketing department at headquarters has determined that a new form of

Figure 13.3   Functional Organizational Chart

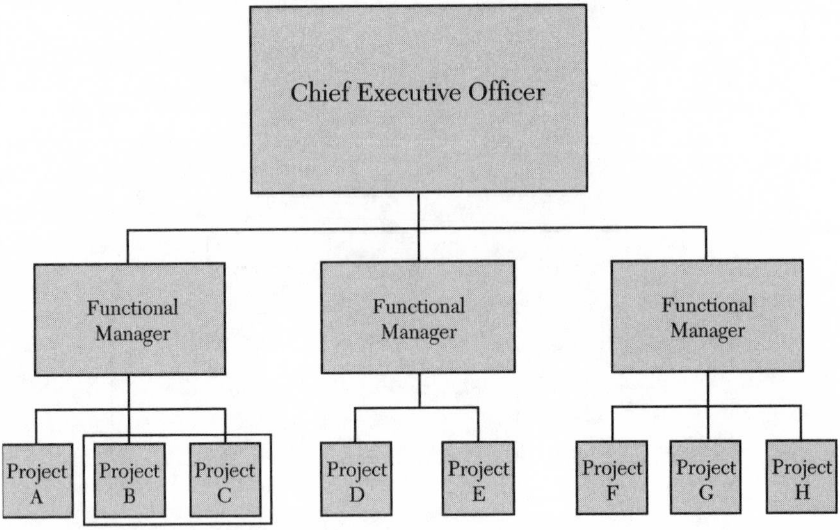

coverage is needed for a specific class of insured people and has started pre-liminary work on a design. Simultaneously, a branch office has discovered the same need and has found a way to modify an existing policy to meet it. Each part of the business continues to work on the project, unaware of what the other department is doing. The two projects are not completed quickly because day-to-day functional responsibilities take priority over these special projects. When they are finished, two redundant and conflicting offerings are in place.

For this type of structure to succeed, the functional area must possess the necessary expertise within its microcosm of the business. The team members are assigned on a part-time basis, when their skills and services are needed. The functional manager (who assumes the role of manager of projects) or his or her delegate now has total responsibility for:

- Defining requirements
- Scheduling work efforts
- Setting project priorities
- Providing necessary facilities
- Acquiring and managing resources
- Adhering to company policies and rules
- Reaching completion dates of projects
- Implementing the final solution
- Producing an effective deliverable

This organization structure can be described as a project "for us, because of us, within us, by us." The advantages and disadvantages of working on a functional project within an organization are explored below.

Advantages

- Because the activity will be centralized under the jurisdiction of a single functional manager, there will be a more unified approach and a bonding of the team toward a quality product.
- Turnaround time will be shortened because a number of different departments/groups will not be required to buy-in.
- Because the deliverable has been developed by a single functional group, there is a strong probability that fewer changes or adjustments will be requested in the finished product.
- Because functional areas are accountable for their own results, they may accept the benefits of success for the outcome of the project. However, should the project run into problems, there is no substitute for the adage, "The buck stops here."
- Generally, when the necessary skills are situated in a single functional area, the ramp-up or learning time will be compressed into a shorter time period.
- The requirements and scope can be evaluated on a more rational and intelligent basis, given the fact that outside sources need not be contacted to gain clarification or explanation.
- In the areas of definition and design, the contributions of a single functional group should ensure that these two phases will be more thorough and complete.
- Without the involvement of a large number of departments or divisions (and their attending political and ego problems), there is a greater probability that a practical and serviceable end-product will be designed, with fewer unnecessary bells and whistles.
- In this close, unified environment, the enhanced communications are more likely to support the recognition of problem situations and the initiatives that will be necessary to resolve them.

Disadvantages

- Large projects that do not involve the contribution of many departments and/or divisions lack the perspective of a broad-based company background. In some projects, this can mean a deficiency in breadth and leadership.
- Similarly, the lack of a broad involvement of major departments and/or divisions may result in a general lack of awareness or in limited

oversight, which leads to a failure to follow all company policies and procedures.

- In the functional environment, there is minimal, if any, conformance to standardized status and project-control reports to upper management.
- Without proper orientation and support, there is no guarantee that one functional area will maintain accounting records in the form and substance that are prescribed by broad company standards.
- Without the support of specific areas of the organization, this structure has difficulty in defining, maintaining, and enforcing common standards of work and independent quality control criteria.
- The relatively narrow confines of a single functional area may impede individual employees from pursuing career objectives outside of their function. Their needs may have to be subordinated to the requirements and priorities of their individual functions.
- Given the fact that functional areas are small and discrete, there is no guarantee that they will possess the essential mix and depth of skills needed to meet the requirements of a major project.

In summary, although this structure is a more bureaucratic approach to running projects, the clear lines of reporting and the efficient use of resources recommend this type of organization for a limited number of projects that are managed *within* a limited functional area.

Matrixed Organization

Most projects in today's project-driven organizations require commitment and support from many organizational areas. However, as noted previously, performing projects within the traditional pyramid structure does not support that requirement. A managerially different structure—the matrixed structure—has emerged to suit this type of project environment.

The matrixed organization structure allows pools of specialized staff with related talents to remain intact. Functional managers continue to oversee the use and scheduling of the persons in their employee pool. Managers of projects draw upon these pools by requesting the skilled staff members that they require when the need arises. Figure 13.4 represents a matrixed organization.

There are three functional areas. In each function, there are employees working for their functional manager. Employees D and E report to one functional manager. In this structure, projects cut across functional groups and pull the appropriate personnel from each group. Notice employees from all three functions are working on project XYZ. Also notice that employee D

Figure 13.4   Matrixed Organization Chart

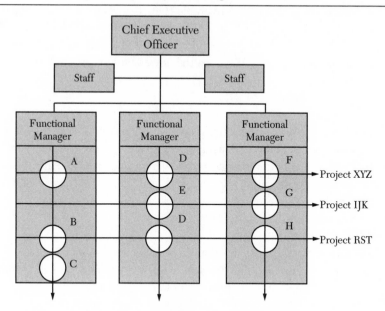

is contributing to both project XYZ and project RST. This is the committee or cross-functional team approach to managing projects.

One of the questions is who will become the manager of the XYZ project? It will be a choice amongst persons A, D, or F. The choice should not be based on subjective, political reasons. The manager of the project should be chosen because he or she has the greatest vested interest in the success of the project and/or because they possess the best project management competency.

At first, this structure may seem ideal. However, occasions arise when managers of projects go to particular pools only to find that they have "run dry," or have no more resources to offer. Functional managers, unaware that their talent pools are shrinking, may commit their departments to deadlines that are difficult, if not impossible, to meet. Project team members who are working on several projects simultaneously may be so torn among their many project efforts that they cannot do their project work well and may not address their functional assignments adequately. This structure requires a continuous and monumental effort at communication between the manager of the project and the functional managers.

In a matrix structure, project resources have dual reporting responsibility. Project personnel report to their functional manager for administrative activities (e.g., vacations, training, performance reviews as well as for the technical performance of the deliverable that they produce), and they look to the manager of the project to define tasks and manage the effort. The manager of the project has responsibility for the ultimate success/failure in meeting the promised goals. Here are the advantages and disadvantages of a balanced matrix.

Advantages

- Combines the best of the traditional functional structure with the involvement of varied functional areas to create the best product possible
- Is the least costly for an organization which performs major projects
- Retains the leadership, technical, and management skills of functional managers
- Allows scarce expertise to be applied more flexibly and efficiently to different projects
- Accommodates changes in resource requirements more easily
- More readily isolates and resolves conflict between project requirements and functional organization policies

Disadvantages

- Increased time and effort to define and communicate policies
- More time required for handling complex issues and coordinating various tasks
- Difficulty in resolving multiple priorities and conflicts in schedules
- Biases of functional division heads may conflict with priorities desired by general management
- Inability to achieve reaction time fast enough to meet project requirements
- Potential competition and conflict between functional managers and managers of projects

Pure Projectized Organization

When this structure is used, people are assembled for a specific project effort from various departments, on a *full-time basis*. This type of project team is referred to as a pure projectized project team. In sharp contract to the matrix structure, this organizational structure uses a completely dedicated task force of talent. This approach works well for completing highly visible projects or a specific phase of any project that needs total dedication. However, pure projectized team members may have times during the project when they are not fully utilized, and they might be out of a job when the project is finished.

Imagine, for example, that you are a business specialist. Although part of the ongoing project is strictly technical, the team will need you back after the technical effort is completed. In the interim, however, there is nothing significant that you can contribute. So as not to lose you, the manager of projects keeps you on the team, working in an auxiliary role but not on core work efforts, until you are required again. Or suppose that you are in charge of developing a new line of summer products. You and the members of your team complete the assignment and then learn that the company is not interested in expanding its products to a year-round line. Your entire group is disbanded.

Maintaining a dedicated team solves the problems of part-time contribution and conflicting priorities, but it creates a continuing overhead cost that can only be justified by speed to market. The justification for a dedicated task force is that a group of highly trained professionals can complete a project sooner, thus lowering costs and/or generating revenues more quickly.

As you can see in Figure 13.5, the pure projectized team (or task force) is comprised of representatives from the various functional areas. In this

Figure 13.5   Pure Projectized Organization Chart

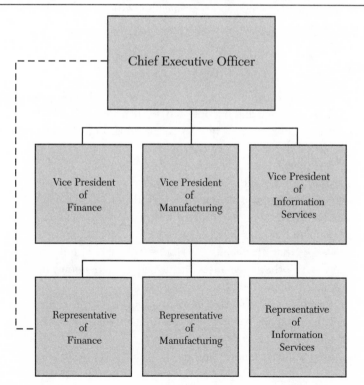

example, the representatives are reassigned temporarily to the Chief Executive Officer (CEO). Pure projectized teams often are not lucky enough to be assigned to the top management person. But they should be directed by someone who does not have a vested interest so that they are managed in a truly objective manner.

This Team is expected to be available for the limited duration of the project and until a specific completion date when the group will be disbanded and the members will be returned to the organization units from whence they came. The manager of the project has total control and authority for the scheduling, management, completion, and quality of the ultimate objective. The manager of the project may be someone selected from the functional or management levels, or may be picked from another area for his or her objectivity in resolving problems that may occur.

An option for managing pure projectized teams is to establish an overseeing steering committee. Historically, however, attempts to manage projects by task force or committee have not been very successful. One, and only one, manager is the key to effectively supervising the group work effort. However, a review committee that monitors progress, makes policy decisions, and provides resources may be a very helpful entity, as we'll see later in this chapter. Nevertheless, day-to-day management must be vested in one individual.

Here are the various advantages and disadvantages of the projectized team structure.

Advantages

- This type of project team can generally be assembled very rapidly, both from internal and outside sources, if necessary.
- The group can react very quickly to changing project conditions or possible shifts in direction or priorities.
- *Esprit de corps* is usually high; the special status of the effort creates a cohesive team feeling.
- Members of the group enjoy high visibility to upper management because they have been handpicked for an important company effort.
- Although individuals have been selected for the specific skills and knowledge that they can contribute, the opportunity to work very closely with other specialists will broaden their knowledge and make them more valuable for future assignments.
- This group can be effective in solving short-term problems.
- From the company's standpoint, team members make an ethical commitment to see the project through to a successful completion. This may help reduce turnover and the need for retraining.

- Common standards within the project will lead toward a uniformly produced final deliverable.
- Management is generally kept very well informed as to the status and progress of the project.
- The assumption that either the principal or the entire responsibility of the team members is to the project(s) results in fewer distractions or interruptions that would otherwise reduce their effectiveness.

Disadvantages

- Functional organizations may resent the encroachment into their territories of a special group that cuts across company lines.
- Asking one person to control the many activities of a very large project may prove cumbersome and unwieldy.
- Team members may be frightened by a temporary assignment. How will it impact their career paths? Where will it lead them—or leave them?
- Reports to upper management may be in a different form or format than those for other company projects, so comparisons can become more difficult.
- Standards may be bent by the group and may vary from those applied for smaller projects or those used in common practice.
- The urgency of the effort may lead to overloading the group.

This discussion has traced the continuum of project structures, ranging from the traditional but limited functional structure to the more applicable matrix structure, and, finally, to the ultimate, but seldom justified, pure projectized team. Now let's look at how an autonomous form of matrix structure that is focused on project management has emerged.

The Emergence of the Project Office

The Project Management Institute's *Project Management Body of Knowledge (PMBOK)* suggests that there are three types of matrixed project structures: (1) the weak matrix, (2) the balanced matrix, and (3) the strong matrix. The weak matrix has a project team composed of team members from various functional departments. No one is named as the manager of projects; this is a self-directed team. In a balanced matrix, one team member from one of the functional departments is named the manager of the project and directs all the other team members. A strong matrix is defined as one in which the organization has isolated a project office and given it responsibility to oversee the project management discipline and in some cases to provide managers of projects to run major initiatives. We have already explored the balanced matrix form. Let's now look at how the strong matrix employing a project office emerged, and at the advantages and disadvantages of this type of structure.

As projects have become more pervasive, in corporations/agencies as a whole and in the project-driven departments mentioned previously, a new unit has emerged: the centralized project management group. This group may be called the Project Office, the Project Management Services Group, or the Project Management Center of Excellence. For our discussion here, we will refer to it as the Project Office. As you can see in Figure 13.6, the Project Office is added to the matrix structure.

The next chapter will delve into the Project Office in more detail. The advantages and disadvantages of this strong matrix structure are listed below. They relate to all project-driven departments, such as Information Systems, Advertising, and, most specifically, the corporate or divisional Central Project Management Office.

Advantages

- Common standards can be adopted relative to the way projects are run within a discipline or within the entire organization.
- Highly skilled project management personnel are developed, and their knowledge is made available for the benefit of all.
- Personnel are kept better informed about changes in deadlines, resource requirements, and/or budgets. The centralized group acts as an information focal point.
- Adjustments for changes in priorities can be accommodated more quickly when one group is coordinating projects and can weigh decisions relative to total organizational business strategies.
- Project control and status reports are delivered to upper management in one format rather than at the discretion of various managers.
- If projects fall behind schedule, it may be possible to "pack" a team in order to get back on track.
- Members of the project-driven unit gain an increased sense of cooperation and loyalty by associating closely with similar professionals.
- Personnel are treated equally, or at least consistently, in all areas of human resources development—performance appraisals, salary increases, promotions, training classes, warnings, dismissals, and so on.

Disadvantages

- The centralized project department can face demands that far exceed its resource capacity.

Figure 13.6   Matrixed Organization Chart with Project Office

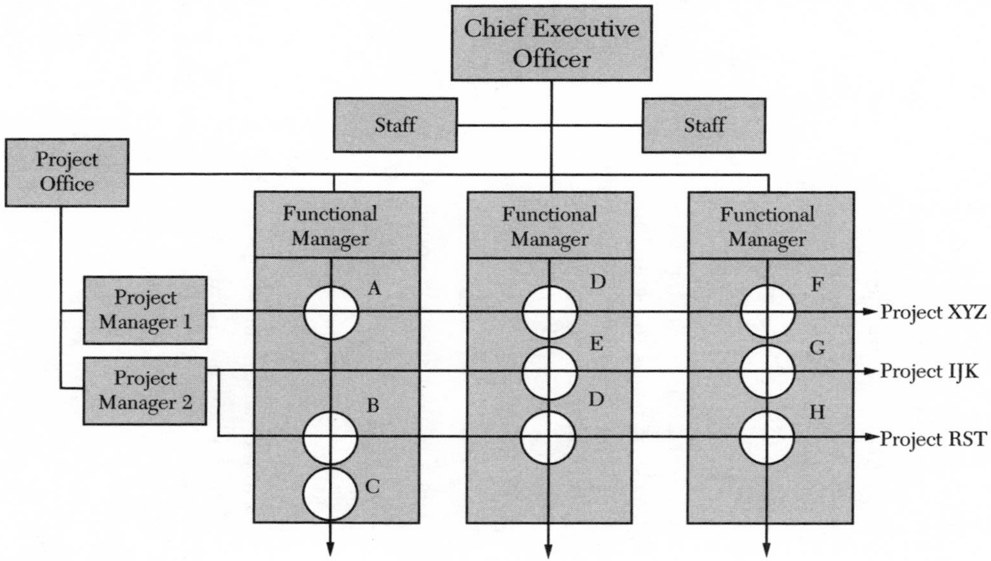

- Standards and documentation may tend to be overdone; the result is an abundance of red tape.
- The total project management cost to the requesting department may be inflated to the extent that project management personnel may wait relatively long periods between assignments or not have enough work to keep them busy.
- It may be difficult to find personnel with the right mix of administrative and people skills, as well as project management skills and, possibly, technical skills.
- Organizational independence may encourage the group to depart from proven administrative practices and indulge in reinventing the wheel.
- The manager of projects has the responsibility and accountability—but not the authority—to acquire the resources needed. This is a very difficult position to be placed in.
- This structure can engender a them-versus-us atmosphere.

Whichever structure is used, the more project-driven the organization becomes, the more it needs direction and support from top management. The next section offers a perspective and some guidelines for establishing a project steering committee.

PROJECT STEERING COMMITTEE

What impact can a project steering committee have on the project community? Far more than an omniscient Big Brother who watches over projects and expects them to be completed on time, within budget, and with renown for their high quality.

This top management team can and should contribute to the success of the project discipline within the entire organization. To do this, many companies are creating a new organizational group to support the project management discipline—the project steering committee. Its genesis comes from acceptance that a project-driven organization requires coordination from the top level.

Steering committees are not new organizational entities. In many enterprises, steering committees for strategic planning or long-range planning have been setting the direction for the organization as a whole. Various disciplines within organizations (e.g., Information Systems) have employed steering committees as focal points for priority setting and dispute resolution.

The project steering committee is composed of line and staff managers from across the organization. The resident line managers are those who use project management the most: managers of Engineering, Manufacturing, Marketing, Sales, Data Processing, and so on. The staff committee members (e.g., the managers of strategic or long-range planning, human resources, and the project office) support the project management discipline.

The overall charter of this committee is to set direction, provide support, and remove obstacles for project teams. This section addresses the roles and responsibilities of the project steering committee. The implication is not that every project steering committee assumes all these roles but that each project steering committee considers which of these roles is appropriate and productive for its unique charter within the organization.

Priority Setting

A steering committee is almost always expected to establish priorities. The project steering committee is no exception. As we discussed in Chapter 7, "Portfolio Management," this Review Board is asked to evaluate the relative order of importance of all projects being done by a corporation or agency. The established priority of each project sends a message to the organization concerning where time, effort, and resources should be expended. The differing priorities clarify decisions concerning how resources will be allocated to various projects. Let's revisit the role of the project steering committee or the Project Review Board in the setting of project priorities.

In many organizations, the complaint is that more than one project is considered to be number 1. They are *all* number 1, or at least there seems to be a number 1a, 1b, and 1c, all of which are considered priorities. That is hypocritical. If no one knows what to work on, the priority setting has been a farce.

Thus, the committee must evaluate the relative merits of multiple approved projects, delineating the top priority from the second, third, and twenty-third priority projects. There are various ways to accomplish this task. Some organizations rank projects in the order in which they think projects will support the strategic goals of the corporation or agency. This is often done arbitrarily, allowing politics to play a more than reasonable role in the process.

For example, one company for which I consulted had each manager rank the 100+ projects in the queue. Then each of the project's rankings was averaged, and the averaged ranking became the official priority. This was done without a discussion of the importance of the project to the organization as a whole, nor to the functional area sponsoring it. Also, this priority-setting process had not gained consensus among the managers. The priority order stayed in place for less than a week; then a high-powered manager demanded resources for one of his pet projects. Although that project had not ranked anywhere near number 1, his position and influence got him the resources that he needed. The priorities that had been established obviously meant nothing.

A more formalized priority-setting process must be used and must include the criteria that are established and weighted. For example, one of the criteria on which a project's priority can be based is its Alignment to the Strategic Goals of the Corporation.

As each project is evaluated, the committee decides whether that project meets these criteria. If the project meets the criteria, it scores a 1; if it does not, it scores a 0. At the end of the evaluation of all criteria, the project with the highest cumulative score is ranked as priority number 1, and so forth down the line.

The committee may want to consider a variation of the priority-setting methodology—one that is more refined and delineating. Rather than scoring each criterion on a binary Yes/No basis, each criterion is given several weighting factors (or scores) associated with different levels of meeting these criteria. For example, Alignment to the Strategic Goals of the Corporation might suggest these weightings:

1. The project is in direct alignment to the corporation's strategic goals.
2. The project has a limited alignment to the corporation's strategic goals.
3. The project has no alignment to the corporation's strategic goals but is directly related to another project that does.
4. The project has no alignment to the corporation's strategic goals.

As in the first scenario, all the weighting factors or scores for all criteria on which one project is being evaluated are added up, and the highest-scoring projects become the top-priority projects. This technique is a more logical process than rank-ordering the projects in a subjective manner. This process ensures discussion, a rational determination of priorities, and a reasonable degree of consensus.

Remember that when a priority system is implemented, the message communicated is that certain projects are more important than others, and that lower-priority projects will not be given the same consideration for resources as higher priority projects. When this is true, the project steering committee must consider allocating additional time (i.e., a time contingency) for the lower-priority projects.

This means, for example, that the top 10 projects are expected to meet their deadlines because these projects presumably will have the leverage to get needed resources. Projects ranked as 11–20 in priority will have a 5 percent time contingency. In other words, these projects will not have the same access to resources; therefore, it will be acceptable to extend their total elapsed time to completion by 5 percent, if necessary. Following that same logic, priority projects 21–30 are allocated a possible 10 percent time contingency; projects 31–40 are given 15 percent; and projects 41 to 50 are given 20 percent. The contingency can only be used if the steering committee receives proof that the needed resources are not available and the time contingency is necessary.

Resource Allocation

The second key role of this project steering committee involves resource management. Participating committee members own the resources that will be assigned to the projects that support the organization. This committee decides the allocation of these resources across the top-ranked projects.

To accomplish this, calculations must be performed to determine how many resources of a particular skill mix are required by each project. These are often called resource-loading calculations. Then the resources required for high-priority projects are allocated, until no more resources are available within the organization. For more information on resource allocation, refer to Chapter 7.

Keep in mind, for our present discussion, that this is one of the roles assigned to the project steering committee. The committee has several choices: (1) all lower-level projects will be put on hold until completion of some of the higher-level projects frees up resources; (2) lower-level projects are important enough to be done, and outside resources will therefore be hired to accommodate these projects as well as the higher-level projects; (3) the deadlines of some high-level projects are extended, which makes some resources available for work on lower-level projects; and/or (4) it is decided that these lower-level projects should not be at such a low level; they are reranked to a higher position, which bumps a currently high-level project down and possibly out of the running for available resources.

We have discussed the two main functions of the project steering committee: priority setting and resource allocation. In addition to these key responsibilities, the committee can and should address a variety of organizational issues.

Organizational Issues

The following issues focus on policies and procedures that the steering committee positions in order to support the project management discipline. Some of these policies and procedures are officially established and supported by the committee; others are informal, yet key to the way in which the committee works with the rest of the project community.

Project Office

A Project Office may be established to support administrative functions performed by the steering committee. This office would be responsible for collecting planned and actual resource allocation data, and for communicating, to all interested parties, the priority ranking of multiple projects. Beyond the administrative role, it is recommended that the project office serve as an internal consultative entity. Staff within the project office then become mentors to managers of projects and project team members by offering advice and hands-on support for planning, monitoring, and tracking projects.

Performance Appraisal Reviews

Managers of projects need to have input into the performance appraisal review process for their team members, even if those team members do not report to them directly. This is not done just so that the manager of projects can highlight his or her role as a manager (albeit part-time) of a team member; it gives the team member due credit for the time and effort he or she has expended on a project.

Communication Plan

The project steering committee should distribute a communication plan to all participants in the project community. For example, how often will priorities be reevaluated? What input does the committee need from managers of projects and project clients in order to reestablish priorities? How frequently will a project team be asked to present to the committee? What information should the team be prepared to present? What feedback will the committee give, and how quickly will it be given? Communication plans should be taken seriously and planned carefully.

The above organizational issues are tangible and are backed up with written policies and procedures. The following issues are more intangible.

Changing from a Functionally Oriented Organization to a Project-Driven Organization

Recognize that this is a significant cultural change. The transition needs to be orchestrated, and roles, accountabilities, and authorities must be clearly defined and communicated. If the project-driven concept is not well positioned and supported by management, the self-contained empires of functional departments will continue to be secretive, noncommunicative, competitive, and antagonistic. If a functional manager does not get the message of how important cross-functional management is in his or her culture, the instinct will be to keep the strongest staff members on functional duties and, by default, assign the weaker members to projects.

Responsibility/Authority

Although most people know that their responsibility is to support projects approved by and prioritized by the project steering committee, clarification of the accountability of not performing these project duties on time and within budget should be communicated to one and all. The authority that people possess or do not possess must be communicated to them, their managers, the manager of projects, and peers with whom they have to deal.

Empowerment to Say "No," with Proof and Alternate Recommendations

In countless organizations, many people do not know how saying "No" will be perceived. As a result, they try as hard as they can to pull off their part of the project. With inordinate effort, they often do pull it off, but they resent the dilemma into which they have put themselves. This scenario occurs because the manager of projects and the project team do not know: how much they can reforecast the project's baselines without informing the committee; how to get what they need to accomplish their goals; or how to approach the steering committee to professionally renegotiate what they need.

In summary, the project steering committee needs to make sure that everyone understands the committee's expectations relative to: preparing briefing presentations, making day-to-day decisions based on the published project priorities, asking or not asking for help, and so on. After the organizational issues are decided, the project steering committee must address itself to the planning effort that will be required of all project teams.

Planning Issues

The success of project management is based on the credibility of the planning effort. If the plans are not credible, then all the work to manage plans will center on replanning, reforecasting, and pure frustration. Here are some areas in which the steering committee can play a very positive role.

Product Development Life Cycle (PDLC)

As noted in Chapter 1, the product development life cycle (PDLC) is a template or model of all tasks that must be performed in order to produce the end-product/deliverable from the project. This template decomposes the project into a standard to-do list of activities that need to be performed. This to-do list is called a Work Breakdown Structure (WBS). A standardized WBS lets everyone work from the same book and brings consistency to the planning process.

Organizations need to be thinking about developing a generic PDLC that is appropriate for all similar projects being performed by their various divisions. Plans will be completed much more quickly, and everyone will have a better understanding of the tasks they are being asked to perform. Furthermore, a consistent PDLC provides an opportunity to collect historical data as a basis from which to plan similar projects in the future.

Project Management Life Cycle (PMLC)

Superimposed over the product development life cycle is a project management life cycle (PMLC), also discussed in Chapter 1. This life cycle is also a template or a model; but it is composed of steps that need to be taken to initiate, plan, execute, change, and close a project. As in the product life cycle, there are supporting procedures, forms that must be filled out, and rules and regulations that must be followed.

Estimating

After the activities in the product development life cycle and the project management life cycle are identified, the required effort and duration of each activity must be determined. Estimating can be better accomplished if an estimating model is in place—a checklist of variables that need to be considered when extrapolating a best guess into an estimate that will be used in the scheduling process. These variables may introduce concerns such as:

- Will resources be available?
- Will the correct skills be available?
- What else do these resources/project team members have to do, other than work on projects?

This last question is important. Typically, people do not spend 100 percent of their work time on projects. Meetings, emergencies, sickness, and vacation detract from their work hours. The rule of thumb is: 60 percent of a person's time can be spent on preplanned WBS task work. If eight hours is considered the base, a person will be giving 4.8 to five hours of his or her day to project-related work. The project steering committee needs to be aware of this limitation and accept it when receiving estimates.

Resource Availability for Projects

Each functional department should determine the categories of work that its people perform. One of my clients said that his staff's time was divided among officially approved corporate projects; technical services offered by his department to other departments; internal cost/savings projects not under the corporate umbrella; exploration of new technology; and dealing with regulatory issues. If all these efforts are part of the whole, then each functional department must decide what percentage of a person's time is to be allocated to each category. This information should be communicated to the project steering committee as a more realistic base for resource allocation than eight hours per day per resource.

Knowledge-Based Systems (KBS)

A history database—a record of the accumulated activities performed, and the effort and duration expended, on past similar projects—can support all the planning topics discussed above. These data can be accumulated if a consistent PDLC is employed and if the resource allocation software is designed to archive the data for future use. Lessons learned from the project closeout as discussed in Chapter 12 also need to be archived on the knowledge-based system. Only the clout of the management on the project steering committee can mandate that project players populate this KBS and that they use it during the project process.

Rolling Wave or Phased Approach

Phasing or chunking projects is a process of decomposing a project into discrete work efforts that are approved and funded separately. For example, a feasibility study is planned in detail, approved, and funded by the project steering committee. After the feasibility study is presented and approved, the design effort is planned in detail, presented to, and funded by the committee. Finally, after the design effort is complete, the project team comes back to the committee with a detailed plan requesting funding for the development and roll-out/implementation efforts.

This chunking of projects keeps the project steering-committee members continually in the loop and allows them to make considered business decisions throughout the entire development life cycle. If canceling a project is appropriate, the committee has timely information for making that decision. If the members decide to fund subsequent phases of the project, they are doing so on an informed basis.

Adequate Time for Planning

This is quite obvious, but the committee must ensure that people responsible for getting the project completed on time, within budget, and with the expected quality will be given the time needed to develop a thorough and adequate plan. After the project is planned, the project steering committee will want to keep informed through scheduled project review meetings.

Project Review Meeting

The importance of setting expectations for project review meetings is discussed in Chapter 9, "Execution Management." Let's review what the project steering committee expects.

Preparation for the Meeting.   The project steering committee must make sure that everyone understands the guidelines for these project review meetings; such as, what does the committee want to see, and how does the committee want to see it? People should not spend valuable time making slick and glitzy overheads that may not be of interest to the committee. A list of the key questions and/or concerns that the committee will expect the team to answer and discuss should be in the team's hands long before the presentation is to take place. Also, the team should know the criteria used for choosing the projects that they are being asked to present. Some folks may think they are being asked to present because the committee thinks they are doing a bad job, when, in fact, the committee is just interested in the status of a major upcoming deliverable.

During the Meeting.   Project review meetings are high-energy, show-off meetings, sobered (if necessary) by requests for management's help. They are not "Let's-beat-up-on-the-team-for-the-mistakes-they-made" bashing sessions nor "Let's-kill-the-messenger-if-he-or-she-brings-bad-news" lashings. People who are presenting at these meetings need the committee to set direction, provide support, and remove obstacles. The project team has worked hard on its project and on preparing the presentation. Beating up the team will only lead to poor morale and lowered commitment and energy after the meeting is adjourned.

This does not mean that the committee can let the meeting go by without giving the team any feedback. The committee will want to converse about what they've heard after the meeting is over, but they should also give as much immediate feedback and positive reinforcement as possible during the meeting. Furthermore, the committee owes the project team a date by which any further feedback will be given to them.

Training

If all of the above exchanges are to occur, the entire project community must continually be growing, learning, and developing competencies in the discipline of project management. The project steering committee members need to take responsibility for their own growth as well as the growth of others in the project community. This development may be in the form of classroom training, either internally or externally presented. It may be self-paced training for individual personal development. It may be open forums or brown-bag lunches sponsored by the steering committee. The committee needs to be creative in considering all the different ways that people who work on projects can hone their skills and become better at this part of their jobs.

The project steering committee, like all organizational entities, is a living, growing organism. How should the committee position itself for growth?

Evolution of the Committee

The committee itself needs to grow. Limiting itself to setting priorities and monitoring the allocation of resources is wrong. The committee can make many other contributions to the project community. The project steering committee should convene focus groups quarterly or semiannually, from various parts of the organization. These focus groups would include members of the committee and five to seven of the "best practices" managers of projects, project team members, and project clients. The objective of the focus group is to have the committee listen to members of the project community in order to understand their feelings and suggestions as to how the committee could better support the project management discipline within the organization. The session needs to be somewhat structured and should be led by a strong facilitator who can direct the discussion toward generating meaningful action plans that will be implemented by the committee over a set period of time.

This may sound like a lot of work. It probably is. But if projects are the way your company's business gets done, then it is necessary to invest in this effort—not all at once, but one step at a time. First, start the committee and formalize the priority setting and resource allocation efforts. Then pick and choose from the above and from other ideas, and turn them into projects to be done in a logical and methodical way.

CONCLUSION

When you manage a project, organizational issues must be considered so that the project environment can survive. The effect of these issues depends on the involvement, commitment, and accountability of the various functional areas throughout the organization, and on how well they support the project effort. The project management discipline addresses these issues by imposing organizational structures to facilitate communication and accountability among all the project players.

In summary, a *functional organization structure* decentralizes the organization so that each department carries on only those projects that pertain to its own needs. Thus, the staff of each department is willing to work hard on projects because they know that completing them may simplify their own jobs. However, this solution may cause redundancy and inefficiency within the organization. The *matrix structure* orchestrates assembling a team of subject matter experts from various functional departments who then work together to accomplish a single project objective. The *pure projectized* approach is similar, but the project team members and the manager of the project are dedicated full-time to the effort. Lastly, the matrixed form of structure can be designed so that it aids not only in the management of the project endeavor itself but in the inculcation of the project management discipline throughout the entire enterprise. This strong version of the matrix positions a *project office* as an autonomous group with one goal: To support project management.

The role of the *project steering committee* can cover a broad scope, from setting priorities to allocating resources. Committee members can and should insert themselves in various organizational issues, from establishing performance appraisal review procedures to clarifying the roles, responsibilities, and authority of project players. In addition to this contribution, the project steering committee gives direction in the ways teams can better plan—by using product development life cycles and project management life cycles, good estimating techniques, and sound knowledge-based systems, to name a few. To keep communication channels open with the project community, the committee may ask for periodic reviews and provide clear direction as to what is expected in these reviews. Finally, this group must take responsibility for seeing that they and all the other project players grow by investing in training and other techniques, and by exploring new and better ways of doing the business of project management.

To extract Tillie from the fray involving her bosses—her resource manager and the manager of her project—it is imperative that the appropriate organizational structure, which fits with the unique culture of the enterprise, be designed, implemented, managed, and maintained.

Effects of Organizational Alternatives on Success Criteria

Structure

	Functional	Matrix	Project Office	Pure Projectized[a]
Time	Low	Medium	High	High
Performance	High	Medium	Low	High
Satisfaction	High	High	Low	Medium
Change	Low	Medium	High	High
Commitment	Low	Medium	High	High
Integration	Low	Medium	High	High
Termination	High	Medium	Low	Low
Visibility	Low	Medium	High	High[b]–Low[c]
Security	High	Medium	Low	Low

[a] = Relevant to short-term projects only
[b] = Is successful
[c] = Not successful

Source: Joan Knutson, How to Be a Successful Project Manager (2nd ed.). American Management Association, 1988.

ASSESSMENT TOOL
Cultural Assessment

General Questions	Response Answer each question in the space provided.
1. Think of a metaphor for your organization's project culture.	
2. What policies and procedures most influence how you work on projects?	
3. What helps you manage projects?	
4. What hinders?	
5. Does your organizational structure help you manage projects?	Yes _____ No _____
6. What hinders?	
7. What practices or techniques have really helped you manage projects?	
8. Who in your organization is really good at managing projects? What do they do?	
9. What have managers in your organization done that really helped you manage projects?	

CHAPTER 14

The Evolution of the Project Office

Wave your magic wand and tomorrow an enterprise-wide, fully functioning Project Office will appear.

Imagine that, after tomorrow, all the systems and procedures will be in place to satisfy the project management process—systems such as project initiation, project planning, and project change control. Can you envision everyone in the organization accepting project management and being willing to do whatever it takes to support the discipline with no selling, no public relations program, no training? Can a culture that has had minimal structure related to the way projects are handled possibly change on a dime and embrace rigor and discipline? How can a business that is just transitioning from a transaction-driven world to a project-driven environment convert to a new way of doing work in a short time?

Change takes time and, as shown in Figure 14.1, a magic wand is not the solution. It takes time for the infrastructure to be built and put in place. Time for the people to be willing to accept the change. And time for an organizational/political platform that will support the change to be established. As the old chestnut goes, "You can't turn the *Titanic* in an alley quickly."

Figure 14.1   Is the Project Office Magic?

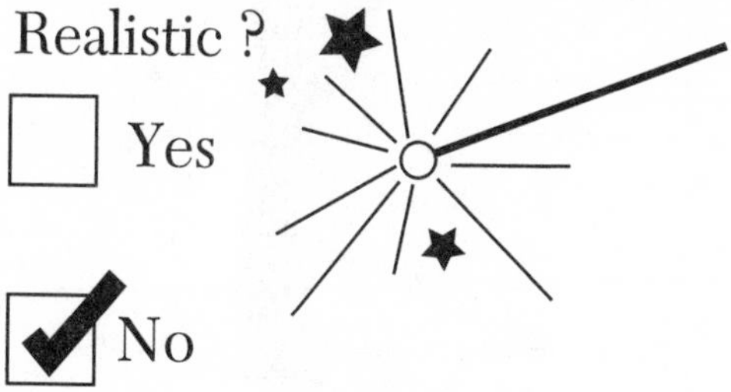

Realistic ?

☐ Yes

☑ No

Try two things. First stand up and cross your arms. Look down and notice which arm is on the top. Then uncross your arms, raise them to the ceiling, and immediately cross your arms again, placing the other arm on the top. It wasn't easy, was it? You had to think about what you needed to do to get the other arm on the top. Now try this. If you aren't wearing a coat/jacket, go get one. Put it on. Pay attention to which arm you put into a sleeve first. Now take off the jacket and put it on again. This time, put the other arm into a sleeve first. What did you notice about both activities? That it was difficult to perform a rote, routine action differently? But more importantly, that it took thought and therefore the activity took longer to perform? The same thing happens when you introduce a new discipline, such as project management, into a culture. People cannot cope if it is introduced too quickly. They will be clumsy. They will need time to get used to each new process. Therefore, a new business system such as project management should be introduced slowly. It should be allowed to evolve over time.

CHAPTER OVERVIEW

Organizations are not prepared to assimilate easily a centralized Project Office that has total authority and accountability. The reasons are:

1. The infrastructure to support the discipline is not in place.
2. The organization is unprepared for the cultural change.
3. The politics are too difficult to overcome overnight.

Implementing the discipline of project management is undertaken with the belief that it will potentially reduce a project's duration (by improving the time:money ratio), contain costs (by increasing net profits), and manage resource utilization (by establishing higher productivity without adding personnel). It is also undertaken with a belief, among top management, that the long-term benefits of professionally applying the discipline of project management will prove to be a prudent investment. However, in spite of these expectations, project players who implement and ultimately maintain a project discipline need help and ongoing management support when they are establishing project processes and procedures. Recognizing the cultural constraints, top management may decide to provide support for product/project management in the form of a Project Office.

This chapter explores the concept of the organizational platform called the Project Office. The chapter consists of two sections. The first section, "The Project Office: The Concept," explores what the Project Office is and is not. The second section, "The Evolutionary Plan: The Three Stages of Project Office Evolution," presents three possible options for inculcating this functional entity into the organizational culture. The Project Office starts out in a staff or advisory role. Then it expands its role to collect and disseminate project information across the enterprise. As a mature entity, it makes available experienced professionals who can take over and actually manage high-visibility or troubled projects. Performance Support Tool 14.1 at the end of this chapter presents the job description of the Director of the Project Office. This Performance Support Tool is available for download at www.pmsi-pm.com.

THE PROJECT OFFICE: THE CONCEPT

The first step in understanding the development and structure of the Project Office is to acquire an understanding of the concept—what a Project Office essentially is and is not.

What It Is

The *Project Office* refers to an autonomous group (or individual) that provides project management support services. This group or individual should be viewed as a service to be shared by all functions within the organization. The job of this group is focused on the discipline of project management—in other words, how to efficiently and effectively plan, organize, and manage projects within a project-driven organization.

In general, the Project Office performs one or all of these generic services:

- Maintains central historical archives of all types of projects
- Functions as a group of internal consultants whose expertise is project management
- Coordinates multiproject and interdepartmental reporting within the organization
- Provides supplemental mentoring and coaching on the techniques of project management and project management software
- Takes accountability for running major initiatives (large projects) within the organization
- Facilitates the continuous improvement process related to project management processes

What It Is Not

The Project Office is not a data-collection or administration function, nor is it an agent of management that follows project teams around and reports to management any variances from the baseline plan without working with the team to find a resolution.

THE EVOLUTIONARY PLAN: THE THREE STAGES OF PROJECT OFFICE EVOLUTION

Imagine a continuum. At the far left of the continuum is a Project Office that provides advice and support to project teams on an as-needed basis. In the middle of the continuum is a Project Office with a purview broadened to provide enterprise-wide information management for better corporate decision making. At the far right of the continuum is a Project Office to which a cadre of managers of projects report. These managers assume accountability for the successful completion of strategic project initiatives for the entire organization.

In the continuum displayed in Figure 14.2, the Project Office evolves through three stages: (1) the Project Office in a Consultative Role, (2) the Project Office in an Enterprise-wide Information Role, and (3) the Project Office in a Managing Role. Each variation on the Project Office continuum represents a stage in its evolution; the Project Office matures as the organizational unit moves from the left side of the continuum to the right. As the Project Office evolves, it increases its areas of responsibility and it grows both in its credibility within the organization and in its expertise and self-confidence.

Figure 14.2   The Evolution of Project Office

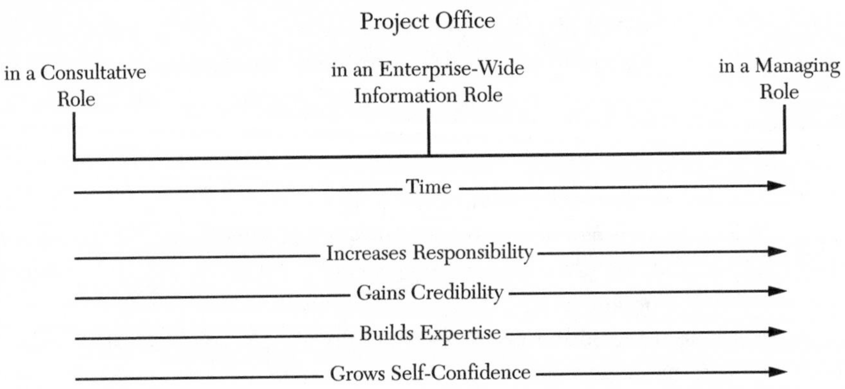

This chapter describes: the role the Project Office plays in each of the three stages; where the Project Office resides in the organizational structure; who will request the Project Office's services; the appropriate skills for the people working in the Project Office; the job duties of the department; and the critical factors needed for the success of each stage in the evolution of the Project Office.

Stage 1: The Project Office in a Consultative Role

The Role of the Project Office

The Project Office in this role provides project management expertise, advice, and guidance to managers of projects and to project players throughout the organization. In other words, the Project Office acts as an internal consultant. Here are several scenarios in which a project player might call on the assistance of the Project Office:

- A project client needs help preparing a business case.
- The project team wants advice for putting together a top management briefing.
- A task leader finds a major variance in the cost of his or her effort but doesn't know how to track down the cause.
- A manager of a project has a political problem: one of the functional areas is not living up to its commitment of resources.

In some cases, the staff member in the Project Office will listen and give guidance. In other cases, he or she might help the project player create the project management deliverables, or intercede on behalf of the project player in political issues. In short, in a consultative role, the Project Office provides support to project teams on an as-needed basis.

Reporting Relationship

The Project Office sometimes resides within a specific business unit such as Engineering, Finance, or Information Systems. In this situation, the Project Office is seen as an advocate for the functional area to which it reports. However, if the staff of the Project Office conduct themselves in an unbiased fashion, they can be viewed as ombudspersons for the entire project discipline throughout the organization. Other functional areas will then seek and be given their advice and guidance.

In some companies, the Project Office reports to top management and serves as a consultative function for the entire enterprise. The Project Office then becomes an advocate for project management to all the functional areas at one time. Giving the Project Office exposure to all the functional areas in the business brings a level of commonality and equality to all projects within the enterprise.

Requesters

The Project Office at this stage is positioned as a service organization: The customer comes to the supplier. The Project Office is the supplier of project management expertise, and requests for internal consultative assistance can come from a variety of customers. The customer might be the project client, a resource manager, a manager of the project, a team leader, or a team member.

Some Project Offices are organized in such a way that project consultants spread the workload among the entire staff so that no one is overcommitted. When a request comes into the Project Office, a project consultant who has available time gets that assignment. Other Project Offices are organized into functional areas; each project consultant is responsible for a part of the business. For example, Sean might respond to all the requests from the Human Resources area; Jamie might deal with the questions and requests for support coming from the Research and Development group.

When project consultants are assigned to a functional area, they become more familiar with that part of the business and with the players employed there. This familiarity allows them to perform their jobs more effectively. However, on the down side, Sean might have a significant amount of work and Jamie may not be steadily busy. This scenario might occur because Sean's functional area has more issues and concerns or because Human Resources believes that project management can be helpful and, therefore, is looking to Sean more frequently.

Staffing

As consultative members, Project Office personnel "mentor"—as opposed to "manage"—the community. The Project Office's credibility within the corporation, agency, or industry is often as important as any actual expertise in project management.

The desired perception, among potential customers, is that the staff in the Project Office understands their organization and their industry and therefore can be trusted to help them use the project management discipline. If the Project Office is organized around functional assignments, the project consultant typically has that functional background. In other words, Sean probably has worked in Human Resources and Jamie has come from Research and Development.

The position of the employees within the Project Office may be permanent. Alternately, the Project Office may be staffed on a revolving basis by successful "project practitioners" within the organization.

Job Duties

The types of project management responsibilities performed by the Project Office in a Consultative Role are: keeper of the methodology, mentor/coach, librarian, source of information, prescreener of phase reviews, and general all-around adviser. Let's explore each of these roles in detail.

Keeper of the Methodology.   The Project Office maintains and updates project management and/or product development *methodologies*—the processes or guidelines that provide structure to the way in which projects are run. These processes or guidelines consist, at a minimum, of the tasks that need to be performed; who will take responsibility for performing those tasks; and the deliverable that will be produced in each task—in other words, each step to take from the beginning of the project until the end. The product development methodology (or life cycle) defines the specific steps needed to create a specific deliverable; on the other hand, the project management methodology is an approach to initiating, defining, planning, executing, controlling, and closing any project.

Mentor/Coach.   The Project Office offers guidance on sociological as well as technical subjects. For example, the project consultant might advise a team on how to use certain project management tools, either automated, such as scheduling packages, or nonautomated, such as a network diagram. Or, the project consultant might attempt to build camaraderie in a newly established team. The Project Office is charged with providing assistance in applying the product and/or the project methodology. In some cases, its task is to ensure compliance with the processes set forth in these methodologies. This role may extend to conducting classroom training. A more informal part of mentoring and coaching requires just listening, being available to the project players, and helping them to traverse the political jungle that comes with working in a matrixed environment.

Librarian.   The Project Office archives documentation from past projects and maintains project "notebooks" for active projects. The Project Office directs managers of projects to sources of best-practice projects that offer history in the form of work breakdown structure (WBS) templates, dependencies, estimates, resource assignments, risk management, and other data.

In its role as librarian, the Project Office becomes the central repository of historical and current project documentation. As technology improves, the

Project Office will want to accumulate these data on automated "knowledge-based systems." Until then, bookcases organized for easy retrieval of past best-practices project documentation will serve. As to best practices, while there seems no logic in making available documentation from prior projects that were unsuccessful, if the failed project was completed with a professional closeout phase and a thorough post-project review was conducted, the records may be of value.

History can be used in many ways: to jump-start project planning with a model work breakdown schedule, dependencies, estimates, and resource assignments; to verify plans already in place by comparing the realities, requirements, and specifications of similar completed projects; and/or to become aware of and prepared for risks encountered in previous projects. The rigorous application of history to the planning of projects will put the planning process on a fast track and make it more accurate.

The Project Office should keep, at a minimum, a registry of all the active projects that have been approved through the selection and prioritization process. This database should contain the information that was documented during the registration phase of the portfolio management process. Specifically, this information includes: (1) the name of the project, (2) when it was approved, (3) a short description, (4) a benefit statement, and (5) the key players, including the names of the project client and the manager of the project. This is the beginning of an enterprise-wide inventory of projects in progress and the positioning of the move into the next stage, the Enterprise-wide Information stage.

Source of Information.   The Project Office directs requesters to sources of information that they need, for example:

- *Education.* The Project Office identifies internal and external classes being given on project management or related subjects, as well as self-study options via CD-ROM, Web training, and audio/videotapes.
- *Automated tool support.* If the enterprise has not chosen a standard scheduling package, the Project Office will provide guidance on what packages are available and will help evaluate the alternatives. If the enterprise has selected a standardized scheduling package, the Project Office will see that the software is made available and will provide help getting the requester up and running. The Project Office can help the requester explore other companion software products that deal with risk management, WBS diagramming, or report-writing tools.
- *Team building.* The Project Office institutes interventions that will coalesce a team at the beginning of a project or at any time when conflict erupts within the group. These interventions may be one-on-one

or may involve the entire group. The project consultant may perform these interventions or may direct the requester to an internal company support program or external resource.

- *Specific procedures and policies.* The Project Office will help a requester find the documentation for specific procedures such as change control, management of issues, or post-project review closeout
- *Names of people to contact within the organization.* The Project Office directs requesters to the people in the organization who can best address the requesters' problem or concerns.

The last item above is probably the most important. Many companies have an undocumented, unmapped network of people who can get things done or who know someone who knows someone who has the appropriate information. These company networks can be difficult if not impossible to traverse, especially for people who are new to the enterprise. The Project Office can minimize the frustration of being sent from one person to the next without ever getting the necessary/correct answer. Some Project Offices maintain databases that help employees find the right people to approach for needed answers or information; other Project Offices are excellent sources for the name with which to begin.

Prescreener of Phase Reviews

The Project Office ensures that end-of-phase-review presentations are ready for top management or the project client. This is accomplished by reviewing the content and conducting dress rehearsals with project teams. The Project Office coaches project teams to be sure that consistent agenda items and standards are observed.

Project players are not in the business of reviews or briefings. They are in the business of running projects. Therefore, reviews should be simply designed, easy for the project players to pull together, and represent current status, variance, and resolution of important aspects of a project.

General All-Around Adviser.   As shown in Figure 14.3, the Project Office in a Consultative Role involves an internal advisory function that offers expertise, advice, and guidance to managers of projects and to project teams. This department may reside within one specific business unit, servicing only that unit, or it may report at a level that is high enough to service the entire organization. Requests for service may come from project clients, resource managers, managers of projects, and members of the team.

Critical Success Factors

This role is consultative and requires a high degree of tact and diplomacy on the part of the Project Office "consultant." No one is mandated to use the

Figure 14.3   Responsibilities, Reporting Relationships, and Sources of Requests from Project Office in a Staff Role

Project Office in a Consultative Role

Responsibility	Resides	Request From
Internal Consultant • Guidance • Advice • Expertise	Within One Specific Business Unit Servicing That Business Unit or the Entire Organization	Project Client Resource Manager Project Manager Team Leader Team Member

Project Office's services. The Project Office must "sell" itself as a help aid and must provide support *without assuming a clerical role*. This is an important point. The Project Office *cannot allow itself* to be relegated to an administrative data-entry and report-generating department. If that is what management requires, competent administrative assistants are needed—not professional managers of projects.

Transition to the Next Stage

As shown in Figure 14.4, during this stage in its evolution, the Project Office earns the trust of the various project players. Knowing that the Project Office is dedicated to supporting them, the project players are now willing to share their information and their problems. After gaining this trust, the Project Office in a Consultative Role can move into Stage 2.

Stage 2: Project Office in an Enterprise-wide Information Role

The Project Office's Enterprise-wide Information Role can be approached in the same way as its Consultative Role. We will consider its role within the organization, where it resides in the organizational structure, who will request its services, the appropriate skills for the staff, the duties of the department, and the critical factors needed to make this stage successful.

Figure 14.4   The Transition of Project Office in a Staff Role to the Enterprise-Wide Role

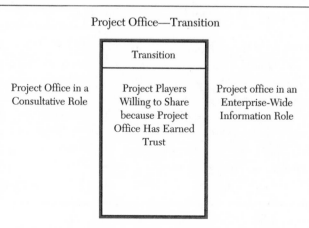

Project Office—Transition

The Role of the Project Office

The Project Office earns the project players' confidence when it performs its staff support role. As time goes on, the project players in the organization become more willing to share their information with the Project Office. They begin to trust that the Project Office will use such information to the betterment of the process and not to the detriment of any functional area, project team, or individual. At this stage, the role of the Project Office broadens.

In its Enterprise-wide Information Role, the Project Office takes on the responsibilities of gathering data relative to a multiproject environment, and of generating and disseminating consolidated reports. What the Project Office does with this information may vary. In the version of the Enterprise-wide Information Role with the least authority, the Project Office merely compiles data and provides reports to management and/or the project client. In a stronger version of this role, the Project Office analyzes the data, finds trouble spots, investigates the causes of problems, and is required to help the troubled project team correct the problem(s).

Here is a sampling of the progressive types of information that the Project Office produces in this stage of its evolution:

1. Resource utilization data show, for each person and for each department, the number of hours planned to do project and nonproject work, as compared to the number of person-hours available. If the planned hours are greater than the person-hours, management has several choices:

- Postpone or cancel the lower-priority projects.
- Hire more employees who possess the required skill mix.
- Contract the work to outside vendors who can fulfill the job needs.

2. By multiplying the person-hours planned (see Step 1) by their charge-out rate, the expenditure of labor dollars is calculated and reported. Management can then decide, on a project-by-project basis, whether this is where the organization's monies are to be spent.

3. When total project expenditures in all the categories of expense are tallied, management can determine whether an unreasonable amount is being spent in any category. Management may ask for an evaluation of any large expenditures and may then recommend how to reduce those costs. For example, if travel expenses were inordinately high, the Project Office might suggest that management should find and implement technology that facilitates meetings without the necessity of traveling to a central location.

4. Along with schedule and quality, payments to outside vendors can be tracked through this system. The Project Office may ask, for example, whether any vendor is processing significantly more change orders than other comparable vendors. If the answer is Yes, a change order process should be reestablished with this overzealous vendor.

5. Which projects are coming in ahead of or behind schedule? This information allows management to set expectations with the customer/client, the board, and the community. Management might then rethink the current strategies, take advantage of opportunities, and prepare for shortfalls. Management might also regard this as an opportunity to reprioritize projects and/or rebalance the utilization of resources.

Reporting Relationship

The Project Office in the Enterprise-wide Information stage reports to a function that has visibility and access across all functional lines. The ideal reporting structure is through the president, CEO, or COO of the organization. However, departments such as Strategic Planning, which have no functional bias, are also appropriate overseers.

Requesters

Because personnel in this Project Office stage still have the duties that they had in the Consultative Role, requests for assistance will still come from the project client, the resource manager, and the manager of the project. Now, however, more sophisticated requests come from management and from customers.

Top management may need substantiating data in a timely manner so that top-level business decisions can be made. The Project Office may, for example, provide data indicating that the firm's hiring rate has increased 20 percent during the past two years, and revenue has increased only 7 percent. Or, only 10 new projects may have been added to the project portfolio during the past year, whereas new projects had been averaging 15 to 20 during the prior two years. In another example, planned utilization of personnel for project-related and nonproject-related work might be more than 50 full-time equivalents over current staffing. These are issues that management must address, but, in the absence of a Project Office that performs an enterprise-information role, they may be unknown to management.

Even if project-related business is going well, top management needs confirming information that can be presented to appropriate parties—the board of directors, for example. Sound information grounded in quantifiable data makes it easier for management to tout the project successes of the company. As shown in Figure 14.5, Project Office in an Enterprise-wide Information Role has responsibility for providing, reporting, and, in some cases, evaluating data, as requested by management, project clients, line managers, and managers of projects.

Staffing

At this stage, the role of the Project Office has expanded to provide support to top management as well as to the manager of the project and the project team. This support consists of collecting data regularly and consolidating

Figure 14.5   Responsibilities, Reporting Relationships, and Sources of Requests from Project Office in an Enterprise-Wide Information Role

Project Office in an Enterprise-Wide Role

Responsibility	Resides	Request From
Gathers Multiproject Data and Helps Facilitate Priority Setting and Generation of Reports	Reporting to High-Level Management Function	Management Customer Project Client Line Manager Project Manager

those data into meaningful management reports. The Project Office's functions are now more dependent on project management expertise than on the credibility that the staff has within the corporation/agency and the industry. Project Office personnel must now have the analytical skills needed to be astute problem solvers. In other words, the balance of the Project Office staff is shifting from organization/industry expertise to project management expertise, and from awareness of a specific area of the business to awareness of the entire business.

The mix of personnel now changes within the department. Some project consultants will continue as advisers assigned to specific projects or functional areas; other project consultants will be retrained, or new staff will be hired. The resulting mix will be expected to:

- Understand the entire business rather than just a segment of the business
- Traverse politics across functional areas
- Perform a needs analysis, to determine the types of project information required by management
- Translate those needs into specifications that will be submitted to the report producing department
- Be familiar with enterprise-wide systems (automated and nonautomated) that are available inside and outside the organization and are capable of collecting and summarizing data
- Analyze project management reports and identify problems
- Identify problems and work with teams to present information to top management with conviction and integrity

Job Duties

The types of project management responsibilities performed by the Project Office in an Enterprise-wide Information Role are: multiproject reporter, priority-setting coordinator, resource tracker, administrator, monitor, and change controller.

Multiproject Reporter. The Project Office generates reports relative to resource utilization, budgetary expenditures, and/or contract status. The enterprise or organization as a whole can only operate if the management has information concerning all of the enterprise—each department within each division within each subsidiary. This information needs to be consolidated so that management is informed of variances compared to planned revenue, costs, resource utilization, profit, and other baselines. This information can be acquired through operational reports prepared by functional departmental managers. However, because projects have become a major component in the operation of most companies/agencies, management also needs information concerning how much time and money projects are costing, compared to the benefits (revenue or cost savings) they are returning.

Priority-Setting Coordinator.   The Project Office coordinates the project solicitation, selection, and priority-setting process. The Project Office works with the project client to ensure that the business case that goes into the solicitation process is prepared correctly. When the Project Review Board or the Project-Setting Committee meets, the Project Office ensures that new projects are presented according to procedure. The project consultant can also act as the facilitator at the project selection and priority-setting meetings.

Resource Tracker.   The Project Office manages a resource allocation system, which tracks the assignment and utilization of all project players within the organization determining any overloading or underloading of staff.

Administrator.   The Project Office classifies approved projects and opens and closes projects in the enterprise-wide system; in other words, it performs the registration function of the Portfolio Management System.

Monitor.   The Project Office raises red flags to managers of projects when project deviations occur, and it ensures that a post-project review is held and that lessons learned are documented and archived for future use.

Change Controller.   The Project Office manages the project change control process to ensure that any changes in the requirements of the final product are evaluated, and that the impacts to schedule, budget, and resource allocation are determined and approved before the change is made. The Project Office also escalates any "major" changes, as appropriate, to management for final approval.

In summary, the Project Office in an Enterprise-wide Information role gathers multiproject data and generates consolidated reports. In some organizations, this information is provided without comment; in other organizations, the Project Office also identifies problem areas and works with the project team to make recommendations for solutions. The Project Office in this stage typically reports to a high level that has control and visibility over the entire enterprise. The Project Office staff is knowledgeable concerning the business and the politics of the entire organization, but more importantly is skilled in the preparation of meaningful information reports at a top management level. The job duties revolve around consolidation of data into information, and dissemination of this information so that good business decisions can be made in a timely manner.

Critical Success Factors

To be successful, the Project Office in this stage needs:

- Standardization of all data elements to allow for cross-enterprise consolidation and reporting of data
- A powerful automated tool to manipulate this mass of data
- True top-management support to ensure that the necessary data are provided by the project players accurately and in a timely manner

Transition to the Next Stage

As shown in Figure 14.6, the transition from the Enterprise-wide Information Role to the Line Role occurs when the organization realizes that it is truly a project-driven organization and that it is in need of focused project management direction and support. This means that the entire organization now sees the need of employing full-time managers of projects who will manage total enterprise initiatives.

Stage 3: Project Office in a Managing Role

We now look at the Project Office in a Managing Role in the same way that we looked at it in a Consultative Role and an Enterprise-Wide Information

Figure 14.6 The Transition of Project Office from Enterprise-Wide Information to Line Role

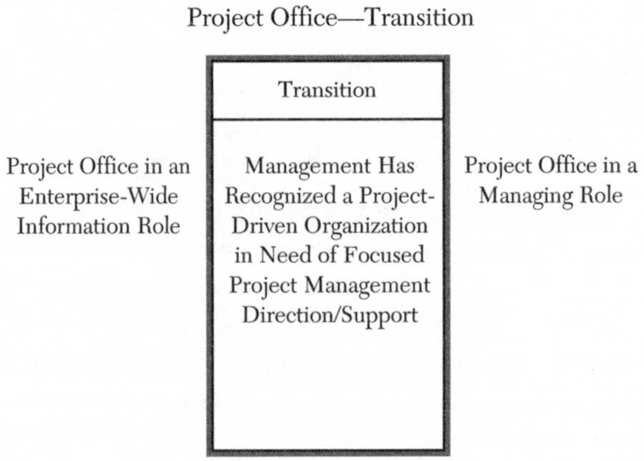

Project Office—Transition

	Transition	
Project Office in an Enterprise-Wide Information Role	Management Has Recognized a Project-Driven Organization in Need of Focused Project Management Direction/Support	Project Office in a Managing Role

Role: its role within the organization; where it resides in the organizational structure; who will request its services; the appropriate skills for the staff; the duties of the department; and the critical factors needed to make this stage successful.

The Role of the Project Office

The positioning of the Project Office in a Managing Role is typically that of a "shared service" within the organization. The Project Office offers all the services provided in the Consultative and Enterprise-Wide Information roles, continues to provide consultative support to projects and to managers of projects, and delivers consolidated reports and decision-making information to interested parties across the enterprise. This next variation of the Project Office employs a staff of knowledgeable and experienced managers of projects who are capable of managing—and available to manage—selected major initiatives/projects.

Managers of projects in this Project Office typically do not manage the smaller, less visible, less integrative projects. The Project Office is asked to provide managers of strategic initiatives which:

- Have higher visibility,
- Are larger in scope in the use of resources and in criticality to the organization's business success,
- Impact across many functional areas of the business.

Reporting Relationship

The Project Office in this stage reports to the same high level as does the Enterprise-Wide Information Project Office. The Project Office can be part of an oversight function, such as Strategic Planning, or it can report directly to the president or CEO of the organization.

There is no doubt, in this final stage of maturation, that the Project Office is an autonomous group. It has the visibility and authority to directly influence the application of project management throughout the enterprise. Besides capturing and providing business reporting to the top levels of management, this function is being chartered to run crucial initiatives within the organization.

Requesters

When this type of Project Office described above is in place, the project client or the top management sponsor may request the project management expertise of a manager from the Project Office. A functional or enterprise

Steering Committee may also require the direction of a manager from this variation of the Project Office. Say, for example, the Information Systems Steering Committee has been asked to implement a new Personnel/Payroll system across the entire organization. Because of the initiative's widespread impact on the organization and because of the cost of the effort, the Steering Committee may choose to approach the Project Office and engage one of the managers of projects.

As shown in Figure 14.7, the manager of projects from the Project Office in a Managing Role is the logical candidate for enterprise-wide project management because the selected manager of projects has the following characteristics, competencies, and support:

- Is perceived as having no bias toward any functional area and therefore can make objective decisions
- Has proven project management competencies and is a seasoned project management practitioner
- Is familiar with many areas within the organization and can talk to all the project players
- Has the backing and the clout of top management because of the Project Office's position within the organization
- Yet is able to bring to bear consultation and information-generation expertise from the Project Office and can consult other colleagues for advice and counsel

Figure 14.7   Responsibilities, Reporting Relationships, and Sources of Requests from Project Office in a Managing Role

Project Office in a Managing Role

Responsibility	Resides	Request From
• Provide All Services Offered inTwo Previous Variations • "Shared Service" • Manage Strategic Initiatives	• Autonomous Functional Area	• Project Client • Steering Committee

Staffing

As a line function, the Project Office employs highly qualified managers of projects who report to the unit. *Manager of projects* is a discrete position, not just a role being performed by people throughout the organization. Attached to the position are: a job description, a performance appraisal review procedure specifically related to the job of the manager of projects, and a development plan to improve the manager's project management skills.

Job Duties

The Project Office in a Managing Role has two major responsibilities, as explained next.

Manager of Projects.   The Project Office plans, organizes, monitors, tracks, and controls major strategic initiatives, and takes full accountability for the project's success or failure. These projects are very important to the success of the enterprise; therefore, accountability is taken seriously by both the manager of projects and the Director of the Project Office.

Leader.   This person models the best practices relative to adhering to the process and discipline of project management. He or she enhances and improves the project management process and becomes an advocate for the discipline of project management throughout the entire organization.

The Project Office in a Managing Role provides all the services offered in the two previous stages, but, having now evolved into a true source for the managment of projects, it employs seasoned managers of projects who possess high levels of expertise in managing major initiatives. This Project Office is an autonomous functional area that responds to requests from project clients, Review Boards, and senior management.

Only a top-notch project management professional can perform these two jobs while fulfilling all the duties required in the previous two stages. Furthermore, the Project Office must have a functional manager who can help coordinate all this work. (See Performance Support Tool 14.1, "Job Description of the Director of the Project Office.")

Critical Success Factors

This final and most mature variation of the Project Office can succeed only if the people throughout the enterprise have recognized that the company has become a project-driven organization. In other words, the first critical success factor is to have all project players, from resource managers to top management, become aware that the majority of the work being performed is organized as projects, and to communicate that these projects cannot be successful without the active engagement of the discipline of project management.

The second critical success factor for the Project Office in a Managing Role is for the project consultants to be highly proficient, professional, skilled, trained, and steeped in the whats, whys, and wherefores of project management.

The third critical success factor is management support. Top management must politically champion and empower the Project Office. If, for example, it is company policy for a business case to be submitted seven working days before the priority-setting meeting so that the committee has time to review it, then a business case that is turned in two days before the meeting will not be considered. Management cannot allow the project client presenting the business case to break that rule unless special permission is granted by the Project Office. The quickest way to undermine the Project Office would be for management to allow any project player to violate major rules in the absence of the Project Office's agreement.

CONCLUSION

A full-blown Project Office cannot be implemented overnight. The evolution of the Project Office through the three stages of development requires the gradual development of infrastructure to support it, the willingness of the culture to invest authority in and accept direction from the Project Office, and the cultivation of pro-project management politics.

The implementation of the Project Office is most effectively accomplished by gradually progressing through three stages into a highly professional, respected, and productive business unit within an organization. The Project Office starts out in a Consultative Role: a knowledgeable project consultant provides guidance and support to any manager of projects or project team member within the organization. Then the Project Office evolves to stage 2—an Enterprise-wide Information role in which it provides information and decision-making support to management by collecting data on a repetitive basis and consolidating those data into management reports. This may include offering top management and the project client evaluations and recommendations based on the information that is reported or working with the team to provide that information. In its most evolved stage, the Project Office in a Managing Role not only advises project teams and provides enterprise-wide information but also takes on a leadership role by managing key initiatives—major projects—within the organization. As shown in Figure 14.8, as the Project Office evolves, it acquires more numerous responsibilities, but it never relinquishes the duties performed during its previous stage(s) of growth.

The services of the Project Office may be provided in three different ways:

1. On a noncost basis, the effort that the Project Office personnel provided to a project is not charged to the project but is considered overhead. This is typical in the first two stages: the Project Office in a Consultative Role, and the Project Office in an Enterprise-wide Information Role.

2. The services of the Project Office may be offered on a charge-back basis, whereby the services provided by personnel in the Project Office are billed to the project(s) on which the manager of the project is working. This charge-back approach would obviously be most appropriate for the third stage, the Project Office in a Managing Role.

3. In a hybrid approach, effort directly related to the management of the project is billed to the project, but the advisory effort, concerning processes or tools, is provided as nonbilled overhead. The enterprise-wide reporting effort can either be paid by the company as overhead or prorated across the functional areas that are using the information. As shown in Figure 14.9, the Project Office evolves through the three stages, gaining more visibility and authority while simultaneously becoming more accountable and exposed.

The greatest challenge is to gain the respect and trust of the functional areas and the project teams so that they request the support of the Project Office. The objective is to get one of the project players—and then the next and the next—to recognize the value of the support that the Project

Figure 14.8   The Evolution of Responsibilities to Project Office in a Managing Role

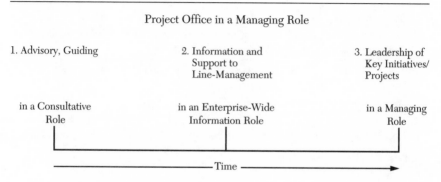

Project Office in a Managing Role

1. Advisory, Guiding

2. Information and
   Support to
   Line-Management

3. Leadership of
   Key Initiatives/
   Projects

in a Consultative
Role

in an Enterprise-Wide
Information Role

in a Managing
Role

Time

Figure 14.9   The Evolution of Accountability, Authority, Visibility, and Vulnerability to Project Office in a Managing Role

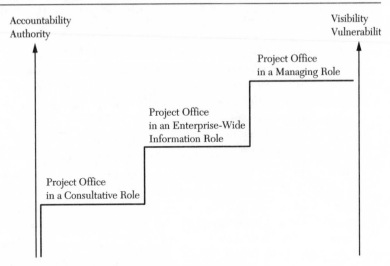

Office can provide. To establish their credibility, the project consultants need to promote the discipline of project management. They can mount their own public relations effort by:

- Seeing that articles published in the company newsletter tout the services that the office can provide or share success stories of specific projects or specific functional areas
- Dropping by the offices of various functional managers and establishing a relationship
- Asking to be invited to project team meetings and then tactfully and slowly offering suggestions and guidance
- Offering awareness and educational events such as brown-bag lunches or symposia to the project players

The assimilation of a Project Office into a corporation/agency will require a cultural change. Cultural changes are more successful if they evolve over time rather than being forced on a population overnight. Consider the evolution of the Project Office as described in this chapter, and allow it to mature and take root in its own time.

Take a few moments to review the job description of the Director of a Project Office, which follows. This Performance Support Tool describes what the Director's job should entail and defines the functions and jobs that the Project Office performs.

PERFORMANCE SUPPORT TOOL 14.1

Job Description of the Director of the Project Office

The Project Director is responsible for providing direction concerning the project management discipline throughout the organization. This position requires the Project Director to monitor the progress of crucial projects being performed at all times. The Project Director will coordinate the project selection and prioritization process and the presentation of the competing projects to management in a professional manner. The Project Director will review all active projects from the planning phase through the closeout phase. The Project Director will provide training, mentoring, and tools to the project team. He or she will establish a standard product life cycle and project management life cycle and make sure that these methodologies are revised and reissued as necessary. These life cycles will be the basis of standard processes and procedures for planning and controlling projects. The Project Director will provide to all staff members project management consultation and support that may consist of:

- Building and maintaining Product Life Cycle models relative to the initiation and definition, development, and creation phases of product development
- Building and maintaining Project Life Cycle models relative to selection, prioritization, planning, controlling, and change management of a project process
- Building and maintaining a multiproject resources management system in order to achieve all project and nonproject work objectives
- Ensuring that quality is planned and achieved
- Providing appropriate training to all project players relative to the above product and project life cycles
- Coordinating the project selection and prioritization process with the functional teams and the priority review team
- Ensuring that the project team is formed in a timely manner with appropriate representation from all areas of the organization and with the necessary commitment of functional managers
- Working with the project teams to ensure that activities are being completed on time, within budget, and of the quality required; and that corrective action is taken if any unacceptable variance occurs in any of these variables
- Managing a change control process that identifies and analyzes the impact of changes of scope and presents them to management for approval or disapproval
- Managing a risk management process to identify and prepare preventive and response plans and to monitor these risks and activate contingency plans when necessary.
- Arranging formal milestone (or phase) reviews that include the following:
  —Maintaining a calendar of scheduled reviews
  —Supporting project teams in preparation of the review and facilitating these meetings when appropriate
  —Producing Executive Summaries that reflect the official status of each formal review held
- Facilitating resolution of issues

- Facilitating cross-department/division communications
- Identifying and arranging for review of projects at the team level
- Escalating project-related concerns to the attention of appropriate management as needed
- Archiving historical project management files to be used in planning future projects
- Supporting the training and application of the chosen scheduling software, and making available any other automated tools that support the project management discipline

✧   ✧   ✧

The Project Director will report to _____ and take his or her direction from that person and from the Project Management Committee. The Project Director has direct line responsibility only for the staff in the Project Office. All other relationships with project team members are dotted or matrixed relationships. However, the Project Director (or a member of his or her department) will be expected to provide performance appraisal review input for all participants on all projects in which the Project Office becomes involved.

PART V
CONCLUSION

CHAPTER 15

Measurements of Project Management Success

Congratulations! You have just earned $500,000! You worked very hard to earn that $500,000. This money is important to your well-being and to the well-being of the people around you.

I approach you and ask you to give *me* $500,000 to invest in a business venture that I assure you is rational and meaningful and will be a positive contribution to your world. You justifiably ask me what return you can anticipate after I have invested your money for you. How much money, above the $500,000, will you get back, and how soon? My response to you is that you won't get any tangible money back, and you probably won't get the $500,000 back. You are shocked and want to know why you should give the money to me at all. "Trust me," I say. "The money will be well used. It will make a difference."

How do you feel about giving me the money under those conditions? Probably not all warm and fuzzy. But that is precisely what we are asking our management to do. We are asking them to pay the salaries of project managers, to pay for the time needed for project clients and project team members to work on projects, and to pay for the training, software, and other expenditures necessary to support the project management discipline. And we are doing this without guaranteeing any return on their investment.

Your top management people feel that *they* have worked very hard to help earn the $500,000. That money is important to *their* well-being and *their* future careers. It is important to all the people who are employed in their organization. And we, as project practitioners, are asking them to give us this $500,000 (plus a lot more) with no visible means of return on that investment. Wrong!

Project management in a project-driven organization is becoming more and more visible, and more and more money is being spent to support the discipline of project management. Like you, top management is going to start asking where this money is going and what they are getting out of it. We'd better be ready to answer.

CHAPTER OVERVIEW

Measurement of project management success will be required by our management and by our customers as the discipline becomes more visible and more expensive. As managers of projects, we can validate, quantitatively and qualitatively, that the discipline of project management is not only successful but adds significant value to the organization. This chapter explains what we are measuring and presents four possible yardsticks of measurement and a set of practical measurement procedures.

The success of any staff or support service can be difficult to measure because of the relatively intangible results that the function produces. However, it is widely believed that any support service—for project management or any other discipline—can be measured by the reactions to it, by the skills and competencies the people possess, by the behavior associated with it, and by its results.

- *Reaction* is the awareness that people have of the subject, and their attitudinal response.
- *Learning* refers to the level of knowledge—and, to some degree, the skills—that people possess.
- *Behavior* takes learning one step farther; it asks: Are people applying the competencies, skills, and processes appropriately?
- *Results,* the ultimate goal, suggest that sound business outcomes are being produced.

Keep these measurement guides in mind. We will refer to them later in this chapter.

Four measurement plateaus allow us to track the return on investment (ROI) that companies are realizing from the implementation and execution of the discipline of project management. As portrayed in Figure 15.1, they are:

- Measurement Plateau 1: Comprehension and Acceptance (gauging reaction and learning)

Figure 15.1   Four Measurement Plateaus

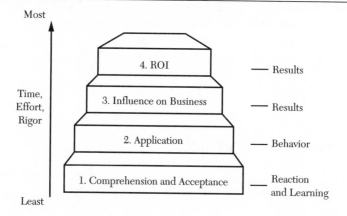

- Measurement Plateau 2: Application (gauging behavior)
- Measurement Plateau 3: Influence on Business (gauging results)
- Measurement Plateau 4: Return on Investment (gauging more tangible results)

Measurement Plateau 1 takes the least time, rigor, and effort; Measurement Plateau 4 takes the most time, rigor, and effort. Measurement Plateau 1 is the least quantifiable and relies on subjective observation; Measurement Plateau 4 is grounded in solid mathematical calculations that yield variations of return on investment based on credible, quantifiable data. As you move from Measurement Plateau 1 to Measurement Plateau 4, you move from measuring how the environment "senses" the success or failure of project management to how the environment can be shown the additional "cents" (and dollars) generated.

After the measurement plateaus are agreed on, we must decide what we are measuring. Specific metrics, or standard units of measure, must be set. These metrics are the criteria by which we will evaluate progress over time, set levels of commitment, and position accountability to reach these targets. Next, a process must be designed to measure project management success in any or all of the four plateaus, as defined by the metrics that have been established. The process of monitoring, tracking, and managing these metrics consists of the following steps:

- Step 1: Data collection
- Step 2: Data analysis
- Step 3: Results compilation
- Step 4: Action plan implementation

Performance Support Tool 15.1, "Project Management Measuring Models," introduces models that provide a rough blueprint of the methods one might pursue in determining whether project management has succeeded in terms of specified project management criteria. This Performance Support Tool and all others referenced in this book are available for download at www.pmsi-pm.com.

Let's start by considering what we need to measure.

WHAT ARE WE MEASURING?

Generically, business success is measured by the following outcomes: tangible outputs, the mind-set of the affected employees, financial impacts, and the reaction of the internal and/or external clients. Let's explore each outcome individually.

Tangible outputs show how much has been produced. Outputs can be tangible things that are produced or transactions that are processed; they can also be intangible services that are offered to internal or external customers. Not only must there be a satisfactory number; these outputs must also meet a quality standard that is acceptable to the organization and, sometimes, to the marketplace.

The mind-set of the affected employees is crucial. If the employees are not willing to produce the products, process the transactions, or support the services, the discipline will not be successful. The employees' attitude toward this discipline of project management and the projects in which they are asked to participate can make an enormous difference.

Financial impacts revolve around the revenue generated as compared to the expenses paid—in other words, the profit. However, financial impact can also be influenced by levels of productivity, avoidance of financial penalties, positioning for future opportunities, and similar influences.

The reaction of internal and/or external clients yields a rating of customer satisfaction. Are potential clients willing to buy what we are selling? Are they happy with it when it is implemented? Do they come back to us for more products and/or services?

The outcomes that measure business success are:

- Tangible outputs
  plus
- Mind-set of affected employees
  plus

- Financial impacts
plus
- Reaction of internal and/or external clients

By what specific criteria can we measure business success in a project-management-driven organization? As shown in Figure 15.2, the quantification of business success relies on sound metrics, or measurements, that could be based on a combination of *hard* (quantifiable) and *soft* (more subjective) data. The hard data relate to output, quality, costs, time, and/or the project client's satisfaction. These translate into the generic success outcomes discussed above, with the exception of the mind-set of the affected employees, which can be evaluated in soft data such as work habits, work climate, and attitudes.

First, however, we must ask ourselves several questions: Should we be evaluating the success or failure of single projects, or do we measure the success or failure of the total project management system and thus the initiatives (or subsystems) that make up the project management discipline? The success of project management can be validated by correlating its success to that of individual projects. This is a valid and clean approach. However, evaluating project management in this way can produce unreliable findings if we fail to recognize that a project might be unsuccessful not because the project management discipline is ineffectual but because of external factors that are beyond the control of the technical or sociological components of project management.

Figure 15.2   Hard and Soft Metrics

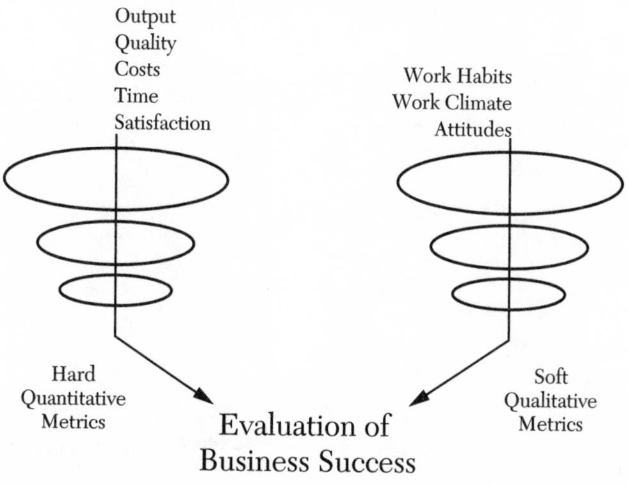

Output
Quality
Costs
Time
Satisfaction

Work Habits
Work Climate
Attitudes

Hard
Quantitative
Metrics

Soft
Qualitative
Metrics

Evaluation of
Business Success

Next, we must ask: What is our goal? Are we attempting to measure the success of projects, or of project management, in terms of the criteria displayed in Figure 15.3? If we are attempting the former, we are concerned primarily with being on time, on budget, and delivering a quality product or service. If we are attempting the latter, we need to focus on initiatives pertinent to project management, such as methodologies, automated support, organizational structure, performance management, information creation and dissemination, and so on. Therefore, although it is also appropriate to apply these measurement techniques to single projects, the thrust of this chapter is to use the techniques to measure the multiple initiatives that make up the business and cultural discipline of project management.

With that in mind, we can narrow down the general success factors, arrive at a list of the specific outcomes of successful project management, and determine the criteria by which the discipline of project management might be evaluated:

- Success criterion 1: Adherence to a standard project management process
- Success criterion 2: More satisfied project customers
- Success criterion 3: More accurate plans
- Success criterion 4: More meaningful and timely project status

Figure 15.3   Success Measured

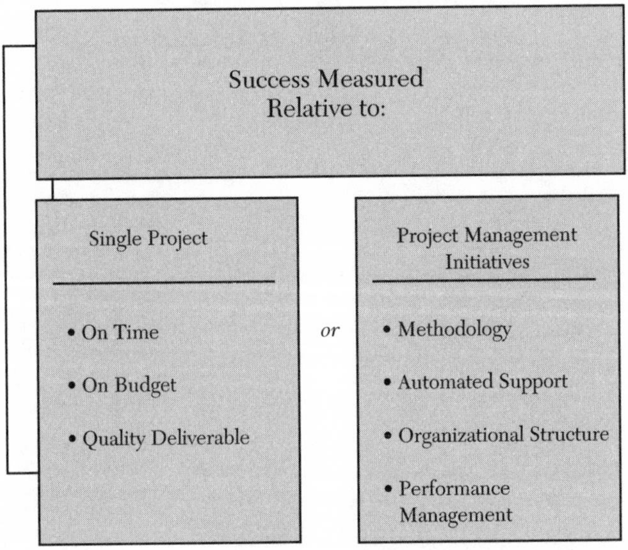

- Success criterion 5: Applied continuous improvement
- Success criterion 6: Effective change control

Each criterion, in turn, can be evaluated in terms of the four general outcomes: tangible output, mind-set of employees, financial impact, and the reaction of internal or external clients. (Performance Support Tool 15.1 offers measurement models by which to determine whether project management has succeeded in an enterprise, according to each of these success criteria.)

In summary, project management can be measured by the success of each of the projects as a composite, or by the total success of the project management discipline. Even if projects are considered bellwethers of project management success, time spent evaluating the project management business system (and its components) is time very well spent.

Project management could be measured against a myriad of criteria, but the six suggested above—and any others that you may choose to add—can be evaluated in terms of generic business-success outcomes such as volume and quality of outputs, acceptance and support by the employees, financial rewards, and customer satisfaction.

Let's explore each measurement plateau in detail, to determine how we can measure the discipline of project management.

THE FOUR MEASUREMENT PLATEAUS

As illustrated in Figure 15.1, there are four measures of project management success within an enterprise: (1) comprehension and acceptance, (2) application, (3) influence on business, and (4) return on investment (ROI). As these measures progress through the series of plateaus, they range from more subjective evaluations based on more qualitative data (sense) to more objective evaluations of hard business results based on quantitative dollars and cents, as follows.

Measurement Plateau 1: Comprehension and Acceptance

This plateau is evaluated by the senses—seeing, hearing, talking, and feeling become indicators that project management is being used successfully. On this plateau, success is measured in terms of reactions and learning. Comprehension suggests cognitive understanding of the benefits of using project management and its tools, techniques, and behaviors. Acceptance is a willingness to try the discipline and to adhere to the associated project management processes and specific procedures.

Three techniques can be used to determine the comprehension and the acceptance of project management within an organization (see Figure 15.4): (1) evaluation of the knowledge and acceptance of the practitioners, (2) validation by gauging the atmosphere and activity as you wander around, and (3) performance of individual competency assessments. These techniques are allied to the following activities:

1. Accumulate Data Relative to the Maturity of the Project Practitioners

The practitioners can be measured by years of experience and/or levels of education. Years of experience can be quantified by the average number of years spent practicing the discipline or filling a project-management-related job. Level of education is shown by academic achievement: the number of degrees earned or classes taken, and/or a passing grade on the Project Management Institute's (PMI) Project Management Professional (PMP) certification exam.

2. Wander Around

Play the role of a cultural archaeologist. Validate your impressions by seeing, hearing, talking, and feeling to determine if project management is being applied successfully. Take a walk with a pencil and a pad of paper in hand. Observe, make notes, ask a predetermined series of questions from technical *and* sociological project management perspectives. You will be able to sense whether project management is being used and whether the people who are using it are supportive of the discipline.

Figure 15.4   Comprehension and Acceptance

Three Evaluation Techniques

1	2	3
Knowledge of Practitioners	Validation by Wandering Around	Individual Competency Assessment

3. Administer a Competency Assessment

Have the project players do a self-assessment. Give them a questionnaire based on the project management competencies required by individuals working in your project environment. These competencies can be acquired from an internal company analysis-and-development effort, from a reputable consulting firm's competency model, and/or from an industry standard, such as PMI's *Project Management Body of Knowledge (PMBOK)*. Each individual who is part of the study is asked to fill out the questionnaire and self-evaluate his or her awareness and knowledge of project management. The results of the study will provide a meaningful cross-section of how the project players view their own comprehension and acceptance of the discipline, and will offer information that identifies deficiencies and facilitates the creation of individual career development plans.

Basic Premise   The basic premise behind the Comprehension and Acceptance Plateau is that the more knowledgeable (learning) and the more accepting (reaction) the project players are, the more successful the project management effort will be.

Measurement Plateau 2: Application

This plateau is judged by the frequency and accuracy with which the technical and sociological behaviors of project management are applied. Three potential techniques can be employed in this plateau, as shown in Figure 15.5:

Figure 15.5   Application

Three Evaluation Techniques

1	2	3
Project Management Documentation	Project Team Meeting— Observations	Organizational Gap Analysis

(1) reviewing project management documentation, (2) observing project team meetings, and (3) identifying organizational gap analysis.

1. Review Project Management Documentation

Conduct an audit to review project definition documents, schedule charts, risk management plans, change control logs, and other deliverables produced by various project processes that are in place. First, determine whether these documents are being produced. If the answer is Yes, the discipline of project management is being applied. Next, decide whether these documents are of an acceptable quality. If Yes, the discipline is being used correctly.

2. Invite Yourself to Project Team Meetings

Observe the dynamics. Have a list of metrics criteria to score what you see. Rate the application of these criteria from 1 (low compliance) to 5 (high compliance). Sample criteria for measuring the application of project management to project teamwork are displayed in Table 15.1.

The results of these observations will indicate (1) whether the team is applying the technical mechanics of project management and (2) the behaviors necessary to work in a cross-functional team.

3. Administer an Organizational Assessment

A gap analysis can be used for this purpose. This organizational assessment may be administered in the form of a questionnaire or via a series of one-on-one interviews or focus group meetings conducted by a strong facilitator. Questions are asked: How do the participants of the survey see the current state of project management within their organization? What do

Table 15.1 Criteria to Measure Application of Project Management

Criteria	Score 1 = Low compliance 5 = High compliance
Schedules are being used to determine on-time performance.	1 2 3 4 5
People are being held accountable for producing quality deliverables.	1 2 3 4 5
Project players are being publicly recognized for successful actions.	1 2 3 4 5

they see as the ideal future state? Diagnosis of the data collected will provide information relative to how people perceive project management being applied and how they envision that project management should be applied. The delta or gap indicates the organization's deficiencies in the application of project management. It establishes areas in which additional work needs to be performed to reach the success metrics goals and objectives.

Basic Premise   The basic premise behind the Application Plateau is that if the tools, techniques, and processes of project management, as well as the behaviors associated with their use in a team environment, are being used—and used correctly—the success of project management as a discipline has increased.

Measurement Plateau 3: Influence on the Business

This plateau is assessed by quantifying the business results that are produced by virtue of the discipline of project management within the enterprise. Two techniques are possible on this plateau:

1. Use trend or forecast analysis to compare what might have been expected to happen without the project management discipline and what did happen with it in place.
2. Administer a 360-degree assessment.

These two techniques are displayed in Figure 15.6.

Figure 15.6   Influence on Business

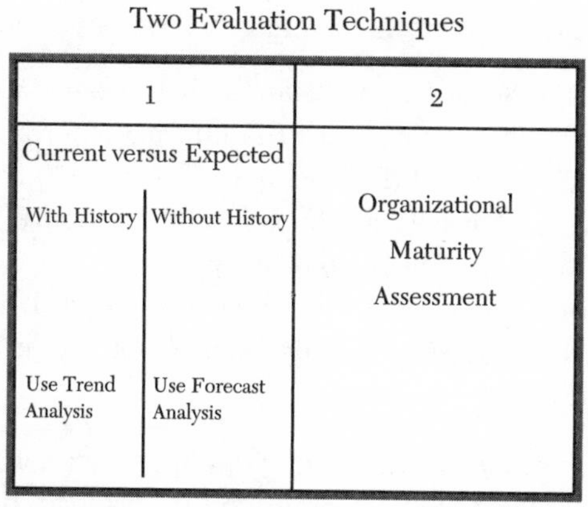

Two Evaluation Techniques

1		2
Current versus Expected		Organizational Maturity Assessment
With History	Without History	
Use Trend Analysis	Use Forecast Analysis	

1. Analyze the Impact of Business Results on the Current Business State

To get the most value from this technique, you will need to measure three data points. The first is the "current business state"—in other words, the current success metrics relative to the chosen success criterion described above. The second data point is the "expected business state"—what the business state would be, in the absence of intervention to improve project management. The third data point is the "actual business state"—the success or failure of the defined outcomes when project management is actually being applied within the organizational environment. The "expected business state" can be based on historical data or on forecast data that were established before the project or the project initiative was implemented, as explained below.

Using Historical Data as Your Base.   If you plan to use historical data as your base, create a trend analysis line, plot historically what has occurred, and then plot a projected trend if no project management intervention had been implemented. After the project management initiative has been implemented, begin accumulating and plotting actual data against the expected trend. If the actual is better than the projected trend, the project management intervention has made a difference.

> **Example** There are currently no top-management project review meetings. The unforeseen problems that require emergency top-management meetings average about 10 per month, and they have been increasing at a rate of about one per quarter. Each of these surprises has cost the organization approximately $100,000. If the trend continues during the next four quarters, instead of 10 surprises costing $1 million, there will be 14 emergencies at a price of $1.4 million. With enough history, it should be possible to plot on the calendar when these expenditures occurred and then track whether frequent top-management project reviews lowered these expenditures.

Using Forecasted Data as a Base.   If historical data are unavailable, perform a forecasting analysis. Determine, with the information available, what business result could be expected if all possible variables are considered and no project management intervention is implemented. As above, once the project management initiative has been implemented, begin accumulating actual data and comparing them against the expected forecast. If the actual is better than the forecasted business result, then the project management intervention has added value.

> **Example** Currently, no top-management project review meetings are scheduled. We know that a group of unforeseen problems require

emergency top-management meetings. Each of these surprises has cost the organization additional dollars. How much? We are not sure. We do know that, for all of the projects that the enterprise completed last year, an additional $2 million (over the planned project budgets) was spent. We can assume that half of that expense could easily have been avoided if top management had been informed of problems early and, as a group, had the time to work out solutions. Therefore, we can forecast that we could save $1 million by instituting top-management project review meetings, and we can establish a metric, or objective, for reducing the project's over-budget estimate by $250,000 per quarter in the next four quarters.

2. Administer a 360-Degree Assessment

This instrument is administered to each project player as well as to the sphere of people with whom the project player works. The sphere consists of people on a higher, lower, and peer level on the organization chart, as well as contacts outside the firm, if appropriate. All of the people who come in contact with a player who is being assessed—whether downward, upward, or sideways on the chart—should evaluate him or her in terms of project competency.

When the 360-degree view is completed, the results indicate how each person is making a difference by using project management. From this evaluation comes the information needed to implement an ongoing performance improvement process. The theory is: If the people performing the project management effort are perceived as performing it well and are continually being groomed and developed, the project management discipline itself will generate better business results.

Basic Premise   The basic premise behind the Influence on Business Plateau is that when Comprehension/Acceptance and Application of project management from the first two plateaus is accomplished, and when appropriate inspection and management are in place, tangible financial and productivity results will be produced because of the presence of the project management discipline.

Measurement Plateau 4: Return on Investment (ROI)

Generically, return on investment evaluates the earnings derived from a venture as compared to the investment expended to complete the venture. To make the venture viable, the earnings need to be equal to or, preferably, greater than the investment.

Return on investment takes the most time, effort, and rigor. However, if and when it becomes necessary to persuade the powers-that-be to approve or continue funding the project management discipline, it will be worth every moment and "cent" invested.

Calculating the project management return on investment requires determining the benefits (expressed in monetary terms) of employing the project management discipline as compared to the monetary costs of implementing and/or maintaining the project management discipline. This is the final and ultimate plateau from which we can provide more quantifiable data and substantively prove the value and worth of project management.

Return on Investment: Series of Calculations

Two methods can be used to determine whether the monies spent to sustain project management in an organization are generating a positive return. The first option is a dollar evaluation called the *Benefit-to-Cost Ratio (BCR);* the second option is the traditional *Return on Investment (ROI)* calculation. Let's look at each one.

Benefit-to-Cost Ratio (BCR).   This calculation determines the ratio of dollars returned to dollars invested. If the ratio is positive, the venture is pulling its weight. However, if the result is negative, the venture is not returning its investment. The specific formula is:

$$\frac{\$Benefits}{\$Costs} = BCR \left(\text{Benefits-to-Cost Ratio} \right)$$

Example   If the benefits were $100 and the costs were $50, the benefits-to-cost ratio would be 2 : 1 or, expressed as a dollar amount:

$$\frac{\$100}{\$50} = \$2.00$$

Two dollars were returned for every dollar invested. Getting double one's money on an investment isn't half bad.

Return on Investment.   The result from this calculation is shown as a percentage. The calculation portrays the percentage of every invested dollar that has been recouped. A result of 0 percent indicates that the investment has reached a break-even point—that is, the dollars spent have been recouped, no more and no less. If the result is less than 0 percent, the investment has not yet paid off. If the result is greater than 0 percent, the investment has paid itself off and has a surplus.

Two formulas are used to calculate return on investment. The *Net Benefits (NB)* formula indicates in monetary terms whether the costs are more or less than the benefits. The formula for calculating Net Benefits is:

$$\text{\$ Benefits} - \text{\$ Costs} = \text{Net benefits}$$

Example The benefit derived from enhancing the project management process was $100; in other words, the $ Benefits = $100. The cost (in dollars) to attain the benefit was $50:

$$\$100 - \$50 = +\$50 \text{ (Net benefits)}$$

The ratio of the Net Benefits to the cost of attaining those net benefits is calculated as a percentage of return on investment. The calculation looks like this:

$$\frac{\text{\$Net benefits}}{\text{\$Costs}} \times 100 = \text{ROI\%}$$

Example In the example above, the Benefits were $100, the Cost was $50, and the Net Benefit was $50. The Net Benefit of $50 divided by the cost of $50 is given as a percentage. The calculation looks like this:

$$\frac{\$50}{\$50(100)} = 100\% \text{ ROI}$$

The return on investment is 100%. In other words, not only has the venture broken even it has also returned 100% on its investment.

Either of these calculations—presenting a dollar return (BCR) or a ratio shown as a percentage return (ROI)—is acceptable as evidence of whether the project management discipline is making "a positive difference" within the organization.

The goal is to place a value on each unit of data that can be collected to measure the success or failure of project management. These data can relate to single projects or to specific project management initiatives, such as a project management methodology, an organizational infrastructure, or an automated-support suite. The BCR or the ROI can be presented as individual "success metrics" or can be "rolled up" to a composite number; the resultant BCR or ROI for each project being evaluated could be consolidated, and an average or a mean could be determined. This approach could also be employed using the BCR or ROI of all the project management initiatives (subsystems) that are in place. This composite number defines the success of the project management discipline as a whole.

Basic Premise: The basic premise behind the ROI Plateau is to further evaluate, in financial terms, the Influence on Business calculated in the third plateau in order to prove that the project management discipline is making a positive financial business impact on the organization.

The information that we have just learned is pulled together in the following integrated example:

Example: Return on Investment Calculation

Project Management Success Criterion 1: There is a documented project management process and it is being applied.

Benefits Metric: Appropriate project management outputs are generated as required by the project management process.

Target Value: 70 percent of projects produce schedule, resource, and cost reports in the appropriate phase, which will reduce the number of status review meetings required.

Costs Metric: Expenditure of core team's salaries and benefits to develop and rollout the report-generating portion of the project management process.

Monetary Benefits from the status review meeting reduction include the following:

- Value of one meeting = $1,000
- Annual number of meetings for one project = 50 (one per week)
- Half of the meetings will not be required because we are following a standard process; therefore, the total number of meetings required per project will be 25.
- 70% of the total number of projects in progress = 10
- Reduced number of meetings = 250
- Savings are $1,000 × 250 = $250,000

Monetary Costs:

To develop a status-reporting segment of a project management process.

• Labor (indirect; i.e., internal staff)	$100,000
• Labor (direct; i.e., outside consultant)	50,000
• Materials (binders, reproduction)	5,000
• Training	25,000

To maintain the status-reporting segment of a project management process.

- Labor (indirect; i.e., internal staff per year)   20,000

Total cost for one year including development
and maintenance $200,000

Benefit-to-Cost Ratio (BCR)

$$\frac{\$Benefit}{\$Cost} = BCR$$

$$\frac{\$250,000}{\$200,000} = 1.25{:}1$$

In other words, for every dollar invested, $1.25 has been returned.

Return on Investment (ROI)

$$\$ \ Benefit - \$ \ Cost = \$ \ Net \ Benefit$$

$$\$250{,}000 - \$200{,}000 = \$50{,}000$$

$$\frac{\$Net \ Benefit}{\$Costs} \times 100 = ROI$$

$$\frac{\$50{,}000}{\$200.00} \times 100 = 25\%$$

In other words, there has been a 25% return on the investment.

Now that we have some grasp of the specific calculations to determine the benefit-to-cost ratio and the return on investment—and have provided an example—let's consider where to find the benefit and cost data so that we can perform these calculations.

Categories of Benefits Used in the Return-on-Investment Calculations

Because project management is used in a wide array of industries, the following is an essentially generic list of sources from which project management benefits can be ascertained. The list ranges from very tangible dollar benefits to more subjective, yet valid, units of measure:

- Contribution to profit
- Savings of costs
- Increased volume; that is, number of units produced or number of transactions processed
- Increase in quantity of output, converted to a dollar value

- Quality improvements translated into the previous four items
- Value of time; reduced employee effort interpreted into loaded labor dollars (salary plus benefits)
- Comparison to the following benchmarks:
  —Your organization's historical database(s)
  —A similar organization's history
  —Professional or trade organizations such as the Project Management Institute
  —Government statistics
- Evaluation gathered through satisfaction surveys from the following:
  —Project clients
  —Operational customers
  —Management steering committee
  —Project managers and project team members
  —Internal or external subject matter experts

Categories of Costs Used in the Return-on-Investment Calculations

This list is much more tangible than the benefits list and includes less subjective data:

- Cost to design and develop preferably prorated over the expected life of the program rather than totally absorbed at the beginning of the measurement process
- Recurring costs to maintain
- Cost of materials
- Cost of quality
- Cost of travel and expenses
- Cost of facilities
- Cost of management
- Cost of labor (salary and benefits) of the participants
- Administration and overhead costs

In summary, there are four plateaus of success in project management, and each can be measured through specific techniques, as summarized in Table 15.2. Each plateau can measure single projects or project management initiatives, either of which can be consolidated to make up a comprehensive report card on the project management discipline. The measurements or metrics are based on technical or hard data, which are quantifiable, and sociological or soft data, which are more intangible.

Now let's explore the process of collecting this information.

Table 15.2   Overview of Measurement Techniques

Plateau	Measurement Technique
Comprehension and acceptance	1. Accumulate data relative to years of experience and/or levels of education. 2. Wander around. 3. Administer a competency assessment.
Application	1. Review project management documentation. 2. Observe project team meetings. 3. Administer an organizational assessment.
Influence on business	1. Analyze the impact of business results on the current business state. 2. Administer a 360-degree assessment.
Return on investment	1. Calculate a benefit-to-cost ratio. 2. Calculate a pure return on investment percentage.

THE MEASUREMENT PROCESS

As one develops the process of measuring project management success in any one of the four plateaus, metrics (data, or units of measure) must be established. These metrics are required to evaluate progress over time, set levels of commitment, and position accountability to reach these targets. Actual metrics are acquired through individual, 360°, or organizational assessments; through action plans and performance contracts; and/or through performance monitoring.

The best process of monitoring, tracking, and managing these metrics balances feasibility, credibility, and simplicity, as demonstrated in the following methodology:

- Step 1: Data Collection
- Step 2: Data Analysis
- Step 3: Results Compilation
- Step 4: Action Plan Implementation

NOTE For these four steps in the measurement process to be successful, a structure and rigor must be established to mandate that the process will be managed and maintained.

Step 1: Data Collection

This first step is critical. Only legitimate and accurate data collected in this step can ensure that valid reports and credible action plans are generated at the other end of the process. It is therefore important to generate a data collection plan before beginning Step 1.

These questions need to be answered to create this plan:

- Which of the measurement plateaus are we addressing, and what information are we trying to ascertain?
- What type of data do we want to collect—financial, attitudinal, performance of specific competencies, designated project success relative to schedule, resource, cost and/or quality?
- What medium are we going to use to collect the data—conduct one-on-one interviews, facilitate focus groups, administer an assessment tool, or observe and document the observations, to name a few?
- What is the sphere of collection—the entire project management community or a sampling of the community? Internal, external, or both?
- How frequently will data be collected and reported out?
- Who will collect and process the information—an internal project management council, the Project Office, or a staff position reporting to senior management?

Some examples of the countless creative ways you can collect data are listed below and shown in Figure 15.7:

- Administer an organizational maturity assessment throughout the entire enterprise to determine the stage of growth that the organization has achieved.
- Choose several work-in-progress projects and conduct an interim audit.
- Administer a competency exam to a select control group of project players.
- Monitor each project player's performance objectives and developmental objectives. (They are part of the performance management system.)
- Establish personal performance contracts with project players prior to beginning a project or prior to rolling out a project management initiative. Track those contracts as the project progresses.
- Examine various business performance records and operational data.
- Query project players, users of the outcomes of projects, senior management, external experts, or customers as to what percentage of improvement and/or what degree of positive impact (low, medium, or

Figure 15.7   Step 1: Data Collection

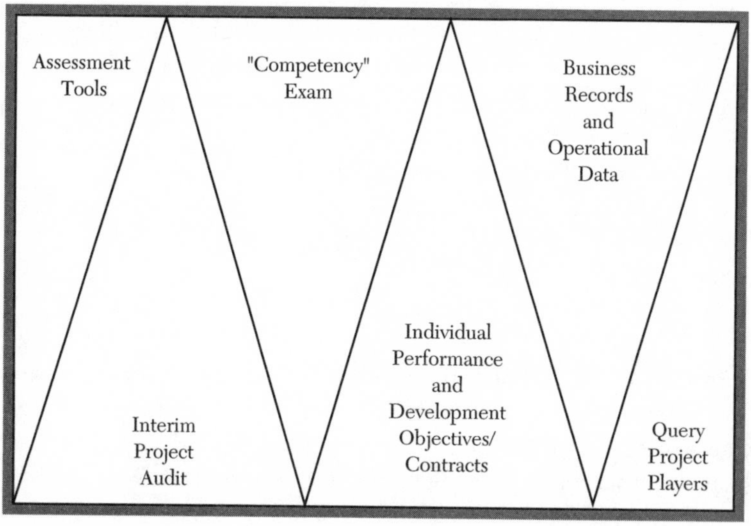

high) and/or what increased benefits/reduced expenses are a result of the intervention of project management.

Step 2: Data Analysis

This step identifies output performance that is directly related to project management and evaluates how this output performance has generated specific improvements in the production and/or performance within the organization.

As summarized in Figure 15.8, there are several approaches to compartmentalizing the data:

Control Group

Compare the same data elements from a group that is using a specific project initiative and from another group that is not using that initiative.

For example: The Information Systems (IS) group in Corporate in Chicago will use the new Change Control Process for the next three months. They will be the pilot or prototype group. They are physically close to the champion of the project management discipline and therefore can be monitored more carefully. However, the IS group in Des Moines will not use the

Figure 15.8   Step 2: Data Analysis

Three Approaches to Compartmentalizing the Data

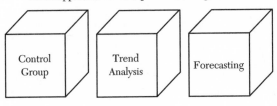

Don't Ignore Intangible Benefits

new process. At the end of three months, the number of changes of scope that have been documented, evaluated, and funded by their requester will be analyzed for the control and the noncontrol groups. Taking into consideration any external forces that might skew the comparison, we can use these data to determine whether the Change Control process is passing the Comprehension/Acceptance, Application, and Business Results plateaus. It may be difficult to perform an ROI calculation at this time; but it would be worthy of consideration.

Trend Analysis

Plot historical data prior to the implementation of project management or of a project management initiative. Then extrapolate what the metrics would be (at predetermined time checkpoints), if a project management intervention were never implemented. Lastly, for those specified checkpoints, collect and plot actual data. If the actual data are better than the projections, the intervention is successful.

Forecasting

This process is similar to trend analysis, except that there are no historical data on which to rely.

With regard to soft data, the goal is to convert intangible benefits into some tangible interpretation of success. If the intangible benefits are too subjective, don't throw them away. Intangible benefits can be as impressive as tangible ones. Create a list of intangible benefits, and let them speak for themselves. Intangible benefits might be:

- Happier employees
- Less communication required

- Better image to customers and/or the community
- Professional development for the staff

After analyzing the data, we need to compile the results for distribution and communication.

Step 3: Results Compilation

Results are compiled by documenting the techniques of the data analysis, which were discussed in Step 2. As shown in Figure 15.9, the documentation may be in the form of graphic representations such as line graphs or columnar charts. Tables or matrices also lend themselves to communicating this type of data. Lists that have been sorted and extracted, relative to specific segments of data, can be very meaningful. And of course, straight text, if organized well, can accomplish the purpose.

Let's say that the results have indicated a problem. That problem must be fixed. The next step is to implement appropriate action plans.

Step 4: Action Plan Implementation

As diagrammed in Figure 15.10, the creation of the action plan is accomplished by taking the reports compiled in Step 3 and isolating any metrics that are not being met or are being met slower than expected. Action plans

Figure 15.9   Step 3: Results Compilation

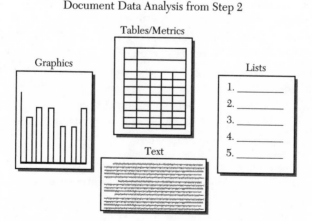

Document Data Analysis from Step 2

Figure 15.10   Step 4: Action Plan Implementation

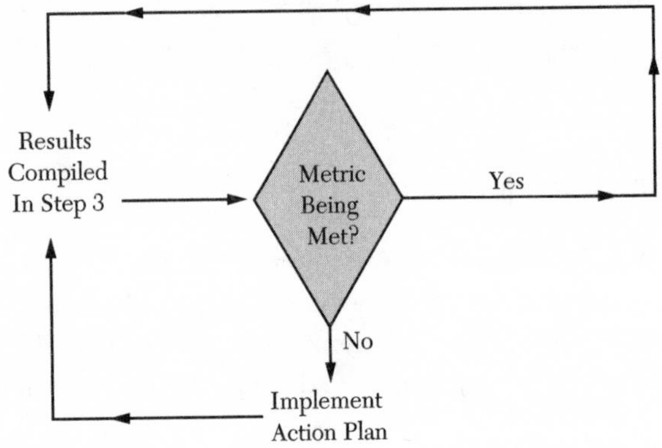

are then created and implemented with more frequent review checkpoints until the metric is accomplished.

When creating these types of action plans, keep in mind the following factors:

- All concerned parties must be involved and must commit to accomplishing their part of the plan.
- The posture should be that the metric is meaningful.
- The expectation is: People will be held accountable for meeting the metric.
- If the original metric is found to be unrealistic or unattainable, it should be discarded or changed.

This is a cyclical process. After creating these action plans, we return to Steps 1 through 3 of the process: collecting, analyzing, and reporting the impact of the action plan. The report then suggests how the action plan could be revisited and changed, as necessary, and the cycle begins anew.

To ensure that specific objectives are accomplished at each of the four measurement plateaus, a collection and analysis process must be established and must mandate that the project management measurement process is to be managed and maintained. A successful ongoing measurement process should have the following characteristics:

- Be simple, economical, and easily implemented
- Be routinely embedded into the daily operational project management effort

- Be practical and credible, and account for external factors
- Be applicable to all projects/initiatives
- Address both hard and soft data

The process of measuring project management success is a classic methodology that can be applied either to the success of a composite of individual projects or to a specific project management initiative.

CONCLUSION

Success in any support service can be measured in terms of reactions to, learning about, behavior around, and results of that undertaking, and the major outcomes of success can be measured in tangible outputs, the mindset of employees, financial impacts, and the reaction of clients. In project management, four plateaus can measure success: Comprehension and Acceptance (measures of knowledge and reaction); Application (measures of behavior); Influence on Business (measures of results); and Return on Investment (even more quantifiable measures of results). On each plateau, two or three techniques can be used to evaluate outcomes. The measurement or metric is based on technical or hard data, which are quantifiable, as well as on sociological or soft data, which are more intangible and qualitative.

Each of these plateaus can measure the success or failure of a single project or a single project management initiative. These single-project or single-initiative metrics can be consolidated to create a comprehensive report card on the discipline of project management.

The procedure used to process these data consists of four steps: (1) Data Collection, (2) Data Analysis, (3) Results Compilation, and (4) Action Plan Implementation. Each of these steps has alternative methodologies.

The objective of project management measurement is not a one-time snapshot of success or failure. The objective is to set a benchmark from which ongoing evaluation of the project management discipline will continue. This is a continuous improvement process.

The first challenge is to articulate the criteria on which project management success can and should be measured. The second challenge is to convert what are often ethereal, subjective criteria into quantifiable units of measure. The final challenge is to implement a process that gathers, analyzes, and reports the results.

With those challenges in mind, it is no wonder that we in project management can be reluctant to implement a measurement system. Many believe there is little value in investing our time and energy in a project management measurement system because:

- Managers don't care whether project management is successful.
- Managers haven't asked specifically for a measurement system; therefore, they don't expect one and don't want one.
- We are all professionals; we all do a good job, so there is no need to measure.
- Project management as a discipline is impossible to measure.
- Project management is so desperately needed that we do not have to justify ourselves. We'll continue to get funded, no matter what.

All of the above statements are false. More and more money is being spent on project management. Project management is becoming more and more visible. It therefore behooves us to step up and measure what project management is doing for our organizations, to shout its successes to the skies, and to continually raise the bar.

The Age of Quality and the Age of Reengineering have had their day. We are now entering the Age of Project Management. There are many reasons why a project management measurement system might not be implemented. But if we hope to prolong our moment in the sun, we need to step up to the next level, which demands that we prove our worth and continue to fight for the funding to grow.

Lastly, complete the assessment tool at the end of this chapter. This assessment addresses Plateau 1, Comprehension and Acceptance and Plateau 2, Application, while Performance Support Tool 15.1 addresses Plateau 3, Business Results.

Project Management Measurement Models

Each of the six models outlined below gives a standard criterion for project management success, followed by various recommended metrics that can be used to measure success. Each metric is accompanied by the specific target values that must be achieved. These general models are meant to be modified for the project environment in which you work. To tailor this tool to your environment, select the most appropriate criteria and then rank and determine the most appropriate metrics and target values for each criterion.

1. SUCCESS CRITERION: THERE IS A DOCUMENTED PROJECT MANAGEMENT PROCESS, AND IT IS BEING USED.

Ranking: To be determined

Possible Metrics:

1. A training course in the discipline is developed and delivered to project management practitioners. *Target Value: xx% by (date).*
2. Appropriate project management outputs are generated. *Target Value: xx%* of projects have the following project management documents produced in the appropriate phase: *(list documents).*
3. Project status reports indicate conformance to the process. *Target Value: xx% by (date).*
4. The product development life cycle is documented, published, and distributed to project management practitioners. *Target Value:* To distribution list by *(date).*

2. SUCCESS CRITERION: PROJECT CUSTOMERS (PROJECT CLIENT, PROJECT TEAM, AND SENIOR MANAGEMENT) ARE MORE SATISFIED WITH PROJECT PERFORMANCE.

Ranking: To be determined

Possible Metrics:

1. More customers indicate satisfaction with the project management aspect of their projects as indicated in surveys. *Target Value:* Percentage indicating satisfaction increases by *xx%* by *(date),* or *xx%* of customers indicate they are more satisfied now than on previous projects.

3. SUCCESS CRITERION: IMPROVED ACCURACY OF PROJECT PLANNING

Ranking: To be determined

Possible Metrics:

1. More projects are meeting schedule. *Target Value: xx%* increases in the number of projects meeting approved schedule within *xx%* tolerance of project duration.
2. Average schedule delays reduced. *Target Value:* Of those projects not meeting schedule, the percentage of overrun is less than pre-project management initiative by *xx%.*
3. More projects are meeting budget or estimated effort.

4. Average budget overruns reduced. *Target Value:* Of those projects not meeting budget, the percentage of overrun is less than pre-project management initiative by *xx%*.

5. Database of project estimates and actuals is created and being maintained. *Target Value:* Database is designed by (*date*). Database is implemented by (*date*). Effective update process exists by (*date*). Analytical reports being produced by (*date*).

6. More projects have an approved schedule and budget developed by the project team. *Target Value: xx%* increases in the number of projects with approved schedule and budget developed by the team.

4. Success Criterion: Improved Ability to Monitor Project Status

Ranking: To be determined

Possible Metrics:

1. Monthly project status reports contain timely and accurate data. *Target Value: xx%* of projects have monthly status reports that give accurate and timely information, as judged by presence of (*list specific types of data*).

2. Project status and tracking documents contain consistent information per the published project management process. *Target Value: xx%* of projects have tracking documents, specifically (*list documents*), that contain consistent information per the published project management process.

3. Significant project dates on key documents are updated or confirmed in a timely and regular fashion. *Target Value: xx%* of projects have been updated on appropriate tracking documents, and the updates are not older than *xx* weeks.

4. Project managers and project clients have access to and are trained in (*list the project management-scheduling package of choice*). *Target Value: xx%* of projects are using the automated tool. *xx%* of project management practitioners have been trained in the automated tool.

5. Milestone predictions for project completion are more accurate. *Target Value: xx%* of predicted project/phase completion dates given at (*specified*) milestones are within *xx%* of actual date. *xx%* of projects include trend analysis at (*specified*) milestones.

6. Standard project tracking documents are defined and being produced regularly by more projects. *Target Value: xx%* of projects conform by (*date*).

5. Success Criterion: There Is a Mechanism in Place for Collecting and Disseminating Lessons Learned.

Ranking: To be determined

Possible Metrics:

1. Project work plans include tasks for project closeout analysis and documentation of lessons learned. *Target Value: xx%* of projects conform by (*date*).

2. Project closeout process is defined, documented, and distributed. *Target Value:* Completed by (*date*).

3. Projects follow the defined closeout process. *Target Value: xx%* of projects conform by (*date*).

4. New projects take advantage of lessons learned in past projects. *Target Value:* By *(date)*, *xx%* of projects include a step during project planning to review available/applicable lessons-learned data.

5. Project lessons-learned information is made accessible. *Target Value:* By *(date)*, *xx%* of completed projects have published lessons learned by *(indicate media)*, have made this information accessible across the organization, and have integrated this information into the project history database.

6. Success Criterion: There Is a Process for Documenting a Change of Scope/Requirements and Its Impact on the Project.

Ranking: To be determined

Possible Metrics:

1. Change management process is defined, documented, and distributed. *Target Value:* Completed by *(date)*.

2. Projects use the change management process. *Target Value: xx%* of projects maintain a change log by *(date)*.

3. Projects document the amount of schedule delay attributable to scope/requirements change. *Target Value: xx%* of projects conform by *(date)*, as evidenced by *(type of data)*.

These six criteria are only the start of what can be a long list of ways to measure the success of the project management disciple in a project-driven organization.

ASSESSMENT TOOL

General Project Management Practices

Objective:
- To determine the general state of project management within the organization
- To identify challenges facing the project client and opportunities for the project manager

Schedules, Budget, Scope	Response
1. What percentage of your projects are completed: • On or before their original schedule commitments? • Within an acceptable amount of delay? • With delays that seriously impact the organization?	_____ % _____ % _____ %
2. What percentage of your projects are completed: • On or under their original budgets? • Within an acceptable level or budget? • With cost overruns that seriously impact the organization? • We don't usually worry about project costs.	_____ % _____ % _____ % _____ %
3. What percentage of your projects are completed while achieving their original scope and technical objectives? • Fully • Partially, but acceptably • Marginally, with serious impact to the company.	 _____ % _____ % _____ %
4. How confident are you that any particular project will meet the currently scheduled completion date at the: • Time of project approval and initiation • Half-way point in its execution • 90% completion point	 _____ % _____ % _____ %

Project Planning and Managing Practices				
Questions	Always	Sometimes	Never	Not Familiar
1. Do you: Appoint a project manager and identify core project team members?				
2. Define the project scope and deliverables?				
3. Prepare a written project objective statement?				
4. Develop the project work breakdown structure?				
5. Define deliverables for each task?				
6. Identify key project interface events?				
7. Develop preliminary schedule using PERT/CPM network planning?				
8. Refine estimates and analyze resource commitments?				
9. Optimize tradeoffs between schedule, scope and budget?				
10. Analyze risk and develop contingency plans?				
11. Manage and control the key project interface events?				
12. Set the baseline plan and schedule?				
13. Report progress and expenditures at defined intervals?				
14. Analyze variances and document their impact?				
15. Identify and control open issues?				
16. Systematically replan and take adaptive action?				
17. Report project status to management and customers?				
18. Conduct periodic project review meetings?				
19. Maintain necessary project documentation?				

Organizational Project Practices				
Questions	Always	Sometimes	Never	Not Familiar
1. We use a documented, integrated project management process for all projects.				
2. Each project is planned, scheduled and monitored on an ad hoc basis using whatever system the project manager or the customer wants.				
3. Only selected, high priority projects are formally planned and managed, with an assigned project manager. All other projects somehow flow through the organization on their own.				
4. We assign experienced PM to projects.				
5. We have effective cross-functional teamwork on projects.				
6. Our project roles and responsibilities are well defined and understood.				
7. Effective PM training is provided to all our project contributors.				
8. Career paths in project management are defined.				
9. Continuous improvements are made in the project management process and related practices.				
10. Our functional managers often double as project managers.				
11. Our project managers are selected mainly because of availability.				
12. Is project planning and control support provided to project managers and project teams?				

Human Side of Project Management

1. Team work on most projects in our organization:

   a. _____ Is excellent on most projects

   b. _____ Is good within the technical functions, but poor between the technical, marketing/ sales, manufacturing/production, and field service people

   c. _____ Depends heavily on the abilities of the project manager

   d. _____ Can be improved with proper training

   e. _____ Cannot be improved with proper training

Barriers to Effective Project Management

1. What barriers have you observed to achieving effective project management?

   a. _____ People generally don't like to plan

   b. _____ Managers and team members don't understand the importance of project management

   c. _____ Too many conflicts emerge between project and functional managers

   d. _____ Project managers are not well trained

   e. _____ Project team members are not trained in project management methods

   f. _____ No staff support for project planning, scheduling and monitoring

   g. _____ No time is made available for doing the PM tasks

   h. _____ Project management software tools are not available

Impact of Ineffective Project Management

1. What are the impacts of ineffective project management practices?

   a. _____ Late completion reduces market share

   b. _____ Technical objectives are not fully met, causing customer dissatisfaction and reducing market acceptance of the product or service

   c. _____ Cost overruns reduce profit

   d. _____ Excessive conflicts, too much overtime and high stress lead to low morale and high turnover

   e. _____ Lack of confidence in project schedules and promise dates, causing unpredictability for customers and in forecasting financial results

   f. _____ Other _____

Impact of Effective Project Management

1. If increased use of project management would make a positive impact on your product, where would you apply the gains?

   a. _____ All gains would be applied to shorten the length of the project

   b. _____ All gains would be applied to increase functionality and quality

   c. _____ All gains would be applied to reducing the cost of the project

   d. _____ Gains would be spread over the difficult areas:

   _____ Schedule _____ Scope _____ Budget

   e. _____ Appreciation of gains would vary on a project by project basis

---

GLOSSARY

baseline   The original plan for a project, work package, or activity, plus or minus approved changes. Usually used with a modifier, as in cost, schedule, or performance measurement baseline.

control   The process of comparing actual performance with planned performance, analyzing variances, evaluating possible alternatives, and taking appropriate corrective action as needed.

corrective action   Changes made to bring expected future performance of the project into line with the plan.

critical path   The series of activities that determines the earliest completion of a project, generally defined in terms of activities with no float. The critical path can change as activities are completed ahead of or behind schedule. Normally calculated for the entire project, the critical path can also be determined for a milestone or a phase.

earned value   A method for measuring project performance; compares the amount of work that was planned with what was accomplished, to determine whether cost and schedule performance is as planned.

float   The amount of time that an activity can be delayed from its early start without delaying the project finish date. This is a mathematical calculation that can change as the project progresses and as changes are made to the project plans.

functional manager   A manager responsible for activities in a specialized department, function, or resource (such as engineering, manufacturing, marketing); also called a resource manager.

Gantt Chart or Gantt Schedule Chart   A bar chart that consists of a graphic display of schedule-related information. Typically, it lists activities or project elements down the left, dates at the top, and activity durations as date-placed horizontal bars.

knowledge-based system (KBS)   A system for recording the accumulation of activities performed, and the effort and duration expended, on past projects. These data also include lessons learned and are easily accumulated if resource allocation software is designed in a way that archives these data for future use.

matrixed organizational structure   An environment in which functional, departmental, or resource managers essentially lend their resources/staff to projects run by various managers of projects, who often report outside of the resource manager's sphere of influence. Staff members report to both their resource manager and the manager of the project. The purpose of this structure is to gather various subject matter experts from different functional areas into one project team to accomplish a specific business objective.

organizational maturity model   Evaluates the stage of growth that the organization has achieved.

performance metric   A quantifiable measurement by which to determine whether project management success criteria are met. Generally, this metric is based on historical data or benchmarks.

PMBOK   The Project Management Institute's *Project Management Body of Knowledge.*

product development life cycle (PDLC)   A collection of generally sequential project phases, the name and number of which are determined by the control needs of the organizations involved. This generally takes the form of a template or model of all tasks that must be performed in order to produce the end-product/deliverable from the project, a standard to-do list of work activities.

project initiative   The overall project statement that commits the organization to begin a project or a project phase.

project management (PM)   The application of knowledge, skills, tools, and techniques to project activities to meet or exceed stakeholder needs and expectations from a project.

project management life cycle (PMLC)   Superimposed over the product life cycle, this is a template or a model composed of steps that need to be taken to initiate, plan, execute and control, and close a project.

project plan   A formal, approved document used to guide both project execution and project control. The primary uses of the project plan are: to document planning assumptions and decisions, to facilitate communication among stakeholders, and to document approved scope, cost, and schedule baselines. A project plan may be summarized or detailed.

Request for Proposal (RFP)   A type of bid document used to solicit proposals from prospective vendors of products or services. Also known as a Request for Quotation (RFQ).

resource leveling   Any form of network analysis in which scheduling decisions (start and finish dates) are driven by resource management concerns (such as limited resources availability). This generally involves adjusting the staffing plan to accommodate overloading or underloading of specific resources in a project.

resource loading   The mathematical calculation of the effort each individual is exerting on various tasks in a single time frame. When all resources/staff have been loaded onto a schedule chart, some individuals may be found to be overcommitted, and the staffing plan must be leveled.

resource manager   A manager responsible for activities in a specialized department, function, or resource (such as engineering, manufacturing, marketing); also called a functional manager.

risk event   A discrete occurrence that may affect the project for better or worse.

scope   The sum of the products and services to be provided as a project.

stakeholder   Individuals and organizations involved in or affected by project activities and outcomes.

360-degree assessment   An instrument that is administered to each project player or team member to evaluate the project management competency of the individual being assessed. All of the people who come in contact with the person being assessed, whether downward, upward, or sideways on the chart, evaluate him or her. An assessment of competency and a performance improvement plan are then derived.

work breakdown structure (WBS)   A hierarchical grouping of project elements that organizes and defines the total scope of the project. This list or diagram represents all tasks that must be completed to finish the project. Each descending level represents an increasingly detailed definition. This becomes the foundation on which all baseline plans are built.

INDEX